GRAMMAR FOR THE WELL-TRAINED MIND: CORE INSTRUCTOR TEXT

Also by Susan Wise Bauer

The Writing With Ease Series
(Well-Trained Mind Press, 2008-2010)

The Writing With Skill Series
(Well-Trained Mind Press, 2012-2013)

The Story of Western Science:
From the Writings of Aristotle to the Big Bang Theory
(W.W. Norton, 2015)

The Well-Educated Mind:
A Guide to the Classical Education You Never Had
updated & expanded ed. (W.W. Norton, 2015)

The Story of the World: History for the Classical Child
(Well-Trained Mind Press)
Volume I: Ancient Times, rev. ed. (2006)
Volume II: The Middle Ages, rev. ed. (2007)
Volume III: Early Modern Times (2003)
Volume IV: The Modern Age (2004)

The History of the World Series
(W.W. Norton)
The History of the Ancient World (2007)
The History of the Medieval World (2010)
The History of the Renaissance World (2013)

WITH JESSIE WISE
The Well-Trained Mind: A Guide to Classical Education at Home, 4th ed.
(W.W. Norton, 2016)

GRAMMAR
FOR THE WELL-TRAINED MIND
CORE INSTRUCTOR TEXT

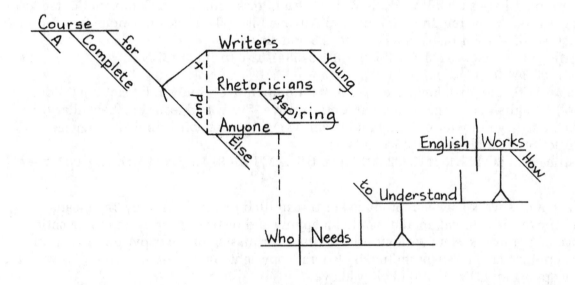

BY SUSAN WISE BAUER
AND AUDREY ANDERSON,
DIAGRAMS BY PATTY REBNE

WELL-
TRAINED
MIND
PRESS

Publisher's Cataloging-In-Publication Data
(Prepared by The Donohue Group, Inc.)

Names: Bauer, Susan Wise. | Anderson, Audrey, 1986- | Rebne, Patty, illustrator.
Title: Grammar for the well-trained mind. Core instructor text, years 1-4 / by Susan Wise Bauer and Audrey Anderson ; with illustrations by Patty Rebne.
Other Titles: Core instructor text, years 1-4
Description: Charles City, VA : Well-Trained Mind Press, [2017] | "A Complete Course for Young Writers, Aspiring Rhetoricians, and Anyone Else Who Needs to Understand How English Works." | For instructors of grades 5 and above.
Identifiers: LCCN 2017942359 | ISBN 978-1-945841-02-6 (print) | ISBN
   978-1-945841-03-3 (ebook)
Subjects: LCSH: English language--Grammar, Comparative--Study and teaching (Middle school) | English language--Grammar, Comparative--Study and teaching (Secondary) | English language--Rhetoric--Study and teaching (Middle school) | English language--Rhetoric--Study and teaching (Secondary)
Classification: LCC LB1631 .B392 2017 (print) | LCC LB1631 (ebook) | DDC 428.00712--dc23

TABLE OF CONTENTS

FOREWORD

Welcome to *Grammar for the Well-Trained Mind!*

This innovative grammar program takes students from basic definitions ("A noun is the name of a person, place, thing, or idea") all the way through detailed analysis of complex sentence structure. The student who completes this program will have all the skills needed for the study of advanced rhetoric—persuasive speech and sophisticated writing.

WHAT MAKES UP THE FULL PROGRAM

Each year of study in *Grammar for the Well-Trained Mind* requires three books.

The nonconsumable *Core Instructor Text* is used for each year of study. It contains scripted dialogue for the instructor, all rules and examples, and teaching notes that thoroughly explain ambiguities and difficulties.

There are four *Student Workbooks* with accompanying *Keys*. Each consumable workbook provides a full course of exercises and assignments. Each corresponding key gives complete, thoroughly explained answers. Your goal is to complete all four *Workbooks* before the student finishes high school. (See *How the Program Works*, below.)

Two optional reference books are also available. All rules and definitions, with accompanying examples, have been assembled into a handy reference book, *The Grammar Guidebook*. This handbook will serve the student for all four years of study—and will continue to be useful as the student moves through advanced high school writing, into college composition, and beyond. In addition, all diagramming rules covered in the course are summarized in *The Diagramming Dictionary: A Complete Reference Tool for Young Writers, Aspiring Rhetoricians, and Anyone Else Who Needs to Understand How to Diagram English Sentences.*

HOW THE PROGRAM WORKS

Language learning has three elements.

First: Students have to understand and memorize rules. We call this "prescriptive learning"—grasping the explicit principles that govern the English language and committing them to memory. *Grammar for the Well-Trained Mind* presents, explains, and drills all of the essential rules of the English language. Each year, the student reviews and repeats these rules.

Second: Students need examples of every rule and principle ("descriptive learning"). Without examples, rules remain abstract. When the student memorizes the rule "Subjunctive verbs express situations that are unreal, wished for, or uncertain," she also needs to memorize the example "I would not say such things if I were you!" Each year, the student reviews and repeats the *same* examples to illustrate each rule.

Third: Students need *practice*. Although the four workbooks repeat the same rules and examples, each contains a completely new set of exercises and writing assignments, along with complete answers.

The combination of *repetition* (the same rules and examples each year) and *innovation* (brand-new practice materials in every workbook) leads the student to complete mastery of the English language.

HOW TO USE GRAMMAR FOR THE WELL-TRAINED MIND

When you first use the program, begin with the *Core Instructor Text* and any *Student Workbook/Key to Student Workbook* combination. Keep the *Grammar Guidebook* and the *Diagramming Dictionary* on hand for reference.

During this first year, you shouldn't expect the student to grasp every principle thoroughly. Simply go through the dialogue for each week's lessons (there are four lessons per week), ask the student to complete the exercises, check the answers, and discuss any mistakes.

If you're working with a high school student, you'll ideally complete the *Student Workbook* in one year. Some students will need longer—and that's absolutely fine. Feel free to take as much time as necessary to finish this workbook. When the first *Student Workbook* is completed (whether in one year, or more!), go back to the beginning of the *Core Instructor Text* and start over, this time using another *Student Workbook/Key* combination. You'll go over the same dialogue, the same rules, and the same examples—with an entirely fresh set of exercises for the student to practice on. This combination of repeated information along with new and challenging exercises will truly begin to build the student's competence in the English language. Follow this same procedure for the third and fourth years of study, using the remaining *Student Workbooks* and matching keys.

Regular reviews are built into the program. Every three weeks the student takes some extra time to do six exercises reviewing what was covered in the three weeks before. After Week 27, the reviews double in scope: twelve exercises review the material all the way back to the beginning of the course. These reviews, beginning with Review 9, become one week's work each. During review weeks, students should try to do three exercises per day, and then should go back and review the rules and principles of any exercise in which they miss two or more sentences/examples.

If you are working with a student in grades 5-8 or an older student who struggles with language work, you may find that it will take you a full year to go through the first twenty weeks of the program. The exercises increase in complexity and difficulty after Week 20. A student who needs a full year to complete Weeks 1-20 should return to the same material (Weeks 1-20) the following year, using another *Student Workbook/Key* combination. Only when the concepts in these lessons are mastered should you move on to Weeks 21 and following.

Students who begin the program in fifth or sixth grade might then spend several years working through the Weeks 1-20 lessons in all four workbooks, and then move on to the Weeks 21-36 lessons during the high school years. Your goal is simply to complete the entire series of Weeks 1-36 at least twice (and ideally, all four times) before the student graduates.

Once the Weeks 1-36 sequence has been completed four times, the student has mastered all the grammar needed for good writing!

BRINGING NEW STUDENTS INTO THE PROGRAM

Because each workbook makes use of the same rules and examples, if you are teaching more than one student (or in a classroom or co-op setting), you may bring new students in at any workbook level. If you've already completed one *Student Workbook/Key* combination with your student or class, you may bring a new student in with the next *Student Workbook/Key* combination in any following year. The workbooks cover the same essential material.

IMPORTANT PRINCIPLES OF TEACHING

As you teach, keep the following in mind.

- Language is a rich complicated tapestry. It is occasionally logical, and sometimes irrational. Mastering its complexities takes time and patience. Don't expect the student to master—or even completely understand—every principle the first time through. Do your best, but be willing to accept imperfect learning the first couple of times through the program. The repetition and practice will eventually bring clarity. Be diligent—don't abandon the curriculum because of frustration! But accept confusion as a natural part of learning the more advanced language concepts.

- Always prompt the student for answers if she becomes confused. This is not a test. It is a learning process. Give as much help as necessary.

- From Week 19 (halfway through the course) on, the student is encouraged to read sentences out loud. Reading out loud is an important part of evaluating your own writing. Do not allow the student to simply read silently—help him develop this skill by following the directions to read aloud.

- Take as long as you need to finish each lesson. As noted above, it's perfectly acceptable to take more than one year to finish a workbook (particularly the first time through). The earlier lessons are shorter and simpler; they increase in both complexity and length as the book goes on. But especially in the later lessons, don't worry if you need to divide a lesson over two days, or take more than one week to complete a week's worth of lessons. In subsequent years, the student will go much more quickly through the earlier lessons, giving you time to stop and concentrate on areas of challenge later on.

- The first time through, ask the student to complete each exercise. In subsequent repetitions, however, you adjust the student's workload in the earlier (and simpler) lessons so that you can spend more time on the later exercises. If the student remembers and understands the concept, ask her to do the first four or five sentences in the exercise. If she completes them correctly, skip the rest of the exercise and move on. This will allow you to customize the program to each student's strengths and weaknesses.

- In my previous grammar and writing programs, I have recommended that students answer all questions in complete sentences. This is essential practice for younger students. However, older students who are writing fluently AND have already had plenty of practice answering in complete sentences do not need to keep this up. As material gets more complex, complete sentence answers simply become too long and unwieldy.

If, however, you are working with a struggling writer, you may wish to ask her to answer in complete sentences rather than following the script as written. So, for example, where the instructor text reads:

> Instructor: What gender do you think the word grandfather has?
> → *Student: Masculine.*
> Instructor: What gender does grandmother have?
> → *Student: Feminine.*

you may instead ask the student to answer:

Instructor: What gender do you think the word grandfather has?
→ *Student: "Grandfather" is masculine.*
Instructor: What gender does grandmother have?
→ *Student: "Grandmother" is feminine.*

ABOUT DIAGRAMMING

Grammar for the Well-Trained Mind uses diagramming exercises throughout.

Diagramming is a learning process. The student should think of the diagrams as experimental projects, not tests. He should attempt the diagram, look at the answer, and then try to figure out why any differences exist. Expect these assignments—particularly in the second half of the book—to be challenging. Give all necessary help using the key, and don't allow the student to be frustrated. Always ask the student to diagram with a pencil (or on a whiteboard or blackboard), and expect him to erase and redo constantly.

Also remember that diagramming is not an exact science! If the student can defend a diagram, accept it even if it's different from the key. To quote a 1914 grammar text: "Many constructions are peculiar, idiomatic, and do not lend themselves readily to any arrangement of lines" (Alma Blount and Clark S. Northup, *An English Grammar for Use in High and Normal Schools and in Colleges*).

A FINAL NOTE

Whenever possible, *Grammar for the Well-Trained Mind* quotes from *real* books (novels, histories, science books, biographies, and more). This shows how grammar works in the real world.

However, just because I quote from something doesn't mean it's appropriate for your child to check out of the library. I quote from books that contain profanity, sex, and death. Whether or not your child is ready to read the entire thing is a family decision.

Introduction to Nouns and Adjectives

— LESSON 1 —

Introduction to Nouns
Concrete and Abstract Nouns

Instructor: Look around the room. Tell me the names of four things that you see.

→ *Student: [Names things in room.]*

Instructor: All of those names are **nouns. A noun names a person, place, thing, or idea.** You will see that rule in your book. Repeat it after me: A noun names a person, place, thing, or idea.

→ *Student: A noun names a person, place, thing, or idea.*

> **Note to Instructor:** If the student has not previously memorized this definition, ask him to repeat it five times at the beginning of each lesson until he has committed it to memory.

Instructor: You listed four nouns for me: [Repeat names of things]. These are all things that you can see. Can you see me?

→ *Student: Yes.*

Instructor: Of course you can. I am a person that you can see. Can you see a kitchen?

→ *Student: Yes.*

Instructor: Can you see a supermarket?

→ *Student: Yes.*

Instructor: Kitchens and supermarkets are both places that you can see. Persons, places, and things are special kinds of nouns called **concrete nouns.** We use the word *concrete* for the hard substance used to make parking lots and sidewalks. Concrete nouns are *substantial* nouns that we can see or touch—or those we can experience through our other senses. *Dog* is a concrete noun, because you can see and touch (and smell!) a dog. *Wind* is a concrete noun, because you can feel the wind, even though you can't see or touch it. *Perfume* is a concrete noun because you can smell it, even though you can't feel or see it. Is *tree* a concrete noun?

→ *Student: Yes.*

Instructor: Is *poem* a concrete noun?

→ *Student: Yes.*

Instructor: Yes, because you can see a poem on the page of a book or hear a poem when it is spoken out loud. Is *tune* a concrete noun?

→ *Student: Yes.*

Instructor: Yes, because you can hear a tune. Is *truth* a concrete noun?

→ *Student: No.*

Instructor: You can't see, taste, touch, smell, or hear truth. *Truth* is an **abstract noun.** An abstraction can't be experienced through sight, taste, feel, smell, or hearing. Truth is real, but we can't observe truth with our senses. Is *justice* an abstract noun?

→ *Student: Yes.*

Instructor: Is *liberty* an abstract noun?

→ *Student: Yes.*

Instructor: Repeat after me: Concrete nouns can be observed with our senses.

→ *Student: Concrete nouns can be observed with our senses.*

Instructor: Abstract nouns cannot.

→ *Student: Abstract nouns cannot.*

Instructor: Let's repeat that definition together three times.

→ *Together:* ***Concrete nouns can be observed with our senses. Abstract nouns cannot.***

> **Note to Instructor:** Like most grammatical definitions, this one does not cover every possible use in the English language. For example, *music* can be a concrete noun ("I hear music") or an abstract noun ("Music transports us to another world").
>
> If the student asks about exceptions, tell him that the line between abstract and concrete nouns is not always clear, but this definition helps us to identify ideas, beliefs, opinions, and emotions as nouns.

Instructor: Do the Lesson 1 exercises in your workbook now. Read the instructions and follow them carefully.

— LESSON 2 —

Introduction to Adjectives
Descriptive Adjectives, Abstract Nouns
Formation of Abstract Nouns from Descriptive Adjectives

Instructor: What is a noun?

→ *Student: A noun names a person, place, thing, or idea.*

Instructor: In the last lesson, we talked about abstract nouns like *peace* and *intelligence* and concrete nouns like *mud* and *earthworms*. Repeat after me: Concrete nouns can be observed with our senses. Abstract nouns cannot.

→ *Student: Concrete nouns can be observed with our senses. Abstract nouns cannot.*

Instructor: Look at the shirt [or dress] you're wearing. Is *shirt* a concrete or abstract noun?

→ *Student: Concrete.*

Instructor: Let's describe this concrete noun. What words can you use to tell me more details about this shirt? What color is it? Is it short-sleeved or long-sleeved? Is it soft, or rough and scratchy?

→ *Student: [Soft, short-sleeved, blue . . .]*

Instructor: The words that you used to describe the noun *shirt* are **adjectives**. Adjectives are words that tell us more about concrete and abstract nouns—as well as pronouns, which we will talk about soon. We could define an adjective as a word that describes a noun or pronoun. But some adjectives do more than simply describe nouns. They *change* or *modify* nouns as well. To *modify* a noun is to alter its meaning a little bit. We'll learn more about adjectives that alter the meaning of nouns later on, but for right now let's just prepare for those lessons by modifying (changing) our description. Repeat the definition of an adjective after me: **An adjective modifies a noun or pronoun.**

→ *Student: An adjective modifies a noun or pronoun.*

Instructor: "Modifies" means "describes" or "tells more about."

Now look at the next sentence with me: Adjectives answer four questions about nouns: What kind, which one, how many, and whose. Say that after me: **Adjectives tell what kind, which one, how many, and whose.**

→ *Student: Adjectives tell what kind, which one, how many, and whose.*

Instructor: In later lessons, we will learn about adjectives that answer the questions which one, how many, and whose. Today, let's talk about adjectives that tell *what kind.* Are you a boy or a girl?

→ *Student: I am a [boy or girl].*

Instructor: [Boy or girl] is a concrete noun. Are you hungry or full?

→ *Student: I am [hungry or full].*

Instructor: You are a [hungry or full] [boy or girl]. [Hungry or full] tells *what kind* of [boy or girl] you are. Are you quiet or loud?

→ *Student: I am [quiet or loud].*

Instructor: You are a [quiet or loud] [boy or girl]. Are you cheerful or grumpy?

→ *Student: I am [cheerful or grumpy].*

Instructor: You are a [cheerful or grumpy] [boy or girl]. These words—hungry, full, quiet, loud, cheerful, grumpy—all answer the question *what kind* of [boy or girl] you are. When an adjective answers the question *what kind*, we call it a **descriptive adjective**. Repeat after me: **Descriptive adjectives tell what kind.**

→ *Student: Descriptive adjectives tell what kind.*

Instructor: Descriptive adjectives have a special quality about them. They can be changed into abstract nouns. **A descriptive adjective becomes an abstract noun when you add -*ness* to it.** If you are hungry, you are experiencing *hungriness.* If you are full, you are experiencing . . .

→ *Student: Fullness.*

Instructor: If you are cheerful, you are filled with cheerfulness. If you are grumpy, you are filled with . . .

→ *Student: Grumpiness.*

Instructor: -*Ness* is a *suffix.* A suffix is added onto the end of a word in order to change its meaning. At the end of this lesson, you will do an exercise changing descriptive adjectives into abstract nouns. You will see a spelling rule at the beginning of this exercise. When you add the suffix -*ness* to a word ending in -*y*, the *y* changes to *i*. Be sure to pay attention to this rule! Repeat it after me: When you add the suffix -*ness* to a word ending in -*y* . . .

→ *Student: When you add the suffix -ness to a word ending in -y . . .*

Instructor: . . . the *y* changes to *i*.

→ *Student: . . . the* y *changes to* i.

Instructor: Most words need a suffix when they change from an adjective to a noun. However, there is one category of words that never needs a new form to cross the line between nouns and adjectives. These words are colors! The names for colors can be used as nouns or adjectives, without changing form. If I say to you, "I like blue," *blue* is a noun. It is the name of the color I like. But if I say, "You are wearing your blue shirt," *blue* is a descriptive adjective. It explains what kind of shirt you are wearing. In a sentence, tell me a color that you *don't* like.

→ *Student: I don't like [color].*

Instructor: In that sentence, [color] is a noun. It is the name of the color you don't like! Now, in a sentence, tell me what color [pants or dress] you are wearing.

→ *Student: I am wearing [brown] pants.*

Instructor: What kind of [pants or dress] are you wearing? Brown [pants or dress]! Brown is a descriptive adjective that tells *what kind*.

Instructor: Complete the exercises at the end of the lesson. If you do not understand the instructions, ask me for help.

— LESSON 3 —
Common and Proper Nouns
Capitalization and Punctuation of Proper Nouns

Instructor: You are a person, but we don't just call you "Hey, [boy or girl]." (Or, "Hey, [man or woman]!") Your name is [name]. That is the proper name for you. [Boy or girl] is a **common noun. A common noun is a name common to many persons, places, things, or ideas.** There are many [boys or girls] in the world. But there is only one of you! **A proper noun is the special, particular name for a person, place, thing, or idea.** *Book* is a common noun that names a thing. Give me the name of a particular book.

→ *Student: [Names book.]*

Instructor: *[Name of Book]* is a proper noun. *Mother* is a common noun that names a person. There are many mothers in the world! What is the special, particular name of your mother?

→ *Student: [First, last name.]*

Instructor: *[First, last name]* is a proper noun. *Store* is a common noun that names a place. Give me the name of a particular store that is near us.

→ *Student: [Names store.]*

Instructor: *[Store]* is a proper noun. **Proper nouns always begin with capital letters.** The capital letter tells us that this is a special, particular name. The rules in your workbook tell you what kinds of names should begin with capital letters. Read each rule out loud, but after each rule, stop while I explain it. Then I will read you the examples beneath each rule.

→ *Student: **1. Capitalize the proper names of persons, places, things, and animals.***

Instructor: We have already talked about proper names of persons, places, and things. Animals often have proper names too—if they're pets! Follow along as I read the examples out loud to you.

boy	Peter
store	Baskin-Robbins
book	*Little Women*
horse	Black Beauty

Instructor: Sometimes proper names of places may have two- or three-letter words in them. Normally, we do not capitalize those words unless they are at the beginning of the proper name. Follow along as I read the following examples to you.

sea	Sea of Galilee
port	Port of Los Angeles
island	Isle of Skye

→ Student: **2. Capitalize the names of holidays.**

Instructor: Holidays are particular, special days. Follow along as I read the examples out loud to you.

Memorial Day
Christmas
Independence Day
Day of the Dead

→ Student: **3. Capitalize the names of deities.**

Instructor: We treat the names of gods and goddesses, of all religions, the same way we would treat the names of people: We capitalize them! Follow along as I read the examples out loud to you. Remember that in Christianity and Judaism, *God* is a proper name!

Minerva (ancient Rome)
Hwanin (ancient Korea)
God (Christianity and Judaism)
Allah (Islam)
Gitche Manitou or Great Spirit (Native American—Algonquin)

→ Student: **4. Capitalize the days of the week and the months of the year, but not the seasons.**

Instructor: The seasons are spring, summer, winter, and fall. Those are written with lowercase letters. Follow along as I read the examples out loud to you.

Monday	January	winter
Tuesday	April	spring
Friday	August	summer
Sunday	October	fall

→ Student: **5. Capitalize the first, last, and other important words in titles of books, magazines, newspapers, movies, television series, stories, poems, and songs.**

Instructor: Titles of works are proper nouns that require special attention! First, notice that small, unimportant words in titles—like *a, an, the, and, but, at, for*, and other very short words—do not need to be capitalized in titles, unless they are the first or last word. I will read each common noun in the list that follows. Answer me by reading the proper noun that names the particular book, magazine, newspaper, and so on. As you read, notice which words in the proper nouns are not capitalized.

Note to Instructor: Begin by saying "book." The student should answer by saying *"Alice's Adventures in Wonderland."* Continue on in the same pattern.

book	*Alice's Adventures in Wonderland*
magazine	*National Geographic*
newspaper	*The Chicago Tribune*
movie	*A River Runs Through It*
television series	*The Waltons*
television show	"The Chicken Thief"
story	"The Visit of the Magi"
poem	"The Night Before Christmas"
song	"Joy to the World"
chapter in a book	"The End of the Story"

Instructor: You will notice that some of these titles are in italics. Others have quotation marks around them. Titles of longer works, such as books, movies, and television series, are put into italics. (When you write by hand, you show italics by underlining those titles.) Shorter works—stories, individual poems, single songs, chapters in books, single television shows—have quotation marks around them instead. *The Waltons* is an entire long television series. "The Chicken Thief" is one episode in one of the seasons.

→ *Student:* **6. Capitalize and italicize the names of ships, trains, and planes.**

Instructor: When a ship, train, or plane has a proper name, you should capitalize it. But if the name has short words in it, you shouldn't capitalize those. We also put those names into italics—or underline them, if we're writing by hand. Follow along as I read the examples out loud to you.

ship	*Titanic*
train	*The Orient Express*
plane	*The Spirit of St. Louis*

Instructor: Which short word is not capitalized in those proper names?

→ *Student: Of.*

Instructor: Now complete the exercises at the end of the lesson. If you do not understand the instructions, ask me for help.

—LESSON 4—

Proper Adjectives
Compound Adjectives (Adjective-Noun Combinations)

Instructor: In the last lesson, you looked at the difference between a common noun and a proper noun. What kinds of persons, places, things, and ideas can a common noun name?

→ *Student: Many different [or a similar answer].*

Instructor: What kind of name is a proper noun?

→ *Student: A particular, special name [or a similar answer].*

Note to Instructor: If the student cannot answer, ask her to reread the definitions at the beginning of Lesson 3 out loud.

Instructor: Review the rules for capitalizing proper nouns quickly by reading them out loud to me.

→ *Student: 1. Capitalize the proper names of persons, places, things, and animals.*
2. Capitalize the names of holidays.
3. Capitalize the names of deities.
4. Capitalize the days of the week and the months of the year, but not the seasons.
5. Capitalize the first, last, and other important words in titles of books, magazines, newspapers, movies, television series, stories, poems, and songs.
6. Capitalize and italicize the names of ships, trains, and planes.

Instructor: Proper nouns can often be used as adjectives. For example, what kind of tiger comes from the region of Bengal?

→ *Student: A Bengal tiger.*

Instructor: If someone speaks fluent Japanese, what kind of speaker is she?

→ *Student: A Japanese speaker.*

Instructor: A proper adjective is an adjective that is formed from a proper name. Read the definition of a proper adjective from your workbook.

→ *Student: **A proper adjective is formed from a proper name. Proper adjectives are capitalized.***

Instructor: Read the examples of proper nouns and proper adjectives in your workbook.

→ *Student: Aristotle, the Aristotelian philosophy; Spain, a Spanish city; Valentine's Day, some Valentine candy; March, March madness.*

Instructor: Some proper nouns change their form when they are used as adjectives. Read the next two pairs of sentences in your workbook out loud.

→ *Student: Shakespeare wrote a number of sonnets. I was reading some Shakespearean sonnets yesterday. Mars is the fourth planet from the sun. The Martian atmosphere is mostly carbon dioxide.*

Instructor: Other times, proper names become adjectives just because they are placed in front of a noun. Read the next pair of sentences now.

→ *Student: On Monday, I felt a little down. I had the Monday blues.*

Instructor: In the second sentence, *Monday* answers the question, "What kind of blues?" So you know that *Monday* has become an adjective. Read the next pair of sentences now.

→ *Student: The English enjoy a good cup of tea and a muffin. Gerald enjoys a good English muffin.*

Instructor: What four questions do adjectives answer?

→ *Student: What kind, which one, how many, whose.*

Instructor: What kind of muffin does Gerald enjoy?

→ *Student: An English muffin.*

Instructor: Sometimes, proper adjectives are combined with other words that are *not* derived from proper names. Read the next two sentences in your workbook out loud.

→ *Student: The German-speaking tourists were lost in Central Park. The archaeologist unearthed some pre-Columbian remains.*

Instructor: *German* and *Columbian* are both proper adjectives. (They're derived from the place name *Germany* and the personal name *Columbus*.) But notice that *German* is connected by a hyphen to the word *speaking*, and *Columbian* is connected to the prefix *pre-*. Those words are not capitalized just because they are combined with a proper adjective. **Words that are not usually capitalized remain lowercase even when they are attached to a proper adjective.** Repeat that rule out loud.

→ *Student: Words that are not usually capitalized remain lowercase even when they are attached to a proper adjective.*

Instructor: *Pre-Columbian* and *German-speaking* are **compound adjectives**. A compound adjective combines two words into a single adjective so that they function together. In the sentence "The German-speaking tourists were lost in Central Park," *German-speaking* is a single word. The tourists were not "speaking tourists." And they weren't necessarily all "German tourists." *German-speaking* is two words, but it has one meaning. Read me the definition of a compound adjective.

→ *Student:* **A compound adjective combines two words into a single adjective with a single meaning.**

Instructor: There are many different kinds of compound adjectives. *Pre-Columbian* is an adjective and a prefix. *German-speaking* is an adjective and a verb form called a participle. You'll learn about these compound adjectives and more over the course of this year. Today, let's look at one particular kind of compound adjective, made up of one adjective and one noun—the two parts of speech we've just covered. Read the next two sentences in your workbook out loud.

→ *Student: When the mine collapsed, it sent a plume of dust sky high. I just had a thirty-minute study session.*

Instructor: *Sky high* and *thirty-minute* are both compound adjectives made up of one noun and one adjective. Read the list of compound adjectives in your workbook. As you do, notice that each one is made up of one noun and one adjective. You don't need to read the abbreviations *N* and *ADJ* out loud!

→ *Student:*   N   ADJ
          sky   high

          ADJ   N
          thirty minute

            N   ADJ
          user friendly

          ADJ   N
          high speed

Instructor: Now look back at the two sentences about the plume of dust and the thirty-minute workout. Something is different about *sky high* and *thirty-minute*. What is it?

→ *Student: Thirty-minute* has a hyphen.

> **Note to Instructor:** If the student calls the hyphen a *dash*, agree, but then point out that *hyphen* is a better name. Technically, a dash is twice as long as a hyphen and is used to separate the parts of a sentence, rather than to connect two words. In typesetting, a dash is known as an *em dash* (—). A hyphen is half the length of an em dash. (Just for your information, there is a third mark in typesetting called an *en dash*, which is halfway between a hyphen and an em dash in length and has two major technical uses—one: it indicates range, and two: it joins words in compound adjectives if one part of the adjective is already hyphenated. Now you know. But there's no need to go into this with the student.)

Instructor: When a compound adjective made up of one adjective and one noun comes right before the noun that it modifies, it is usually hyphenated. If it *follows* the noun, it is usually *not* hyphenated. Look at the next pair of sentences. When *sky-high* comes right before *plume*, it is hyphenated, but when *thirty minutes* comes after *study session*, the hyphen disappears. Read the next two pairs of sentences out loud. Notice that the compound adjectives *user friendly* and *high speed* are only hyphenated when they come immediately before the nouns *directions* and *connections*.

→ *Student: Those directions are not user friendly! I prefer user-friendly directions. The connection was high speed. He needed a high-speed connection.*

Instructor: When an adjective comes right before the noun it modifies, as in *user-friendly directions*, we say that it is in the **attributive position**. When it follows the noun, it is in the **predicative position**. Attributive compound adjectives are hyphenated. Predicative compound adjectives aren't.

You don't necessarily have to remember those terms for this lesson. Just remember when to add the hyphen: when the compound adjective comes before the noun!

Complete the exercises in your workbook now.

Introduction to Personal Pronouns and Verbs

—LESSON 5—

Noun Gender
Introduction to Personal Pronouns

Note to Instructor: Ask the student to complete Exercise 5A before the lesson begins. Provide any answers that the student doesn't know (this exercise is for fun).

Instructor: We often use different names for male and female animals. Male and female animals have different **gender**. In English, we say that the words we use to name these animals also have *gender*. Nouns that name male animals are **masculine**. The words *bull* and *rooster* are masculine. Give me three more names from Exercise 5A that have masculine gender.

→ *Student: [Reads three names from the "male" column of Exercise 5A.]*

Instructor: Nouns that name female animals are **feminine** in gender. *Cow* and *hen* are feminine nouns. Give me three more names from Exercise 5A that have feminine gender.

→ *Student: [Reads three names from the "female" column of Exercise 5A.]*

Instructor: We also use masculine and feminine nouns to talk about other living things, including people. What is the masculine noun for a grown male person?

→ *Student: Man.*

Instructor: What is the feminine noun for a young female person?

→ *Student: Girl.*

Instructor: In English, nouns can have masculine or feminine gender. Nouns can also be **neuter** when it comes to gender. A *neuter* noun can refer to a living thing whose gender is unknown. In the list above, is a calf male or female?

→ *Student: It could be either or neither.*

Instructor: A calf can be either masculine or feminine. So can a chick. When we don't know the gender of a living thing, we say that it is *neuter*. The words *bull* and *rooster* have masculine gender, the words *cow* and *hen* have feminine gender, and the words *calf* and *chick* have neuter gender. What gender do you think the word *grandfather* has?

→ *Student: Masculine.*

Instructor: What gender does *grandmother* have?

→ *Student: Feminine.*

Instructor: What about *grandchild*?

→ *Student: Neuter.*

Instructor: We also use the word *neuter* for nouns that refer to nonliving things. Furniture, rocks, and clouds aren't either male or female. So we say that the nouns *table, boulder,* and *cloud* have neuter gender. Look around the room and name three things that have neuter gender.

→ *Student: [Names three things.]*

Instructor: Repeat after me: **Nouns have gender.**

→ *Student: Nouns have gender.*

Instructor: **Nouns can be masculine, feminine, or neuter.**

→ *Student: Nouns can be masculine, feminine, or neuter.*

Instructor: **We use *neuter* for nouns that have no gender, and for nouns whose gender is unknown.**

→ *Student: We use* neuter *for nouns that have no gender, and for nouns whose gender is unknown.*

Instructor: In some languages, the gender of a noun changes that noun's form. A masculine noun will have one kind of ending; a feminine noun, another. In English, we usually only pay attention to gender in one particular situation: when we're replacing a noun with a pronoun. Read me the next brief paragraph in your workbook.

→ *Student: Subha Datta set off for the forest, intending to come back the same evening. He began to cut down a tree, but he suddenly had a feeling that he was no longer alone. As it crashed to the ground, he looked up and saw a beautiful girl dancing around and around in a little clearing nearby. Subha Datta was astonished, and let the axe fall. The noise startled the dancer, and she stood still.*

Instructor: In the second sentence, who is *he*?

→ *Student: Subha Datta.*

Instructor: In the third sentence, what is *it*?

→ *Student: The tree.*

Instructor: In the final sentence, what is *she*?

→ *Student: The beautiful girl or the dancer.*

Instructor: *He, it,* and *she* are **pronouns. A pronoun takes the place of a noun.** Repeat that definition after me.

→ *Student: A pronoun takes the place of a noun.*

> **Note to Instructor:** If the student is not familiar with this definition, have him memorize it by repeating it three times at the beginning of the next few lessons.

Instructor: The pronoun *he* is a masculine pronoun; it takes the place of the proper noun Subha Datta. The pronoun *it* is a neuter pronoun. Why do we call the tree *it*?

→ *Student: We don't know what gender it is.*

Instructor: *He* is a masculine pronoun. *It* is a neuter pronoun. *She* is a feminine pronoun. In the following sentence, replace the correct noun with the feminine pronoun *she*: Sarah was ready to eat lunch.

→ *Student: She was ready to eat lunch.*

Instructor: There is a special word for the noun that the pronoun replaces: the **antecedent**. *Ante-* is a Latin prefix that means "before." *Cedent* comes from a Latin word meaning "to go." So *antecedent* literally means "to go before." Usually, the antecedent noun *goes before* its pronoun. Read me the next sentence in your workbook.

→ *Student: Subha Datta thought he was dreaming.*

Instructor: *Subha Datta* is the antecedent of the pronoun *he*. Repeat after me: **The antecedent is the noun that is replaced by the pronoun.**

→ *Student: The antecedent is the noun that is replaced by the pronoun.*

Instructor: Less often, the antecedent noun follows the pronoun. Read the next sentence out loud.

→ *Student: Although she did not yet know it, the fairy had not convinced Subha Datta.*

Instructor: What is the antecedent of the pronoun *she*?

→ *Student: The fairy.*

Instructor: Let's read the list of pronouns together.

→ *Together: I, you, he, she, it, we, you (plural), they.*

Instructor: These pronouns are called ***personal pronouns***. **Personal pronouns replace specific nouns.** They show who is speaking, who or what is being spoken about, and who or what is being spoken to. You will learn about other kinds of pronouns in later lessons. Just like the nouns they replace, these personal pronouns have gender. Which of these pronouns is masculine?

→ *Student: He.*

Instructor: Which pronoun is feminine?

→ *Student: She.*

Instructor: The pronoun *it* is neuter. The other pronouns—*I, you, we,* and *they*—can be either masculine or feminine, depending on whether their antecedent is male or female.

Complete the exercises at the end of the lesson. If you do not understand the instructions, ask for help.

—LESSON 6—

Review Definitions
Introduction to Verbs
Action Verbs, State-of-Being Verbs
Parts of Speech

Instructor: What is your favorite kind of animal?

→ *Student: [Names animal.]*

Instructor: Is the word [*animal*] a noun or an adjective?

→ *Student: Noun.*

Instructor: What is a noun?

> **Note to Instructor:** If the student cannot answer, direct him to the definitions in his workbook.

→ *Student: A noun names a person, place, thing, or idea.*

Instructor: Is it a common or a proper noun?

→ *Student: Common.*

Instructor: Repeat after me: A common noun is a name common to many persons, places, things, or ideas.

→ *Student: A common noun is a name common to many persons, places, things, or ideas.*

Instructor: Is it a concrete or an abstract noun?

→ *Student: Concrete.*

Instructor: Repeat after me: Concrete nouns can be observed with our senses. Abstract nouns cannot.

→ *Student: Concrete nouns can be observed with our senses. Abstract nouns cannot.*

Instructor: Now think of some descriptive adjectives that apply to this animal. Remember, an adjective modifies a noun or pronoun. Repeat after me: Adjectives tell what kind, which one, how many, and whose.

→ *Student: Adjectives tell what kind, which one, how many, and whose.*

Instructor: Descriptive adjectives tell what kind. (Repeat!)

→ *Student: Descriptive adjectives tell what kind.*

Instructor: Have you thought of some descriptive adjectives for your animal? See if you can list at least three.

→ *Student: [Answers will vary: Hairy, scaly, black, white, spotted, small, huge, wrinkled, whiskered, carnivorous . . .]*

Instructor: You can turn many descriptive adjectives into abstract nouns by adding -ness. Can you turn any of your adjectives into abstract nouns?

→ *Student: [Answers will vary: Whiteness, hairiness, smallness, hugeness . . .]*

Instructor: Now, tell me some things this animal can do. Try to use single words; for example instead of saying *stalk and catch an antelope*, say, *Stalk, catch, eat.*

→ *Student: [Answers will vary: Bark, sleep, crawl, swim . . .]*

Instructor: These words are **verbs**. Read me the definition of a verb.

→ *Student: **A verb shows an action, shows a state of being, links two words together, or helps another verb.***

Instructor: We have just talked about the verbs that your animal can do. When a verb is doing an action, it is called an action verb. Repeat after me: A verb shows an action.

→ *Student: A verb shows an action.*

Instructor: List five actions that you can do. Begin with, *Talk!*

→ *Student: Talk, [answers will vary: write, eat, think, sleep, clean, dress, walk, run].*

Instructor: Those are actions that you do. Now let me ask you a question. Where are you?

→ *Student: I am [in the kitchen, in Virginia, in the United States].*

Instructor: Where am I?

→ *Student: You are [in the kitchen, in Virginia, in the United States].*

Instructor: Those answers don't tell anything about actions that you and I might be doing. Instead they state where you and I *are*—where we exist at this particular moment. Where is [a male friend or member of the family]?

→ Student: *He is [answers will vary].*

Instructor: Where is [a female friend or member of the family]?

→ Student: *She is [answers will vary].*

Instructor: *Am, are*, and *is* are state-of-being verbs. A state-of-being verb just shows that something exists. Read the list of state-of-being verbs out loud.

> **Note to Instructor:** If the student has not previously learned the state-of-being verbs, have him repeat them five times before each grammar lesson until they are memorized.

→ Student: *Am, is, are, was, were, be, being, been.* 5 x's

Instructor: Now you understand the first half of the definition. Go ahead and repeat the whole definition for me now.

→ Student: *A verb shows an action, shows a state of being, links two words together, or helps another verb.*

Instructor: We will discuss the last part of that definition in the next lesson.

Now you have learned the definitions of four **parts of speech**: nouns, adjectives, pronouns, and verbs. **Part of speech is a term that explains what a word does.** Let's review those parts of speech one more time. What does a noun do?

→ Student: *A noun names a person, place, thing, or idea.*

Instructor: What does an adjective do?

→ Student: *An adjective modifies a noun or pronoun.*

Instructor: What does a pronoun do?

→ Student: *A pronoun takes the place of a noun.*

Instructor: What does a verb do?

→ Student: *A verb shows an action, shows a state of being, links two words together, or helps another verb.*

Instructor: Now complete the exercises at the end of the lesson. If you do not understand the instructions, ask me for help.

— LESSON 7 —

Helping Verbs

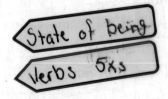 State of being Verbs 5xs

Instructor: What is a part of speech? If you can't remember the definition, you may read it from your workbook.

→ Student: *Part of speech is a term that explains what a word does.*

Instructor: What does a verb do? See if you can repeat the definition from memory.

→ Student: *A verb shows an action, shows a state of being, links two words together, or helps another verb.*

> **Note to Instructor:** If the student cannot repeat the definition from memory, continue to have him repeat it five times before each grammar lesson until it is memorized.

Instructor: List three action verbs that a horse can do.

→ Student: [Answers will vary: *Walk, trot, gallop, neigh, eat, drink, sleep, roll, bite.*]

Instructor: List the state-of-being verbs for me. See if you can do this from memory.

→ Student: *Am, is, are, was, were, be, being, been.*

> **Note to Instructor:** If the student cannot list the verbs from memory, continue to have him repeat them five times before each grammar lesson until they are memorized.

Instructor: We'll talk about verbs that link two words together a little later. Right now, let's discuss the last part of that definition: A verb can help another verb. Look at Exercise 7A now. In the second column of sentences, the main verbs are each *helped* by a state-of-being verb. Complete this exercise now.

Instructor: In these sentences, the helping verbs together with the action verb form the complete verb. Read the list of helping verbs out loud.

→ Student: *Am, is, are, was, were, be, being, been, have, has, had, do, does, did, shall, will, should, would, may, might, must, can, could.*

> **Note to Instructor:** If the student has not previously learned the helping verbs, have him repeat them five times before each grammar lesson until they are memorized.

Instructor: You'll notice that the first eight helping verbs are the same as the state-of-being verbs. The state-of-being verbs can either stand alone or help another verb. Repeat after me: I am.

→ Student: *I am.*

Instructor: I am speaking.

→ Student: *I am speaking.*

Instructor: In the first sentence, *am* is all alone and is a state-of-being verb. In the second sentence, *am* is helping the verb *speaking* (you can't just say, "I speaking"). Helping verbs make it possible for verbs to express different times and different sorts of action; we'll learn about these times and actions in later lessons. For now, complete Exercise 7B.

> **Note to Instructor:** If the student has difficulty supplying the helping verbs, you may suggest answers. The purpose of this exercise is to teach the student to be aware of helping verbs when they occur.

—LESSON 8—

Personal Pronouns
First, Second, and Third Person
Capitalizing the Pronoun *I*

Instructor: Answer me in a complete sentence: How old are you?

→ Student: *I am [age].*

Instructor: What part of speech does that sentence begin with?

> **Note to Instructor:** If necessary, tell the student to look at the first set of words in the workbook.

→ *Student: A pronoun.*

Instructor: Tell me all the personal pronouns now. Try not to look at your workbook.

→ *Student: I, you, he, she, it, we, you, they.*

	Personal Pronouns	
	Singular	**Plural**
First person	I	we
Second person	you	you
Third person	he, she, it	they

Instructor: Now look at the list of personal pronouns in your workbook. You might notice something different about this list: Each pronoun has a *person* and a *number.*

There are three kinds of *persons* that pronouns refer to. You can find the first kind of person by pointing to yourself.

> **Note to Instructor:** Point to yourself and prompt the student to do the same.

Instructor: I am pointing to myself. What are you doing?

→ *Student: I am pointing to myself.*

Instructor: The first person is the one who is pointing, or speaking, or just *being.* If you're all by yourself, you use the pronoun *I* about yourself. That is the *first person singular personal pronoun.* Say that phrase after me.

→ *Student: First person singular personal pronoun.*

> **Note to Instructor:** Move over and stand next to the student. Emphasize the word *we*.

Instructor: Now there are two of us. *We* is plural. What is the *first person plural personal pronoun*?

→ *Student: We.*

> **Note to Instructor:** As you speak, leave the room and speak to the student through the door.

Instructor: Now *we* are both *I* again. Who is in the room?

→ *Student: I am.*

Instructor: There is only one person in the room—until now. [Step back through the door.] Now there is a second person in the room. Who is the second person?

→ *Student: You are.*

Instructor: For the second person, we use the pronoun *you.* In English, *you* can be either singular or plural. If there were two of me here, you would still say "You are." *You* is both the *second person singular* and the *second person plural personal pronoun.* Who is the second person, again?

→ *Student: You are.*

Instructor: And what would you say if there were two of me?

→ *Student: You are.*

Instructor: Imagine that a third person has just walked into the room and you and I are talking to each other about this third person. If the third person happens to be Luke Skywalker, I would say, "He is in the room (and he has a light saber)." *He* is the *masculine third person singular pronoun.* Now imagine that Tinkerbell has followed Luke Skywalker into the room. What pronoun would you use to tell me that Tinkerbell is in the room?

→ *Student: She is in the room.*

Instructor: Now a horse has poked its head into the room. You don't know whether the horse is male or female. What pronoun would you use for the horse?

→ *Student: It.*

Instructor: *He, she,* and *it* are all *third person singular personal pronouns,* with three different genders. There's only one personal pronoun left. If the horse, Tinkerbell, and Luke Skywalker all set off on a quest together, we would say, "They have gone on a quest." *They* is the *third person plural personal pronoun.* Say that after me.

→ *Student:* They *is the third person plural personal pronoun.*

Instructor: Read the next sentence.

→ *Student: Although they are not very hungry, I certainly am.*

Instructor: There are two personal pronouns in this sentence. What are they?

→ *Student: They and I.*

Instructor: What person and number is the pronoun *they*?

→ *Student: Third person plural.*

Instructor: What person and number is *I?*

→ *Student: First person singular.*

Instructor: There's one more difference between the pronouns. Can you figure out what it is?

> **Note to Instructor:** If necessary, prompt the student by saying, "What kind of letter is *t*? What kind of letter is *I*?"

→ *Student:* I *is a capital letter and* they *begins with a small letter.*

Instructor: The personal pronoun *I* is always capitalized. No one really knows why. In Old English, the first person singular pronoun was *ich.* Middle English uses *ich, ic,* and *i.* But by the end of the Middle English period, most writers were using the capital *I* all by itself. Maybe the small *i* looked lonely all by itself. We'll never know. All you need to remember is that *I* is always capitalized.

Let's use this sentence to quickly review a couple of other things. There are two verbs in the sentence. What are they?

→ *Student: Are and am.*

Instructor: What kinds of verbs are these?

→ *Student: State-of-being verbs.*

Instructor: What part of speech is *hungry*?

> **Note to Instructor:** If necessary, prompt the student by saying, "*Hungry* modifies *he.* What part of speech modifies a noun or a pronoun?"

→ *Student: An adjective.*

Instructor: Read the next sentence for me.

→ *Student: As the German-built plane rose into the air, I experienced a strange loneliness.*

Instructor: What are the two verbs in that sentence?

→ *Student: Rose and experienced.*

Instructor: What kinds of verbs are those?

→ *Student: Action verbs.*

Instructor: What are the three nouns in the sentence?

→ *Student: Plane, air, loneliness.*

Instructor: One of those nouns is an *abstract* noun. Which is it?

→ *Student: Loneliness.*

Instructor: Even though loneliness can be experienced, it is an abstract noun because it is a feeling that cannot be touched, seen, smelled, or heard. What kinds of nouns are *plane* and *air?*

→ *Student: Concrete nouns.*

Instructor: You can't see air, but it is a real thing that has a physical effect on your body—so *air* is definitely concrete! What part of speech is *German-built?*

→ *Student: An adjective* OR *A compound adjective.*

> **Note to Instructor**: If the student says *adjective*, ask, "What kind of adjective?"

Instructor: Why is *German* capitalized?

→ *Student: It is a proper adjective.*

Instructor: Is *German-built* in the attributive or predicative position?

→ *Student: Attributive.*

Instructor: It is hyphenated because it is in the attributive position.

Complete the exercises in your workbook now.

Introduction to the Sentence

—LESSON 9—

The Sentence
Parts of Speech and Parts of Sentences
Subjects and Predicates

> **Note to Instructor:** This lesson begins with a series of instructor questions and statements that are intended to be confusing. Say the first one and then wait for the student to look puzzled (or say "What?") before continuing on; do the same for the next three.

> **Note to Instructor:** Today's lesson teaches the terms *subject* and *predicate*. The difference between simple and complete subjects and predicates will be covered in Lesson 12. If the student has already learned these terms and asks about them, you may tell her that *subject* and *predicate* in Lessons 9-11 is shorthand for *simple subject* and *simple predicate*.

Instructor: Today's lesson.

Instructor: For a little while.

Instructor: If raining.

Instructor: Caught a ball.

Instructor: You probably didn't understand anything I just said. That's because I wasn't using sentences. Read me the first definition.

→ Student: ***A sentence is a group of words that contains a subject and a predicate.***

Instructor: Look at the first sentence, "The cat sits on the mat." The word *cat* is underlined. What part of speech is the word *cat*—noun, adjective, pronoun, or verb?

→ Student: *Noun.*

Instructor: The correct part of speech is written above the word. Look at the word *sits*. What part of speech is *sits*?

→ Student: *It is a verb.*

Instructor: Most sentences have two basic parts—the **subject** and the **predicate. The subject of the sentence is the main word or term that the sentence is about.** Repeat that definition.

→ Student: *The subject of the sentence is the main word or term that the sentence is about.*

Instructor: Who or what is the first sentence about?

→ Student: *The cat.*

Instructor: *Cat* is the subject. If I ask, "What part of speech is *cat*?" you would answer *noun*. But if I ask, "What part of the sentence is *cat*?" you would answer *subject*. Look at the definitions below the example sentence and read me the second definition found there.

→ *Student: Part of speech is a term that explains what a word does.*

Instructor: Now read me the third definition.

→ *Student: **Part of the sentence is a term that explains how a word functions in a sentence.***

Instructor: Look at the second example sentence. What is the *subject* of that sentence—the main word or term that the sentence is about?

→ *Student: Tyrannosaurus rex.*

Instructor: Write *subject* on the line under *Tyrannosaurus rex*, across from the label *part of the sentence*. What *part of speech* is the subject *Tyrannosaurus rex*?

→ *Student: A noun.*

Instructor: Write *noun* above *Tyrannosaurus rex*, across from the label *part of speech*.

Now look back at the first sentence. The double-underlined word *sits* is a verb; it shows an action. *Verb*, the correct part of speech, is written on the line above it. In the second sentence, what part of speech is the double-underlined word?

→ *Student: Verb.*

Instructor: Write *verb* on the line above *crashes*. Now look back at the first sentence. Earlier, I said that each sentence has two parts—the subject and the predicate. The subject of the sentence is the main word or term that the sentence is about. **The predicate of the sentence tells something about the subject.**

The word *predicate* comes from the Latin word *praedicare* [preh-dee-car-eh], meaning "to proclaim." The predicate of the sentence is what is said or *proclaimed* about the subject. Read that definition out loud.

→ *Student: The predicate of the sentence tells something about the subject.*

Instructor: In the first sentence, the predicate tells us something about the subject—it tells us that the cat is *sitting*. *Sits* is the predicate of the first sentence. What is the predicate of the second sentence?

→ *Student: Crashes.*

Instructor: Write *predicate* on the *part of the sentence* line beneath *crashes*. Now let's review. What is a part of speech? You may look back at your book for the answer.

→ *Student: Part of speech is a term that explains what a word does.*

Instructor: What four parts of speech have you learned so far?

→ *Student: Noun, adjective, pronoun, verb.*

Instructor: What is a part of the sentence?

→ *Student: Part of the sentence is a term that explains how a word functions in a sentence.*

Instructor: Most sentences have two parts—a subject and a predicate. What is a subject?

→ *Student: The subject of a sentence is the main word or term that the sentence is about.*

Instructor: What is a predicate?

→ *Student: The predicate of the sentence tells us something about the subject.*

part of speech   <u>noun</u>   <u>verb</u>
The <u>*Tyrannosaurus rex*</u> <u>crashes</u> through the trees.
part of the sentence   <u>subject</u>   <u>predicate</u>

Instructor: Complete the Lesson 9 exercises now.

— LESSON 10 —

Subjects and Predicates
Diagramming Subjects and Predicates
Sentence Capitalization and Punctuation
Sentence Fragments

Instructor: What was the definition of a sentence that we read in the last lesson? You may read it from your workbook if you can't remember.

→ *Student: A sentence is a group of words that contains a subject and predicate.*

Instructor: The next three groups of words in your workbook are sentences, even though each sentence is only two words long. Read them out loud now.

→ *Student: He does. They can. It is.*

Instructor: Each group of words has a subject and a predicate. The subjects are underlined once, and the predicates are underlined twice. Read me the definition of a subject.

→ *Student: The subject of the sentence is the main word or term that the sentence is about.*

Instructor: Read me the definition of a predicate.

→ *Student: The predicate of the sentence tells something about the subject.*

Instructor: You can usually find the subject by asking, "Who or what is the sentence about?" What is the subject of the next sentence?

→ *Student: Hurricanes.*

Instructor: Underline the word *hurricanes* once. This is the subject. What do hurricanes do?

→ *Student: Form.*

Instructor: Underline the word *form* twice. This is the predicate.

> **Note to Instructor:** If the student answers, "Form over warm tropical waters," ask him to answer with a single word.

Instructor: You've marked the subject and predicate by underlining them, but there's a better way to show how the parts of a sentence work together. When you diagram a sentence, you draw a picture of the logical relationships between the different parts of a sentence. The first step in diagramming any sentence is to diagram the subject and predicate. Look at the diagram of *Hurricanes form.*

Instructor: Which comes first on the diagram—the subject or the predicate?

→ *Student: The subject.*

Instructor: When you diagram a simple sentence like this one, you begin by drawing a straight horizontal line and dividing it in half with a vertical line. Make sure that the vertical line goes straight through the horizontal line. Write the subject on the left side of the vertical line and the predicate on the right side. Before we go on, write *subject* on the left side of the blank diagram in your book and *predicate* on the right side.

subject | predicate

Instructor: A sentence is a group of words that contains a subject and a predicate—but that's only the first part of the definition. Look at each one of the sentences in your workbook. What kind of letter does each sentence begin with?

→ *Student: A capital letter.*

Instructor: What is at the end of each sentence?

→ *Student: A period.*

Instructor: This is the second part of the definition. A sentence begins with a capital letter and ends with a punctuation mark. Read me the two-part definition of a sentence.

→ *Student: A sentence is a group of words that contains a subject and a predicate. A sentence begins with a capital letter and ends with a punctuation mark.*

Instructor: Sometimes, a group of words begins with a capital letter and ends with a punctuation mark—but doesn't have a subject and a predicate. Read me the next sentence.

→ *Student: No running in the kitchen.*

Instructor: Do you understand that sentence?

→ *Student: Yes.*

Instructor: *No running in the kitchen* and *Caught a ball* are both groups of words without a subject and predicate. But *No running in the kitchen* makes sense, and *Caught a ball* doesn't. Sometimes a group of words can function as a sentence even though it's missing a subject or predicate. Read me the next paragraph.

→ *Student: Can we measure intelligence without understanding it? Possibly so; physicists measured gravity and magnetism long before they understood them theoretically. Maybe psychologists can do the same with intelligence. Or maybe not.*

Instructor: The group of bolded words makes complete sense, but there's no subject *or* predicate in them. On the other hand, the next two groups of words have subjects *and* predicates, but *don't* make complete sense. Read them out loud.

→ *Student: Because he couldn't go. Since I thought so.*

Instructor: Any time a group of words begins with a capital letter and ends with a period, it should make sense on its own. So we need to add one word and one more line to our definition. Read the new definition out loud.

→ *Student: **A sentence is a group of words that usually contains a subject and a predicate. A sentence begins with a capital letter and ends with a punctuation mark. A sentence contains a complete thought.***

Instructor: What word did we add to that definition? (It's in the first line.)

→ *Student: Usually.*

Instructor: What line did we add?

→ *Student: A sentence contains a complete thought.*

Instructor: If a group of words is capitalized and ends with a punctuation mark, but doesn't contain a complete thought, we call it a sentence fragment. When you're writing, avoid sentence fragments. Not every sentence *has* to have a subject and a predicate. But every sentence has to make sense when you read it on its own. Now finish the exercises at the end of the lesson.

— LESSON 11 —
Types of Sentences

Instructor: Let's begin by reviewing the definition of a sentence. Read that definition out loud.

→ *Student: A sentence is a group of words that usually contains a subject and a predicate. A sentence begins with a capital letter and ends with a punctuation mark. A sentence contains a complete thought.*

Instructor: Read me the next sentence. Notice that it is written with a capital letter and a punctuation mark.

→ *Student: A purple penguin is playing ping-pong.*

Instructor: Read the sentence again, but this time read it with great excitement.

→ *Student: (with great excitement) A purple penguin is playing ping-pong!*

Instructor: Now read the sentence as though you were asking a question.

→ *Student: (in a questioning tone) A purple penguin is playing ping-pong?*

Instructor: When we are speaking, we can use expression in our voices and faces to convey feelings about what we are saying. When we are writing, however, we do not have expression, so we use punctuation as a tool to show the reader our feelings about a sentence. Read the definition of the first sentence type out loud.

→ *Student: **A statement gives information. A statement always ends with a period.***

Instructor: A statement simply explains a fact. Statements declare that something is so. Make a statement about your shoes.

→ *Student: My shoes are [Answers will vary: blue, on my feet, dirty].*

Instructor: You will sometimes see statements called **declarative sentences.** *Declarative sentence* is another way to refer to a *statement*. What kind of sentences are statements?

→ *Student: Statements are declarative sentences.*

Instructor: Read the definition of the second type of sentence.

→ *Student: **An exclamation shows sudden or strong feeling. An exclamation always ends with an exclamation point.***

Instructor: When we want to convey particularly strong emotion behind our statements, we can use an exclamation point. If we are surprised or excited about the purple penguin, we can write that sentence as an exclamation, and convey our surprise or excitement with an exclamation point. *A purple penguin is playing ping-pong!* Make an exclamation about your shoes!

→ *Student: My shoes are [Answers will vary: blue, on my feet, dirty]!*

Instructor: You will sometimes see exclamations called **exclamatory sentences.** "Exclamatory sentence" is another word for an exclamation. What kinds of sentences are exclamations?

→ *Student: Exclamations are exclamatory sentences.*

Instructor: Sometimes exclamations begin with question words like *how* or *what,* and do not have complete subjects and predicates. Examples of this type of exclamations are *What a strange bug!* or *How nice to see you!* What would you say if you wanted to make an exclamation about how fun this grammar lesson is?

→ *Student: What fun this grammar lesson is!*

Instructor: Read the definition of the third sentence type.

→ *Student: **A command gives an order or makes a request. A command ends with either a period or an exclamation point.***

Instructor: When you tell someone to do something, you are giving a command. When you say, *Please pass the butter*, you are making a request; that is a command. If you say *Be quiet!* you are giving an order. That is also a command. Make a request of me, beginning with *please.*

→ *Student: Please [Answers will vary: sit down, walk to the door, stop giving me a grammar lesson].*

Instructor: That is a command. But I'm not going to follow it. Now give me an order.

→ *Student: Sit down [Answers will vary: walk to the door].*

Instructor: I'm not going to follow that command either. But you're doing a good job. Depending on the emotion behind the command, you can use a period or an exclamation point. Stand up.

→ *Student [Stands up.]*

Instructor: That command ended with a period. Now sit down!

> **Note to Instructor:** Use a strong tone of voice for the second command.

→ *Student: [Sits down.]*

Instructor: That command ended with an exclamation point. When you give someone a command, you are acting in an **imperative** manner—like a king or an emperor. "Imperative" comes from the Latin word for "emperor": *imperator.* What kind of sentences are commands?

→ *Student: Commands are imperative sentences.*

Instructor: Look at the three commands in your workbook. Those commands are actually complete sentences—but they're missing one of the basic sentence parts. What's missing—the subject or the predicate?

→ *Student: The subject.*

> **Note to Instructor:** If the student has difficulty answering this question, ask whether the commands are verbs or nouns. When the student answers "verbs," point out that predicates contain verbs.

Instructor: The subject of a command is almost always *you.* If I say, "Sit!" what I really mean is, "You sit!" We say that the subject of a command is *understood to be you*, because the *you* is not spoken or written. Repeat after me: **The subject of a command is understood to be *you.***

→ *Student: The subject of a command is understood to be* you.

Instructor: When we diagram a command, we write the word *you* in parentheses in place of the subject. Look at the diagram in your workbook. Notice that *you* is in parentheses and that *Sit* is capitalized in the diagram because it is capitalized in the sentence. Is the exclamation point on the diagram?

→ *Student: No.*

Instructor: Read the definition of the fourth type of sentence.

→ *Student: **A question asks something. A question always ends with a question mark.***

Instructor: Ask me a question about my shoes.

→ *Student: Are your shoes* [Answers will vary: *blue*]?

Instructor: Stop interrogating me! To *interrogate* someone means to ask them questions. What are questions also known as?

→ *Student: Questions are known as interrogative sentences.*

Instructor: When you diagram a question, remember that English often forms a question by reversing the subject and the predicate. Read me the statement and the question in your workbook.

→ *Student: He is late. Is he late?*

Instructor: Look at the two diagrams of these two sentences. What is the difference between them?

→ *Student: The word* He *is capitalized in the first diagram, and the word* Is *is capitalized in the second.*

Instructor: When you diagram a question, you may want to turn it into a statement first. This will remind you that the subject still comes first on the diagram and the predicate comes second. Now complete the exercises at the end of the lesson. If you do not understand the instructions, ask me for help.

— LESSON 12 —

Subjects and Predicates
Helping Verbs
Simple and Complete Subjects and Predicates

Instructor: I'm going to begin a sentence and I want you to finish it. If you don't know what to say, look down at your workbook for a hint. Mary . . .

→ *Student: . . . had a little lamb.*

Instructor: Its fleece . . .

→ *Student: . . . was white as snow.*

Instructor: And everywhere that Mary went, the lamb . . .

→ *Student: . . . was sure to go.*

Instructor: All three of those sentences have a *subject* and a *predicate.* The subject of "Mary had a little lamb" is *Mary.* What did Mary do?

→ *Student: Had [a little lamb].*

Instructor: *Had* is the predicate. But there are actually more precise names for *Mary* and *had*. Mary is the **simple subject** and *had* is the **simple predicate**. First, let's talk about the simple subject. The simple subject is *just* the main word or term that the sentence is about. Read the next two sentences in your workbook out loud.

→ Student: *The subject of the sentence is the main word or term that the sentence is about.* **The simple subject of the sentence is just the main word or term that the sentence is about.**

Instructor: In the next sentence, *fleece* is the *simple subject*. Underline *fleece* one time and then circle the phrase *its fleece*. *Its fleece* is the *complete subject*. The **complete subject** of the sentence is the simple subject and all the words that belong to it. Read the definition of complete subject out loud now.

→ Student: **The complete subject of the sentence is the simple subject and all the words that belong to it.**

Instructor: You can probably guess what the complete predicate is. It's the simple predicate (the verb of the sentence) and all the words that belong to it. Read the next three sentences out loud.

→ Student: *The predicate of the sentence tells something about the subject.* **The simple predicate of the sentence is the main verb along with any helping verbs. The complete predicate of the sentence is the simple predicate and all the words that belong to it.**

Instructor: In the sentence in your workbook, *was white as snow* is the complete predicate, and *was* is the simple predicate. Underline *was* twice and circle *was white as snow*.

Now, look at the next two sentences. Each one has been divided into the complete subject and the complete predicate. In each, the simple subject is underlined once and the simple predicate is underlined twice. Notice that the simple predicate is made up of both the main verb and the helping verb. Recite the helping verbs for me now.

→ Student: *Am, is, are, was, were, be, being, been, have, has, had, do, does, did, shall, will, should, would, may, might, must, can, could.*

Instructor: Here's a summary of this whole lesson: You can divide any sentence into two parts: the simple subject and the words that belong to it, and the simple predicate and the words that belong to *it*.

Complete the exercises in your workbook now.

— REVIEW 1 —

The review exercises and answers are found in the Student Workbook and accompanying Key.

Verb Tenses

— LESSON 13 —

Nouns, Pronouns, and Verbs
Sentences
Simple Present, Simple Past, and Simple Future Tenses

Instructor: Let's do a quick review of some of your definitions. What does a noun do?

→ *Student: A noun names a person, place, thing, or idea.*

Instructor: What does a pronoun do?

→ *Student: A pronoun takes the place of a noun.*

Instructor: What does a verb do?

→ *Student: A verb shows an action, shows a state of being, links two words together, or helps another verb.*

Instructor: List the state-of-being verbs for me.

→ *Student: Am, is, are, was, were, be, being, been.*

Instructor: List the helping verbs for me.

→ *Student: Am, is, are, was, were, be, being, been, have, has, had, do, does, did, shall, will, should, would, may, might, must, can, could.*

Instructor: Read me the definition of a sentence.

→ *Student: A sentence is a group of words that usually contains a subject and a predicate. A sentence begins with a capital letter and ends with a punctuation mark. A sentence contains a complete thought.*

Instructor: Repeat these sentences after me: I sing.

→ *Student: I sing.*

Instructor: I eat.

→ *Student: I eat.*

Instructor: I learn.

→ *Student: I learn.*

Instructor: Each one of those sentences tells about something I am doing in the present—right now. Give me some other two-word sentences explaining what you are doing right now, in the present.

→ *Student: I [Answers will vary: sit, study, look, read, breathe].*

> **Note to Instructor:** If the student uses *I am sitting*, *I am studying*, or a similar form, remind her that she can only use two words.

Instructor: You have learned that verbs do four things—show action, show state of being, link two words together, or help other verbs. But while verbs are doing these four things, they also give us information about *when* these things are happening. In your sentences, everything is happening right now—in the present. A verb can show present time, past time, or future time.

In grammar, we call the time a verb is showing its **tense**. *Tense* means "time." Repeat after me: **A verb in the present tense tells about something that happens in the present.**

→ *Student: A verb in the present tense tells about something that happens in the present.*

Instructor: I might sing today, but yesterday, I sang. Repeat these sentences after me: Yesterday, I ate.

→ *Student: Yesterday, I ate.*

Instructor: Yesterday, I learned.

→ *Student: Yesterday, I learned.*

Instructor: Each one of those sentences tells about something I did on a day that has passed— yesterday. Give me some other two-word sentences explaining what you did yesterday.

→ *Student: I [Answers will vary: sat, studied, looked, read, breathed].*

> **Note to Instructor:** If the student uses *I was sitting*, *I was studying*, or a similar form, remind her that she can only use two words.

Instructor: Repeat after me: **A verb in the past tense tells about something that happened in the past.**

→ *Student: A verb in the past tense tells about something that happened in the past.*

Instructor: I might sing again tomorrow. Repeat these sentences after me: Tomorrow, I will sing.

→ *Student: Tomorrow, I will sing.*

Instructor: Tomorrow, I will eat.

→ *Student: Tomorrow, I will eat.*

Instructor: Tomorrow, I will learn.

→ *Student: Tomorrow, I will learn.*

Instructor: Each one of those sentences tells about something I will do in the future. Give me some other three-word sentences explaining what you will do tomorrow.

→ *Student: I [Answers will vary: will sit, will study, will look, will read, will breathe.]*

> **Note to Instructor:** If the student uses *I will be sitting*, *I will be studying*, or a similar form, remind her that she can only use three words in her sentence.

Instructor: Repeat after me: **A verb in the future tense tells about something that will happen in the future.**

→ *Student: A verb in the future tense tells about something that will happen in the future.*

Instructor: In English, we have three tenses—past, present, and future. The verbs we've been using are in the **simple past, simple present**, and **simple future**. There are more complicated forms of past, present, and future, but we will talk about those another time. Right now, look at Exercise 13A. Fill in the missing tenses of each verb.

> **Note to Instructor:** Give the student all necessary help in filling out this chart. The student may find it helpful to say the subject out loud with each form of the verb: *I will grab. I grab. I grabbed.*

Instructor: Look at the verbs in the *simple future* column. What did you add to each one?

→ *Student: Will.*

Instructor: We **form the simple future by adding the helping verb** *will* **in front of the simple present.** Now look at the verbs in the *simple past* column. What two letters did you add to each one?

→ *Student: -Ed.*

Instructor: -*Ed* is a **suffix. A suffix is one or more letters added to the end of a word to change its meaning.** Repeat that definition now.

→ *Student: A suffix is one or more letters added to the end of a word to change its meaning.*

Instructor: When you add the suffix -*ed* to the end of a verb, it changes the verb from simple present to simple past tense. That changes the meaning of the verb. Now read me the rules for forming the simple past of regular verbs. (Some verbs are *irregular* and don't follow these rules. You'll study the most common irregular verbs later.)

→ *Student: To form the past tense, add* -ed *to the basic verb.*

> *sharpen–sharpened*
> *utter–uttered*

If the basic verb ends in -e *already, only add* -d.
> *rumble–rumbled*
> *shade–shaded*

If the verb ends in a short vowel sound and a consonant, double the consonant and add -ed.
> *scam–scammed*
> *thud–thudded*

If the verb ends in -y *following a consonant, change the* y *to* i *and add* -ed.
> *cry–cried*
> *try–tried*

Instructor: Complete the remaining exercises in your workbook now.

— LESSON 14 —

Simple Present, Simple Past, and Simple Future Tenses
Progressive Present, Progressive Past, and Progressive Future Tenses

Instructor: In the last lesson, you learned about simple tenses—ways a verb changes to show you whether it is happening in the past, present, or future. Repeat after me: I study, I studied, I will study.

→ *Student: I study, I studied, I will study.*

Instructor: Is the verb *study* past, present, or future?

→ *Student: Present.*

Instructor: A verb in the present tense tells about something that happens in the present. Is the verb *will study* in the past, present, or future?

→ *Student: Future.*

Instructor: A verb in the future tense tells about something that will happen in the future. Is the verb *studied* in the past, present, or future?

→ *Student: Past.*

Instructor: A verb in the past tense tells about something that happened in the past. Look at the verb *study* in your workbook. What did we add to it to make it future?

→ *Student: Will.*

Instructor: What did we add to it to make it past?

→ *Student: The suffix -ed.*

Instructor: Read me the rules for forming the simple past.

→ *Student: To form the past tense, add -ed to the basic verb. If the basic verb ends in -e already, only add -d. If the verb ends in a short vowel sound and a consonant, double the consonant and add -ed. If the verb ends in -y following a consonant, change the y to i and add -ed.*

Instructor: Complete Exercise 14A now.

Instructor: Verbs in the simple past, simple present, and simple future simply tell you when something happened. But these simple tenses are *so* simple that they don't give you any more information. If I say, *I cried,* I might mean that I shed a single tear. Or I might mean that I wept and wept and wept for hours. Today we're going to learn about three more tenses. They are called the **progressive past**, **progressive present**, and **progressive future**. Read me the next two sentences.

→ *Student: Yesterday, I cried. I was crying for a long time.*

Instructor: The verb *was crying* is progressive past. It tells you that the crying went on for a while in the past. Read me the next two sentences.

→ *Student: Today, I learn. I am learning my grammar.*

Instructor: The verb *am learning* is progressive present. It tells you that the learning is progressing on for some time today. Read me the next two sentences.

→ *Student: Tomorrow, I will celebrate. I will be celebrating all afternoon.*

Instructor: The verb *will be celebrating* is progressive future. It tells you that the celebration will go on for more than just a minute. Now read me the definition of a progressive verb.

→ *Student: **A progressive verb describes an ongoing or continuous action.***

Instructor: Look at the list of progressive verbs in Exercise 14B. Each one of those progressive verbs has the same suffix, or ending. What is it?

→ *Student: The ending -ing.*

Instructor: Circle the ending of each verb. Then, underline the helping verbs that come in front of each verb.

Instructor: To form a progressive tense, you add helping verbs and the suffix *-ing*. Repeat after me: **The progressive past tense uses the helping verbs *was* and *were*.**

→ *Student: The progressive past tense uses the helping verbs* was *and* were.

Instructor: **The progressive present tense uses the helping verbs *am, is,* and *are*.**

→ *Student: The progressive present tense uses the helping verbs* am, is, *and* are.

Instructor: **The progressive future tense uses the helping verb *will be*.**

→ *Student: The progressive future tense uses the helping verb* will be.

Instructor: There are two spelling rules you should keep in mind when you add *-ing* to a verb. Read them out loud, along with the examples.

→ *Student: **If the verb ends in a short vowel sound and a consonant, double the consonant and add -ing.***
    sk<u>ip</u>–skipping
    dr<u>um</u>–drumming

If the verb ends in a long vowel sound plus a consonant and an -e, drop the e and add -ing.
    sm<u>ile</u>–smiling
    tr<u>ade</u>–trading

Instructor: Complete the remaining exercises now.

— LESSON 15 —

Simple Present, Simple Past, and Simple Future Tenses
Progressive Present, Progressive Past, and Progressive Future Tenses
Perfect Present, Perfect Past, and Perfect Future Tenses

Instructor: This week, we have learned about tenses—verb forms that tell us when actions take place. We have also learned about two different kinds of tenses—simple and progressive. A simple tense *simply* tells us when an action takes place. But a progressive tense tells us when an action takes place—*and* that the action lasted for a while. Read me the first definition in your workbook.

→ *Student: A progressive verb describes an ongoing or continuous action.*

Instructor: Read me the next sentence.

→ *Student: Yesterday, I was studying tenses.*

Instructor: The verb *was studying* is progressive past. It tells you that the studying went on for a while in the past. Read me the second sentence.

→ *Student: Today, I am studying tenses.*

Instructor: The verb *am studying* is progressive present. It tells you that the studying is still progressing for some time today. Read me the third sentence.

→ *Student: Tomorrow, I will be studying something else!*

Instructor: The verb *will be studying* is progressive future. It tells you that the studying will still be progressing for some time tomorrow. But will you be studying about tenses?

→ *Student: No!*

Instructor: You've learned about simple and progressive tenses. Today, we will be studying the third kind of tense. Read me the imaginary news bulletin in your workbook.

→ *Student: NEWS BULLETIN! A diamond theft occurred at the National Museum yesterday. The thief had already fled the scene when a security guard discovered that the diamond was missing.*

Instructor: When did the theft occur?

→ *Student: Yesterday.*

Instructor: The verb *occurred* is simple past. It just tells that sometime yesterday, the theft occurred. What did the security guard do?

→ *Student: He discovered that the diamond was missing.*

Instructor: What tense is the verb *discovered* in?

→ *Student: Simple past.*

Instructor: What happened *before* the security guard discovered the missing diamond?

→ *Student: The thief fled.*

Instructor: By the time the security guard discovered the theft, the thief was finished fleeing. But was the diamond still missing?

→ *Student: Yes.*

Instructor: *Discovered* is the simple past. *Was missing* is the progressive past—the missing was going on yesterday, and it is still going on today. But *had fled* is the third kind of tense: the **perfect tense.** Repeat after me: **A perfect verb describes an action which has been completed before another action takes place.**

→ *Student: A perfect verb describes an action which has been completed before another action takes place.*

Instructor: The thief had completed his fleeing before the security guard discovered the theft. Read me the next three sentences.

→ *Student: I practiced my piano. I was practicing my piano all day yesterday. I had practiced my piano before I went to bed.*

Instructor: The first sentence is in the simple past. You simply practiced. The second sentence is in the progressive past. The practicing went on for some time. The third sentence is in the perfect past. You finished practicing the piano—and *then* you went to bed. There are three perfect tenses—just like there are three simple tenses and three progressive tenses. They are perfect present, perfect past, and perfect future. Look at the chart in your workbook and read me the three sentences underneath *perfect past.*

→ *Student: I had practiced yesterday. I had eaten before bed. I had seen the movie a week ago.*

Instructor: Each one of those actions was finished in the past before something else happened. Repeat after me: **Perfect past verbs describe an action that was finished in the past before another action began.**

→ *Student: Perfect past verbs describe an action that was finished in the past before another action began.*

Instructor: You usually form the perfect past with the helping verb *had.* Now read me the three sentences underneath *perfect present.*

→ *Student: I have practiced. I have eaten already. I have seen the movie once.*

Instructor: Each one of those actions was finished in the past, but we don't know exactly when— just that they're finished *now.* Repeat after me: **Perfect present verbs describe an action that was completed before the present moment.**

→ *Student: Perfect present verbs describe an action that was completed before the present moment.*

Instructor: You usually form the perfect present with the helping verbs *have* and *has.* Read me the three sentences underneath *perfect future.*

→ *Student: I will have practiced tomorrow. I will have eaten by bedtime tomorrow. I will have seen the movie before it leaves the theater.*

Instructor: Those actions haven't even happened yet—but they will be finished, in the future, before something else happens. Repeat after me: **Perfect future verbs describe an action that will be finished in the future before another action begins.**

→ *Student: Perfect future verbs describe an action that will be finished in the future before another action begins.*

Instructor: You should use the helping verbs *will have* for the perfect future. Complete your exercises now.

— LESSON 16 —

Simple Present, Simple Past, and Simple Future Tenses
Progressive Present, Progressive Past, and Progressive Future Tenses
Perfect Present, Perfect Past, and Perfect Future Tenses
Irregular Verbs

Instructor: Read the first line of verbs in your workbook now.

→ *Student: Go, run, are, know, make.*

Instructor: These are some of the most common and frequently used verbs in English. And because English speakers have used them *so* often, something weird has happened to them. Read the second list of verbs, making each word two syllables.

→ *Student: Go-ed, run-ned, ar-ed, know-ed, mak-ed.*

Instructor: That should sound very strange to you. But that's what these verbs would sound like if they formed the simple past by adding *-ed,* like most other verbs. The suffix would make each word two syllables long—and for common verbs, that's too long! Here's what you should remember about people: We're lazy and in a hurry at the same time. It takes more time and effort to say two syllables than to say one. That's why names like Robert and Michael and Christopher usually get shrunk down to Bob, Mike, and Chris—and that's why each one of these common verbs has gotten reduced down to a quick one-syllable version of itself. Read those one-syllable versions now.

→ *Student: Went, ran, were, knew, made.*

Instructor: We call these **irregular verbs** because they don't follow the rule for the simple past. You probably know all of these irregular forms already, because you've been using them in speech since you learned how to talk. Your first exercise is a chart of irregular verbs. Fill out the Exercise 16A chart now.

Instructor: Once you know the simple past and simple present of an irregular verb, you can usually form the progressive tenses without any problem. But the perfect tenses are often irregular too. Read all nine forms of the irregular verb "go" from the chart in your workbook.

→ *Student: Went, go, will go; was going, am going, will be going; had gone, have gone, will have gone.*

Instructor: Notice that the progressive tenses add the suffix *-ing* to the simple present and use helping verbs—just like a regular verb. But what does the verb *go* change to, in the perfect tenses?

→ *Student: It becomes gone.*

Instructor: That's an irregular perfect. If it were regular, you would say *had went, have went, will have went.* Sometimes you'll hear people who don't know their grammar use this form: *I had went to the store.* But you're learning the correct forms now, so *you* will always say, *I had gone to the store.* Now look at the verb *eat.* What irregular form does *eat* take in the perfect tenses?

→ *Student: Eaten*

Instructor: Would you ever say, *I will have ate my dinner*?

→ *Student: No!*

Instructor: We'll study more irregular verbs in later lessons. But the rest of this lesson is simple: fill out the chart in Exercise 16B with the correct forms. You have been given the simple present of each verb; use the 16A chart for reference if necessary. If you're not sure about the irregular perfects, just ask me.

More About Verbs

— LESSON 17 —

Simple, Progressive, and Perfect Tenses
Subjects and Predicates
Parts of Speech and Parts of Sentences
Verb Phrases

> **Note to Instructor:** The student will probably begin yawning as soon as you mention the word. Make a joke out of it; this verb was used on purpose to break up the tedium of review!

Instructor: In the last lesson, I promised you that you'd study something other than verb tenses. You will—but first we have to do a quick review! Read the first line in your workbook out loud.

→ *Student: I yawn today. Yesterday, I yawned. Tomorrow I will yawn.*

Instructor: Those three sentences are in the simple present, the simple past, and the simple future. The verbs *yawn, yawned,* and *will yawn* don't tell you how long the yawning goes on—or when it ends. Read the second line out loud.

→ *Student: I am yawning today. Yesterday, I was yawning. Tomorrow, I will be yawning.*

Instructor: Those three sentences are in the progressive present, the progressive past, and the progressive future. Read me the definition of progressive tense.

→ *Student: A progressive verb describes an ongoing or continuous action.*

Instructor: If you say, *Yesterday, I was yawning,* that tells me that the yawning went on for at least a little while. Now read me the next three sentences.

→ *Student: I have yawned today already. Yesterday, I had yawned before I had my dinner. Tomorrow, I will have yawned by the time the sun goes down.*

Instructor: Those three sentences are in the perfect present, the perfect past, and the perfect future. Read me the definition of perfect tense.

→ *Student: A perfect verb describes an action which has been completed before another action takes place.*

Instructor: I think that we should complete our yawning before we go on with our lesson! Hop up and do five jumping jacks, and then we'll go on.

> **Note to Instructor:** Jumping jacks are optional, but the student will probably need to do something physical to stop the yawning.

Instructor: Look at Exercise 17A and follow the directions.

Instructor: Read me the next two sets of words in your workbook.

→ *Student: Had rejoiced, will have rejoiced.*

Instructor: *Had rejoiced* is a perfect past verb. *Will have rejoiced* is a perfect future verb. In each of these examples, the helping verb and the main action verb act together as a single verb. We call these **verb phrases**. Read me the definition of a phrase.

→ *Student: **A phrase is a group of words serving a single grammatical function.***

Instructor: In a verb phrase, a group of words serves a single grammatical function by acting as a verb. Read me the next two sets of words.

→ *Student: Have greatly rejoiced, they will have all rejoiced.*

Instructor: A word comes between the helping verb and the main verb in each of those verb phrases. *Greatly* and *all* are not part of the verb phrases! Only helping verbs and main verbs belong in a verb phrase.

When you diagram a verb phrase, all of the verbs in the verb phrase go on the predicate space of the diagram. You can see this illustrated in your workbook.

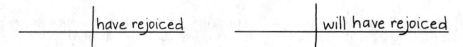

Instructor: Before you complete Exercise 17B, let's review both predicates and subjects. Repeat after me: The subject of the sentence is the main word or term that the sentence is about.

→ *Student: The subject of the sentence is the main word or term that the sentence is about.*

Instructor: The simple subject of the sentence is *just* the main word or term that the sentence is about.

→ *Student: The simple subject of the sentence is* just *the main word or term that the sentence is about.*

Instructor: The predicate of the sentence tells something about the subject. Repeat that after me.

→ *Student: The predicate of the sentence tells something about the subject.*

Instructor: The simple predicate of the sentence is the main verb along with any helping verbs.

→ *Student: The simple predicate of the sentence is the main verb along with any helping verbs.*

Instructor: When we studied subjects and predicates, we also talked about the difference between parts of speech and parts of a sentence. Repeat after me: Part of speech is a term that explains what a word does.

→ *Student: Part of speech is a term that explains what a word does.*

Instructor: Noun and pronoun are both parts of speech. Main verb and helping verb are both parts of speech. Tell me what a noun does.

→ *Student: A noun names a person, place, thing, or idea.*

Instructor: Tell me what a pronoun does.

→ *Student: A pronoun takes the place of a noun.*

Instructor: These parts of speech can also function, in sentences, as subjects. *Subject* refers to the *part of the sentence* that the noun or pronoun is in. Read me the definition of *part of the sentence*.

→ *Student: Part of the sentence is a term that explains how a word functions in a sentence.*

Instructor: A main verb does an action, shows a state of being, or links two words together. A helping verb helps the main verb. Read me the definition of a verb.

→ *Student: A verb shows an action, shows a state of being, links two words together, or helps another verb.*

Instructor: A verb is a part of speech. In a sentence, a main verb and its helping verbs form the predicate. A predicate is a part of the sentence. When you underline a main verb and its helping verbs, you are locating a part of speech. When you put the entire verb phrase on the diagram, you are showing that the verb and its helping verbs function, in the sentence, as a predicate. They tell more about the subject. Now for the last part of the review: Find the subject of a sentence by asking, *Who or what is the sentence about?* Find the predicate by asking, *Subject what?*

Try that now as you complete Exercise 17B.

— LESSON 18 —

Verb Phrases
Person of the Verb
Conjugations

Instructor: Several lessons ago you completed a chart showing the progressive tenses. Look over these verbs from that chart now.

	Progressive Past	Progressive Present	Progressive Future
I run	I was running	I am running	I will be running
You call	You were calling	You are calling	You will be calling
He jogs	He was jogging	He is jogging	He will be jogging
We fix	We were fixing	We are fixing	We will be fixing
They call	They were calling	They are calling	They will be calling

Instructor: In the progressive future column, all of the helping verbs are the same. But in the middle column, what three helping verbs are used to help form the progressive present?

→ *Student: Am, are, is.*

Instructor: In the progressive past column, two different helping verbs are used. What are they?

→ *Student: Was and were.*

Instructor: Because the helping verbs change, the entire verb phrases change. Verbs and verb phrases change their form because of the person or thing that does the verb. When verbs change for this reason, we say that they are in the first, second, or third person. Look at the next chart.

PERSONS OF THE VERB

	Singular	Plural
First person	I	we
Second person	you	you
Third person	he, she, it	they

Instructor: We talked about the first-, second-, and third person pronouns in Lesson 8. Let's review now—and connect those pronouns to verbs.

> **Note to Instructor:** Point to the student in a dramatic fashion.

Instructor: Say after me, *I understand!*

→ *Student: I understand!*

Instructor: The first person is the one who is speaking. If you're all by yourself, you would use the pronoun *I.* If someone is with you, you use the pronoun *we.*

> **Note to Instructor:** Move over and stand next to the student.

Instructor: Say with me, *We understand!*

→ *Together: We understand!*

Instructor: The second person is the one who's in the room, but who isn't . . . [Point to the student again.] Who is the second person in this room?

→ *Student: You.*

Instructor: For the second person, we use the pronoun *you.* In English, *you* can be either singular or plural. If there were two of you here, I would still use the pronoun *you.* Say with me, and point to me, *You understand!*

→ *Together [Pointing at each other]: You understand!*

Instructor: The third person who might be doing an action is the person who isn't you, and isn't me. We use four different pronouns to refer to *that* person—the third person. If that person is male, we say, *He understands.* What do we say if that person is female?

→ *Student: She understands.*

Instructor: Imagine that my dog is sitting here, listening and looking very intelligent, but you don't know whether my dog is a he or a she. What pronoun would you use to point out that the dog also understands?

→ *Student: It understands.*

Instructor: What if there were a whole crowd of third persons in the room, all understanding? What pronoun would you use for them?

→ *Student: They understand.*

Instructor: Together, let's team up the first, second, and third person with the action verb *pretend.* When we say the first person, we'll point to ourselves. When we say the second person, we'll point to each other. When we say the third person, we'll point to an imaginary person in the room. Follow along as I read. I'll start with the first person:

→ *Together: I pretend. [Point to self.]*
>   *You pretend. [Point to student as student points to you.]*
>   *He, she, it pretends. [Point to imaginary person.]*
>   *We pretend. [Point to self and student at the same time.]*
>   *You pretend. [Point to student and also to another imaginary person.]*
>   *They pretend. [Point to imaginary group of persons with both hands.]*

Instructor: Look at all six forms of the verb *pretend*. Which one is different?

→ *Student: The third person singular.*

Instructor: In the simple present, most verbs keep the same form except for in the third person singular. We change the third person singular by adding an *-s*. Let's do the same for the verb *wander*.

→ *Together: I wander. [Point to self.]*

> *You wander [Point to student as student points to you.]*
>
> *He, she, it wanders. [Point to imaginary person.]*
>
> *We wander. [Point to self and student at the same time.]*
>
> *You wander. [Point to student and also to another imaginary person.]*
>
> *They wander. [Point to imaginary group of persons with both hands.]*

Instructor: When we go through the different forms of a verb like this, we say that we are **conjugating** the verbs. The chart in your workbook shows the simple present conjugation of the verbs *pretend* and *wander*. Now read through the simple past and simple future of the verb *wander*.

> **Note to Instructor:** Give the student a moment to look at the simple past and simple future charts.

Instructor: Did the verbs change for any of the persons?

→ *Student: No.*

Instructor: Regular verbs don't change in the simple past and simple future—so you'll never have to conjugate them again! They only change in the simple present. Now read through the perfect present conjugation of the verb *wander*. In this tense, the main verb stays the same, but the helping verb changes once. For what person does it change?

→ *Student: The third person singular.*

Instructor: So in the present and in the perfect present, the verb only changes form in the third person singular form. In the present, the verb adds an *-s*. In the perfect present, the helping verb changes from *have* to *has*. Now read through the perfect past and perfect future of the verb.

> **Note to Instructor:** Give the student a moment to look at the perfect past and perfect future charts.

Instructor: Did the verbs change for any of the persons?

→ *Student: No.*

Instructor: Regular verbs don't change in the perfect past and perfect future either—so you'll never have to conjugate *them* again! Do you see a pattern? In the simple and perfect tenses, the form of the verb only changes in one person—the third person singular form. And it only changes in the present tense.

Complete your exercises now.

— LESSON 19 —

Person of the Verb
Conjugations
State-of-Being Verbs

Instructor: What two pronouns refer to the first person?

> **Note to Instructor:** If the student needs a hint, point to yourself, and then go stand next to the student and point to both of you. For second person, point to the student; for third person, point to imaginary people in the room (or to siblings).

→ *Student: I and we.*

Instructor: What pronoun refers to the second person?

→ *Student: You.*

Instructor: What four pronouns refer to the third person?

→ *Student: He, she, it, they.*

Instructor: In the last lesson, you learned that when you team up a verb to each of the persons and change its form when necessary, you are *conjugating* it. The Latin word *conjugare* [con-ju-gar-eh] means "to join together." When you conjugate a verb, you are joining the verb to each person in turn. *Conjugare* itself is made by joining two words together; *con* means "with," and *jugare* means "to yoke." Have you ever heard the word *conjugal*? It means "having to do with marriage" and it too comes from the Latin word *conjugare*. Marriage also joins two things together—in this case, two people.

In the last lesson, you learned that regular verbs don't change form very often when you conjugate them. Look at the simple present of the verb *conjugate*. Which form changes?

→ *Student: The third person singular form.*

Instructor: Regular verbs don't change form in the simple past or simple future, so you only have one example of the verb under each. Look at the perfect present of the verb *conjugate*. Which form changes? HINT: The verb itself doesn't change, but the helping verb does.

→ *Student: The third person singular form.*

Instructor: Regular verbs also don't change form in the perfect past or perfect future—just in the perfect present. We haven't talked about progressive tenses yet. Look at the progressive present. What helping verb does the progressive present use?

→ *Student: Am.*

Instructor: Conjugating *am* is a whole different story. Remember, *am* is a state-of-being verb. What does a state-of-being verb show?

→ *Student: That something just exists.*

> **Note to Instructor:** If the student can't remember, tell him to turn back to Lesson 6 and look at the state-of-being verbs. Tell him, "A state-of-being verb shows that something just exists," and then ask him to recite the state-of-being verbs out loud.

Instructor: Let's read the simple present conjugation together, pointing to the correct person.

→ *Together:*

> *I am. [Point to self.]*
> *You are. [Point to student/instructor.]*
> *He, she, it is. [Point to imaginary person.]*
> *We are. [Point to self.]*
> *You are. [Point to student/instructor.]*
> *They are. [Point to imaginary persons.]*

Instructor: This is an irregular verb, because it doesn't change form like most other verbs. You probably use these forms properly when you speak, without even thinking about it. Repeat after me: We is hungry.

→ *Student: We is hungry.*

Instructor: That sounds strange, doesn't it? So for the most part, you won't need to memorize these forms; you just need to understand why they change. They change because the person of the verb changes. Now look at the progressive present chart. In the progressive present, the state-of-being verbs become helping verbs, showing that action is continuing on for a time.

Complete Exercise 19A by filling in the blanks with the correct helping verbs.

Instructor: When you conjugate a progressive form, you don't really conjugate the main verb. It stays the same! The helping verb is the one that changes. Let's review all the tenses of the state-of-being verb *am* now.

> **Note to Instructor:** Follow the pattern below for each conjugation. Reciting these out loud will give the student a sense of the patterns of the conjugations. Pointing as you recite will reinforce the student's grasp of the first, second, and third person.

→ *Together:*

REGULAR VERB, SIMPLE PRESENT

> *I am. [Point to self.]*
> *You are. [Point to student/instructor.]*
> *He, she, it is. [Point to imaginary person.]*
> *We are. [Point to both self and student/instructor.]*
> *You are. [Point to student/instructor.]*
> *They are. [Point to imaginary persons.]*
> *[etc.]*

STATE-OF-BEING VERB, SIMPLE PAST

	Singular	Plural
First person	I was	we were
Second person	you were	you were
Third person	he, she, it was	they were

STATE-OF-BEING VERB, SIMPLE FUTURE

	Singular	Plural
First person	I will be	we will be
Second person	you will be	you will be

Third person	he, she, it will be	they will be

STATE-OF-BEING VERB, PERFECT PRESENT

	Singular	**Plural**
First person	I have been	we have been
Second person	you have been	you have been
Third person	he, she, it has been	they have been

STATE-OF-BEING VERB, PERFECT PAST

	Singular	**Plural**
First person	I had been	we had been
Second person	you had been	you had been
Third person	he, she, it had been	they had been

STATE-OF-BEING VERB, PERFECT FUTURE

	Singular	**Plural**
First person	I will have been	we will have been
Second person	you will have been	you will have been
Third person	he, she, it will have been	they will have been

STATE-OF-BEING VERB, PROGRESSIVE PRESENT

	Singular	**Plural**
First person	I am being	we are being
Second person	you are being	you are being
Third person	he, she, it is being	they are being

STATE-OF-BEING VERB, PROGRESSIVE PAST

	Singular	**Plural**
First person	I was being	we were being
Second person	you were being	you were being
Third person	he, she, it was being	they were being

STATE-OF-BEING VERB, PROGRESSIVE FUTURE

	Singular	**Plural**
First person	I will be being	we will be being
Second person	you will be being	you will be being
Third person	he, she, it will be being	they will be being

Instructor: In Exercise 19A, you filled in the correct helping verbs for the progressive present; now
do the same thing in 19B for the past and future.

— LESSON 20 —

Irregular State-of-Being Verbs
Helping Verbs

Instructor: I'll ask you a question, and I'd like you to answer with the first person singular pronoun and the state-of-being verb in the correct tense. The question will tell you which tense to use. Here's the first question: Are you learning grammar today?

→ *Student: I am.*

Instructor: Were you learning grammar at some unspecified point in the past week?

→ *Student: I was.*

> **Note to Instructor:** If the student answers with another tense, say, "At some unspecified *simple* point in the *past?*"

Instructor: Will you be learning grammar at some unspecified point *next* week?

→ *Student: I will be.*

> **Note to Instructor:** If the student says, *I will*, point out that *I will* is not a state-of-being verb. *Will* is a helping verb that still needs a state-of-being verb to complete it. If necessary, send the student back to review the lists of state-of-being verbs (your student can find lists in Lessons 6 and 7).

Instructor: Are you being progressively happier and happier today? If so, tell me with the first person pronoun, the correct verb, and the adjective *happy*.

> **Note to Instructor:** Give the student any necessary help to bring out the correct answers.

→ *Student: I am being happy.*

Instructor: How about all day yesterday?

→ *Student: I was being happy.*

Instructor: How about all day tomorrow?

→ *Student: I will be being happy.*

Instructor: Have you been hungry at all today, before eating?

→ *Student: I have been hungry.*

Instructor: Were you hungry yesterday before breakfast?

→ *Student: I had been hungry.*

Instructor: Will you be hungry before dinner tomorrow?

→ *Student: I will have been hungry.*

Instructor: In the last lesson, you learned that state-of-being verbs are often irregular when you conjugate them. *Am, is, are, was, were, be, being,* and *been* are all past, present, and future forms of the irregular state-of-being verb *am.* (When you think about it, there's actually only one verb for *simply existing.*) Knowing the forms of this verb is important, so even though it's tedious, we're going to review one more time. Read me the simple present, simple past, and simple future forms of the verb *am,* first singular and then plural for each. Begin with "I am, you are, he, she, it . . ."

→ *Student: I am; you are; he, she it is; we are; you are; they are. I was; you were; he, she, it was; we were; you were; they were. I will be; you will be; he, she, it will be; we will be; you will be; they will be.*

Instructor: Read me the perfect present, past, and future tenses in the same way.

→ *Student: I have been; you have been; he, she, it has been; we have been; you have been; they have been; I had been; you had been; he, she, it had been; we had been; you had been; they had been; I will have been; you will have been; he, she, it will have been; we will have been; you will have been; they will have been.*

Instructor: Now read the progressive present, past, and future tenses.

→ *Student: I am being; you are being; he, she, it is being; we are being; you are being; they are being; I was being; you were being; he, she, it was being; we were being; you were being; they were being; I will be being; you will be being; he, she, it will be being; we will be being; you will be being; they will be being.*

Instructor: We'll talk more about irregular verbs in the lessons to come, but today we're just going to talk about state-of-being verbs and helping verbs. Now that you've been through that whole long conjugation of the verb *am*, you've covered all of the state-of-being verbs. Tell me the full list of helping verbs now.

→ *Student: Am, is, are, was, were, be, being, been; have, has, had; do, does, did; shall, will, should, would, may, might, must, can, could.*

Instructor: Since the first eight verbs are forms of one verb, *am*, it won't surprise you that *have*, *has*, and *had* are all simple forms of the single verb *have*. Take the time now to fill out the missing forms of *have* in Exercise 20A. Ask me for help if you need it.

> **Note to Instructor:** Throughout this lesson, if this is the first time the student has encountered these forms, give all necessary help. Most students will be able to hear the correct form if they recite the conjugation out loud.

Instructor: Would you like to guess what verb *do*, *does*, and *did* are the simple forms of?

→ *Student: Do.*

Instructor: Fill out the missing forms in Exercise 20B.

Instructor: Now we only need to discuss *shall, will, should, would, may, might, must, can* and *could*. You've already run across *will*; it is the helping verb that helps form the simple future tense of many other verbs. Read the left-hand column in your workbook now.

→ *Student: I will be; you will run; he, she, it will sing; we will eat; you will shout; they will cavort.*

Instructor: In American English, *shall* is simply an alternative version of *will*, but Americans only use *shall* in the first person—and not very often. Read the middle column in your workbook now.

→ *Student: I shall be; you will run; he, she, it will sing; we shall eat; you will shout; they will cavort.*

Instructor: If you're an American, you'll probably only hear *shall* in the form of a question. A waiter might ask *Shall I take your order?* or your ballroom dance partner might say *Shall we dance?* But you're more likely to hear *May I take your order?* or *Would you like to dance?* It is never incorrect to substitute *shall* for *will*, but if you're American, you'll sound odd; *shall* is dying in American usage. In British usage, though, *shall* implies some sort of resolve on the part of the speaker. In British English, *I will go home* is just a statement of fact. *I shall go home* implies that you intend to get home, no matter how many obstacles stand in your way. Read the final column now, and put determination into your voice!

→ *Student: I shall be! You shall run! He, she, it shall sing! We shall eat! You shall shout! They shall cavort!*

Instructor: *Should* and *would* are odd words. Technically, *should* is the past tense of *shall*, and *would* is the past tense of *will*. Read me the next two phrases in your workbook.

→ *Student: I will go to bed early. When I was young, I would always go to bed early.*

Instructor: You can see how *would* indicates the past, and *will* shows the future. But we don't usually use either *would* or *should* as a past tense any more. Read the next two phrases now.

→ *Student: I would like to go to bed early. I should probably go to bed now.*

Instructor: *Would* and *should* generally express your intention to do something. We'll discuss this in a few weeks when we talk about *mode*; so for right now, don't worry about the conjugations of *would* and *should*. Instead, put them side-by-side with *may, might, must, can,* and *could,* and read the next seven sentences out loud.

→ *Student: I would eat the chocolate caramel truffle. I should eat the chocolate caramel truffle. I may eat the chocolate caramel truffle. I might eat the chocolate caramel truffle. I must eat the chocolate caramel truffle. I can eat the chocolate caramel truffle. I could eat the chocolate caramel truffle.*

Instructor: All of these sentences concern hypothetical situations. You haven't eaten the truffle yet, but in the future you will eat it—depending on various conditions. We will discuss these hypothetical situations when we get to the lessons on subjunctive and modal verbs. For right now, you just need to remember the statements in your workbook. Read them out loud for me now.

→ *Student: Am, is, are, was, were, be, being, and been are forms of the verb am. Have, has, and had are forms of the verb has. Do, does, and did are forms of the verb do. Shall and will are different forms of the same verb. Should, would, may, might, must, can, and could express hypothetical situations.*

Nouns and Verbs in Sentences

— LESSON 21 —

Person of the Verb
Conjugations
Noun-Verb/Subject-Predicate Agreement

Instructor: Let's review a few conjugations. We'll start with a simple one—the simple present of *enjoy*. That, of course, is a word you would use when you talk about your grammar lessons. Read through the simple present with me, pointing to each person as we say it.

→ *Together: I enjoy. [Point to self.]*
You enjoy. [Point to student as student points to you.]
He, she, it enjoys. [Point to imaginary person.]
We enjoy. [Point to self and student at the same time.]
You enjoy. [Point to student and also to another imaginary person.]
They enjoy. [Point to imaginary group of persons with both hands.]

Instructor: Which of these are first person pronouns?

→ *Student: I, we.*

Instructor: Second person pronouns?

→ *Student: You.*

Instructor: Third person pronouns?

→ *Student: He, she, it, they.*

Instructor: Now let's review the perfect past of the state-of-being verb *I am*.

→ *Together: I had been. [Point to self.]*
You had been. [Point to student as student points to you.]
He, she, it had been. [Point to imaginary person.]
We had been. [Point to self and student at the same time.]
You had been. [Point to student and also to another imaginary person.]
They had been. [Point to imaginary group of persons with both hands.]

Instructor: Finally, let's review the progressive future of the verb *run*.

→ *Together: I will be running. [Point to self.]*
You will be running. [Point to student as student points to you.]
He, she, it will be running. [Point to imaginary person.]
We will be running. [Point to self and student at the same time.]
You will be running. [Point to student and also to another imaginary person.]
They will be running. [Point to imaginary group of persons with both hands.]

Instructor: When you looked at conjugations in the last lesson, you noticed that regular verbs sometimes change form when the person of the verb changes. Look at the conjugation of the regular verb *grab* now. You'll see that some of the tenses simply list the first person and then say, "etc." That's because in those tenses, the verb doesn't change form at all. *I grabbed* and *they grabbed* use the same form of the verb.

> **Note to Instructor:** If the student is not familiar with the abbreviation "etc.," explain that this is short for *et cetera*, Latin for *and the rest*. It is used to show that whatever comes next is the same as what came before.

Instructor: In this complete conjugation of the regular verb *grab*, the verb forms that change are underlined. Which person and number changes in the simple present?

→ *Student: Third person singular.*

Instructor: Which person and number changes in the perfect present?

→ *Student: Third person singular.*

Instructor: Look at the progressive present. The plural forms are all the same. The singular forms are all different! What three helping verbs are used for these forms?

→ *Student: Am, are, is.*

Instructor: Because we use the irregular state-of-being verb *am* to form the progressive present, the forms keep changing. The same thing happens in the progressive past. What two helping verbs are used?

→ *Student: Was and were.*

Instructor: When a pronoun is put together with the proper form of a verb, we say that the pronoun and the verb *agree* in *person* and *number*. If I say, *I am grabbing*, I have paired the first person singular pronoun *I* with the first person singular form *am grabbing*. The pronoun and the verb *agree*. If I say, *I is grabbing*, I've paired the first person singular pronoun with the third person singular verb form. Those forms don't agree.

Complete Exercise 21A now.

Instructor: All of the sentences in Exercise 21A team up pronouns with verbs. But when you put nouns and verbs together to form the subject and predicate of a sentence, those nouns and verbs should also agree. Look at the next section in your workbook. Singular nouns take the same verb forms as third person singular pronouns. Plural nouns take the same verb forms as third person plural pronouns. This is called *noun-verb agreement* or *subject-predicate agreement*. Now, read with me straight across each line of the simple present chart, beginning with *He, she, it grabs* and *They grab*.

→ *Together: He, she, it grabs   They grab*
  The man grabs   The men grab
  The woman grabs   The women grab
  The eagle grabs   The eagles grab

Instructor: Now read through the perfect present, progressive present, and progressive past charts out loud, in the same way. It's important to be able to *hear* if the subject and predicate agree with each other.

→ *Student: He, she, it has grabbed; they have grabbed. The boy has grabbed; the boys have grabbed . . . [etc.]*

Instructor: Sometimes the subject of a sentence will be followed by phrases that describe it.

These phrases do not affect the number of the subject. However, they can sometimes be confusing. Listen to the following sentence: *The wolves howl. Wolves* is a plural subject that takes the plural verb *howl*. I'm going to add a phrase to this sentence so it reads *The wolves in their den howl.* Our verb is still *howl*. Who or what howls?

→ *Student: Wolves.*

Instructor: *Wolves* is still our subject. However, we now have the singular word *den* right before our verb. We have to be careful to make the verbs agree with the subjects, and not with any sneaky words in between. I can add many phrases to describe my subjects, and it will not affect the verb. For example, I can say: *The moon, shimmery and bright in the dark sky, rises.* The phrases *shimmery and bright in the dark sky* do not affect the number of my subject. Always ask *Who or what* before the verb to find the real subject, and make your verb agree with the true subject, instead of any words in between.

Complete Exercises 21B and 21C now.

— LESSON 22 —

Formation of Plural Nouns
Collective Nouns

Instructor: Several lessons ago, just for fun, we talked about the names for animals and groups of animals. Let's try a few out. What do you call a group of chickens?

→ *Student: Brood.*

> **Note to Instructor:** *Flock* is acceptable, but tell the student that *brood* is actually more correct.

Instructor: How about a group of deer?

→ *Student: Herd.*

Instructor: A group of owls?

→ *Student: Parliament.*

Instructor: The words *brood, herd*, and *parliament* are special words that describe groups of animals as one unit. These words are called **collective nouns**. Read me the definition of a collective noun.

→ *Student: **A collective noun names a group of people, animals, or things.***

Instructor: Even though collective nouns refer to more than one thing, they are usually considered singular nouns. Repeat this after me: Collective nouns are usually singular.

→ *Student: Collective nouns are usually singular.*

Instructor: Complete Exercise 22A now.

Instructor: Even though collective nouns like *brood* are singular, the word *chickens* is plural, describing more than one chicken. We say *a brood of chickens* because there's only one brood, but there are many chickens. We say *a gaggle of geese* because there's only one gaggle, but many geese. We say *a herd of deer* because there's only one . . .

> **Note to Instructor:** Pause to let the student complete your sentence. Provide the answers to this and the following questions if necessary.

→ *Student: Herd.*

Instructor: . . . but there are many . . .

→ *Student: Deer.*

Instructor: The nouns *chickens, geese,* and *deer* are all plural nouns. The singular of *chickens* is *chicken.* What is the singular of *geese?*

→ *Student: Goose.*

Instructor: What is the singular of deer?

→ *Student: Deer.*

Instructor: Singular nouns usually become plural nouns when you add an *-s* to the end—but not always! *Goose* and *deer* have irregular plurals; *goose* changes spelling instead of adding *–s,* and *deer* doesn't change at all.

Exercise 22B explains the rules for making words plural, and Exercise 22C gives you a chance to practice. Complete both exercises now.

— LESSON 23 —

Plural Nouns
Descriptive Adjectives
Possessive Adjectives
Contractions

Instructor: Hold up your workbook for me. That book belongs to you; it is [student's name]'s book. This book that I am holding belongs to me. It is [instructor's name]'s book. We can turn common and proper nouns into special words called **possessives** to show ownership. *To possess* something means to own it. The punctuation mark called the apostrophe makes a word possessive. Read the definition of an apostrophe out loud.

→ *Student: **An apostrophe is a punctuation mark that shows possession. It turns a noun into an adjective that tells whose.***

Instructor: **Possessive adjectives tell whose.** Read that rule out loud.

→ *Student: Possessive adjectives tell whose.*

> **Note to Instructor:** Some grammarians classify these as possessive nouns rather than adjectives. Since the focus of this book is on teaching students to use language properly, and the possessive noun is *used* as an adjective, we will continue to call these possessive adjectives.

Instructor: What is the definition of an adjective?

> **Note to Instructor:** Prompt the student as needed by saying, *An adjective modifies* . . .

→ *Student: An adjective modifies a noun or pronoun.*

Instructor: What questions do adjectives answer?

→ *Student: What kind, which one, how many, whose.*

Instructor: You have already learned about adjectives that tell *what kind*. Read the next line out loud, to remind yourself.

→ *Student: Descriptive adjectives tell what kind.*

Instructor: You have now learned about two different kinds of adjectives—descriptive and possessive. Do you remember how to turn a descriptive adjective into an abstract noun?

→ *Student: Add the suffix* -ness.

> **Note to Instructor:** Prompt the student with the correct answer if necessary.

Instructor: Turn the descriptive adjective *happy* into an abstract noun.

→ *Student: Happiness.*

Instructor: Turn the descriptive adjective *slow* into an abstract noun.

→ *Student: Slowness.*

Instructor: When you form a possessive adjective from a noun, you're doing the opposite. Instead of turning an adjective into a noun, you're taking a noun and making it into an adjective. For singular nouns, you do this by adding an apostrophe and an *-s*. Read me the rule out loud, and look at the examples.

→ *Student:* **Form the possessive of a singular noun by adding an apostrophe and the letter -s.**

Instructor: Practice this now by completing Exercise 23A.

Instructor: Read me the next rule, and look at the example.

→ *Student:* **Form the possessive of a plural noun ending in -s by adding an apostrophe only.**

Instructor: Since plural nouns usually end in *-s*, we do not need to add another *-s* to plural nouns to make them possessive; we simply add an apostrophe. *Puppies* and *the Wilsons* are both plural nouns, so we only need to add an apostrophe to each to make them possessive. Now read me the last rule about forming a possessive.

→ *Student:* **Form the possessive of a plural noun that does not end in -s as if it were a singular noun.**

Instructor: The nouns *man, woman,* and *goose* have irregular plurals that don't end in *-s*. So you would simply add an apostrophe and an *-s* to turn them into possessive adjectives. Practice these three rules now by completing Exercise 23B.

Instructor: You can turn a noun into a possessive adjective—but you can also turn a pronoun into a possessive adjective. Look at the chart in your workbook. As you can see, you don't turn a pronoun into a possessive adjective by adding an apostrophe and *-s* the way you do with a noun. Instead, each personal pronoun changes its form to become a possessive adjective. Go down to the next chart now. Read the *Incorrect* column out loud, and see how strange the pronouns would sound with an apostrophe and *-s* ending.

→ *Student: I's book, you's candy, he's hat, she's necklace, it's nest, we's lesson, they's problem.*

Instructor: Instead, each pronoun changes its form to become a possessive adjective. Read down the *Correct* column now.

> **Note to Instructor:** These possessive adjectives are also sometimes classified as possessive pronouns; we will continue to call them possessive adjectives until Week Thirteen, Lesson 49.

→ *Student: My book, your candy, his hat, her necklace, its nest, our lesson, their problem.*

Instructor: A noun turned into a possessive adjective *always* has an apostrophe. A pronoun turned into a possessive adjective *never* has an apostrophe! You should remember that, because pronouns are sometimes combined with other words to form contractions that might look like possessives. Look at the first line of your next chart. What does *he's* stand for?

→ *Student: He is.*

Instructor: What does *she's* stand for?

→ *Student: She is.*

Instructor: What does *it's* stand for?

→ *Student: It is.*

Instructor: What does *you're* stand for?

→ *Student: You are.*

Instructor: What does *they're* stand for?

→ *Student: They are.*

Instructor: *He's, she's, it's, you're,* and *they're* are all **contractions**. A **contraction is a combination of two words with some of the letters dropped out.** The word *contraction* comes from two Latin words: *con,* meaning "together," and *tractio* [trak-she-oh], meaning "drag." In a contraction, two words are *dragged together*. The apostrophe in the contraction tells us where the letters were dropped.

In Exercise 23C, you will see a list of words that are often contracted. The letters which are usually dropped are in grey print. Complete that exercise now.

In the next lesson we will talk about how to avoid confusing these contractions with possessive forms.

— LESSON 24 —

Possessive Adjectives
Contractions
Compound Nouns

Instructor: What is a contraction?

→ *Student: A contraction is a combination of two words with some of the letters dropped out.*

Instructor: Two of the contractions that you studied in the last lesson are occasionally misused—and three more are *often* misused! Look at the chart in your workbook. As you can see, *he's* means "he is," not "his." And *she's* means "she is," not "her." You probably won't misuse those two, but almost every student trips up on the next one! What does *i-t-apostrophe-s* mean?

→ *Student: It is.*

Instructor: That is not the same as the possessive adjective *its!* Never, never, never, use *i-t-apostrophe-s* as a possessive adjective. *I-t-s* is a possessive adjective. *It's* is a contraction. Read me the first set of three sentences below the chart.

→ *Student: It's hard for a hippopotamus to see its feet. It is hard for a hippopotamus to see its feet.*
It's hard for a hippopotamus to see it is feet.

Instructor: If you're not sure whether to use *its* or *it's,* substitute *it is* for the confusing pronoun
and see what happens. If it makes sense, use *it's* with the apostrophe. If not, use *its* with no
apostrophe. What does *you-apostrophe-r-e* mean?

→ *Student: You are.*

Instructor: That is not the same as the possessive adjective *your.* Read me the next set of
three sentences.

→ *Student: You're fond of your giraffe. You are fond of your giraffe. You're fond of you are giraffe.*

Instructor: If you can substitute *you are,* use *you're* with the apostrophe. If not, use *your* with no
apostrophe. What does the contraction *they-apostrophe-r-e* mean?

→ *Student: They are.*

Instructor: That is not the same as the possessive adjective *their!* Read the next set of
sentences out loud.

→ *Student: They're searching for their zebra. They are searching for their zebra. They're searching
for they are zebra.*

Instructor: If you can substitute *they are,* use *they're* with the apostrophe. If not, use *their* with no
apostrophe.

   Complete Exercise 24A before we move on.

Instructor: Let's finish out this week of nouns and verbs with a look at one more kind of noun.
Contractions aren't the only words formed by combining two other words. **Compound nouns** are
also formed by bringing two words together—in this case, two other nouns that work together to
form a single meaning. Read me the definition of a compound noun.

→ *Student: **A compound noun is a single noun composed of two or more words.***

Instructor: Compound nouns can be written as one word, more than one word, or a hyphenated
word. Let's talk about each kind of compound noun. Did you just hear me use the contraction
let's? What does that contraction stand for?

→ *Student: Let us.*

Instructor: Let us move on. The first kind of compound noun is the simplest—if you put *ship*
and *wreck* together, you have a new word. What new word do you get if you join the words
wall and *paper*?

→ *Student: Wallpaper.*

Instructor: The word *wallpaper* has a different meaning from either *wall* or *paper.* It's a new word.
Haircut and *chalkboard* are also compound nouns formed by putting two words together.

   Now look at the next kind of compound noun. Some compound nouns are formed by joining
two nouns with a hyphen. Read me the three examples from your workbook.

→ *Student: Self-confidence, check-in, pinch-hitter.*

Instructor: And, finally, some compound nouns consist of two or more words that aren't joined at
all. They have a space between them, but together they still form a new meaning. Read me the
three examples from your workbook.

→ *Student: Air conditioning, North Dakota, The Prince and the Pauper.*

Instructor: When a compound noun is the subject of a sentence, *all* of the words that make up the noun are included in the simple subject.

Complete Exercise 24B now.

Instructor: Now imagine that you have a handful of snow in your left hand and a handful of snow in your right hand. In that case, you would have two . . .

→ Student: *Handfuls of snow.*

> **Note to Instructor:** If student says "handsful," say, "No, you would have two handfuls of snow" and ask him to repeat "handfuls of snow" after you.

Instructor: Sometimes it's difficult to know exactly how to make a compound noun plural. If one person walking by your house is a passerby, what are two people walking past your house—passerbys, or passersby? If you're unsure about how to form the plural of a compound noun, you can always look it up. But here are four simple rules that will work for most compound nouns.

First: **If a compound noun is made up of one noun along with another word or words, pluralize the noun.**

In the word *passerby, passer* is more central than *by* because *passer* is a noun referring to the actual walking person, while *by* simply tells you where that person is walking. Circle the word *passersby*, and cross out the word *passerbys*.

passerby   (passersby)   ~~passerbys~~

Instructor: Now read me the second rule.

→ Student: **If a compound noun ends in -ful, pluralize by putting an -s at the end of the entire word.**

Instructor: For common nouns ending in *-ful*, it used to be common to pluralize the noun, so that *truckful* became *trucksful*. But that's hard to say, so it is now much more widely accepted to simply add an *-s* to the end of the word: truckfuls. Either is correct, but when you write, you should be consistent. For the purposes of your exercises in this book, add the pluralizing *-s* to the end of the word. Circle the word *truckfuls* to remind yourself that you'll be using this form.

truckful   trucksful   (truckfuls)

Instructor: Read me the third rule.

→ Student: **If neither element of the compound noun is a noun, pluralize the entire word.**

Instructor: In the word *grown-up, grown* is an adjective and *up* is an adverb describing the adjective. So which of the forms is correct?

→ Student: *Grown-ups.*

Instructor: Cross out the form *growns-up* and circle *grown-ups*.

grown-up   ~~growns-up~~   (grown-ups)

Instructor: The final rule is: **If the compound noun includes more than one noun, choose the most important to pluralize.** In the noun *attorney at law, attorney* and *law* are both nouns, but *attorney* is more important because it describes the actual person practicing law. Cross out the incorrect plural form and circle the correct choice.

attorney at law   (attorneys at law)   ~~attorney at laws~~

Instructor: Complete Exercise 24C now. Ask for help if you need it; some of the words are tricky!

— REVIEW 2 —

The review exercises and answers are found in the Student Workbook and accompanying Key.

WEEK 7

Compounds and Conjunctions

— LESSON 25 —

Contractions
Compound Nouns
Diagramming Compound Nouns
Compound Adjectives
Diagramming Adjectives
Articles

Instructor: In the last lesson you learned about contractions. Read me the definition of a contraction.

→ *Student: A contraction is a combination of two words with some of the letters dropped out.*

Instructor: To make a contraction, you usually combine a helping verb with another word.
Complete Exercise 25A before we go on.

Instructor: Look at the sentence in your workbook, and examine the two diagrams beneath it.

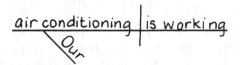

Instructor: The first diagram is done correctly. *Air conditioning* forms a single meaning. It is a compound noun that acts as the subject of the sentence, so both of the nouns are placed together on the subject line of the diagram. What word is written on the slanted line beneath the subject?

→ *Student: Our.*

Instructor: *Our* is a possessive adjective that describes air conditioning. It answers the question, *Whose air conditioning?* When you diagram a sentence, you write adjectives on a slanted line below the nouns they modify. Look at the second diagram.

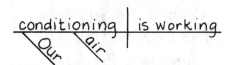

Instructor: What other word is now written on an adjective line?

→ *Student: Air.*

55

Instructor: This is incorrect because *air* is a noun. It names a thing. It doesn't go on an adjective line. And *conditioning* is different from *air conditioning*. If you split up the words *air* and *conditioning*, you don't have the same noun any more. When you're diagramming, compound nouns go together on the same line, even if there is a space between them. Adjectives go on the slanted line beneath the nouns they modify.

Complete Exercise 25B before we go on.

Instructor: Read the next sentence out loud.

→ *Student: The large-headed monster had twenty-seven teeth.*

Instructor: What punctuation mark do you see in the words *large-headed* and *twenty-seven*?

→ *Student: A hyphen.*

Instructor: You have already learned about compound adjectives. Do you remember why *large-headed* and *twenty-seven* are both hyphenated? HINT: It has to do with their position in the sentence.

Note to Instructor: Provide the correct answer if necessary.

→ *Student: They are in the attributive position.*

Instructor: Look at the diagram beneath the sentence. It shows the subject, the predicate, and the adjectives modifying the subject.

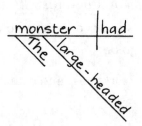

Instructor: Notice that a compound adjective, like a compound noun, goes on a single line. Also notice that the word *The* is written on an adjective line. The words *the, a,* and *an* are adjectives, but they have a special name. They are called **articles.** Read me the next definition.

→ *Student: **The articles are a, an, and the.***

Instructor: Like other adjectives, articles are diagrammed on slanted lines beneath the nouns they describe.

Complete the remaining exercises now.

— LESSON 26 —

Compound Subjects
The Conjunction *And*
Compound Predicates
Compound Subject-Predicate Agreement

Instructor: You've learned that compound nouns and adjectives are composed of two or more words. Think about the compound noun *backstroke*. How many words compose this noun?

→ *Student: Two.*

Instructor: What two words compose the compound noun *backstroke*?

→ *Student:* Back *and* stroke.

Instructor: Think about the compound adjective *old-fashioned*. What two words compose this adjective?

→ *Student:* Old *and* fashioned.

Instructor: The word *compound* means "made up of two or more parts." Nouns and adjectives are parts of speech that can be compound. But there are also parts of sentences that can be compound. Read the first sentence.

→ *Student: The fireman hurries.*

Instructor: What is the predicate (the verb) in this sentence?

→ *Student: Hurries.*

Instructor: What is the subject? Who or what hurries?

→ *Student: Fireman.*

Instructor: What is *the*?

→ *Student: An article.*

Instructor: This sentence has only one subject and one predicate. Read the second sentence out loud.

→ *Student: The policeman hurries.*

Instructor: What is the predicate in this sentence?

→ *Student: Hurries.*

Instructor: What is the subject?

→ *Student: Policeman.*

Instructor: This is also a sentence with a single subject and a single verb. These two sentences have the same predicate, so we can combine these two sentences to make one sentence: *The fireman and the policeman hurry.* We still have a single verb: *hurry.* What is the subject in this sentence? Who or what hurry?

→ *Student: The* fireman *and the* policeman.

Instructor: *Fireman* and *policeman* are the subjects in this sentence. Because there is more than one subject, this sentence has a **compound subject**. Now look at the predicate. Is the verb *hurries* singular or plural? If you're not sure, look at the simple present conjugation of *hurry*.

→ *Student: Singular.*

> **Note to Instructor:** If the student isn't sure, ask, "Is the fireman an *I*, a *you*, or a *he*?" If necessary, review Lesson 21, where the student learned the rule *Singular nouns take the same verb forms as third person singular pronouns.*

Instructor: How many firemen are hurrying?

→ *Student: One.*

Instructor: How many policemen are hurrying?

→ *Student: One.*

Instructor: When the fireman and the policeman are both hurrying, how many men are hurrying?

→ *Student: Two.*

Instructor: The compound subject is plural, so we change the verb from the third person singular form to the third person plural form. Read me the next rule.

→ *Student:* ***Compound subjects joined by*** *and* ***are plural in number and take plural verbs.***

Instructor: When we join sentences together to create a compound subject or predicate, we use the word *and*. *And* is a part of speech called a **conjunction**. *Conjunction* means "joined together." Read the definition of a conjunction out loud.

→ *Student:* ***A conjunction joins words or groups of words together.***

Instructor: You can use the conjunction *and* to join compound subjects. You can also use it to join compound predicates. Read me the next sentence.

→ *Student: The farmer plants.*

Instructor: What is the predicate in this sentence?

→ *Student: Plants.*

Instructor: What is the subject?

→ *Student: Farmer.*

Instructor: The next sentence has the same subject, but a different predicate. What is it?

→ *Student: Harvests.*

Instructor: These two sentences have the same subject, so we can combine them to make one sentence with two predicates—a compound predicate. *The farmer plants and harvests.* What is the compound predicate in this sentence?

→ *Student: Plants and harvests.*

Instructor: What word connects them?

→ *Student: And.*

Instructor: What part of speech is *and*?

→ *Student: A conjunction.*

Instructor: Now study the diagrams of compound subjects and compound predicates.

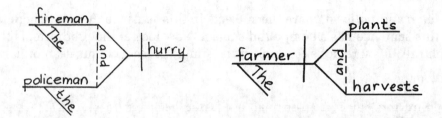

Instructor: Notice that the conjunction *and* is written sideways on a dotted line connecting the compound parts of the sentence. Follow this pattern as you complete the exercises.

— LESSON 27 —

Coordinating Conjunctions
Complications in Subject-Predicate Agreement

Instructor: What is a conjunction? You may look in your book if you can't remember the definition.

→ *Student: A conjunction joins words or groups of words together.*

Instructor: There are several different kinds of conjunctions, and each kind works in a different way. The first conjunction you've learned, *and,* is a **coordinating conjunction**. Read the definition of a coordinating conjunction out loud.

→ *Student:* **A coordinating conjunction joins similar or equal words or groups of words together.**

Instructor: You've learned that *and* can join two subjects, or two predicates. These are similar parts of the sentence. Read the full list of coordinating conjunctions out loud.

→ *Student: And, or, nor, for, so, but, yet.*

Instructor: *And, or,* and *nor* can be used to join single subjects or single words together. Each has a slightly different meaning. Read the first sentence.

→ *Student: Indonesia and Greater Antilles are groups of islands.*

Instructor: When you use *and,* you are adding two nouns, or two verbs, or two of something else together. *Indonesia* and *Greater Antilles* are both proper nouns serving as subjects. When you use *or,* you are suggesting alternatives—one *or* the other. Read the next sentence in your workbook.

→ *Student: I will nap or go running.*

Instructor: You're only going to choose one of those verbs to do, not both (and certainly not at the same time). *Nor* is an interesting word. It's like *and,* but you usually use it only in a negative sense. Read the next sentence.

→ *Student: They will not help me, nor you.*

Instructor: Using *nor* as a coordinating conjunction is a little bit old-fashioned; today, we usually use *nor* with *neither,* which is a different kind of conjunction. You'll be learning more about that combination in a later lesson.

And, or, and nor can join single words, but *for, so, but,* and *yet* usually join longer groups of words. *For* has the sense of *since* or *because.* Read the next sentence.

→ *Student: I ran after them, for I needed help.*

Instructor: *For* connects the sentence *I ran after them* with the sentence *I needed help. So* implies *with the result that.* Read the next sentence.

→ *Student: I stubbed my toe, so now my foot hurts.*

Instructor: Use *but* and *yet* to show contrast. Read the next two sentences.

→ *Student: I was exhausted, but my sister was still full of energy. He was laughing, yet he seemed sad.*

Instructor: You'll revisit these last four conjunctions in a few weeks. For right now, practice using all of these by completing Exercise 27A.

Instructor: Read me the next rule.

→ Student: **Compound subjects joined by and are plural in number and take plural verbs.**

Instructor: Look at the examples below. Does the pronoun *I* take a singular or plural verb?

→ Student: *Singular.*

Instructor: Does the compound subject *George and I* take a singular or plural verb?

→ Student: *Plural.*

Instructor: Because there is more than one subject acting together, the verb is *plural*. But not all compound subjects take plural verbs. Another common conjunction that we can use to combine single subjects into a compound subject is the word *or*. We can say, *The fireman or the policeman hurries.* In this case, we use a singular verb, because either the fireman or the policeman hurries. Only one person hurries—not both. I'll give you another example: *The dog and the cat are sleeping on the sofa.* What is the verb in this sentence?

→ Student: *Are sleeping.*

Instructor: What is the compound subject?

→ Student: *Dog and cat.*

Instructor: In this sentence, we use the plural verb *are*, because the compound subject is joined by the conjunction *and*. The dog and cat are *both* sleeping. Two animals are sleeping, so they take a plural verb.

Now let's join the compound subject with the conjunction *or*: *The dog or the cat is sleeping on the sofa.* We use the singular verb *is* because the compound subject is joined by *or*. Only one of those animals is sleeping on the sofa—not both of them. The single sleeping animal takes the singular verb.

Read me the next sentence out loud.

→ Student: *The dogs or the cat is sleeping on the sofa.*

Instructor: Is the verb *is sleeping* singular or plural?

→ Student: *Singular.*

Instructor: Read the rule about compound subjects joined by *or*.

→ Student: **When compound subjects are joined by or, the verb agrees with the number of the nearest subject.**

Instructor: In the sentence *The dogs or the cat is sleeping on the sofa*, we use the singular verb *is sleeping*, even though *dogs* is plural—because the closest subject to the verb, *cat*, is singular.

As you can see, subject-predicate agreement is not always simple! For the rest of this lesson (and most of the next), we'll look at some cases in which it might not be so easy to figure out whether the subject takes a singular or plural verb. Let's start with an easy one. Read me the next sentence.

→ Student: *The pies were scrumptious.*

Instructor: What is the verb?

→ Student: *Were.*

Instructor: Is *were* a singular or plural verb?

→ Student: *Plural.*

Instructor: Is *pies* singular or plural?

→ *Student: Plural.*

Instructor: We have a plural subject and a plural verb. Good—the predicate and the subject agree! Now let's add a phrase to describe the subject, so that our sentence says: *The pies on the table were scrumptious.* Does the phrase *on the table* change the fact that *pies* is plural?

→ *Student: No.*

Instructor: Most of the descriptive phrases do not change the number of the subject. When choosing a verb to agree with the subject, you should usually ignore any phrases between subject and verb. Read me the next sentence.

→ *Student: The box of pencils is on the top shelf.*

Instructor: Underline *box* one time. This is the subject, and it is singular. Underline the verb *is* twice. The verb agrees with the subject, so it is also singular. *Pencils* is plural, but this does not change the number of the verb. In the next two sentences, underline the subject once and the predicate twice. Ignore the phrases that come between the subject and verb. Follow along as I read these sentences:

> A <u>can</u> of red beans <u>sits</u> on the table.
>
> The young <u>man</u> at all of the meetings <u>was bored</u>.

Instructor: Each one of the subjects is singular. The phrases *of red beans* and *at all of the meetings* do not change the verb.

However, there is *one* case in which we must look in the phrases after the subject in order to determine the number of the subject. Read the next two rules about fractions.

→ *Student: **Fractions are singular if used to indicate a single thing. Fractions are plural if used to indicate more than one thing.***

Instructor: A fraction can describe just one thing, or more than one thing. Read the two examples out loud, and pay special attention to the verbs.

→ *Student: Three-fourths of the pie was missing. Three-fourths of the socks were missing.*

Instructor: These two sentences have the same subject. What is the subject in these sentences?

→ *Student: Three-fourths.*

Instructor: In the first sentence, *three-fourths* describes a single part of a pie so we use the singular verb *was*. In the second sentence, *three-fourths* describes more than one sock (probably a whole heap of socks!), so we use the plural verb *were*. When fractions are used as the subject, you must look at the descriptive phrase following the fraction to determine the number of the subject. In other words, you have to think about the *meaning* of the sentence, not just the grammatical form!

The same is true when you're talking about amounts of money, segments of time, or measures of weight or distance. Read the next rule.

→ *Student: **Expressions of money, time, and quantity (weight, units, and distance) are singular when used as a whole, but plural when used as numerous single units.***

Instructor: Read the next two sentences.

→ *Student: Thirty dollars is too much to pay for that shirt. Thirty dollars are spread across the table.*

Instructor: Both of these sentences have the same subject. HINT: It's modified by the adjective *thirty*. What is the subject?

→ *Student: Dollars.*

Instructor: We use a singular verb when referring to the single price of something, but we use a plural verb when referring to the money itself as actual plural things. Read the next two sentences.

→ Student: *Seven years is a long time to wait. The minutes tick by.*

Instructor: In the first sentence, *Seven years* is a single unit, but in the second sentence, the minutes are passing one by one—and there are many of them. *They tick by* (not *It ticks by*). Read the third set of sentences now.

→ Student: *A thousand pounds is far too heavy for that truck. Fifty gallons of water are divided among the refugees. Four miles is too far to walk.*

Instructor: In the first and third sentences, *thousand pounds* and *four miles* are both single units—one weight, one distance. In the second sentence, the fifty gallons are portioned out—one gallon here, another gallon there, a third gallon somewhere else.

There are some rules in English grammar that seem to have nothing to do with common sense! But when you're talking about subject-predicate agreement, use your brain. Is the subject a single *thing,* or plural *things?*

Use this same common sense for collective nouns. Read the next rule in your workbook.

→ Student: **Collective nouns are usually singular. Collective nouns can be plural if the members of the group are acting as independent individuals.**

Instructor: This is a complicated rule. You must think about the entire meaning of the sentence before deciding which rule to use. Read the two examples out loud, and pay attention to the verbs used.

→ Student: *The herd of cattle was grazing quietly. The herd of cattle were scattered throughout the plains.*

Instructor: When the herd grazes together as a single unit doing one thing, the singular verb *was* can be used. When the herd acts as many different independent individual cows, the plural verb *were* should be used.

When in doubt, use a singular verb with collective nouns.

Try using your brain on the rest of the exercises now.

— LESSON 28 —

Further Complications in Subject-Predicate Agreement

Instructor: We're not done with complicated subject-predicate relationships yet! You'll have to continue using your common sense as we go through the rules in the lesson. Read the next rule out loud.

→ Student: **Many nouns can be plural in form but singular in use: measles, mumps, rickets, politics, mathematics, economics, news.**

Instructor: These nouns look like they are plural but are actually singular in their use and meaning. This category of nouns includes the names of diseases, like measles, or words ending in *–ics*, like politics. Read the example out loud. Pay attention to the verb used.

→ Student: *Mathematics is my favorite subject.*

Instructor: Read the next rule.

→ *Student:* **Singular literary works, works of art, newspapers, countries, and organizations can be plural in form but are still singular in use.**

Instructor: This rule is very similar to the last one. These categories of nouns often look plural in form, but they are singular in use and take singular verbs. Read the two example sentences, and pay attention to the verb.

→ *Student:* Little Women *was written by Louisa May Alcott. The United States is south of Canada.*

Instructor: By themselves, the words *women* and *states* are plural nouns, but when they are the title of one book or a single country, they are singular and take singular verbs. Read the next rule out loud.

→ *Student:* **Many nouns are plural in form and use but singular in meaning: pants, scissors, pliers, glasses.**

Instructor: These nouns each describe a single thing, but they are plural in form and take a plural verb. Usually nouns in this category are single objects composed of two parts. Read the example sentence, and pay attention to the verb.

→ *Student: Pants are too hot in the summertime.*

Instructor: *Pants* is just one thing—a pair of pants. But you would not say *Pants is too hot* because *pants* takes a plural verb. You might also say, "My scissors are missing" with a plural verb—not "My scissors is missing!" with a singular verb.

Read the next rule out loud.

→ *Student:* **In sentences beginning with** There is **or** There are, **the subject is found after the verb.**

Instructor: These sentences are tricky! Because the word *there* comes at the beginning of the sentence, it looks like the subject. In these special sentences, however, the true subject is found after the verb. We must find the true subject and make our verb agree with it. Read the two examples, and pay attention to the verbs.

→ *Student: There is a skunk in the brush. There are three skunks in the brush.*

Instructor: In order to find the true subject, sometimes it is helpful to change the sentence around to read *A skunk is there in the brush* or *Three skunks are there in the brush*. What is the true subject in the first sentence?

→ *Student: Skunk.*

Instructor: Because *skunk* is singular, we use the singular verb *is*. What is the subject in the second sentence?

→ *Student: Skunks.*

Instructor: Because *skunks* is plural, we use the plural verb *are*. Four more rules to go! Read the next.

→ *Student:* **Each** and **every** always indicate a singular subject.

Instructor: These two words can be either adjectives or pronouns. Read the next three sentences in your workbook.

→ *Student: In Masai villages, each woman cares for her own cattle. In Masai villages, each of the women cares for her own cattle. In Masai villages, each cares for her own cattle.*

Instructor: In the first sentence, *each* is a descriptive adjective that tells more about *woman*. In the second and third sentences, *each* is a pronoun that stands for the noun *woman*. The sentences all refer to single, individual women, so the verb is singular. You can compare it to the plural subject and predicate in the sentence below.

Now, read the two sentences making use of *every*.

→ *Student: Every man needs friends. Men need friends.*

Instructor: The first sentence refers to all men, but the adjective *every* implies that you are considering them one at a time, so the verb is singular. The second sentence simply uses the plural form *men*, so it takes the plural form of the verb.

Read the next rule and the sentence that follows it.

→ *Student: **Compound nouns that are plural in form but singular in meaning take a singular verb.** Fish and chips is my favorite British dish.*

Instructor: *Fish and chips* looks like two nouns linked by the coordinating conjunction *and*, but actually it's one dish—a compound noun that stands for *one* thing. It is plural in form, but single in meaning. Your next rule (and sentence) illustrates a similar situation.

→ *Student: **Compound subjects joined by** and **take a singular verb when they name the same thing.** The owner and manager of the ice cream shop is also working behind the counter.*

Instructor: Since the owner is the same person as the manager, the subject of this sentence is only one person—and takes a singular noun. Read the last rule and example now.

→ *Student: **Nouns with Latin and Greek origins take the singular verb when singular in form and the plural verb when plural in form.** The data suggest otherwise.*

Instructor: *Data* is the plural form of the Latin word *datum*, so it is correct to say *data suggest* rather than *data suggests*—even if this sounds odd to your ears. Read through the chart of the most commonly used Greek and Latin words so that you become a little more familiar with their singular and plural forms.

→ *Student: Medium, media; datum, data; criterion, criteria; phenomenon, phenomena; focus, foci; appendix, appendices.*

Instructor: Practice all of these rules now by completing the exercises. You may look back at the rules if necessary.

Introduction to Objects

— LESSON 29 —

Action Verbs
Direct Objects

Note to Instructor: You will need a ball for this lesson.

Instructor: This is a ball. I can throw this ball up into the air. I can catch this ball. If I am not careful, I could lose this ball. Tell me three more things that I could do with this ball.

→ *Student: [Answers will vary. Bounce, kick, drop . . .]*

Instructor: *Throw, catch, lose, bounce, kick*, and *drop* are all action verbs. What is the definition of a verb?

→ *Student: A verb shows an action, shows a state of being, links two words together, or helps another verb.*

Instructor: All of these verbs belong to the first part of the definition—they show actions. And all of those actions directly affect another object—the ball. We have a name for an object that is directly affected by an action verb: **direct object**. Read the definition of a direct object.

→ *Student: **A direct object receives the action of the verb.***

Instructor: You can find the direct object in a sentence by asking the questions *whom* or *what* after reading the subject and verb together. Listen to this sentence: *Cara built a bonfire.* What is the verb?

→ *Student: Built.*

Instructor: What is the subject?

→ *Student: Cara.*

Instructor: Now let's find the object by asking *whom* or *what* after the subject and verb. Cara built what?

→ *Student: A bonfire.*

Instructor: *Bonfire* is the direct object. It receives the action of the verb *built*. Let's try another sentence. *We roasted marshmallows over the bonfire.* What is the verb?

→ *Student: Roasted.*

Instructor: What is the subject?

→ *Student: We.*

Instructor: What is the object? We roasted what?

→ *Student: Marshmallows.*

Instructor: *Marshmallows* is the direct object. *Bonfire* isn't, because if you put it together with the subject and verb you would have "We roasted the bonfire." Sometimes there will be confusing phrases after the verb like *over the bonfire.* Remember that a direct object is always a single noun, never a phrase. In the next sentence, what are the subject and the verb?

→ *Student: Tom ate.*

Instructor: What is the direct object?

→ *Student: Cookie.*

Instructor: In the next sentence, name the subject, verb, and direct object.

→ *Student: Julia, drank, lemonade.*

Instructor: Direct objects are not always objects that we can see and touch. They can be people or abstract nouns as well. For example, in the sentence *She visited her grandfather,* the word *grandfather* is the direct object. What is the direct object in the sentence *He had forgotten her name?*

→ *Student: Name.*

Instructor: What is the direct object in the sentence *She found peace?*

→ *Student: Peace.*

Instructor: Now let's diagram direct objects. Look carefully at the frame in your workbook. Direct objects are diagrammed to the right of the verb, separated by a short, straight line. Let's try the sentence *We roasted marshmallows.* First, write your verb to the right of the center line.

Next, write your subject to the left of the center line. Remember to use the same capitalization as the sentence.

Finally, write your direct object to the right of the short vertical line. The line that separates the verb from the direct object should never go through the horizontal line.

$$\underline{We \mid roasted \mid marshmallows}$$

Instructor: A verb can have a compound direct object. For example: *We roasted soft marshmallows and beefy hot dogs.* What two things did we roast?

→ *Student: Marshmallows and hot dogs.*

Instructor: There are two direct objects—marshmallows and hot dogs. Put the subject, predicate, and compound direct object on the frame provided. Write *and* on the vertical line connecting the direct objects. Notice that *hot dogs* is a compound noun written with a space between the words—if you just put *dogs* on the direct object line, you'd have a whole different sentence! Write the adjectives on the adjective lines provided.

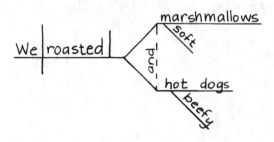

Instructor: A sentence can have compound subjects, compound predicates, *and* compound direct objects. Read the next sentence.

→ *Student: My friend and I rode roller coasters and ate popcorn and cotton candy.*

Instructor: This sentence has a compound subject. What are the two subjects?

→ *Student:* Friend *and* I.

Instructor: Write those onto the subject lines of the diagram. Write *and* on the correct line. What part of speech is *my?*

→ *Student: Adjective.*

Instructor: Write it onto the correct line. This sentence has a compound predicate. What are the two things that my friend and I did?

→ *Student: Rode [roller coasters] and ate [popcorn and cotton candy].*

> **Note to Instructor:** If the student includes the bracketed phrases, say, "What two single verbs show the actions that my friend and I took?"

Instructor: Write those action verbs onto the predicate lines in the diagram. Write *and* on the correct line. Now ask "Whom or what?" after the first verb to find the direct object: My friend and I rode what?

→ *Student: Roller coasters.*

Instructor: Write that on the direct object line after the verb *rode.* Notice that *roller coasters* is a compound noun—both words should go on the line. Now ask "Whom or what?" after the second verb: My friend and I ate what?

→ *Student: Popcorn and cotton candy.*

Instructor: This is a compound direct object. Both words receive the action of the verb *ate.* Write them on the object lines that follow the verb *ate.* Write *and* on the correct line. Notice that both *popcorn* and *cotton candy* are compound nouns! Now you have diagrammed a sentence with compound subjects, compound verbs, compound direct objects, *and* compound nouns.

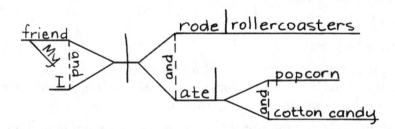

Instructor: Complete the next exercises now.

— LESSON 30 —

Direct Objects
Prepositions

Instructor: Read me the first sentence in your workbook.

→ *Student: I broke my breakfast plate!*

Instructor: What is the subject and predicate of that sentence?

→ *Student:* I *and* broke.

Instructor: What did you break?

→ *Student: My plate.*

Instructor: *Plate* is the direct object of the action verb *broke*. Now read me the second sentence.

→ *Student: The pottery plate broke into pieces.*

Instructor: What is the subject and predicate?

→ *Student: Plate, broke.*

Instructor: This sentence has the same action verb as the first sentence. But instead of a direct object, this sentence ends with something else—a prepositional phrase. Let's take a minute to talk about prepositions. Place your hands on your workbook.

→ *(Student places hands on book.)*

Instructor: Place your hands under your workbook.

→ *(Student places hands under book.)*

Instructor: Place your hands beside your workbook.

→ *(Student places hands beside book.)*

Instructor: Place your hands above your workbook.

→ *(Student places hands above book.)*

Instructor: Place your hands near your workbook.

→ *(Student places hands near book.)*

Instructor: By changing just one word in each of these commands, I changed the relationship between your hands and the book. These words—*on, under, beside, above, near*—are called **prepositions**. Read me the definition of a preposition.

→ *Student:* **A preposition shows the relationship of a noun or pronoun to another word in the sentence.**

Instructor: If you can recognize a preposition when you see one, you'll find it much easier to recognize the parts of a sentence. We're going to practice the chart of prepositions three times. The first time, I want you to turn around in a circle after each section. Stand up and begin now.

> **Note to Instructor:** The directions in this lesson are intended to keep the student active so that he will stay alert. You may choose to skip them. However, it is important that the student memorize the list of prepositions. If he has not already memorized them in a previous year of study, have him chant the chart out loud three times a day until all of the prepositions have been learned.

→ *Student: Aboard, about, above, across.*
  After, against, along, among, around, at. [Turns around.]
  Before, behind, below, beneath.
  Beside, between, beyond, by. [Turns around.]
  Down, during, except, for, from.
  In, inside, into, like. [Turns around.]
  Near, of, off, on, over.
  Past, since, through, throughout. [Turns around.]
  To, toward, under, underneath.
  Until, up, upon.
  With, within, without. [Turns around.]

Instructor: For the second time, try to say each section only taking one breath per section. For example: (Take one breath) Aboard, about, above, across, after, against, along, among, around, at. Whew! Now I can take another breath for the next section. Ready? Go!

→ *Student: [Breathes.] Aboard, about, above, across.*
  After, against, along, among, around, at.
  [Breathes.] Before, behind, below, beneath.
  Beside, between, beyond, by.
  [Breathes.] Down, during, except, for, from.
  In, inside, into, like.
  [Breathes.] Near, of, off, on, over.
  Past, since, through, throughout.
  [Breathes.] To, toward, under, underneath.
  Until, up, upon.
  With, within, without.

Instructor: For the third and final time, alternate walking and jogging around the room while you say each section. Walk as you say the prepositions that begin with *A*, jog as you say the prepositions beginning with *B*, and so on.

→ *Student: [Walks.] Aboard, about, above, across.*
  After, against, along, among, around, at.
  [Jogs.] Before, behind, below, beneath.
  Beside, between, beyond, by.
  [Walks.] Down, during, except, for, from.
  In, inside, into, like.
  [Jogs.] Near, of, off, on, over.
  Past, since, through, throughout.
  [Walks.] To, toward, under, underneath.
  Until, up, upon.
  With, within, without.

Instructor: Now that you've learned the prepositions, complete the next three exercises. Check them with me when you've finished.

— LESSON 31 —

Definitions Review
Prepositional Phrases
Object of the Preposition

Instructor: In the last lesson, you learned the definition of a new part of speech. Let's review the definitions of the six parts of speech we've covered so far. If you can't remember the definitions, you may look in your book. What is a noun?

→ Student: *A noun names a person, place, thing, or idea.*

Instructor: What is an adjective?

→ Student: *An adjective modifies a noun or pronoun.*

Instructor: What is a pronoun?

→ Student: *A pronoun takes the place of a noun.*

Instructor: What is a verb?

→ Student: *A verb shows an action, shows a state of being, links two words together, or helps another verb.*

Instructor: What is a conjunction?

→ Student: *A conjunction joins words or groups of words together.*

Instructor: What is a coordinating conjunction?

→ Student: *A coordinating conjunction joins similar or equal words or groups of words together.*

Instructor: What is a phrase?

→ Student: *A phrase is a group of words serving a single grammatical function.*

Instructor: What is a preposition?

→ Student: *A preposition shows the relationship of a noun or pronoun to another word in the sentence.*

Instructor: List as many prepositions as you can. If you get stuck, you may look at the list in your workbook.

> **Note to Instructor:** If the student does not know the list of prepositions, have him repeat it three times every day until it is learned.

Instructor: In the last lesson, you practiced circling prepositions. In your workbook, you will see three sentences with the prepositions circled. Take your pencil and underline the preposition and all the words after it, in each sentence.

> A brook sluggishly flows (through) low ground.
>
> Dark draperies hung (upon) the walls.
>
> The tunnel wound (into) the green hill.

Instructor: In each sentence, those three words contain a preposition, and a noun that comes after the preposition. What is the noun that follows the preposition in the first sentence?

→ Student: *Ground.*

Instructor: In the second sentence?

→ *Student: Walls.*

Instructor: In the third?

→ *Student: Hill.*

Instructor: Each one of these nouns is modified. What adjective modifies *ground?*

→ *Student: Low.*

Instructor: What adjective modifies *walls?*

→ *Student: The.*

Instructor: What adjectives modify *hill?*

→ *Student: The and green.*

Instructor: Each set of preposition, noun, and adjectives belonging to the noun is called a **prepositional phrase.** Prepositions are always found in prepositional phrases. Read the definition of a prepositional phrase.

→ *Student: **A prepositional phrase begins with a preposition and ends with a noun or pronoun.***

Instructor: You've learned that a direct object receives the action of the verb. In a prepositional phrase, the noun that follows the preposition is also an object. We call it the object of the preposition. Read the next rule in your workbook.

→ *Student: **That noun or pronoun is the object of the preposition.***

Instructor: A prepositional phrase contains the preposition, the object of the preposition, and any words that describe the object. In the three sentences in your workbook, you have already underlined the prepositional phrases. To find the whole prepositional phrase, you can ask *whom* or *what* after the preposition. Look at the next sentence. What is the preposition?

→ *Student: Beneath.*

Instructor: Circle the preposition. Beneath what?

→ *Student: Your workbook.*

Instructor: Write *OP* for *object of the preposition* above the noun *workbook.* Underline the prepositional phrase *beneath your workbook.* Now you have found the preposition, the object of the preposition, and the prepositional phrase.

OP
Put your hand (beneath) <u>your workbook.</u>

Instructor: What is the preposition in the next sentence?

→ *Student: Across.*

Instructor: Circle the preposition. Across what?

→ *Student: The floor.*

Instructor: Write *OP* above the noun *floor.* Underline the prepositional phrase *across the floor.*

OP
Calvin ran (across) <u>the floor.</u>

Instructor: Look at the last sentence. What is the preposition?

→ *Student: For.*

Instructor: Circle the preposition. For whom?

→ *Student: My mother.*

Instructor: Write *OP* above the noun *mother*. Underline the prepositional phrase *for my mother*.

OP
I baked a pie (for) <u>my mother</u>.

Instructor: Now that you have learned how to identify prepositional phrases, complete your exercises.

— LESSON 32 —

Subjects, Predicates, and Direct Objects
Prepositions
Object of the Preposition
Prepositional Phrases

Instructor: In the last lesson, you learned about prepositions and prepositional phrases. If you can identify the prepositional phrases in any sentence, you'll find that it's much, much easier to locate the other parts of the sentence—the subject, predicate, and direct object. Let's do one more quick review of those sentence parts. Read the next three definitions in your workbook now.

→ *Student: The subject of the sentence is the main word or term that the sentence is about. The simple subject of the sentence is just the main word or term that the sentence is about. The complete subject of the sentence is the simple subject and all the words that belong to it.*

Instructor: Look at the next sentence in in your workbook. Who or what is the sentence about?

→ *Student: The warrior.*

> **Note to Instructor:** If the student gives another answer, say, "Who or what is seeing?"

Instructor: *Warrior* is the simple subject. Underline it once. *The warrior* is the complete subject. Circle it now.

(The <u>warrior</u>) saw on the opposite mountain two great globes of glowing fire.

Instructor: Now read the next three definitions.

→ *Student: The predicate of the sentence tells something about the subject. The simple predicate of the sentence is the main verb along with any helping verbs. The complete predicate of the sentence is the simple predicate and all the words that belong to it.*

Instructor: Everything that doesn't belong to the complete subject belongs to the complete predicate. Circle the rest of the sentence now. What single word tells you what the warrior actually did?

→ *Student: Saw.*

Instructor: That is the simple predicate. Underline it twice.

(The <u>warrior</u>) <u>saw</u> on the opposite mountain two great globes of glowing fire.)

Instructor: Read the next definition in your workbook.

→ *Student: A direct object receives the action of the verb.*

Instructor: What did the warrior see? Answer with one word.

→ *Student: Globes.*

Instructor: *Globes* receives the action of *seeing*. Put the initials *DO* over *globes* to indicate that it is the direct object.

$$\text{DO}$$
(The warrior) saw on the opposite mountain two great globes of glowing fire.)

Instructor: What is a preposition?

→ *Student: A preposition shows the relationship of a noun or pronoun to another word in the sentence.*

Instructor: Recite the list of prepositions for me now.

> **Note to Instructor:** If the student has not memorized the list of prepositions, continue to ask the student to repeat this list three times per day until it is committed to memory.

→ *Student: Aboard, about, above, across, after, against, along, among, around, at, before, behind, below, beneath, beside, between, beyond, by, down, during, except, for, from, in, inside, into, like, near, of, off, on, over, past, since, through, throughout, to, toward, under, underneath, until, up, upon, with, within, without.*

Instructor: Read the next two definitions now.

→ *Student: **A prepositional phrase begins with a preposition and ends with a noun or pronoun. That noun or pronoun is the object of the preposition.***

Instructor: Look at the next sentence in your workbook. The simple subject is underlined once, the simple predicate is underlined twice, and the direct object is labeled. The complete subject is divided from the complete predicate by a vertical line.

There are two prepositional phrases in the sentence. What is the object of the preposition *on*?

→ *Student: Mountain.*

Instructor: What is the object of the preposition *of*?

→ *Student: Fire.*

Instructor: Draw a box around each preposition, and then circle each prepositional phrase.

$$\text{DO}$$
The warrior | saw (on] the opposite mountain) two great globes (of] glowing fire.)

Instructor: Now read me the next sentence in your workbook.

→ *Student: The warrior saw two great globes.*

Instructor: Once you remove prepositional phrases from a sentence, it's much easier to find the subject, predicate, and direct object. Even long, complicated sentences can be made manageable if you identify the prepositional phrases before you start to identify the main parts of the sentence. The next sentence in your workbook has *five* prepositional phrases in it. Underline each one, and then rewrite the sentence without the prepositional phrases on the line below.

The Dragon King <u>with his retainers</u> accompanied the warrior <u>to the end of the bridge</u>, and took leave <u>of him</u> <u>with many bows and good wishes</u>.

<u>The Dragon King accompanied the warrior, and took leave.</u>

Instructor: In your rewritten sentence, underline the subject once, the predicate twice, and label
   the direct objects.

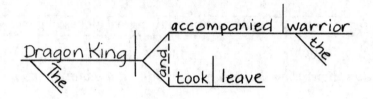

Instructor: Now diagram the sentence on the frame in your workbook.

Instructor: Complete the remaining exercises now.

Adverbs

— LESSON 33 —

Adverbs That Tell How

Instructor: In the last eight weeks, you've learned the names and definitions of six parts of speech. Can you name those six parts of speech?

→ Student: Noun, adjective, pronoun, verb, conjunction, preposition.

> **Note to Instructor:** Prompt student if necessary.

Instructor: This week, you'll learn about the seventh part of speech: the adverb. Read me each sentence. Be sure to read the sentences in the same way that the squirrel stole the sock.

> **Note to Instructor:** The student should read the first sentence very slowly, the second in a sleepy voice, the third in a happy voice, and the fourth very quickly.

→ Student: [Slowly] A sneaky squirrel stole my sock slowly. [Sleepily] A sneaky squirrel stole my sock sleepily. [Cheerfully] A sneaky squirrel stole my sock cheerfully. [Very fast] A sneaky squirrel stole my sock rapidly.

Instructor: You said these sentences slowly, sleepily, cheerfully, and rapidly. These words describe the way you spoke. They modify, or describe, the action verb *said*. In the sentences about the squirrel, the words *slowly, sleepily, cheerfully,* and *rapidly* describe how the squirrel stole. They modify, or describe, the verb *stole*. These words are **adverbs**. Adverbs describe verbs, just as adjectives describe nouns and pronouns. Read the definition of an adverb.

→ Student: **An adverb describes a verb, an adjective, or another adverb.**

Instructor: All of the adverbs in the first four sentences described verbs. Read the next two sentences out loud.

→ Student: An exceptionally sneaky squirrel stole my sock slowly. A sneaky squirrel stole my sock very rapidly.

Instructor: In the first sentence, the bolded adverb describes the adjective *sneaky*. In the second, the bolded adverb describes the adverb *rapidly*. In this week's lessons, we will discuss all three kinds of adverbs. Read me the next part of the definition.

→ Student: **Adverbs tell how, when, where, how often, and to what extent.**

Instructor: Today we are only going to study adverbs that describe verbs and answer the question *how*. In the sentence *A sneaky squirrel stole my sock rapidly*, the word *rapidly* tells **how** the squirrel stole. Many adverbs that answer the question *how* end in *-ly*, like *cheerfully, slowly,* and *sleepily*. If you add *-ly* to the end of most adjectives, you can turn them into adverbs that answer the question *how*. For example, the adjective *serious* is turned into the adverb *seriously* by adding *-ly*. Let's try this trick together. Add *-ly* to the end of the adjective *fierce* to turn it into an adverb.

→ *Student: Fiercely.*

Instructor: Write that on the blank in your book. Can you turn the adjective *thorough* into an adverb?

→ *Student: Thoroughly.*

Instructor: Write that down. If the adjective already ends in *-y*, change the *y* into an *i* before adding *-ly*. For example, the adjective *crazy* turns into the adverb *crazily*. Using this pattern, can you turn the adjective *scary* into an adverb?

→ *Student: Scarily.*

Instructor: Write that down. Can you turn the adjective *cheery* into an adverb?

→ *Student: Cheerily.*

Instructor: Write that down.

Adjective	Adverb
serious	seriously
fierce	fiercely
thorough	thoroughly
crazy	crazily
scary	scarily
cheery	cheerily

Instructor: All of the adverbs you just formed answer the question *how*.

Adverbs that answer the question *how* can be found anywhere in a sentence. Can you find the adverb in the following sentence? *He left hurriedly.*

→ *Student: Hurriedly.*

Instructor: The adverb *hurriedly* tells how he left. This adverb can go anywhere in the sentence. The sentence could read *Hurriedly, he left* or *He hurriedly left*. All of these sentences are correct.

Now let's see how to diagram adverbs that modify verbs. Look at the diagram.

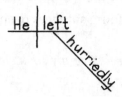

Instructor: What word does *hurriedly* describe or modify?

→ *Student: Left.*

Instructor: The adverb *hurriedly* goes on a slanted line beneath the word it modifies. In the next few lessons we will study adverbs that answer different questions and modify adjectives and adverbs. Right now, complete your exercises.

— LESSON 34 —
Adverbs That Tell When, Where, and How Often

Note to Instructor: Allow five minutes for the student to complete Exercise 34A.

Instructor: Did you get those recipe cards in the right order? Read me the directions in order from one to five.

Note to Instructor: See the Answer Key for the correct order.

Instructor: What words gave you the best clues about the order of these directions?

→ *Student: [First, finally . . .]*

Instructor: The words *first, second, next, later,* and *finally* are adverbs that tell *when.* In the last lesson, we talked about adverbs that describe verbs and tell *how.* Today we are going to talk about adverbs that tell when, where, and how often. Read me the definition of an adverb.

→ *Student: An adverb describes a verb, an adjective, or another adverb. Adverbs tell how, when, where, how often, and to what extent.*

Instructor: Like adverbs that tell how, adverbs that tell when, where, and how often describe verbs. Read me the next sentence.

→ *Student: Yesterday I washed my dog outside.*

Instructor: Which word in this sentence tells *when* I washed my dog?

→ *Student: Yesterday.*

Instructor: Like *later, finally,* and *next, yesterday* is an adverb that tells *when.* Circle the adverb *yesterday.* Which word in this sentence tells *where* I washed my dog?

→ *Student: Outside.*

Instructor: *Outside* is an adverb that tells *where.* Circle the adverb *outside.* In the next sentence, what adverb tells *where* the dog ran?

→ *Student: Away.*

Instructor: Circle the adverb *away.* The next two sentences contain adverbs that tell when *and* adverbs that tell where. What two adverbs tell when?

→ *Student: Then and now.*

Instructor: Circle those two adverbs. What two adverbs tell where?

→ *Student: Down and there.*

Instructor: Circle *down* and *there.*

Yesterday I washed my dog outside.

The dog ran away.

Then the dog lay down.

Now my dog is sleeping there.

Instructor: Let's talk about two more adverbs that tell where: *there* and *here*. When those adverbs come at the end of a sentence, it's easy to recognize them. Read the next two sentences.

→ Student: *My glasses are lying there. My red book is sitting here.*

Instructor: In those two sentences, it's pretty clear that *there* modifies *lying* and *here* modifies *sitting*. Both adverbs answer the question *where?* But sometimes *there* and *here* come at the beginning of a sentence—and, even more confusing, they modify state-of-being verbs.

Read me the next two sentences.

→ Student: *There are my glasses. Here is my red book.*

Instructor: *There* and *here* may look like subjects—but an adverb can't be the subject of a sentence. So they are modifying a verb—the state-of-being verb in each sentence. Where are the glasses?

→ Student: *The glasses are there.*

Instructor: *There* modifies the state-of-being verb *are*. Where is the red book?

→ Student: *The red book is here.*

Instructor: *Here* modifies the state-of-being verb *is*. Now, look at the three diagrams and notice where the adverbs are diagrammed. In the first sentence, when is the dog sleeping?

→ Student: *Now.*

Instructor: Where is the dog sleeping?

→ Student: *There.*

Instructor: So *now* and *there* are both adverbs that are diagrammed beneath the verb *is sleeping*.

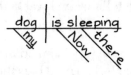

Instructor: What is the subject of the sentence *There are my glasses*?

→ Student: *Glasses.*

Instructor: What is the subject of *Here is my red book*?

→ Student: *Book.*

Instructor: Notice that all the adverbs are diagrammed beneath the verbs they modify—no matter where they come in the sentence.

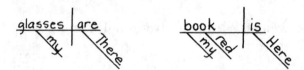

Instructor: Repeat after me: **Here and there are adverbs that tell where.**

→ Student: Here *and* there *are adverbs that tell where.*

Instructor: Adverbs can also tell how often. Listen to the following sentence: *I wash my dog weekly.* What word in that sentence tells how often I wash my dog?

→ Student: *Weekly.*

Instructor: *Weekly* is an adverb that tells how often. Listen to the following question and answer with a complete sentence: Do you always, sometimes, or never eat breakfast?

→ *Student: I [always/sometimes/never] eat breakfast.*

Instructor: Listen: Can you always, sometimes, or never keep secrets?

→ *Student: I can [always/sometimes/never] keep secrets.*

Instructor: Listen: If you were a pirate, would you always, sometimes, or never attack other ships?

→ *Student: If I were a pirate, I would [always/sometimes/never] attack other ships.*

Instructor: *Always, sometimes,* and *never* are adverbs that tell *how often*. They describe verbs. Adverbs that tell *how often* sometimes interrupt verb phrases. Remember, a verb phrase is a main verb plus all of its helping verbs. Read me the next sentence.

→ *Student: Richie is always looking for adventure.*

Instructor: Who is always looking?

→ *Student: Richie.*

Instructor: Richie is the subject. How often is Richie looking for adventure?

→ *Student: Always.*

Instructor: *Always* is an adverb that tells how often. *Is looking* is the verb. The verb phrase *is looking* is interrupted by the adverb *always*. Tell me the adverb in the following sentence: *I will often be eating.*

→ *Student: Often.*

Instructor: Now look at the diagram. Notice that all of the verbs in the verb phrase are in the predicate space, while *often* goes beneath it. Be careful not to put adverbs in the predicate space, even if they come in the middle of the verb phrase.

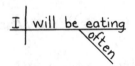

Instructor: Read me the next three sentences.

→ *Student: When will you arrive? Where is my hat? How are you doing?*

Instructor: Each one of those questions begins with an adverb. What question does the adverb *when* answer?

→ *Student: When.*

Instructor: What question does *where* answer?

→ *Student: Where.*

Instructor: What question does *how* answer?

→ *Student: How.*

Instructor: Exactly! When an adverb begins a question, we still diagram it as an adverb. Remember, when you diagram a question, you first turn it into a statement. Read me the first question that has been turned into a statement.

→ *Student: You will arrive When.*

Instructor: The adverb *when* is diagrammed beneath the verb, because it answers the question *when* about the verb *will arrive*.

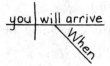

Instructor: Read me the second question that has been turned into a statement.

→ *Student: My hat is Where.*

Instructor: Place the subject, verb, adverb, and adjective in the correct place on the diagram.

Instructor: Now turn the third sentence, "How are you doing?", into a statement and diagram it yourself on your own paper.

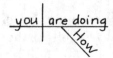

Instructor: Complete the exercises in your workbook now.

— LESSON 35 —

Adverbs That Tell To What Extent

Instructor: Read me the definition of an adverb one more time.

→ *Student: An adverb describes a verb, an adjective, or another adverb. Adverbs tell how, when, where, how often, and to what extent.*

Instructor: We've already talked about adverbs that describe verbs and tell how, when, where, and how often. Today, we'll cover the final kind of adverb—adverbs that describe adjectives or other adverbs, and tell to what extent. Look out the window. Let's describe the weather today. Is it hot or cold?

→ *Student: It is [hot/cold].*

Instructor: Is it extremely [hot/cold] or just somewhat [hot/cold]?

→ *Student: It is [extremely/somewhat] [hot/cold].*

Instructor: Is it sunny or cloudy?

→ *Student: It is [sunny/cloudy].*

Instructor: Is it extremely [sunny/cloudy] or somewhat [sunny/cloudy]?

→ *Student: It is [extremely/somewhat] [sunny/cloudy].*

Instructor: Is it rainy, humid, or dry?

→ *Student: It is [rainy/humid/dry].*

Instructor: Is it extremely [rainy/humid/dry] or somewhat [rainy/humid/dry]?

→ *Student: It is [extremely/somewhat] [rainy/humid/dry].*

Instructor: You've now told me about the temperature and climate, and you've also told me the extent of the temperature and climate. You told me *how* hot/cold and *how* sunny/cloudy it is outside. Now I should know exactly what kind of clothes to wear outside! Let's study the sentence *The extremely humid day was unpleasant.* What is the verb?

→ *Student: Was.*

Instructor: What is the subject?

→ *Student: Day.*

Instructor: What kind of day is it? (Answer with one word.)

→ *Student: Humid.*

Instructor: *Humid* is a descriptive adjective that describes *day*. The word *extremely* is an adverb that describes the adjective *humid*. It tells us *to what extent* the day is humid. Read me the next sentence.

→ *Student: Sharon runs quite quickly.*

Instructor: *Sharon* is the subject and *runs* is the verb. What single word describes the verb *runs* and tells *how* Sharon runs?

→ *Student: Quickly.*

Instructor: The word *quite* does not describe *runs*. We cannot say *Sharon runs quite.* The word *quite* is an adverb that describes the other adverb *quickly*. Look at the following sentence and tell me the two adverbs that you hear: *Larry shrieked especially loudly.*

→ *Student: Especially loudly.*

Instructor: Which adverb describes *how* Larry shrieked?

→ *Student: Loudly.*

Instructor: Larry shrieked loudly. *Loudly* describes the verb *shrieked*. Which word tells to what extent the shrieking was loud?

→ *Student: Especially.*

Instructor: In your workbook, practice diagramming adverbs that describe adjectives or other adverbs. Diagram the subject and verb *Larry* and *shrieked* on the frame provided. Now write the adverb *loudly* on the diagonal line below the verb, because *loudly* describes the verb *shrieked*. Next, write the adverb *especially* on the diagonal line drawn below *loudly,* because *especially* describes *loudly*.

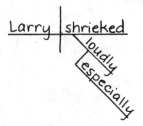

Instructor: When you've finished, read me the next sentence.

→ *Student: Extremely skittish Larry ran away.*

Instructor: Diagram the subject and verb *Larry* and *ran* on the frame provided. *Away* answers the question *how* and describes *ran*, so write the adverb *away* on the diagonal line beneath the verb. What is the adjective that describes the subject *Larry*?

→ *Student: Skittish.*

Instructor: *Skittish* is diagrammed on the straight diagonal line below *Larry*. Now let's find the adverb that describes the adjective *skittish*. To what extent is Larry skittish?

→ *Student: Extremely.*

Instructor: *Extremely* is diagrammed on the diagonal line drawn below *skittish*.

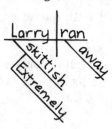

Instructor: Complete the exercises now.

— LESSON 36 —

Adjectives and Adverbs
The Adverb *Not*
Diagramming Contractions
Diagramming Compound Adjectives and Compound Adverbs

Instructor: One more review: What is an adjective, and what do adjectives do?

→ *Student: An adjective modifies a noun or pronoun. Adjectives tell what kind, which one, how many, and whose.*

Instructor: What is an adverb, and what do adverbs do?

→ *Student: An adverb describes a verb, an adjective, or another adverb. Adverbs tell how, when, where, how often, and to what extent.*

Instructor: Read the following sentence out loud. It's a sentence that you might find in an Elizabethan play or a 17th-century poem.

→ *Student: It matters naught.*

Instructor: Examine the diagram in your workbook.

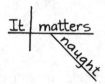

Instructor: *Naught* is an archaic (old-fashioned, no longer in common use) *adverb of negation*—an adverb that reverses or cancels out whatever it modifies. *It matters naught* means the opposite of *It matters*: It doesn't matter at all. Over time, English speakers shortened the adverb *naught* until it reached its present form: *not*. Today, we would express *It matters naught* as *It does not matter*. *Not* is still an adverb, reversing the meaning of the verb *does matter*, so it's diagrammed below the verb, as illustrated in your workbook.

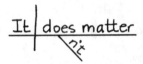

Instructor: Then, English speakers shortened *not* even further and turned it into a contraction. *Does not* became *doesn't*. But *not* is still an adverb—not part of the verb.

Review the definition of a contraction by reading it out loud.

→ *Student: A contraction is a combination of two words with some of the letters dropped out.*

Instructor: When you diagram a contraction, you divide the two words that have been combined apart again, as though they were still two separate words. Then, you diagram each separately. Examine the diagram of the sentence *It doesn't matter* in your workbook.

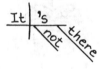

Instructor: *Does* and *n't* have been divided, and *n't* is diagrammed as though it were the full form *not*. Read me the next sentence out loud.

→ *Student: It's not there.*

Instructor: What two words are represented by the contraction *it's*?

→ *Student: It is.*

Instructor: The pronoun *It* is the subject. The contracted verb *'s* is the predicate. So treat *'s* as if it were the full verb *is* and place it on the predicate line. Notice that the adverbs *not* and *there* modify the verb, so they are diagrammed beneath it.

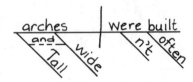

Instructor: Read the next sentence out loud.

→ *Student: Tall and wide arches weren't often built.*

Instructor: What is the predicate?

→ *Student: Were built.*

Instructor: What are the two adverbs diagrammed beneath the predicate?

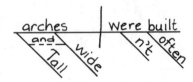

→ *Student: N't and often.*

Instructor: What two adjectives describe the subject noun *arches*?

→ *Student: Tall and wide.*

Instructor: When two adjectives modify the same noun and are linked by *and*, they are often
called *compound adjectives*. Look carefully at the diagram of this sentence. Notice that *tall* and
wide are both diagrammed beneath *arches*, but they are also linked together by the dotted line
with *and* written on it. Read me the final sentence in your workbook now.

→ *Student: The idea was deeply and widely held.*

Instructor: Where are the adverbs *deeply* and *widely* diagrammed?

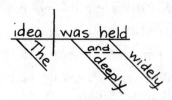

→ *Student: Beneath the predicate.*

Instructor: Where is *and* diagrammed?

→ *Student: On the dotted line connecting the adverbs.*

Instructor: Complete your exercises now.

— REVIEW 3 —

The review exercises and answers are found in the Student Workbook and accompanying Key.

WEEK 10

Completing the Sentence

— LESSON 37 —

Direct Objects
Indirect Objects

Instructor: You should be able to place every word in the following sentence (from *The Odyssey* by Homer) on the frame provided. The bolded word has already been diagrammed for you.

Note to Instructor: Provide all necessary help. You may need to tell the student that *forth* is an old-fashioned way to say *forward*, so it is an adverb that answers the question *where*.

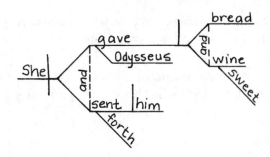

Instructor: This sentence has a compound verb, and one of those verbs has two direct objects. So there are a total of three direct objects in this sentence. What are they?

→ *Student: Bread, wine, him.*

Instructor: Read me the definition of a direct object.

→ *Student: A direct object receives the action of the verb.*

Instructor: *Bread* and *wine* are the objects that were given. But who received the bread and the wine?

→ *Student: Odysseus.*

Instructor: Odysseus did not *directly* receive the action of the verb *give*. Did she pick Odysseus up and give him away to someone else?

→ *Student: No.*

Instructor: So *Odysseus* is not a direct object—but the verb *gave* does have an effect on Odysseus, because he ends up getting the bread and the wine. *Odysseus* is an **indirect object.**

Read me the definition of an indirect object.

→ *Student: **An indirect object is the noun or pronoun for whom or to whom an action is done.***

Instructor: To whom is the bread and wine given?

→ *Student: Odysseus.*

Instructor: So the giving *directly* affects the bread and wine, and *indirectly* affects Odysseus. *Odysseus* is the indirect object of the verb *gave*. Read the next part of the definition now.

→ *Student:* **An indirect object comes between the action verb and the direct object.**

Instructor: In this sentence, *Odysseus* comes between the action verb *gave* and the direct objects *bread* and *wine*. Now read the next sentence about Odysseus out loud.

→ *Student: Odysseus asked the stranger a question.*

Instructor: What is the action verb in that sentence?

→ *Student: Asked.*

Instructor: What is the subject? Who or what asked?

→ *Student: Odysseus.*

Instructor: What is the direct object? Odysseus asked what?

→ *Student: A question.*

Instructor: What is the indirect object? Odysseus asked the question to whom?

→ *Student: The stranger.*

Instructor: Sentences that have indirect objects will always have direct objects. You can have a direct object with no indirect object, but you cannot have an indirect object without a direct object.

Sometimes indirect objects can be compound. We can say *Brandon sent his cousin and uncle an email.* What is the direct object—the thing that is actually *sent*?

→ *Student: The email.*

Instructor: To whom or for whom is the email sent?

→ *Student: His cousin and uncle.*

Instructor: *Cousin and uncle* is the compound indirect object in that sentence. Now look at the two diagrams.

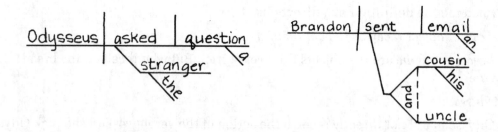

Instructor: In the first sentence, notice that the indirect object is written underneath the verb on a horizontal line connected to the verb by a slanted line. Nothing is written on the slanted line. The slanted line reminds you that the verb *indirectly* affects the indirect object. A compound indirect object, like *cousin and uncle,* is diagrammed on two horizontal lines connected by a dotted line. The conjunction *and* is written on the dotted line.

Finish your exercises now.

— LESSON 38 —

State-of-Being Verbs
Linking Verbs
Predicate Adjectives

Instructor: Yesterday, you learned about indirect objects. Direct objects and indirect objects are parts of the sentence that follow an action verb. Today, we're going to talk about parts of the sentence that follow state-of-being verbs. Read the first sentence in your workbook out loud.

→ Student: *The tiny, jewel-colored hummingbird is strong and frantically energetic.*

Instructor: What is the subject?

→ Student: *Hummingbird.*

Instructor: Underline it once. What is the predicate?

→ Student: *Is.*

Instructor: Underline it twice.

> The tiny, jewel-colored <u>hummingbird</u> <u>is</u> strong and frantically energetic.

Instructor: You've learned that there are four kinds of verbs. What are they? (You may look at your book if you can't remember these definitions.)

→ Student: *A verb shows an action, shows a state of being, links two words together, or helps another verb.*

Instructor: So far, we've talked about action verbs, state-of-being verbs, and helping verbs. But we haven't talked yet about verbs that link words together. **A linking verb connects the subject to a noun, pronoun or adjective in the complete predicate.** Repeat that definition out loud.

→ Student: *A linking verb connects the subject to a noun, pronoun, or adjective in the complete predicate.*

Instructor: Let's talk about each part of this definition. In this sentence, the verb *is* links the subject *hummingbird* to two other words. See if you can find the first one. Answer in one word: The hummingbird is . . .

→ Student: *Strong.*

> **Note to Instructor:** Prompt the student if necessary.

Instructor: There's a second possible answer to that question. The hummingbird is also . . .

→ Student: *Energetic.*

Instructor: *Strong* and *energetic* are both adjectives that describe the hummingbird. There are two more adjectives that describe the hummingbird in this sentence. One is a compound adjective. What are they?

> **Note to Instructor:** Prompt the student if necessary.

→ Student: *Tiny and jewel-colored.*

Instructor: *Tiny* and *jewel-colored* are descriptive adjectives. *Strong* and *energetic* are also descriptive, but because they come after the linking verb, we call them **predicate adjectives.** Read me the definition of a predicate adjective.

→ *Student:* **A predicate adjective describes the subject and is found in the complete predicate.**

Instructor: Attributive adjectives that describe the subject come right before it, and are found in the complete subject; predicate adjectives that describe the subject come after the subject and are found in the complete predicate. Review the definitions of subject and predicate quickly by reading them out loud.

→ *Student: The subject of the sentence is the main word or term that the sentence is about. The simple subject of the sentence is just the main word or term that the sentence is about. The complete subject of the sentence is the simple subject and all the words that belong to it. The predicate of the sentence tells something about the subject. The simple predicate of the sentence is the main verb along with any helping verbs. The complete predicate of the sentence is the simple predicate and all the words that belong to it.*

Instructor: When a state-of-being verb links the simple subject to an adjective found in the complete predicate, it becomes a linking verb. What are the state-of-being verbs?

→ *Student: Am, is, are, was, were, be, being, been.*

Instructor: Read me the first pair of sentences in your workbook.

→ *Student: I am. I am hungry.*

Instructor: In the first sentence, *am* is a state-of-being verb. Write *SB* over the verb. In the second sentence, *am* becomes a linking verb because it is followed by the predicate adjective *hungry*. Write *LV* over the verb and *PA* over the predicate adjective. Do the same thing for the next two pairs of sentences.

SB	SB	SB
I am.	They are being.	The sunset was.
LV PA	LV PA	LV PA
I am hungry.	They are being loud.	The sunset was spectacular.

Instructor: When you diagram a predicate adjective, you place it after the linking verb. You divide it from the linking verb with a slanted line that points back to the subject. This shows that the predicate adjective describes the subject. Look at the diagram.

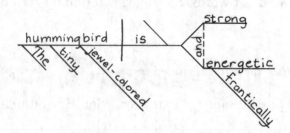

Instructor: Notice where *tiny* and *jewel-colored* are diagrammed—beneath the subject. They are attributive adjectives, found in the complete subject part of the sentence, so they are diagrammed with the subject. *Strong* and *energetic* are diagrammed after the linking verb *is* because they are predicate adjectives. They are found in the complete predicate, so they are grouped with the predicate on the diagram.

Be sure not to confuse predicate adjectives with direct objects! Direct objects follow action verbs. A predicate adjective cannot follow an action verb—and a direct object cannot follow a linking verb. Compare the diagrams of the next two sentences. The first sentence has a linking verb followed by a predicate adjective. The second has an action verb followed by a direct object.

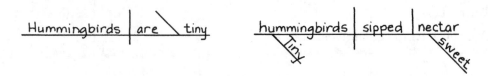

Instructor: Complete your exercises now.

— LESSON 39 —

Linking Verbs
Predicate Adjectives
Predicate Nominatives

Instructor: Let's play a very short version of Twenty Questions. I will give you clues, and you guess what I am thinking about. For every clue I give you, you can have one guess. As soon as you know the answer, tell me.

> **Note to Instructor:** Choose one of the following (save the others for subsequent years of study!). Read the clues, and allow the student one guess after each clue, asking "Are you a _____?" You can keep track of how many guesses it takes the student to guess the correct answer.

I am an animal.	I am a fruit.
I am a mammal.	I am red.
I am unpopular.	I am small.
I am black and white.	I am soft.
I am stinky.	I am a berry.
<u>I am a skunk.</u>	<u>I am a strawberry [or raspberry].</u>
I am a plant.	I am food.
I am yellow.	I am dessert.
I am tall.	I am round.
I am a flower.	I am brown.
I am sunny.	I am gooey and frosted.
<u>I am a sunflower.</u>	<u>I am chocolate cake.</u>

Instructor: In each of these clues, I gave you a linking verb followed by a word in the complete predicate that described the subject *I*. But not all of those words describing *I* were adjectives. Some of them were nouns.

Look at the first sentence in your workbook. The linking verb *am* is followed by the adjective *unpopular*. What do we call an adjective that follows the predicate and describes the subject?

→ *Student: A predicate adjective.*

Instructor: Read me the definition of a predicate adjective.

→ *Student: A predicate adjective describes the subject and is found in the complete predicate.*

Instructor: *Unpopular* is a predicate adjective. Now look at the next two sentences. What two words follow the linking verbs?

→ *Student: Flower, berry.*

Instructor: Are these words adjectives?

→ *Student: No.*

> **Note to Instructor:** If student says "yes," remind her of the definition of a noun: A noun names a person, place, thing, or idea. Flowers and berries are both things.

Instructor: When an adjective follows a linking verb, it describes the subject. But when a noun follows a linking verb, it *gives the subject another name.* Read the definition of a **predicate nominative**.

→ *Student: **A predicate nominative renames the subject and is found in the complete predicate.***

Instructor: The word *nominative* comes from the Latin word *nomen,* which means "name." We also get our English word *name* directly from the Latin *nomen.* This might help you to remember that a predicate nominative *renames* the subject. Now look at the two diagrams in your workbook. In the first diagram, *unpopular* is a predicate adjective. In the second diagram, *berry* is a predicate nominative. They are diagrammed in exactly the same way.

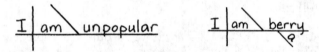

Instructor: Let's practice the difference between predicate adjectives and predicate nominatives just a little more. Read the next sentence.

→ *Student: Iguanas are reptiles.*

Instructor: Is the verb *are* an action verb or a linking verb?

→ *Student: Linking verb.*

Instructor: What *are* iguanas?

→ *Student: Reptiles.*

Instructor: To discover whether this is a predicate nominative or a predicate adjective, first check to see if it is a noun or an adjective. Predicate nominatives are nouns or pronouns, and predicate adjectives are adjectives. Is *reptiles* a noun or an adjective?

→ *Student: Noun.*

Instructor: *Reptiles* is a noun. You can think of the linking verb as an *equals sign* that makes the subject equal the predicate nominative. Let's test this sentence: Iguanas = reptiles. If that formula is true, you've correctly identified the linking verb and predicate nominative. Read the second sentence.

→ *Student: Iguanas are scaly.*

Instructor: Iguanas are what?

→ *Student: Scaly.*

Instructor: Is *scaly* a noun or an adjective?

→ *Student: Adjective.*

Instructor: *Scaly* is an adjective. You can test this by reading the predicate adjective before the subject: *Scaly iguanas.* If that phrase makes sense, you have identified a predicate adjective. Try putting *reptiles* in front of *iguanas.*

→ *Student: Reptiles iguanas.*

Instructor: That doesn't make sense, so you know that *reptiles* isn't a predicate adjective. Does *iguanas* equal *scaly?*

→ *Student: No.*

Instructor: So you know that scaly isn't a predicate nominative. Use those two tests as you complete your exercises.

— LESSON 40 —

Predicate Adjectives and Predicate Nominatives
Pronouns as Predicate Nominatives
Object Complements

Instructor: What does a linking verb do? You may read the definition from your workbook if you can't remember it.

→ *Student: A linking verb connects the subject to a noun, pronoun, or adjective in the complete predicate.*

Instructor: We've talked about nouns that come after the linking verb and rename the subject. What are these nouns called?

→ *Student: Predicate nominatives.*

Instructor: We've also talked about adjectives that come after the linking verb and describe the subject. What are these adjectives in the complete predicate called?

→ *Student: Predicate adjectives.*

Instructor: So far, we haven't talked about pronouns that come after linking verbs. Review the definitions of pronoun and antecedent in your workbook.

→ *Student: A pronoun takes the place of a noun. The antecedent is the noun that is replaced by the pronoun.*

Instructor: Read the list of personal pronouns that we've already covered.

→ *Student: I; you; he, she, it; we; you; they.*

Instructor: These personal pronouns can also follow a linking verb to complete a sentence. Read the next three sentences in your workbook.

→ *Student: It is I. The winner is you. My best friend is she.*

> **Note to Instructor:** The difference between subject and object pronouns will be covered in Week Thirteen, after the linking verb-action verb distinction is more thoroughly explored (in Week Twelve). If the student objects that *It is me* or *My best friend is her* sounds more natural, explain that *me* and *her* can only serve as objects, not as predicate nominatives, and promise a fuller explanation in the lessons to come.

Instructor: In each of these sentences, the linking verb *is* is followed by a personal pronoun that *renames* the subject. Are these personal pronouns serving as predicate nominatives or predicate adjectives?

→ *Student: Predicate nominatives.*

Instructor: The personal pronouns *I, you, he, she, it, we,* and *they* can also serve as predicate nominatives. Complete the next three sentences in your workbook by placing a singular or plural noun, as indicated, along with any necessary modifiers, in each blank.

> **Note to Instructor:** It is more natural to say *We are companions* or *Where are we?* However, insist on a plural noun (and modifiers) for each blank. This lesson lays the groundwork for upcoming lessons on inverted word order, interrogative pronouns, and other constructions where a linking verb is followed by a pronoun. Possible answers might be: *Companions/allies/soldiers/students are we; the loser/the fiercest competitor/the best chef has been you; victors/spies/farmers were they.*

Instructor: Since a pronoun takes the place of a noun, a pronoun can also serve as a predicate nominative. Let's look at one more way to finish out a sentence with a word that *renames* or *describes.* Read the following sentences out loud.

→ *Student: We elected Marissa leader. The explorers found the camp abandoned. He painted the fence white.*

Instructor: Each one of these sentences has an action verb. Underline each action verb twice. Each one of these sentences has a direct object. Label the direct object with *DO*.

$$\text{We } \underline{\text{elected}} \overset{\text{DO}}{\text{ Marissa}} \text{ leader.}$$

$$\text{The explorers } \underline{\text{found}} \overset{\text{DO}}{\text{ the camp}} \text{ abandoned.}$$

$$\text{He } \underline{\text{painted}} \overset{\text{DO}}{\text{ the fence}} \text{ white.}$$

Instructor: Every direct object is followed by another word. What word follows *Marissa*?

→ *Student: Leader.*

Instructor: What part of speech is *leader*?

→ *Student: Noun.*

Instructor: *Leader* is a noun that follows the direct object and *renames* it. We call this an **object complement**. Read the definition of an object complement now.

→ *Student: **An object complement follows the direct object and renames or describes it.***

Instructor: Look at the diagram that follows in your workbook.

We | elected | Marissa \ leader

Instructor: Notice that the object complement *leader* follows the object with a slanted line pointing back towards the object—just like a predicate nominative that renames the subject. The object complement *renames* the object. Now look at the diagrams of the next two sentences.

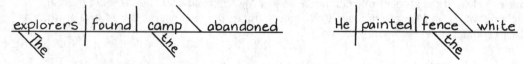

Instructor: What words follow and describe *camp* and *fence*?

→ *Student: Abandoned and white.*

Instructor: What part of speech are these two words?

→ *Student: They are adjectives.*

Instructor: These adjectives are also object complements. We don't diagram them down below the direct object because they are in the *predicative position.* Let me remind you: All the way back in Lesson 4, you learned a rule about hyphenated compound adjectives. Read the next rule in your workbook.

→ *Student: An adjective that comes right before the noun it modifies is in the attributive position.*

Instructor: Compound adjectives are hyphenated if they are in the attributive position. Read me the next rule.

→ *Student: An adjective that follows the noun is in the predicative position.*

Instructor: Compound adjectives in the predicative position are *not* hyphenated. Now you have another rule about the difference between adjectives in the attributive and predicative positions. Adjectives in the attributive position are diagrammed beneath the noun they modify. But when an adjective is in the predicative position after the object, it's diagrammed as an object complement.

Look at the last three examples in your workbook now. Notice that when we move an adjective modifying the direct object from the attributive to the predicative position, it changes the meaning of the sentence. In the first sentence, what color did your friend dye his hair?

→ *Student: Purple.*

Instructor: In the second sentence, your friend already *had* purple hair—and *then* dyed it. We don't know what color until we add another object complement. In the third sentence, what color did your friend dye his purple hair?

→ *Student: Orange.*

Instructor: So we diagram object complements and attributive adjectives that modify the object differently because they have different meanings. Look carefully at the diagrams now.

My friend dyed his hair purple.
My friend dyed his purple hair.
My friend dyed his purple hair orange.

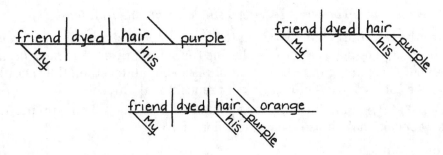

Instructor: When you understand how to diagram an object complement, finish the exercises in your workbook.

More About Prepositions

— LESSON 41 —

Prepositions and Prepositional Phrases
Adjective Phrases

Instructor: How many prepositions can you say in one minute without looking at your book?

> **Note to Instructor:** Time the student as she lists prepositions and count how many of the 46 prepositions she can say in one minute. When she is finished, have her read through the entire list of prepositions (in workbook) for review.

Instructor: What is a preposition? You may look at your book if you cannot remember the definition.

→ *Student: A preposition shows the relationship of a noun or pronoun to another word in the sentence.*

Instructor: Prepositions are always found in phrases. Read the definition of a prepositional phrase.

→ *Student: A prepositional phrase begins with a preposition and ends with a noun or pronoun.*

Instructor: What is the noun or pronoun in the prepositional phrase called?

→ *Student: The object of the preposition.*

Instructor: Review the last definition in your book. What is a phrase?

→ *Student: A phrase is a group of words serving a single grammatical function.*

Instructor: In a verb phrase, all of the words in the group serve a single grammatical function because, all together, they act as a verb. Underline the verb phrase *could have been running* in the next sentence. There are four verbs in that phrase—but all together, they act like one single verb! Today, we're going to take a closer look at prepositional phrases.

You have a list of five song titles in your workbook. In each, circle the preposition and underline the prepositional phrase. The first is done for you.

> Speed (of) Sound
> Ring (of) Fire
> Bridge (Over) Troubled Water
> Time (of) Your Life
> The Sound (of) Silence

Instructor: Each one of those prepositional phrases describes another word in the title. What kind of speed?

→ *Student: Speed of sound.*

Instructor: Which bridge?

→ *Student: The one over troubled water*

Instructor: What kind of sound?

→ *Student: Sound of silence.*

Instructor: Do you remember what part of speech answers the questions, *Which one? What kind? How many? Whose?*

→ *Student: Adjective.*

> **Note to Instructor:** Prompt the student if necessary.

Instructor: When prepositional phrases describe a noun or pronoun and answer those questions, they are behaving like adjectives. Groups of words that behave like adjectives are called *adjective phrases*. There are other kinds of adjective phrases that we'll learn about later, but this is the first. Write *prepositional phrase* in the empty circle on your diagram. We'll be adding other circles with other kinds of phrases to this diagram in later lessons.

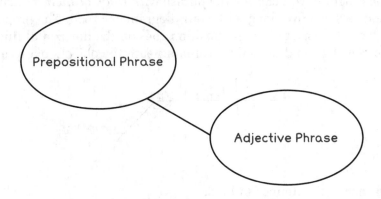

Instructor: Read me the definition beneath the diagram.

→ *Student:* **Prepositional phrases that act as adjectives are also called adjective phrases.**

Instructor: Prepositional phrases usually answer the questions *what kind, which one,* and *whose.* Listen to the sentence that I read and tell me the prepositional phrase that you hear: *The boy with the freckles was whistling.*

→ *Student: With the freckles.*

Instructor: What word does the phrase *with the freckles* describe?

→ *Student: Boy.*

Instructor: The phrase *with the freckles* tells us what kind of boy. Tell me the adjective phrase that you hear in this sentence: *The old man on the bench hummed a tune.*

→ *Student: On the bench.*

Instructor: What word does this phrase modify?

→ *Student: Man.*

Instructor: The phrase *on the bench* tells which man. Let's try one more. Tell me the adjective phrase that you hear in this sentence: *Arthur borrowed a book of mine.*

→ *Student: Of mine.*

Instructor: What word does this phrase modify?

→ *Student: Book.*

Instructor: The phrase *of mine* tells whose book. In each of these sentences, the adjective phrase came directly after the word it modified. Repeat after me: **Adjective phrases usually come directly after the words they modify.**

→ *Student: Adjective phrases usually come directly after the words they modify.*

Instructor: When you diagram an adjective phrase, you can see exactly what word it modifies. Read the next sentence.

→ *Student: Caleb climbed a tree with thick branches.*

Instructor: What is the adjective phrase?

→ *Student: With thick branches.*

Instructor: What word does this phrase modify?

→ *Student: Tree.*

Instructor: In the diagram, you can see the phrase *with thick branches* diagrammed underneath the word it modifies. Follow along with your diagram as I read. The preposition goes on the diagonal line, and the object of the preposition goes on the horizontal line. Any adjectives modifying the object go on diagonal lines underneath the object, just like normal adjectives.

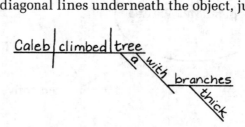

Instructor: Read the next sentence out loud.

→ *Student: The children in the house were sleeping.*

Instructor: Diagram this sentence on the diagram frame below.

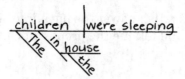

Instructor: Now continue on to your exercises.

— LESSON 42 —

Adjective Phrases
Adverb Phrases

Instructor: Don't look at your book until you answer the next three questions I will ask you. What do we call a prepositional phrase that acts as an adjective?

→ *Student: An adjective phrase.*

Instructor: Where does an adjective phrase usually come in a sentence?

→ *Student: Directly after the word it modifies.*

Instructor: Prepositional phrases can act like adjectives, but they can also act like adverbs. What do you think we call a prepositional phrase that acts like an adverb?

→ *Student: An **adverb phrase**.*

Instructor: Read the definition now.

→ *Student: **Prepositional phrases that act as adverbs are also called adverb phrases.***

Instructor: Review the definition of an adverb by reading me the next two lines.

→ *Student: An adverb describes a verb, an adjective, or another adverb. Adverbs tell how, when, where, how often, and to what extent.*

Instructor: When a prepositional phrase answers one of these questions, it is an adverb phrase. Like adjective phrases, adverb phrases can also be made up of other groups of words—and you'll learn about those later. Right now, write *prepositional phrase* in the empty circle on your diagram.

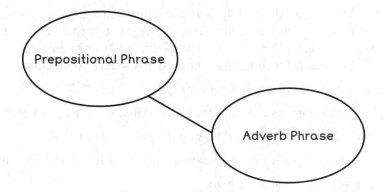

Instructor: Look at the four song titles in your workbook. All of these titles contain prepositional phrases that are also adverb phrases. Circle each preposition and underline each prepositional phrase. The first is done for you.

>   Fly Me (to) the Moon

>   I Fall (to) Pieces

>   Wake Me (at) Sunset

>   Sitting (on) the Dock (of) the Bay

Instructor: All of these prepositional phrases except for one are adverb phrases. *Where* will you fly?

→ *Student: To the moon.*

Instructor: *How* will you fall?

→ *Student: To pieces.*

Instructor: *When* will you wake?

→ *Student: At sunset.*

Instructor: Which song title has two prepositional phrases?

→ *Student: Sitting on the Dock of the Bay.*

Instructor: Which dock?

→ *Student: The dock of the bay.*

Instructor: *Of the bay* is a prepositional phrase that modifies the noun *dock* and answers the question *which one. On the dock* is a prepositional phrase that modifies the noun *sitting* and answers the question *where*. Which phrase is an adverb phrase?

→ *Student: On the dock.*

Instructor: Adverb phrases often come right after the word they modify. But they can also occur elsewhere. Look at the next two sentences. Where does Cameron scuba-dive?

→ *Student: In Hawaii.*

Instructor: This adverb phrase modifies the verb and tells where Cameron scuba-dives. When does Cameron wake up?

→ *Student: At 6:00 a.m.*

Instructor: What word does this phrase modify?

→ *Student: Wakes.*

Instructor: This adverb phrase modifies the verb and tells us when Cameron wakes up. However, it comes at the beginning of the sentence, not directly after the verb. Unlike adjective phrases, which usually come directly after the word they modify, adverb phrases can be found anywhere in a sentence. Repeat after me: **Adverb phrases can be anywhere in a sentence.**

→ *Student: Adverb phrases can be anywhere in a sentence.*

Instructor: Two adverb phrases can modify the same verb. Read me the next sentence.

→ *Student: With great confidence, Hank Aaron swung the bat through the air.*

Instructor: Underline the two prepositional phrases in the sentence. What are they?

→ *Student: With great confidence, through the air.*

Instructor: Both of these phrases modify the verb. They tell how and where Hank Aaron swung the bat. Now look at the diagram of that sentence.

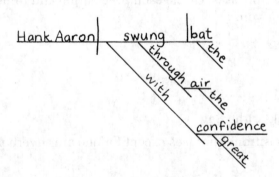

Instructor: Both prepositional phrases are diagrammed beneath the verb, because they both modify the verb. A prepositional phrase that modifies an adjective or an adverb would be diagrammed beneath that word. Read me the next sentence.

→ *Student: In summer, the car was hot beyond belief.*

Instructor: The prepositional phrase *in summer* answers the question *when*. Prepositional phrases that answer the question *when* are always adverb phrases. Diagram *in summer* on the lines beneath the verb. *Beyond belief* describes the predicate adjective *hot*. It tells *to what extent* the car was hot. A phrase that describes an adjective is an adverb phrase. Diagram *beyond belief* on the lines beneath the adjective.

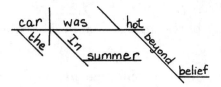

Instructor: Finish your exercises now.

— LESSON 43 —

Definitions Review
Adjective and Adverb Phrases
Misplaced Modifiers

Instructor: Before we begin today's lesson, let's do a quick definition review. In your workbook, complete each definition. Then try to write as many prepositions as you can in the blanks. The first letter of each preposition has been provided for you.

An adjective modifies a noun or pronoun.

Adjectives tell what kind, which one, how many, and whose.

A preposition shows the relationship of a noun or pronoun to another **word in the sentence.**

A prepositional phrase begins with a preposition and ends with a noun **or pronoun.** That noun or pronoun is the **object of the preposition.**

A phrase is a group of words serving a single grammatical **function.**

Prepositional phrases that act as adjectives are also called **adjective phrases.**

Adjective phrases usually come directly after the words they modify.

An adverb describes a verb, an adjective, or another adverb.

Adverbs tell how, when, where, how often, and to what **extent.**

Prepositional phrases that act as adverbs **are also called adverb phrases.**

<u>Prepositions</u>
aboard, about, above, across
after, against, along, among, around, at
before, behind, below, beneath
beside, between, beyond, by
down, during, except, for, from
in, inside, into, like
near, of, off, on, over
past, since, through, throughout
to, toward, under, underneath
until, up, upon
with, within, without

Instructor: Read the next sentence out loud.

→ *Student: The cat scratched Brock's sister with the striped tail.*

Instructor: Something is wrong with this sentence. *With the striped tail* is an adjective phrase. Where do adjective phrases usually come?

→ *Student: Directly after the words they modify.*

Instructor: So, if you just go by the phrase's placement in the sentence, who has the striped tail?

→ *Student: Brock's sister.*

Instructor: Do you think that is what the sentence means?

→ *Student: No.*

Instructor: When an adjective phrase is put in the wrong place, we call it a **misplaced modifier.** Read that definition out loud.

→ *Student: **A misplaced modifier is an adjective phrase in the wrong place.***

Instructor: Try rephrasing the sentence, placing the phrase *with the striped tail* directly after the noun it modifies.

→ *Student: The cat with the striped tail scratched Brock's sister.*

Instructor: That sentence is much better, and not nearly as confusing. Circle the phrase *with the striped tail* and draw a line from it to the space after *cat* to show where the adjective phrase should go.

The cat scratched Brock's sister (with the striped tail.)

Instructor: Now read me the next sentence.

→ *Student: The beautiful girl was dancing with the handsome man in the red dress.*

Instructor: Circle the misplaced adjective phrase and draw a line to the space after the noun it *should* modify.

The beautiful girl was dancing with the handsome man (in the red dress.)

Instructor: Here's an adjective phrase that's misplaced in a way that makes it sound like an adverb phrase. Read the next sentence out loud.

→ *Student: On the pizza, Molly ate the mushrooms.*

Instructor: That sounds as if the prepositional phrase *on the pizza* is answering the question *where*. If that were the case, Molly would be sitting on the pizza eating mushrooms. Circle the prepositional phrase. Where should it go?

→ *Student: After the noun mushrooms.*

Instructor: Draw a line to the space after *mushrooms*. This is not an adverb phrase answering the question *where*—instead, it is an adjective phrase telling us *which mushrooms* Molly ate. You know it is an adjective phrase because it modifies the noun *mushrooms*. Adverbs can't modify nouns! They can only modify verbs, adjectives, and other adverbs.

(On the pizza,) Molly ate the mushrooms.

Instructor: Adverb phrases can also be misplaced—just like single adverbs. Read me the next sentence.

→ *Student: I cut my finger while I was cooking badly.*

Instructor: Bad cooks do sometimes cut their fingers, but I think this sentence means that the *finger* was badly cut. Circle the adverb *badly* and draw a line to the space after the direct object *finger*.

I cut my finger while I was cooking (badly)

Instructor: Read the sentence again.

→ *Student: I cut my finger badly while I was cooking.*

Instructor: Like misplacing an adverb, misplacing an adverb phrase can change the meaning of a sentence. Read the next sentence.

→ *Student: I saw that the toast was burned with a glance.*

Instructor: It sounds as though you burned the toast with a glance—like Superman's heat vision. Where should *with a glance* go?

→ *Student: After the verb* saw.

Instructor: Circle the phrase *with a glance* and draw a line to the space right after the verb.

I saw that the toast was burned (with a glance)

Instructor: Remember, an adverb *doesn't have to* go right after the verb it modifies, but if you put it somewhere else you still need to make sure that the meaning of the sentence is clear. Read me the final sentence.

→ *Student: I spotted the dog chewing on the sofa leg from the stairs.*

Instructor: Who is on the stairs? It's not completely clear, is it? Circle the adverb phrase *from the stairs* and draw a line to the space before the pronoun *I*.

I spotted the dog chewing on the sofa leg (from the stairs)

Instructor: Now reread the sentence.

→ *Student: From the stairs, I spotted the dog chewing on the sofa leg.*

Instructor: Now it's perfectly clear that *you* were on the stairs, not the dog. Continue your practice by finishing the exercises now.

— LESSON 44 —

Adjective and Adverb Phrases
Prepositional Phrases Acting as Other Parts of Speech

Instructor: The English language loves prepositional phrases *so* much that it uses them as stand-ins for other parts of speech. We've already seen how they can act as adjectives and adverbs. Read me the first sentence in your workbook.

→ *Student: The ship went down into the Gulf of Guinea and, with many stops on the way, approached the mouth of the Congo.*

Instructor: Diagram this sentence onto the frame provided. If you need help, ask me.

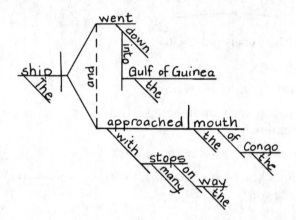

Instructor: This sentence has one subject (ship) and compound verbs. The ship did two things. It went and it approached. Let's talk about *went* first. The ship went down. What part of speech is *down*?

→ *Student: An adverb.*

Instructor: The prepositional phrase *into the Gulf of Guinea* modifies the adverb *down*. It tells you more about the direction *down*. What part of speech modifies an adverb?

→ *Student: Another adverb.*

Instructor: So this is an example of an adverb phrase modifying another adverb. Now look at the action verb *approached* and its direct object, *mouth*. What kind of mouth did the ship approach?

→ *Student: The mouth of the Congo.*

Instructor: This is an adjective phrase, modifying the noun *mouth*. Did the ship approach the mouth of the Congo directly and quickly?

→ *Student: No.*

Instructor: Instead, the ship approached it *with many stops*. This is an adverb phrase answering the question, *How did the ship approach?* So it is diagrammed beneath the verb it modifies. Where were all those stops?

→ *Student: On the way.*

Instructor: This phrase tells you more about the stops. They weren't in Europe, or in North America—they were *on the way*. Because this phrase modifies the noun *stops,* it is acting as an adjective.

   This sentence has two prepositional phrases that act like adverbs, and two that act like adjectives. But that's not all prepositional phrases can do. They can also pretend to be nouns. Read me the next two sentences in your workbook.

→ *Student: A swamp is not a safe place. Under the bridge is not a safe place.*

Instructor: Both of these sentences have the same verb: *is.* Underline that verb twice. What is the subject of the first sentence?

→ *Student: Swamp.*

Instructor: What is a swamp *not?*

→ *Student: A safe place.*

Instructor: In this sentence, the state-of-being verb *is* links the subject, *swamp,* to a noun in the predicate that renames the subject, *place.* What do we call a noun that renames the subject and is found in the complete predicate?

→ *Student: A predicate nominative.*

Instructor: Underline *swamp* once. Label the noun *place* with the letters *PN* for predicate nominative. Draw an arrow from *place* back to *swamp.*

A <u>swamp</u> <u>is</u> not a safe place. [PN]

Instructor: Now look at the second sentence. It has the same predicate nominative. Label it with *PN.* But this time, *place* doesn't rename a single subject. It renames the prepositional phrase *under the bridge.* Circle *under the bridge.* Then, draw an arrow from *place* back to the circled phrase.

(Under the bridge) <u>is</u> not a safe place. [PN]

Instructor: What is not a safe place?

→ *Student: Under the bridge.*

Instructor: The prepositional phrase *under the bridge* is the subject of the sentence. It is acting just like a noun. Now look at the two diagrams in your workbook.

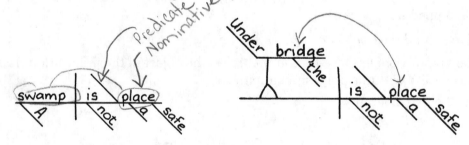

Instructor: First of all, what part of speech is *not?*

→ *Student: An adverb.*

Instructor: *Not* is always an adverb, so it is diagrammed beneath the verb. Now look at the two subjects. *Swamp* and *under the bridge* both occupy the subject place on the diagram. But in order to show that *under the bridge* is actually a prepositional phrase *pretending* to be a noun, we put a little two-legged tree in the subject space and place the prepositional phrase on top of it.

A prepositional phrase can be the subject of a sentence—but it can also be the predicate nominative. Read the next two sentences and look at the diagrams.

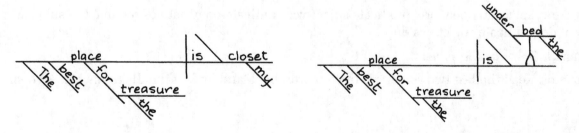

Instructor: In each sentence, *place* is the subject. *Is* is the verb. What is the predicate nominative that renames *place* in the first sentence?

→ *Student: Closet.*

Instructor: What is the prepositional phrase acting as a predicate nominative that renames *place* in the second sentence?

→ *Student: Under the bed.*

Instructor: So far, we've seen prepositional phrases acting as subjects and prepositional phrases acting as predicate nominatives. Here's one more way a prepositional phrase can pretend to be a noun: It can actually serve as the object of a preposition! Read the next two sentences now.

→ *Student: He stepped from the dark. He stepped from behind the tree.*

Instructor: In the first sentence, underline the prepositional phrase *from the dark*. This is an adverb phrase. It modifies the verb *stepped* and answers the question *Where?*

In the second sentence, circle the prepositional phrase *behind the tree*. Then, underline the entire phrase *from behind the tree.*

He stepped <u>from the dark</u>.

He stepped <u>from⟨behind the tree⟩</u>

Instructor: What preposition does the phrase "from behind the tree" begin with?

→ *Student: From.*

Instructor: He stepped from where?

→ *Student: From behind the tree.*

Instructor: The prepositional phrase *behind the tree* is the object of the preposition *from*. It's like a prepositional phrase within a prepositional phrase!

Examine the two diagrams.

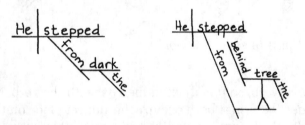

Instructor: Notice how *behind the tree* is diagrammed on a little two-legged tree that sits in the object of the preposition space.

What three parts of speech have we just seen prepositional phrases acting as?

→ *Student: Subject, predicate nominative, object of the preposition.*

Instructor: Let's add one more: predicate adjective. Predicate nominatives rename the subject. What do predicate adjectives do?

→ *Student: Describe the subject.*

Instructor: Read the last two sentences in your workbook and look at the diagrams below them.

→ *Student: The man is happy. The man is in love.*

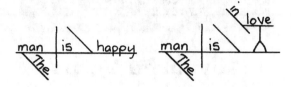

Instructor: What is the predicate adjective that describes *man* in the first sentence?

→ *Student: Happy.*

Instructor: In the second sentence, circle the prepositional phrase *in love.* Draw an arrow from the phrase back to the subject *man.*

The man is (in love.)

Instructor: What is the man?

→ *Student: In love.*

Instructor: The prepositional phrase follows the linking verb and describes the subject, so it is acting as a predicate adjective.

Complete the exercises in your workbook now.

Advanced Verbs

— LESSON 45 —

Linking Verbs
Linking/Action Verbs

> **Note to Instructor:** You will need a wrapped piece of candy for this lesson.

Instructor: Can you tell me the five senses?

> **Note to Instructor:** The student may give the five senses as nouns, verbs, or a combination. Give necessary help by gesturing to prompt the student if necessary.

→ *Student: Taste, touch, smell, sound, sight.*

Instructor: Let's describe this piece of candy with our five senses. Answer in complete sentences—and try to use only one descriptive word in each sentence. How does it look? Finish this sentence: "It looks . . ."

→ *Student: It looks* [Answers may vary: *colorful].*

Instructor: (Rustle wrapping) How does it sound?

→ *Student: It sounds* [Answers may vary: *crackly].*

Instructor: (Give candy to student) How does it feel?

→ *Student: It feels* [Answers may vary: *hard].*

Instructor: Unwrap the candy and sniff it. How does it smell?

→ *Student: It smells* [Answers may vary: *sweet].*

Instructor: Now you can eat the candy! How does it taste?

→ *Student: It tastes* [Answers may vary: *delicious].*

Instructor: You described this candy for me using your five senses. You told me that the candy tastes [delicious]. In this sentence, does the word *[delicious]* describe the candy?

→ *Student: Yes.*

Instructor: *[Delicious]* is a predicate adjective in this sentence. *Tastes* is the linking verb. So far, you have only studied state-of-being verbs that act like linking verbs. What are those state-of-being verbs? Look at your book if you can't remember.

→ *Student: Am, is, are, was, were, be, being, been.*

Instructor: The verbs *taste, feel, smell, sound,* and *look* can act like linking verbs. But you have to be careful when you see these verbs in a sentence—because they can also act like action verbs. Take a bite out of your piece of candy now. Did you taste it?

→ *Student: Yes.*

Instructor: Did it taste delicious?

→ *Student: Yes.*

Instructor: Look at the next two sentences. In the first sentence, the verb *taste* is an action verb. What did you taste?

→ *Student: The candy.*

Instructor: You performed an action—tasting—and the candy received that action, so the candy is the direct object. Write *AV* above *tasted* and *DO* above *candy.*

>   AV   DO
> I tasted the candy.

Instructor: In the second sentence, delicious *describes* candy. It is a predicate adjective linked to the subject by the linking verb *tasted.* When you see the verbs *taste, feel, smell, sound,* and *look,* you can decide whether they are action verbs or linking verbs by examining the word that comes after the verb. If that word describes or renames the subject, the verb is *linking.* If that word is *affected* by the verb, the verb is an *action* verb. Write *LV* above *tasted* and *PA* above *delicious.*

>   LV   PA
> The candy tasted delicious.

Instructor: Read me the next sentence.

→ *Student: The fried chicken tasted crispy.*

Instructor: What word comes after the verb?

→ *Student: Crispy.*

Instructor: Does *crispy* describe or rename fried chicken?

→ *Student: Describe.*

Instructor: Is it a predicate nominative or a predicate adjective?

→ *Student: Predicate adjective.*

Instructor: In this sentence, *tasted* is a linking verb. Write *LV* above *tasted* and *PA* above *crispy.*

>   LV   PA
> The fried chicken tasted crispy.

Instructor: Read me the next sentence.

→ *Student: The chicken tasted the birdseed.*

Instructor: Does *birdseed* describe or rename chicken?

→ *Student: No.*

Instructor: *Birdseed* is affected by the verb *tasted.* It is the direct object, so in this sentence, *tasted* is an action verb. Write AV above *tasted* and DO above *birdseed.*

>   AV   DO
> The chicken tasted the birdseed.

Instructor: If you're not sure whether a verb is action or linking, try substituting *am* or *is* for the verb. If the verb is linking, *am* or *is* will make sense. If it's an action verb, the sentence will sound ridiculous. *The fried chicken is crispy* makes sense, because *tasted* is a linking verb. *The chicken is the birdseed* doesn't—because in that sentence, *tasted* is an action verb. Read me the next two sentences, substituting *is* for the verb *felt* in both.

→ Student: *Thomas is the baby chick. Thomas is sad.*

Instructor: Which sentence makes sense?

→ Student: *The second.*

Instructor: That's because *felt* is a linking verb that connects Thomas with the predicate adjective *sad* in the second sentence. In the first sentence, *felt* is an action verb with a direct object. Now read the complete list of additional linking verbs.

→ Student: *Taste, feel, smell, sound, look, prove, grow, remain, appear, stay, become, seem.*

Instructor: In many cases, these can be either linking or action verbs. Read the first two sentences in the column that says *action* and then the first two in the column that says *linking*.

→ Student: *He proved the theory. The farmer grew wheat. He proved unreliable. The farmer grew tired.*

Instructor: *Theory* and *wheat* are direct objects of the action verbs *proved* and *grew*. *Unreliable* and *tired* are predicate adjectives that describe *he* and *farmer*. Read the next three sentences in the *action* column.

→ Student: *The dog remained on the porch. The cloud appeared in the sky. We stayed home.*

Instructor: All three of those sentences contain action verbs, but none of the verbs have a direct object. You know they are action verbs, though, because there's no predicate adjective or predicate nominative. A linking verb always has to have a predicate adjective or nominative following it. Otherwise, it's not *linking* anything! Read the three sentences under the *linking* column now.

→ Student: *The dog remained wary. The cloud appeared threatening. We stayed happy with our home.*

Instructor: *Wary, threatening,* and *happy* are all predicate adjectives that describe *dog, cloud,* and *we*. Now read me the last two sentences.

→ Student: *The student became confused. The grammar seemed difficult.*

Instructor: *Become* and *seem* are always linking verbs.

    Complete your exercises now.

— LESSON 46 —

Conjugations
Irregular Verbs
Principal Parts of Verbs

Instructor: Before we start today's lesson, take a few minutes to review the tenses you've already learned. Read me the three definitions in your book.

→ *Student: Verbs in the simple past, simple present, and simple future describe actions that simply happen. Verbs in the progressive past, progressive present, and progressive future describe actions that go on for a while. Verbs in the perfect past, perfect present, and perfect future describe actions which have been completed before another action takes place.*

Instructor: Complete the first exercise in your workbook before we go on.

Instructor: The verb in your exercise is a regular verb. It follows the same rules as many other verbs. You form the simple past by adding -*d* or -*ed*, the perfect present by adding the helping verb *have*, the progressive tenses by dropping the final *e* and adding -*ing* along with helping verbs, and so on.

You've already learned that some verbs are irregular. Read me the simple past, present, and future forms of the irregular verbs in your workbook.

Simple Present	Simple Past	Simple Future
build	built	will build
buy	bought	will buy
choose	chose	will choose
sell	sold	will sell

Instructor: If *build* were a regular verb, the simple past would be *builded. Bought* would be *buyed, chose* would be *choosed,* and *sold* would be *selled.* But irregular verbs don't follow the rules when they form past, present, and future.

English has a lot of irregular words, because it has borrowed a lot of words from other languages! In your next exercise, you'll see a list of borrowed English words. Finish Exercise 46B now.

Instructor: Some English verbs are irregular because they follow patterns from other languages. Others are irregular because they've been used so often that their forms have been shortened and made easier to say. If you're going to write and speak properly, you need to know which verbs are irregular. The best way to remember irregular verbs is to understand their **principal parts.**

Every English verb has three principal parts—three forms that will tell you everything you need to know about how the verb is conjugated. Repeat after me: **English verbs have three principal parts.**

→ *Student: English verbs have three principal parts.*

Instructor: The first principal part is the simple present—the same form you would use if you matched the simple present of the verb to the pronoun *I*. Read the example of the first principal part.

→ *Student: Conjugate.*

Instructor: The second principal part is the simple past. Read the example of the second principal part.

→ *Student: Conjugated.*

Instructor: What letter is added to the verb *conjugate* to form the second principal part?

→ *Student: The letter* -d.

Instructor: The verb *conjugate* is a regular verb, because it follows the rule for forming the past tense. The third principal part of a verb is found when you drop the helping verb from the perfect past. What is the third principal part of the verb *conjugate?*

→ *Student: Conjugated.*

Instructor: The second and third principal parts of a regular verb are usually the same. But irregular verbs often have different second and third principal parts. The verb *eat* is irregular. What is the past tense of the verb *to eat*?

> **Note to Instructor:** Prompt the student as needed by saying, "Today I eat. Yesterday I . . ."

→ *Student: Ate.*

Instructor: The third principal part of *to eat* is different. Can you guess what it is? I have . . .

→ *Student: Eaten.*

Instructor: Write those three forms in the blanks in your workbook.

English verbs have three principal parts.
First principal part: The simple present (present)
(I) conjugate   *(I)* eat
Second principal part: The simple past (past)
(I) conjugated   *(I)* ate
Third principal part: The perfect past, minus helping verbs (past participle)
(I have) conjugated   *(I have)* eaten

The three principal parts are called the present, the past, and the past participle. You can remember this by telling yourself that the third principal part is only *part* of the perfect past. That makes it the past *parti*ciple.

Today, you will only use regular verbs so that you can become comfortable with principal parts. Tomorrow, you will learn more about irregular verbs.

Complete the final exercises now.

— LESSON 47 —

Linking Verbs
Principal Parts
Irregular Verbs

Instructor: Read me the entire list of linking verbs.

→ *Student: Am, is, are, was, were, be, being, been, taste, feel, smell, sound, look, prove, grow, remain, appear, stay, become, seem.*

Instructor: Underline the verbs that can also be used as action verbs.

Linking Verbs
am, is, are, was, were
be, being, been
taste, feel, smell, sound, look
prove, grow,
remain, appear, stay
become, seem

Instructor: Look at the three principal parts of *taste, become,* and *feel. Taste* is a regular verb. It forms the past and past participle by adding *-d.* But *become* and *feel* are irregular. The past is formed by changing the spelling of the word. And both of them form the past participle in a different way. The past participle of *become* is the same as the present. What is the past participle of *feel* the same as?

→ *Student: The past.*

Instructor: These irregular verbs have different patterns. There are hundreds of irregular verbs in English—but many of them follow similar patterns. For example, I can say in the present tense, Today I sleep, and in the past tense, Yesterday I slept. Likewise, I can say in the present tense, Today I sweep. What is the past-tense sentence?

→ *Student: Yesterday I swept.*

Instructor: You have already picked up the pattern. In the present tense, I can say, Today I sink, and in the past tense, Yesterday I sank. Likewise, I can say in the present tense, Today I drink. What is the past-tense sentence?

→ *Student: Yesterday I drank.*

Instructor: Even though these verbs are irregular, meaning that they do not use *-d* or *-ed* to form their past tenses, they still follow a pattern: *sleep—slept, sweep—swept* and *sink—sank, drink— drank.* There is a chart of common irregular verbs in your workbook. Let's practice it together. I will read the basic verb, and you read the irregular past tense and past participle. Say the word *have* before the past participle, to remind yourself when you use that form. For example, I will say, *Awake,* and then you will say, *Awoke, have awoken.*

The first verb, *beat,* usually doesn't change form—but some writers prefer to use the second version. Read me both.

Note to Instructor: Prompt the student if necessary by reading the next line of dialogue to him.

→ *Student: Beat, have beat or beat, have beaten.*

Instructor: Burst.

→ *Student: Burst, have burst.*

Note to Instructor: Continue on through the charts in the same pattern.

COMMON IRREGULAR VERBS

Present	Past	Past Participle

SAME PRESENT, PAST & PAST PARTICIPLE:

beat	beat	beat	(OR	beat	beat	beaten)
burst	burst	burst				
cost	cost	cost				
cut	cut	cut				
fit	fit	fit				
let	let	let				
put	put	put				
quit	quit	quit				
hit	hit	hit				
hurt	hurt	hurt				
set	set	set				
shut	shut	shut				

SAME PAST & PAST PARTICIPLE:

bend	bent	bent
send	sent	sent
lend	lent	lent
bleed	bled	bled
feed	fed	fed
feel	felt	felt
keep	kept	kept
lead	led	led
leave	left	left
meet	met	met
read	read	read
sleep	slept	slept
bring	brought	brought
buy	bought	bought
catch	caught	caught
fight	fought	fought
seek	sought	sought
teach	taught	taught
think	thought	thought
lay	laid	laid
pay	paid	paid
say	said	said
sell	sold	sold
tell	told	told
lose	lost	lost
shoot	shot	shot
find	found	found
wind	wound	wound
dig	dug	dug
sit	sat	sat
win	won	won
stand	stood	stood
understand	understood	understood
hear	heard	heard
make	made	made
build	built	built

DIFFERENT PAST AND PAST PARTICIPLE:

awake	awoke	awoken
bite	bit	bitten
break	broke	broken
choose	chose	chosen
forget	forgot	forgotten
freeze	froze	frozen
get	got	gotten
give	gave	given
drive	drove	driven
eat	ate	eaten
fall	fell	fallen
hide	hid	hidden
rise	rose	risen
shake	shook	shaken
speak	spoke	spoken
steal	stole	stolen
take	took	taken
write	wrote	written
ride	rode	ridden

become	became	become
begin	began	begun
come	came	come
run	ran	run

drink	drank	drunk
shrink	shrank	shrunk
ring	rang	rung
sing	sang	sung
swim	swam	swum

draw	drew	drawn
fly	flew	flown
grow	grew	grown
know	knew	known

tear	tore	torn
wear	wore	worn

do	did	done
go	went	gone

lie	lay	lain

see	saw	seen

Instructor: That's enough for one day! No more exercises until tomorrow.

— LESSON 48 —

Linking Verbs
Principal Parts
Irregular Verbs

Instructor: Today, you'll complete exercises in using irregular verbs. Before you do that, let's review a few things you learned this week. Try to answer without looking at your workbook (but the lists and rules are there, if you need them). What are the linking verbs?

→ Student: *Am, is, are, was, were; be, being, been; taste, feel, smell, sound, look; prove, grow; remain, appear, stay; become, seem.*

Instructor: What do verbs in the simple past, simple present, and simple future describe?

→ Student: *Actions that simply happen.*

Instructor: What do verbs in the progressive past, progressive present, and progressive future describe?

→ Student: *Actions that go on for a while.*

Instructor: What do verbs in the perfect past, perfect present, and perfect future describe?

→ Student: *Actions which have been completed before another action takes place.*

Instructor: What are the three principal parts of a verb named?

→ Student: *Present, past, past participle.*

Instructor: What are the principal parts of the regular verb *juggle*?

> **Note to Instructor:** If necessary, remind the student to use the forms for I [simple present], I [simple past], I [perfect past minus helping verb]."

→ Student: *Juggle, juggled, juggled.*

Instructor: What are the principal parts of the irregular verb *rise*?

→ Student: *Rise, rose, risen.*

Instructor: Complete the exercises now.

— REVIEW 4 —

The review exercises and answers are found in the Student Workbook and accompanying Key.

Advanced Pronouns

— LESSON 49 —

Personal Pronouns
Antecedents
Possessive Pronouns

Instructor: Read the first two sentences in your workbook.

→ *Student: Lindsay woke up when Lindsay heard Lindsay's mother call Lindsay. Lindsay ate Lindsay's breakfast and brushed Lindsay's teeth and got ready for Lindsay's day.*

Instructor: This sentence needs pronouns. You learned about pronouns all the way back in Week Two. Read me the definition of a pronoun from your book.

→ *Student: A pronoun takes the place of a noun.*

Instructor: Instead of saying Lindsay so many times, try substituting the pronouns *her* and *she* for the noun, *Lindsay.* I'll start, and you can finish. Lindsay woke up when she heard . . .

→ *Student: . . . her mother call her. She ate her breakfast and brushed her teeth and got ready for her day.*

Instructor: That sounds much better! The pronouns *her* and *she* take the place of the proper noun *Lindsay. Lindsay* is the *antecedent* of the pronouns *her* and *she.* Read the definition of antecedent.

→ *Student: The antecedent is the noun that is replaced by the pronoun.*

Instructor: In Week Two, you learned a list of personal pronouns—pronouns that refer to specific people or things. Read that list now.

Personal Pronouns

	Singular	Plural
First person	I	we
Second person	you	you (plural)
Third person	he, she, it	they

Instructor: A personal pronoun has to be the same *gender* as its antecedent. If the antecedent is male, the personal pronoun has to be . . .

→ *Student: Male.*

Instructor: It also has to be the same *number* as its antecedent. If the antecedent is plural, the personal pronoun has to be . . .

→ *Student: Plural.*

Instructor: Finish your first exercise before we go on.

Note to Instructor: If the student has difficulty identifying gender and number, review Lessons 5 and 8 before going on.

Instructor: The list you learned in Week Two is a useful beginning list of personal pronouns—but there are many more personal pronouns that you need to be familiar with. Read the full list of personal pronouns.

→ *Student: I, me, my, mine; you, your, yours; he, she, him, her, it; his, hers, its; we, us, our, ours; they, them, their, theirs.*

Instructor: In the next couple of lessons, you'll learn how to use all of these pronouns properly. Start by underlining the personal pronouns *I, you, he, she, it, we, you,* and *they* on your list.

Personal Pronouns (Full List)
I, me, my, mine
you, your, yours
he, she, him, her, it
his, hers, its
we, us, our, ours
they, them, their, theirs

Instructor: In Week Two, you practiced using those personal pronouns. But you've also practiced using the pronouns *my, our, your, his, her, its,* and *their.* In the Personal Pronouns list, underline those pronouns twice.

Personal Pronouns (Full List)
I, me, my, mine
you, your, yours
he, she, him, her, it
his, hers, its
we, us, our, ours
they, them, their, theirs

Instructor: You learned about those pronouns in Lesson 23—except that in Lesson 18, we called them *possessive adjectives.* Look at the next chart. These words are adjectives, because they describe nouns. They are also pronouns—because each one takes the place of a noun with an apostrophe and an -s. In the blanks before each noun, write the correct possessive adjective (which is the same as the correct possessive pronoun!).

Peter's sword	his sword
The Pevensie children's wardrobe	their wardrobe
The tree's silver leaves	its leaves
Lucy's cordial	her cordial

Instructor: Each one of those possessive adjectives takes the place of the underlined noun. So the possessive adjectives are *also* possessive pronouns. When they describe a noun, you diagram them just like adjectives. In the sentences you see diagrammed in your workbook, *tree's* and *Its* are both diagrammed as adjectives. *Tree's* is a possessive noun acting like an adjective. *Its* is a possessive pronoun acting like an adjective.

The tree's silver leaves glistened.
Its silver leaves glistened.

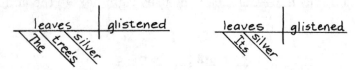

Instructor: Now diagram the next two sentences on the frames provided.

Lucy's cordial healed Edmund.

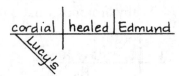

Her cordial healed Edmund.

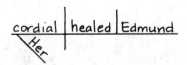

Instructor: There are two more kinds of personal pronouns in that list. Go back up to your Personal Pronouns full list, and circle the pronouns *mine, yours, hers, ours,* and *theirs.*

Personal Pronouns (Full List)
I, me, my, (mine)
you, your, (yours)
he, she, him, her, it
his, (hers), its
we, us, our, (ours)
they, them, their, (theirs)

Instructor: These possessive pronouns only ever occur as *predicate adjectives*. Read me the three sentences about chocolate in your workbook.

→ Student: *The chocolate is my candy. The chocolate is mine candy. The chocolate is mine!*

Instructor: Look at the diagrams of these three sentences.

In the first sentence, *candy* is a predicate nominative—a noun that renames *chocolate. My* is a possessive pronoun acting like an adjective, so it is diagrammed beneath *candy.*

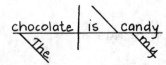

Instructor: The second sentence is just wrong. You would never use *mine* right before a noun, in the attributive position.

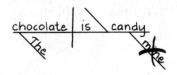

Instructor: In the third sentence, *mine* is a possessive pronoun acting like a predicate adjective. Look at the diagram. It comes after the linking verb *is* and describes the subject, *chocolate*. *Mine* can be a predicate adjective—but it can't be used right next to the noun like a regular descriptive adjective.

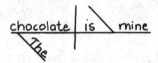

Instructor: Look at the three sentences about the baby brother and the diagrams that come after them. In the first sentence, "He is your baby brother," what part of the sentence is *brother?*

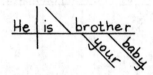

→ *Student: Predicate nominative.*

> **Note to Instructor:** If the student doesn't know the answer, say, "Is *brother* another name for *he?* What do we call a noun that renames the subject and comes after the predicate?"

Instructor: What does the pronoun *your* act like?

→ *Student: An adjective.*

Instructor: Look at the second sentence. Is it correct to say *yours baby brother?*

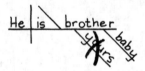

→ *Student: No.*

Instructor: Now look at the diagram of the third sentence, "The baby brother is yours!" *Yours* follows the linking verb. What part of the sentence is it?

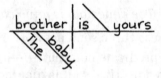

→ *Student: A predicate adjective.*

> **Note to Instructor:** If necessary, prompt the student by saying, "What kind of adjective comes *after* the predicate?"

Instructor: *Mine, yours, hers, ours,* and *theirs* are possessive pronouns that can only act like *predicate adjectives.* Now you know how to use all of these pronouns except for *me, him, us,* and *them.* You'll learn about them in the next lesson.

Complete your exercises now.

— LESSON 50 —

Pronoun Case

Instructor: In the last lesson we talked about three kinds of pronouns. First, we reviewed the basic personal pronouns *I, you, he, she, it, we,* and *they.* Those personal pronouns are underlined once in your workbook. Next, we reviewed personal pronouns that are also called possessive adjectives. Those pronouns are underlined twice in your book. Read them out loud now.

→ *Student: My, your, her, his, its, our, theirs.*

Instructor: Then you learned about personal pronouns that *only* act as *predicate adjectives.* Those pronouns are circled in your book. Read them out loud now.

→ *Student: Mine, yours, hers, ours, theirs.*

> **Personal Pronouns** (Full List)
> I, me, my, mine
> you, your, yours
> he, she, him, her, it
> his, hers, its
> we, us, our, ours
> they, them, their, theirs

Instructor: Label each pronoun in the next sentence as PP (for basic personal pronoun), DA (for possessive pronoun acting as a regular descriptive adjective), or PA (for possessive pronoun acting as a predicate adjective).

>   DA   PP   DA   PA
> My crown, I am; but still my griefs are mine.
>   —William Shakespeare, *Richard II*

Instructor: Four pronouns in your list are still unmarked. What are they?

→ *Student: Me, him, us, them.*

Instructor: These are pronouns that can only be used as objects. Read the definition of **object pronouns**.

→ *Student: **Object pronouns are used as objects in sentences.***

Instructor: The object pronouns are *me, you, him, her, it, us,* and *them. You* and *it* can be either subjects or objects. *Her* can be an object or a possessive pronoun. But *Me, him, us,* and *them* can *only* be used as objects. In the following three sentences, mark whether these pronouns are direct objects, indirect objects, or objects of a preposition.

>   OP   DO   DO
> For **me**, my lords, I love **him** not, nor fear **him**.
>   —William Shakespeare, *Henry VIII*

>   IO
> Give **us** notice of his inclination.
>   —William Shakespeare, *Richard III*

>   OP   OP
> A virtuous and a Christian-like conclusion,/To pray for **them** that have done scathe to **us**.
>   —William Shakespeare, *Richard III*

Instructor: **Subject pronouns are used as subjects and predicate nominatives in sentences.** Let's read the subject pronouns together three times.

➜ *Together: (Three times) I, you, he, she, it, we, they.*

Instructor: *I, he, she, we,* and *they* can *only* be used as subjects and predicate nominatives. In the next three sentences, mark whether these pronouns are subjects or predicate nominatives.

>   S   PN
> **I** am **he**.
>   —William Shakespeare, *Richard III*

>   S   S
> Stand **we** in good array; for **they** no doubt,/Will issue out again and bid us battle.
>   —William Shakespeare, *Henry VI*

> S   S   S
> **I** blame her not, **she** could say little less;/ **She** had the wrong. But what said Henry's queen?
>   —William Shakespeare, *Henry VI, Part III*

Instructor: *You, her,* and *it* can be used in different ways. *You* can be a subject or an object. Read me the next two sentences.

➜ *Student: You need to learn grammar. I will teach you.*

Instructor: In the first sentence, *you* is the subject. In the second *you* is the direct object. Mark them as *S* and *DO*.

>   S   DO
> You need to learn grammar. I will teach you.

Instructor: *Her* can be an object or a possessive adjective. Read me the next two sentences.

➜ *Student: I met her at the park. She was wearing her jacket.*

Instructor: In the first sentence, *her* is the direct object. In the second sentence, *her* is a possessive adjective describing *jacket*. Mark them as *DO* and *DA* (for descriptive adjective).

>   DO   DA
> I met her at the park. She was wearing her jacket.

Instructor: *It* can be a subject or an object. Read me the next two sentences.

➜ *Student: It is not very hard. I will learn it.*

Instructor: In the first sentence, *it* is the . . .

➜ *Student: Subject.*

Instructor: In the second sentence, *it* is the . . .

➜ *Student: Direct object.*

Instructor: Mark them as S and DO.

>   S   DO
> It is not very hard. I will learn it.

Instructor: Look back at your list now, and read me all of the subject pronouns.

➜ *Student: I, you, he, she, it, we, they.*

Instructor: Now read me the object pronouns.

➜ *Student: Me, you, him, her, it, us, them.*

Instructor: When you need a pronoun as the subject or predicate nominative of a sentence, always use a subject pronoun. For example, you would write **She** *is a goalie*, not **Her** *is a goalie*, because *she* is the subject of the sentence. You would also write *The goalie is* **she**, not *The goalie is* **her**, because *she* is the predicate nominative that renames the subject *goalie*. You probably use the correct pronouns as subjects automatically—but be careful to always use subject pronouns for predicate nominatives as well. Read me the next three sets of correct and incorrect sentences. Notice how each correct sentence uses a subject pronoun as a predicate nominative.

→ *Student: I am he. I am him. The students are we. The students are us. The teachers are they. The teachers are them.*

Instructor: When you need to use a pronoun as the direct object, indirect object, or object of a preposition, choose an object pronoun. For example, you would write *Susie passed* **me** *the ball*, not *Susie passed* **I** *the ball*, because *me* is the indirect object. We would also say *Susie called* **them** *yesterday*, not *Susie called* **they** *yesterday*, because *them* is the direct object. In the sentence *The kitten licked Jim*, is the word *Jim* a subject, direct object, indirect object, or predicate nominative?

> **Note to Instructor:** If the student needs help, offer prompts by asking, "Does Jim equal kitten?" or "The kitten licked whom?"

→ *Student: Direct object.*

Instructor: Therefore we need to use the object pronoun *him* in place of *Jim*. Write that in the blank.

> The kitten licked Jim.
> The kitten licked _him_.

Instructor: In the sentence *The winners were Judy and Diane*, how are the words *Judy and Diane* used in the sentence?

> **Note to Instructor:** If the student needs help, ask, "Do Judy and Diane rename the subject winners?"

→ *Student: Predicate nominatives.*

Instructor: Therefore we need to use the subject pronoun *they* in place of *Judy and Diane*. Write that in the blank.

> The winners were Judy and Diane.
> The winners were _they_.

Instructor: There is one more tricky situation to keep in mind. When pronouns are part of a compound subject or object, be careful to choose the correct pronoun. In the sentence *Give the prize to Madison and him*, *Madison* and *him* are both objects of the preposition *to*. So you would not use the subject pronoun *he*. In the sentence *Dad and I made brownies*, is *I* part of the subject or part of the object?

→ *Student: Part of the subject.*

Instructor: So you would not use the object pronoun *me*—even if *Dad and me* sounds right! When you use *I* as part of a compound subject, it's also considered polite to put the personal pronoun *second* in the sentence. So you would say **Dad and I** *made brownies*, not **I and Dad** *made brownies*. If you're not sure which pronoun to use, try dropping the other subject or object and using the pronoun alone. You wouldn't say *Give the prize to he* or *Me made brownies*.

Complete your exercises now.

— LESSON 51 —

Indefinite Pronouns

Instructor: I am going to ask you a few questions, and you can choose one of three answers: *Anyone, everyone,* or *no one.* If you were going to an enormous amusement park with roller coasters, mazes, cotton candy, popcorn, and a huge water slide, whom would you want to invite to go with you? Anyone, everyone, or no one?

→ *Student: [Answer.]*

Instructor: If you were stranded on a deserted island, whom would you want to come rescue you? Anyone, everyone, or no one?

→ *Student: [Answer.]*

Instructor: If you had just begun listening to some of your favorite music, whom would you want to come into your room and tell you to clean it up? Anyone, everyone, or no one?

→ *Student: [Answer.]*

Instructor: Each answer you gave me was a pronoun, but not a *personal* pronoun. Personal pronouns take the place of *particular* nouns. Read me the first two sentences in your book.

→ *Student: Gollum wanted the ring. He longed for it.*

Instructor: Who is he?

→ *Student: Gollum.*

Instructor: What is it?

→ *Student: The ring.*

Instructor: Read me the next sentence.

→ *Student: Everyone hoped that Frodo would succeed.*

Instructor: Who is everyone?

> **Note to Instructor:** The correct answer is "We don't know." If the student comes up with particular answers (Aragorn, Sam, Gandalf, etc.), say, "But do we know *exactly* who everyone is?"

Instructor: *Everyone* is an **indefinite pronoun**. Read me the definition of indefinite pronouns from your workbook.

→ *Student:* **Indefinite pronouns are pronouns without antecedents.**

Instructor: Without antecedents, these pronouns do not refer to definite, specific persons or things. But indefinite pronouns can still provide us with much information. They can tell us if we are describing one person or many people, one thing or many things, a small part of a group or a large part of a group. But it isn't always clear whether indefinite pronouns are referring to one person or thing—or *many* persons or things. Some indefinite pronouns are singular; some are plural; and some can be either singular or plural. You will simply have to learn them in order to use them correctly. First, we will cover the singular indefinite pronouns. Hold up one finger and say, "Singular!"

→ *Student: Singular!*

Instructor: Repeat after me.

> **Note to Instructor:** Practice the singular indefinite pronouns twice. The first time, chant one line at a time with the student repeating. The second time, chant two lines at a time.

anybody	anyone	anything
everybody	everyone	everything
nobody	no one	nothing
somebody	someone	something
another	other	one
either	neither	each

Instructor: Now let's learn the plural indefinites. Hold up two fingers and say, "Plural!"

→ *Student: Plural!*

Instructor: Repeat after me two times: Both, few, many, several.

→ *Student: (Twice) Both, few, many, several.*

Instructor: Now, let's learn the pronouns that can be singular or plural. Hold up one finger on your right hand and two fingers on your left hand, and say, "Singular or plural!"

→ *Student: Singular or plural!*

Instructor: Repeat after me two times: All, any, most, none, some.

→ *Student: (Twice) All, any, most, none, some.*

Instructor: These indefinite pronouns can be singular or plural, depending on their use. We have to think about what the indefinite pronoun is referring to. Sometimes that means we must look in the prepositional phrase that follows the indefinite pronoun. Read me the next sentence.

→ *Student: All of the cake was eaten.*

Instructor: All of what?

→ *Student: The cake.*

Instructor: How many cakes were there?

→ *Student: One.*

Instructor: In this sentence, *all* is singular, because there was only one cake. Remember, the subject of a sentence can never be found in a prepositional phrase. Back in Lesson 32, you practiced circling prepositional phrases *to get them out of the way*, so that you could more easily find the other parts of the sentence. But when your sentence contains *all, any, most, none,* or *some,* you have to examine the prepositional phrase *after* you circle it to figure out whether these pronouns are being used in the singular or the plural sense.

Read me the next sentence.

→ *Student: All of the pieces were eaten.*

Instructor: Circle the prepositional phrase.

All (of the pieces) were eaten.

Instructor: That prepositional phrase tells you whether *all* describes *one thing* or *more than one thing.* Was there more than one piece?

→ *Student: Yes.*

Instructor: In the first sentence, *all* is singular because there is only one cake. In this sentence, *all* is plural, because there were several pieces. Listen to the following phrase and tell me if we should use a singular or plural verb: *Most of the people . . .*

→ *Student: Plural.*

Instructor: We should use a plural verb because there were several people. Listen to another phrase: *None of the water . . .*

→ *Student: Singular.*

Instructor: We should use a singular verb because *water* is a singular noun. Look at the diagrams in your workbook now. Notice the singular verb following *all* in the first sentence and the plural verb following *all* in the second. Those verbs take their number from the nouns *cake* and *pieces* in the prepositional phrases.

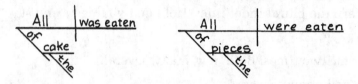

Instructor: There is one more important thing to know about indefinite pronouns. They can be used in the place of nouns—but, like possessive pronouns, they can also be used as adjectives. Read the next sentence.

→ *Student: Many of the guests arrived early.*

Instructor: Put parentheses around the prepositional phrase "of the guests." Now you can clearly see the subject of the sentence. What is it?

→ *Student: Many.*

Instructor: Fill out the diagram frame below the sentence.

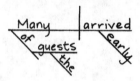

Instructor: Read the next sentence out loud.

→ *Student: Many guests arrived early.*

Instructor: In this sentence, who arrived early?

→ *Student: Guests.*

Instructor: *Guests* is the subject of the sentence, and *many* is an indefinite pronoun acting as an adjective. Fill out the diagram frame below the sentence.

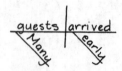

Instructor: Remember that the subject or object of a sentence will never be in a prepositional phrase. Find your prepositional phrases first and circle them! This will help you decide whether an indefinite pronoun is acting as a noun or as an adjective.

Complete the remainder of your exercises now.

— LESSON 52 —

Personal Pronouns
Indefinite Pronouns

Instructor: We've covered a lot of information about pronouns this week, so let's take a few minutes to review. Your workbook has a full list of personal pronouns. Which ones are the subject pronouns? Write them on the first blank.

> **Note to Instructor:** If the student has trouble identifying the subject pronouns, suggest that the student place each pronoun in the subject spaces of the sentences that follow.

Subject pronouns: _I, you, he, she, it, we, they_

Instructor: Now, place each subject pronoun in the blank in front of the correct predicate in your workbook. You can put more than one pronoun in the same blank!

_I_ am delighted to be doing grammar.
You, we, they are delighted to be doing grammar.
He, she, it is delighted to be doing grammar.

Instructor: Which are the object pronouns? Write them on the next blank.

Object pronouns: _Me, him, us, them, you, her, it_

Instructor: Place each object pronoun in the correct blank in the next two sentences.

> **Note to Instructor:** This is a trick question; all object pronouns can serve both as objects of prepositions and as direct objects.

The walrus splattered water all over _me, him, us, them_ .
The rain drenched Kim and _me, him, us, them_ .

Instructor: Which possessive pronouns can act as possessive adjectives in the attributive position?

Possessive pronouns/possessive adjectives in attributive position: _my, your, his, her, its, our, their_

Instructor: Place each possessive adjective into one of the blanks below.

I grabbed _my, your, his, her_ umbrella.
The cloud began dropping _its_ moisture.
The soaked tourists ran for _their_ cars.

Instructor: Which possessive pronouns can act as possessive adjectives, but only in the predicate position?

Possessive pronouns/possessive adjectives in predicate position: _mine, yours, hers, ours, theirs_

Instructor: Place each possessive adjective into one of the blanks below.

That raincoat is _mine, yours, hers_ .
Those waterproof ponchos are _ours, theirs_ .

Instructor: Now let's review indefinite pronouns. What is an indefinite pronoun?

→ *Student: Indefinite pronouns are pronouns without antecedents.*

Instructor: The first 18 indefinite pronouns on your list all take singular verbs. It might help to remember that pronouns ending with *body*, *one*, and *thing* are always singular. Read me all the pronouns ending in *body*, *one*, and *thing*.

→ Student: *Anybody, everybody, nobody, somebody; anyone, everyone, no one, someone, one; anything, everything, nothing, something.*

Instructor: Then you just have to remember the last five. Let's say them together.

→ Both: *Another, other, either, neither, each.*

Instructor: Fill in the blanks with the correct state-of-being verb in the simple present tense.

> Everyone <u>is</u> in the kitchen.
> Nobody <u>is</u> in the dining room.
> Neither of them <u>is</u> in the garden.

Instructor: Read me the indefinite pronouns that always take plural verbs.

→ Student: *Both, few, many, several.*

Instructor: Fill in the blanks with the correct past helping or linking verb.

> Both <u>were</u> cooking eggplants.
> A few of the crowd <u>were</u> objecting to eggplant.
> Several <u>were</u> quite happy with the prospect of eggplant.

Instructor: Now, read me the indefinite pronouns that can take either singular or plural verbs.

→ Student: *All, any, most, none, some.*

Instructor: These pronouns are plural when they refer to a group of things, and singular if they refer to one thing. Fill in the blanks in the next two sentences with the correct past helping or state-of-being verb.

> All of the fire engines <u>were</u> there.
> All of the mansion <u>was</u> destroyed in the fire.

Instructor: There's one more complication to consider when you're using indefinite pronouns—particularly *singular* indefinite pronouns. Look at the next sentence in your workbook. In this sentence, *everyone* is singular. Once everyone *gets* those presents, the presents will belong to everyone. So we need to put a possessive personal pronoun in that blank. Can we say, "Is everyone coming to get their Christmas present"?

→ Student: [Yes/no.]

Instructor: Even though that might sound natural, we can't use the personal pronoun *their*, because *their* is plural and *everyone* is singular. We have to use a singular pronoun instead. What are the three singular possessive pronouns that we can use in attributive position (in front of *Christmas presents*)?

→ Student: *His, her, its.*

Instructor: We don't want to use *its*, because a person is not an *it*. But we also don't know whether the unknown person coming to get a Christmas present should be referred to as *he* or *she!* There are actually three different ways to solve this problem. First of all, the traditional, old-fashioned way to refer to someone of unknown gender is just to call everyone *he*, whether *he* is a *he* or actually a *she*. The masculine pronoun has often been assumed to apply to everyone, just like *mankind* has often been assumed to include both mankind and womankind. So that's the first possible solution. Write *his* into the first blank.

> Is everyone coming to get his Christmas present?

Instructor: This is correct, but it also isn't a perfect solution. Why?

→ *Student:* [Answers may vary: *Not all of the people getting presents were men.*]

> **Note to Instructor:** The student may respond in any appropriate way.

Instructor: Instead of assuming that *his* covers everyone getting a present, you could use both pronouns and put *his or her* in the next blank. Write that down now.

Is everyone coming to get his or her Christmas present?

Instructor: That seems fairer—but it's also a little bit awkward. So a third solution would be to rephrase the sentence. Read me the next sentence out loud.

→ *Student: Are they all coming to get their Christmas presents?*

Instructor: Using the personal pronoun *they* instead of the indefinite pronoun *everyone* solves the problem! When a sentence requires an indefinite pronoun to be matched up to a personal possessive pronoun, be sure to use the correct singular or plural pronoun—and if that sounds awkward, try to think of another way to write the sentence.

Complete the exercises in your workbook now.

Active and Passive Voice

— LESSON 53 —

Principal Parts
Troublesome Verbs

Instructor: Let's begin today with a tongue twister. Can you read it three times fast?

→ Student: *(Three times) She set the set of sorted stuff*
  Beside the seat where she had sat.

Instructor: There are a lot of similar words in this tongue twister, and it's easy to see how these words could get confused. English has a handful of verbs that are regularly misused, even by educated people. Two of these verbs are *sit* and *set,* which are found in our tongue twister. To use them correctly, you need to know their principal parts. Let's quickly review principal parts. How many principal parts do English verbs have?

→ Student: *English verbs have three principal parts.*

Instructor: What is the first principal part?

→ Student: *The first principal part is the simple present.*

Instructor: What is the second principal part?

→ Student: *The second principal part is the simple past.*

Instructor: How do you find the third principal part?

→ Student: *The third principal part of a verb is found by dropping the helping verb from the perfect past.*

Instructor: Complete your first exercise before we go on. Some of the verbs on the chart are regular, but some are irregular.

___

Instructor: Now look at the list of troublesome irregular verbs and read the definition of *sit.*

→ Student: *To rest or be seated.*

Instructor: Stand up and read me the principal parts of *to sit.*

→ Student: *Sit, sat, sat.*

Instructor: Now sit down. What did you just do?

→ Student: *I sat.*

Instructor: Repeat these examples after me: I sat on the porch swing.

→ *Student: I sat on the porch swing.*

Instructor: I have already sat down.

→ *Student: I have already sat down.*

Instructor: When a person or thing is resting or being seated, use the principal parts of the verb *sit.* This verb is sometimes confused with the verb *set.* Read the definition of *set* from your workbook.

→ *Student: To put or place something.*

Instructor: The verb *set* always has a direct object. Let's *set* our pencils on the table and read the principal parts of *to set* two times.

→ *Together: (Setting pencils on table) Set, set, set; set, set, set.*

Instructor: Repeat these examples: Cherie set her heavy backpack down.

→ *Student: Cherie set her heavy backpack down.*

Instructor: Cherie has already set the table.

→ *Student: Cherie has already set the table.*

Instructor: Look at the next set of troublesome verbs. Read the definition of *lie.*

→ *Student: To rest or recline.*

Instructor: Let's take our hands and put them under our head like we are *lying* down to rest and read the principal parts of *to lie* two times.

→ *Together: (With hands under head) Lie, lay, lain; lie, lay, lain.*

Instructor: Repeat these examples after me: Grandma lay down to rest.

→ *Student: Grandma lay down to rest.*

Instructor: Grandma has lain down to rest.

→ *Student: Grandma has lain down to rest.*

Instructor: The verb *lie* is often confused with the verb *lay,* because the past tense of *lie* is *lay.* But they have different meanings. Read the definition of *lay.*

→ *Student: To put or place something.*

Instructor: Like the verb set, *the* verb *lay* always has a direct object. Let's pick up our pencils and *lay* them on the table and say the principal parts of *to lay* two times.

→ *Together: (Placing pencils on table) Lay, laid, laid; lay, laid, laid.*

Instructor: Repeat these examples after me: Grandma laid the new rug on the floor this morning.

→ *Student: Grandma laid the new rug on the floor this morning.*

Instructor: Grandma has already laid the new rug on the floor.

→ *Student: Grandma has already laid the new rug on the floor.*

Instructor: Notice that both sentences have a direct object—the rug. Now read me the definition of the troublesome verb *rise.*

→ *Student: To get up or go up.*

Instructor: Let's *rise* from our chairs together and read the principal parts of *to rise* two times.

→ *Together: (Rising from chairs) Rise, rose, risen; rise, rose, risen.*

Instructor: Repeat these examples after me: I rose at 6:00 this morning.

→ *Student: I rose at 6:00 this morning.*

Instructor: The sun had already risen.

→ *Student: The sun had already risen.*

Instructor: The verb *rise* is often confused with the verb *raise*. Read the definition of *raise* from your workbook.

→ *Student: To cause something to go up or grow up.*

Instructor: Like the verbs *set* and *lay*, the verb *raise* always has a direct object. Let's *raise* our hands together and read the principal parts of *to raise* two times.

→ *Together: (Raising hands) Raise, raised, raised; raise, raised, raised.*

Instructor: *Raise* is a regular verb. Repeat these examples after me: Tasha raised the flag.

→ *Student: Tasha raised the flag.*

Instructor: Tasha has raised three children.

→ *Student: Tasha has raised three children.*

Instructor: Let's look at the next set of verbs, and read the definition of *to let*.

→ *Student: To allow.*

Instructor: Let's make an OK sign with our fingers as if we are *letting* someone do something and read the principal parts of *to let* together.

→ *Together: (Making OK sign with fingers) Let, let, let; let, let, let.*

Instructor: Repeat these examples: Please let me go to the pool party!

→ *Student: Please let me go to the pool party!*

Instructor: Dad has often let me go to pool parties.

→ *Student: Dad has often let me go to pool parties.*

Instructor: *Let* is often confused with the verb *leave*. Read the definition of *leave* from your workbook.

→ *Student: To go away from or to allow to remain.*

Instructor: Let's get up and *leave* the room together and read the principal parts of *to leave*.

→ *Together: (Leaving room) Leave, left, left; leave, left, left.*

Note to Instructor: Be sure to come back!

Instructor: Repeat these examples after me: Leave me alone!

→ *Student: Leave me alone!*

Instructor: Marge left her wallet in the car.

→ *Student: Marge left her wallet in the car.*

Instructor: Complete the remaining exercises now.

— LESSON 54 —

Verb Tense
Active and Passive Voice

Instructor: You already know that verbs have *tense.* A tense can be past, present, or future; a tense can also be simple, progressive, or perfect. Review the definitions of simple, progressive, and perfect tenses by reading them out loud to me.

→ Student: *A simple verb simply tells whether an action takes place in the past, present, or future. A progressive verb describes an ongoing or continuous action. A perfect verb describes an action which has been completed before another action takes place.*

Instructor: Review tenses, before we go on, by completing Exercise 54A in your workbook.

Instructor: Verbs have another quality besides *tense.* They also have *voice.* Read the next sentence in your workbook out loud.

→ Student: *The door had been fastened upon the inner side, and the windows were blocked by old-fashioned shutters with broad iron bars.*

Instructor: Compare that sentence with the next sentence, written below it: *He fastened the door upon the inner side.* In the first sentence, the verb is in the **passive voice**. In the second, the verb is in the **active voice**. Repeat after me: **In a sentence with an active verb, the subject performs the action.**

→ Student: *In a sentence with an active verb, the subject performs the action.*

Instructor: In the sentence *He fastened the door upon the inner side,* who performs the action of fastening?

→ Student: *He.*

Instructor: *He* is the subject, and *he* performs the action. Repeat after me: **In a sentence with a passive verb, the subject receives the action.**

→ Student: *In a sentence with a passive verb, the subject receives the action.*

Instructor: In the sentence *The door had been fastened upon the inner side,* what is the subject?

→ Student: *The door.*

Instructor: Does the door do the fastening?

→ Student: *No.*

Instructor: The verb of this sentence is in the passive voice. The subject, *door,* doesn't perform the action. It *receives* the action, because it is the thing that gets fastened. Let's say that I was very mean, and I punched you for no reason at all. The subject of this sentence is *I,* and I punched you. I actively performed this action. I can also say this sentence as *You were punched by me.* You did not do anything; you were just sitting there passively, minding your own business, and I came along and punched you. You received the punch. Both sentences describe the same situation, but use different subjects. Look at the next sentence, and tell me the verb: *The Egyptians constructed pyramids.*

→ Student: *Constructed.*

Instructor: What is the subject of the sentence? Who or what constructed?

→ *Student: Egyptians.*

Instructor: In this sentence, did the Egyptians perform the action of constructing?

→ *Student: Yes.*

Instructor: The subject is performing the action, so this sentence is active. Let's change this sentence a little bit. *Pyramids were constructed.* What is the verb phrase in this sentence?

→ *Student: Were constructed.*

Instructor: What is the subject? Who or what was constructed?

→ *Student: Pyramids.*

Instructor: *Pyramids* is the subject, but the pyramids did not construct anything! They received the action, so this sentence is passive. In passive sentences, we do not necessarily need to know who performs the action. We can include the performer of the action in a prepositional phrase, for example: *Pyramids were constructed by the Egyptians*, or we can leave that out and simply say *Pyramids were constructed.*

   Passive sentences are useful if we do not know the performer of the action. However, active sentences tend to be more powerful and engaging than passive sentences. Look at the chart of verbs in the active and passive voice. I'll say the active voice example, and you say the passive voice example. Present: Freddy tricks the alligator.

→ *Student: The alligator is tricked by Freddy.*

Instructor: In all of these, you will notice that while the active voice *might or might not* use helping verbs, the passive voice *always* uses helping verbs. Now cover up the passive voice column with your hand. After I read the active voice, try your best to tell me the passive voice without looking. If you need to peek, that's okay. Past: Freddy tricked the alligator.

→ *Student: The alligator was tricked by Freddy.*

Instructor: Future: Freddy will trick the alligator.

→ *Student: The alligator will be tricked by Freddy.*

Instructor: Progressive present: Freddy is tricking the alligator.

→ *Student: The alligator is being tricked by Freddy.*

Instructor: Progressive past: Freddy was tricking the alligator.

→ *Student: The alligator was being tricked by Freddy.*

Instructor: Progressive future: Freddy will be tricking the alligator.

→ *Student: The alligator will be being tricked by Freddy.*

Instructor: That sentence sounds funny, doesn't it? The progressive future tense is not used in the passive form very often. Perfect present: Freddy has tricked the alligator.

→ *Student: The alligator has been tricked by Freddy.*

Instructor: Perfect past: Freddy had tricked the alligator.

→ *Student: The alligator had been tricked by Freddy.*

Instructor: Perfect future: Freddy will have tricked the alligator.

→ *Student: The alligator will have been tricked by Freddy.*

Instructor: Read the very last rule in your workbook.

→ *Student: **State-of-being verbs do not have voice.***

Instructor: A state-of-being verb can't be active or passive. It just *is*.

Complete your exercises now.

— LESSON 55 —

Parts of the Sentence
Active and Passive Voice

Instructor: We're going to review what you've learned in the last few weeks by diagramming the sentences in your workbook together. Use your own paper for this exercise.

> **Note to Instructor:** Use the Answer Key to the student's workbook to complete this lesson.

— LESSON 56 —

Active and Passive Voice
Transitive and Intransitive Verbs

Instructor: Let's review the formation of tenses in the passive voice now. I am going to read you the present active, progressive present active, and perfect present active sentences on your sheet. Then, you read me the present passive, progressive present passive, and perfect present passive versions of those sentences.

The farmer grows wheat. The farmer is growing wheat. The farmer has grown wheat.

→ Student: *Wheat is grown by the farmer. Wheat is being grown by the farmer. Wheat has been grown by the farmer.*

Instructor: Let's do the same with the past active and passive sentences. I made a cake. I was making a cake. I had made a cake.

→ Student: *The cake was made by me. The cake was being made by me. The cake had been made by me.*

Instructor: And now the future tenses. The princess will keep the key. The princess will be keeping the key. The princess will have kept the key.

→ Student: *The key will be kept by the princess. The key will be being kept by the princess. The key will have been kept by the princess.*

Instructor: What are the three direct objects in the sentences with active verbs?

→ Student: *Wheat, cake, and key.*

Instructor: In each transformation of the verb from active to passive, the direct object of the active verb becomes the subject of the passive verb. Now look at the next four sentences. Can you turn these active verbs into passive verbs?

> **Note to Instructor:** Give the student some time to try rephrasing the sentences.

Instructor: You cannot make these active verbs into passive verbs—because there is no object to turn into a subject! Nothing in the sentences receives the action of the verb. We call these kinds of verbs **intransitive** verbs. **Transitive** comes from the Latin word *transire,* which means "to pass over." In a transitive verb, action *passes* from the subject to an object. Read me the definitions of transitive and intransitive verbs from your workbook.

→ Student: **Transitive verbs express action that is received by some person or thing. Intransitive verbs express action that is not received by any person or thing.**

Instructor: Intransitive verbs can only be active. They can't be passive. Read me the list of some of the more common intransitive verbs.

→ Student: *Cough, go, arrive; sit, lie, rise; shine, sneeze, am, is, are, was, were.*

Instructor: Use two of those verbs in a sentence.

→ Student: *[Answers will vary.]*

> **Note to Instructor:** *I coughed all night, The sun is shining on the water,* and *I will arrive at 5 p.m.* are sample sentences. None of the sentences should have direct objects.

Instructor: None of those sentences have direct objects, do they? Now read me the nine examples of transitive verbs.

→ Student: *Love, eat, help; set, lay, raise; cut, hug, save.*

Instructor: Use two of those verbs in a sentence with a direct object.

→ Student: *[Answers will vary.]*

> **Note to Instructor:** *I love roast beef, The man raised the flag in the morning,* and *The chef cut the carrots* are sample sentences. It is completely possible to use a transitive verb *without* a direct object, but all of the student's sample sentences should contain a direct object.

Instructor: Look at the second line of both lists. A few lessons ago, you studied the verbs *sit/set, lie/lay,* and *rise/raise.* These are words which are often confused. Another way to remember the differences between them is to remind yourself that *sit, lie,* and *rise* are always intransitive. They *never* have direct objects. Read the next three sentences out loud now.

→ Student: *I am sitting on the front porch. I lay down on the grass. I will have risen early in the morning.*

Instructor: In those sentences, the progressive present, simple past, and perfect future forms of the intransitive verbs *sit, lie,* and *rise* are all followed by prepositional phrases—*not* by direct objects! No person or thing is receiving the action of those verbs. Now read the next three sentences.

→ Student: *I am setting the heavy box down. I laid my weary head on my arms. I will have raised my hand at least once by the end of class.*

Instructor: In those sentences, the progressive present, simple past, and perfect future forms of the transitive verbs *set, lay,* and *raise* all have direct objects. What is the direct object of *I am setting*?

→ Student: *Box.*

Instructor: What is the direct object of *I laid*?

→ Student: *Head.*

Instructor: What is the direct object of *I will have raised*?

→*Student: Hand.*

Instructor: Some verbs can be either transitive or intransitive. Read the nine examples in your workbook.

→*Student: Turn, break, speak; fly, run, spread; taste, eat, sing.*

Instructor: The first set of sentences below shows how several of these verbs can be used with direct objects, as transitive verbs. Read those out loud.

→*Student: The cook turns the meat on the spit. I will spread gochujang mayonnaise on the burger bun. He is singing a difficult aria.*

Instructor: Each of these verbs has a direct object. Circle the direct object in each sentence.

> The cook turns the (meat) on the spit.
>
> I will spread gochujang (mayonnaise) on the burger bun.
>
> He is singing a difficult (aria)

Instructor: In the second set of sentences, each verb is intransitive. There are no direct objects. Read those sentences now.

→*Student: The captain turned towards the sunset. The mist spread across the river's surface. He's singing in the shower.*

Instructor: Circle the prepositional phrase in each sentence.

> The captain turned (towards the sunset)
>
> The mist spread (across the river's surface)
>
> He's singing (in the shower)

Instructor: These intransitive verbs don't take objects. Instead, they're followed by prepositional phrases that act as adverbs.

There's no way to make those intransitive verbs passive instead of active—but when a verb is used in a transitive way, you *can* make it passive. Finish up today's lesson by rewriting the sentences in your workbook on the blanks below. Remember: The object will become the subject in each sentence, and the subject will go into a prepositional phrase following the verb. Make sure to keep your verb in the same tense—you're only changing the voice, not the tense! Look back at the chart at the beginning of this lesson if you need help

> The cook turns the meat on the spit.
> ___The meat is turned on the spit by the cook.___
>
> I will spread gochujang mayonnaise on the burger bun.
> ___Gochujang mayonnaise will be spread on the burger bun by me.___
>
> He is singing a difficult aria.
> ___A difficult aria is being sung by him.___

Instructor: Complete the exercises in your workbook now.

WEEK 15

Specialized Pronouns

— LESSON 57 —

Parts of Speech
Parts of the Sentence
Intensive and Reflexive Pronouns

Instructor: Read the first sentence in your workbook.

→ *Student: Anita made herself a huge brownie sundae!*

Instructor: Who made the sundae in this sentence?

→ *Student: Anita.*

Instructor: Who gets to eat the sundae?

→ *Student: Anita.*

Instructor: We know this because of the word *herself.* If the sentence had said *Anita made her a huge brownie sundae,* we might think that Anita made the sundae, but another girl gets to eat it. The word *herself* is a **reflexive pronoun.** Read the definition of reflexive pronouns.

→ *Student:* **Reflexive pronouns refer back to the subject.**

Instructor: You can remember this by reminding yourself that the reflexive pronoun *reflects* an action back onto the subject. Did you hear the reflexive pronoun in that sentence? What was it?

> **Note to Instructor:** If the student doesn't remember, repeat, "You can remember this by reminding *yourself.*"

Instructor: **Usually, reflexive pronouns act like objects.** *Reflexive pronoun* is the name of a part of speech. What is a part of speech? The answer is in your workbook.

→ *Student: Part of speech is a term that explains what a word does.*

Instructor: A reflexive pronoun refers to the subject. That is what the word does. But reflexive pronouns can act in different ways as parts of sentences. What is a part of a sentence? The answer is in your workbook.

→ *Student: Part of the sentence is a term that explains how a word functions in a sentence.*

Instructor: The next few sentences are taken from the letters of the scientist Galileo. Read me the first.

→ *Student: He adapted himself to their knowledge.*

Instructor: The subject is underlined once and the predicate twice. What did he adapt?

136

→ *Student: Himself.*

Instructor: In this sentence, the reflexive pronoun *himself* is the direct object of the verb *adapted*. Read me the next sentence.

→ *Student: He gave himself a task.*

Instructor: He gave what?

→ *Student: A task.*

Instructor: *Task* is the direct object. *Himself* is indirectly affected by the verb *gave.* What kind of object is *himself?*

→ *Student: An indirect object.*

Instructor: Read me the third sentence.

→ *Student: He praises in himself what he blames in others.*

Instructor: What part of speech is *in?*

→ *Student: A preposition.*

Instructor: In the prepositional phrase *in himself,* the reflexive pronoun is the object of the preposition. So you can see that the reflexive pronoun can act as different parts of a sentence. Now read me the list of reflexive pronouns.

→ *Student: Myself, himself, herself, itself, yourself, yourselves, ourselves, themselves.*

Instructor: You can see that these all end with -*self* or -*selves.* These same pronouns can also act as **intensive pronouns**. Read me the definition of intensive pronouns.

→ *Student: **Intensive pronouns emphasize a noun or another pronoun.***

Instructor: Look at the following sentence: *The Queen of England herself gave the speech.* In this sentence, the intensive pronoun *herself* is used to emphasize the subject *the Queen of England* and draw special attention to it. You know that *herself* is not a reflexive pronoun, because it isn't an object. Instead, *herself* just renames the subject.

   For your information: This is an appositive. If you haven't studied appositives yet, you'll find out more about them in Lesson 94. For right now, just note that it is *not* an object. The next three sentences show how the sentences would sound if *herself* were an object. Read all three out loud.

→ *Student: The Queen of England gave herself. The Queen of England gave herself the speech. The Queen of England gave the speech to herself.*

Instructor: Those sentences have very different meanings! Read the next sentence out loud now.

→ *Student: Aristotle himself observed these variations.*

Instructor: Is *himself* a reflexive pronoun or an intensive pronoun?

→ *Student: Intensive.*

> **Note to Instructor:** If the student isn't sure of the answer, help her rephrase the sentence as *Aristotle observed himself.* This turns the intensive pronoun into a reflexive pronoun acting as a direct object and changes the meaning of the sentence.

Instructor: Write *INTENSIVE* above the pronoun *himself.*

INTENSIVE
Aristotle himself observed these variations.

Instructor: Read the next sentence out loud.

→ *Student: He jumped into the sea and drowned himself.*

Instructor: Is *himself* a reflexive pronoun or an intensive pronoun? HINT: If it acts as an object, it is a reflexive pronoun.

→ *Student: Reflexive.*

Instructor: Write *REFLEXIVE* above the pronoun. It is the direct object of the transitive verb *drowned.*

REFLEXIVE

He jumped into the sea and drowned himself.

Instructor: When you diagram a reflexive pronoun, put it in the direct object, indirect object, or object of the preposition place on the diagram. But when you diagram an intensive pronoun, place it in parentheses after the noun or pronoun it intensifies. Look at the diagrams in your workbook. Point to the intensive pronoun *himself* in the first diagram, and the reflexive pronoun *himself* in the second diagram.

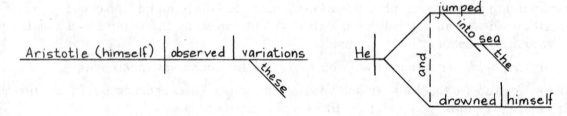

Instructor: There are a few incorrect words that are sometimes used in place of intensive and reflexive pronouns. Look in your book for the words you should avoid, and let's read them out loud together.

→ *Together: Do NOT use theirselves, hisself, or ourself.*

Instructor: Use *themselves, himself,* or *ourselves* instead. Here's the final rule about intensive and reflexive pronouns: Only use them in sentences where they have antecedents. Look at the incorrect sentence: "Diana and myself cooked a casserole." The pronoun *myself* doesn't have any antecedent. There is no word that it refers back to. Cross out the incorrect sentence and read the correct version.

→ *Student: Diana and I cooked a casserole.*

Instructor: Read the next sentence out loud.

→ *Student: I myself cooked a casserole.*

Instructor: That sentence is correct because *myself* refers back to *I. I* is the antecedent. Read the final correct sentence out loud.

→ *Student: Take care of yourself.*

Instructor: This sentence is correct, because the understood subject is *you. You* is the antecedent of *yourself,* and we understand it to already exist in the sentence.

Complete the exercises now.

— LESSON 58 —

Demonstrative Pronouns
Demonstrative Adjectives

Instructor: In your workbook, draw lines from each question in the left column with the correct punch line in the right column to create jokes.

Questions	Punch lines
What did the teacher say to make the student eat his quiz?	That opens up a whole new can of worms.
What did the customer in the butcher shop hear that scared him?	This will be a piece of cake!
What did the fisherman say when he dropped his bucket of bait?	These cost an arm and a leg.

Instructor: Sayings like *a piece of cake* are called idioms. Idioms are sayings that have two meanings. *A piece of cake* can mean an actual slice of cake, or it can mean "something that is very simple or easy." You could not understand these jokes if you didn't already know the double meaning of these idioms. You also couldn't form these jokes without two very important categories of pronouns. We'll be studying those two categories over two lessons.

Look at the sentences in the column on the right. Each punch line begins with a **demonstrative pronoun.** Read the definition and the list of demonstrative pronouns.

→ Student: **Demonstrative pronouns demonstrate or point out something. They can take the place of a single word or a group of words.** *This, that, these, those.*

Instructor: Tell me two things you see that are far away.

→ Student: *[Thing 1 and Thing 2.]*

Instructor: *That* and *those* describe things that are far away from you. Repeat after me: That is [Thing 1].

→ Student: *That is [Thing 1].*

Instructor: Those are [Thing 1 and Thing 2].

→ Student: *Those are [Thing 1 and Thing 2].*

Instructor: Now tell me two things that are close to you.

→ Student: *[Thing 3 and Thing 4.]*

Instructor: *This* and *these* describe things that are close to you. Repeat after me: This is [Thing 3].

→ Student: *This is [Thing 3].*

Instructor: These are [Thing 3 and Thing 4].

→ Student: *These are [Thing 3 and Thing 4].*

Instructor: In the sentences you just formed, *this, that, these,* and *those* are pronouns. Each one takes the place of a noun or nouns—the names of the things you are talking about. But the demonstrative pronouns can also be used as adjectives.

The next four sets of sentences are from the classic American novel *To Kill a Mockingbird*. In the first sentence of each set, the demonstrative pronoun is acting like a pronoun—it takes the place of a person, place, thing, or idea. In the second sentence of each set, the demonstrative pronoun acts like an adjective or adverb. Read me the first sentence now.

→ *Student: "Your cousin wrote this," said Aunt Alexandra. "He was a beautiful character."*

Instructor: The demonstrative pronoun *this* stands for a thing—the book that the cousin wrote. *This* is the direct object of the verb *wrote*. Underline it and write *DO* above it.

DO
"Your cousin wrote <u>this</u>," said Aunt Alexandra. "He was a beautiful character."

Instructor: Now read the second sentence.

→ *Student: "Didn't know it was this dark. Didn't look like it'd be this dark earlier in the evening."*

Instructor: *This* has become an adverb that modifies the adjective *dark*. How dark was it? *This* dark. Circle *this* and draw a line from it to the adjective *dark*.

"Didn't know it was (this) dark. Didn't look like it'd be (this) dark earlier in the evening."

Instructor: When a demonstrative pronoun modifies a noun, it is functioning as a demonstrative adjective. Read me the definition from your workbook.

→ *Student:* **Demonstrative adjectives modify nouns and answer the question** which one.

Instructor: Read the first sentence in the next set, from *To Kill a Mockingbird* by Harper Lee, out loud.

→ *Student: That was the only time I ever heard Atticus say it was a sin to do something . . .*

Instructor: The demonstrative pronoun *that* stands for a thing—the thing that Atticus said. Underline it. *That* is the subject of the verb *was*. Write an *S* above it.

S
<u>That</u> was the only time I ever heard Atticus say it was a sin to do something . . .

Instructor: Now read the second sentence in the set.

→ *Student: "I destroyed his last shred of credibility at that trial, if he had any to begin with."*

Instructor: *That* has become an adjective that modifies the noun *trial*. Which trial? *That* trial. Circle *that* and draw a line from it to the noun *trial*.

"I destroyed his last shred of credibility at (that) trial, if he had any to begin with."

Instructor: Read the first sentence in the next set out loud.

→ *Student: It was times like these when I thought my father, who hated guns and had never been to any wars, was the bravest man who ever lived.*

Instructor: The demonstrative pronoun *these* stands for a plural thing—the times when the narrator thought her father was the bravest man who ever lived. Underline it. *These* is the object of the preposition *like*. Write *OP* above it.

OP

It was times like <u>these</u> when I thought my father, who hated guns and had never been to any wars, was the bravest man who ever lived.

Instructor: Now read the second sentence in the set.

→ *Student: I was beginning to notice a subtle change in my father these days, that came out when he talked with Aunt Alexandra.*

Instructor: *These* has become an adjective that modifies the plural noun *days*. Which days? *These* days. Circle *these* and draw a line from it to the noun *days*.

I was beginning to notice a subtle change in my father these days, that came out when he talked with Aunt Alexandra.

Instructor: Now read the first sentence in the last set out loud.

→ Student: "Dill, those were his own witnesses."

Instructor: The demonstrative pronoun *those* stands for people—the witnesses. Underline it. *Those* is the subject of the verb *were*. Write an *S* above the demonstrative pronoun.

           S
"Dill, <u>those</u> were his own witnesses."

Instructor: Now read the final sentence out loud.

→ Student: Mrs. Merriweather was one of those childless adults who find it necessary to assume a different tone of voice when speaking to children.

Instructor: *Those* has become an adjective that modifies the plural noun *adults*. Which adults? *Those* adults.

Now look at the diagrams. Diagramming demonstrative pronouns is simple. If the pronoun is standing in for a noun, you just diagram it as whatever part of the sentence it is acting as. In the first diagram, *those* is the subject of the sentence, so you diagram it on the subject space. If the pronoun is acting as an adjective or adverb, simply place it on the line where the modifier would go. In the second diagram, *those* is on a slanted line beneath the noun *adults* because it acts as an adjective modifying *adults*.

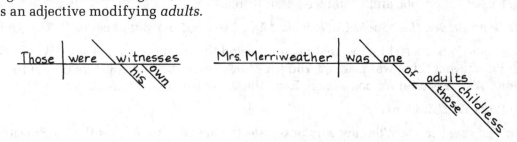

Instructor: The sentences above don't tell you *exactly* what the demonstrative pronouns are replacing. But look again at the second part of your definition. Demonstrative pronouns can replace either a single word or a group of words. Read me the next two sentences.

→ Student: Did you see the coaster? That is one scary ride.

Instructor: What does *that* refer back to?

→ Student: The coaster.

Instructor: Circle *coaster* and draw an arrow from *That* back to the circle.

Did you see the coaster? That is one scary ride.

Instructor: In the second sentence, *these* replaces a whole group of words. What are *these*?

→ Student: Raindrops on roses and whiskers on kittens, bright copper kettles and warm woolen mittens, brown paper packages tied up with strings.

Instructor: Circle that entire list and draw a line from *these* back to the circle.

Raindrops on roses and whiskers on kittens, bright copper kettles and warm woolen mittens, brown paper packages tied up with strings, these are a few of my favorite things.

Instructor: Complete your exercises now.

— LESSON 59 —

Demonstrative Pronouns
Demonstrative Adjectives
Interrogative Pronouns
Interrogative Adjectives

Instructor: Look back at the silly jokes in the last lesson. Each one of the answers begins with a demonstrative pronoun. But each one of the questions begins with an **interrogative pronoun.** Interrogative pronouns are used to ask questions. Read the definition and the list of interrogative pronouns.

→ Student: **Interrogative pronouns take the place of nouns in questions.** *Who, whom, whose, which, what.*

Instructor: Interrogative pronouns usually come at the beginning of questions. There are other words used to ask questions, such as *when* or *why*, but only these five words are pronouns, because they are used in place of nouns. *Who* and *whom* are used for people. *What* is used for things. Read me the next two sentences from *To Kill a Mockingbird.* In these sentences, *who* and *whom* are used for people, and *what* is used for things.

→ Student: *"Who started this?" said Uncle Jack. "Talk like what in front of whom?" he asked.*

Instructor: Uncle Jack doesn't know what *person* started the trouble—so he asks, "Who?" When we don't know what thing was said, or who heard it, we use the interrogative pronouns *what* and *whom*. *Whose* is used for possession. Read the third sentence out loud.

→ Student: *Whose is that blanket?*

Instructor: The speaker doesn't know who possesses the blanket, so he uses the interrogative pronoun *whose.* Read me the final sentence now.

→ Student: *Which is correct?*

Instructor: *Which* is used especially when there is a choice between two or more things.

Now, read me the next three sentences.

→ Student: *Whose blanket is missing? What madness is this? Which shoes are yours?*

Instructor: The last three interrogative pronouns, *whose, what,* and *which,* can also be used as adjectives—just like demonstrative pronouns can be used as demonstrative adjectives. Read me the definition in your workbook.

→ Student: **Interrogative adjectives modify nouns.**

Instructor: For today, there are three more things for you to remember about interrogative pronouns. First, it is easy to confuse the interrogative pronoun *whose* with the contraction *who's.* In the next sentence, *whose* is an interrogative pronoun that asks about the possession of the flip-flops. Read me that sentence out loud.

→ Student: *Whose orange flip-flops are those?*

Instructor: In the following sentence, *who's* is a contraction. Read me that sentence out loud, substituting *who is* for the contraction *who's.*

→ Student: *Who is cooking dinner?*

Instructor: Remember not to use the contraction in the wrong place! If you're not sure whether to write *whose* or *who*-apostrophe-*s,* try substituting the words *who is.* If the sentence makes sense with the substitution, write the contraction; if not, use the interrogative pronoun. Read the next two sentences and cross out the incorrect word.

> I don't know ~~whose~~/who's coming to dinner.
> Whose/~~who's~~ plate is still empty?

Instructor: Here's the second thing you need to remember: The interrogative pronouns *who* and *whom* are never adjectives. They are always pronouns, and they always stand for people, but they have different uses. *Who* always acts as a subject or predicate nominative within a sentence. *Whom* always acts as an object. Read the quote from Uncle Jack again; it is the next sentence in your book.

→ Student: *Who started this?*

Instructor: In this sentence, *who* is used as the subject. We can substitute a noun or another subject pronoun in place of *who,* and the sentence will still be correct: *She started this. They started this. I started this. Jack started this.* Now read the second sentence.

→ Student: *Talk like what in front of whom?*

Instructor: In this sentence, *whom* is used as the object of what preposition?

→ Student: *Of.*

Instructor: We could substitute a noun or another object pronoun in its place, and the sentence will be correct. *In front of him? In front of her? In front of them? In front of Jack?* Read the next two sentences and cross out the incorrect word.

> ~~Whom~~/Who is calling?
> To whom/~~who~~ did you speak?

Instructor: Third: Diagram interrogative adjectives like any other adjective, and diagram interrogative pronouns like any other pronoun. Look at the diagrams in your workbook. In the first diagram, *whose* is the subject and *blanket* is a predicate nominative renaming the pronoun *whose.* In the second diagram, *whose* is an adjective.

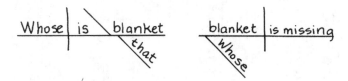

Instructor: Complete your exercises now.

— LESSON 60 —

Pronoun Review
Sentences Beginning with Adverbs

Instructor: Time for one more review! What is a pronoun? Try to answer without looking at your book.

→ Student: *A pronoun takes the place of a noun.*

Instructor: What is an antecedent?

→ *Student: An antecedent is the noun that is replaced by the pronoun.*

Instructor: Read me the full list of personal pronouns.

→ *Student: I, me, my, mine; you, your, yours; he, she, him, her, it; his, hers, its; we, us, our, ours; they, them, their, theirs.*

Instructor: Twelve of these pronouns can also be used as adjectives indicating possession. Underline them twice.

> **Personal Pronouns**
> I, me, <u>my, mine</u>
> you, <u>your, yours</u>
> he, she, him, <u>her</u>, it
> <u>his, hers, its</u>
> we, us, <u>our, ours</u>
> they, them, <u>their, theirs</u>

Note to Instructor: Prompt the student as necessary.

Instructor: Now write *S* above the pronouns that can be used as subjects, and *O* above the pronouns that can be used as objects. If a pronoun can be used either way, write both.

Note to Instructor: If the student needs help, suggest that she use the sentence *They saw you*. Pronouns that can be substituted for *they* are subject pronouns; pronouns that can be substituted for *you* are object pronouns.

Personal Pronouns

>   S   O
> I, me, <u>my, mine</u>
>
>   S O
> you, <u>your, yours</u>
>
>   S   S   O   O SO
> he, she, him, <u>her</u>, it
> <u>his, hers, its</u>
>
>   S   O
> we, us, <u>our, ours</u>
>
>   S   O
> they, them, <u>their, theirs</u>

Instructor: What are indefinite pronouns?

→ *Student: Indefinite pronouns are pronouns without antecedents.*

Instructor: Hold up one finger and say, "Singular!"

→ *Student: Singular!*

Instructor: Read the list of singular indefinite pronouns out loud, one time.

Singular

anybody	anyone	anything
everybody	everyone	everything
nobody	no one	nothing
somebody	someone	something
another	other	one
either	neither	each

Instructor: Hold up two fingers and say, "Plural!"

→ *Student: Plural!*

Instructor: Repeat after me two times: both, few, many, several

→ *Student: (Twice) Both, few, many, several.*

Instructor: Hold up one finger on your right hand and two fingers on your left hand, and say, "Singular or plural!"

→ *Student: Singular or plural!*

Instructor: Repeat after me two times: all, any, most, none, some.

→ *Student: (Twice) All, any, most, none, some.*

Instructor: *All, any, most, none,* and *some* can take either singular or plural verbs. What do reflexive pronouns do?

→ *Student: Reflexive pronouns refer back to the subject.*

Instructor: What are the reflexive pronouns?

→ *Student: Myself, himself, herself, itself, yourself, yourselves, ourselves, themselves.*

Instructor: Those pronouns can be subjects or objects. In the next sentence, what part of the sentence is *herself*?

→ *Student: Direct object.*

Instructor: *Herself* is a reflexive pronoun, acting as the direct object of the verb *hurt.* But in the sentence after that, *herself* has a different function. It is *intensifying* the subject. Read me the sentence.

→ *Student: She herself tripped.*

Instructor: Now read the definition of an intensive pronoun out loud.

→ *Student: Intensive pronouns emphasize a noun or another pronoun.*

> **Note to Instructor:** Say the next sentence loudly and with great emphasis (startle the student, who is probably bored with pronouns by now).

Instructor: WHAT IS THAT?????

I have just used the next two kinds of pronouns in one sentence. Read me the next definition.

→ *Student: Demonstrative pronouns demonstrate or point out something. They can take the place of a single word or a group of words.*

Instructor: What are the demonstrative pronouns?

→ *Student: This, that, these, those.*

Instructor: I used a demonstrative pronoun at the end of my loud question. And I used an interrogative pronoun to begin it. What do interrogative pronouns do?

→ *Student: Interrogative pronouns take the place of nouns in questions.*

Instructor: What are they? (That sentence also has two pronouns in it.)

→ *Student: Who, whom, whose, which, what.*

Instructor: *Whose, which,* and *what* can also be used as adjectives. What do interrogative adjectives do?

→ *Student: Interrogative adjectives modify nouns.*

Instructor: Remember that demonstrative pronouns can also serve as adjectives—as well as subjects and objects. In the next two sentences, label each demonstrative and interrogative as either *A* for adjective or *P* for pronoun.

    P   A

What are you doing? Don't you know what direction to go?

Instructor: Now let's look at a few sentences that seem similar—but are actually very different. Read me the next six short sentences in your workbook.

→ *Student: That is she. What is that? Which is yours? Where are you? There you are. So it is.*

Instructor: Look at the diagrams of the first three sentences. Each of these contains at least one demonstrative or interrogative pronoun that is taking the place of a noun.

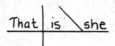

Instructor: In the first sentence, what part of the sentence is *that*?

→ *Student: The subject.*

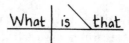

Instructor: In the second sentence, what part of the sentence is *that*?

→ *Student: The predicate nominative.*

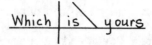

Instructor: In the third sentence, what part of the sentence is *which*?

→ *Student: The subject.*

Instructor: Now look at the next three sentences. *Where are you?* sounds very similar to *What is that?* But *where* is not a pronoun. What kind of word answers the questions *where, when, how, how often, to what extent*?

→ *Student: An adverb.*

Instructor: The second sentence answers the question *Where are you?*

→ *Student: There.*

Instructor: In the third sentence, *so* also answers an adverb question. It tells you *how.* How is it? It is so. Even though these sentences seem to be structured exactly like the first three, *where, there,* and *so* are adverbs.

Diagram those last three sentences on the frames provided.

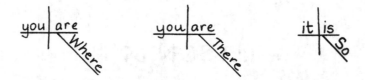

Instructor: Here's something for you to keep in mind, though: Grammar experts can disagree! Some grammarians would classify *where* and *there* in these particular sentences as *pronouns,* because they stand in for *the place you are.* Since *where* and *there* answer the adverb questions, though, we're going to continue to treat them as adverbs.

Complete your exercises now.

— REVIEW 5 —

The review exercises and answers are found in the Student Workbook and accompanying Key.

WEEK 16

Imposters

— LESSON 61 —

Progressive Tenses
Principal Parts
Past Participles as Adjectives
Present Participles as Adjectives

Instructor: Read the first paragraph in your book. It describes a famous fraud that fooled hundreds of people—including Sir Arthur Conan Doyle, who created Sherlock Holmes.

> One Sunday afternoon in 1917, cousins <u>named</u> Frances Griffiths and Elsie Wright, <u>aged</u> nine and fifteen, saw some fairies and took clear snapshots of them with their box camera . . . In 1983, sixty-six years later, Elsie Wright and Frances Griffiths decided that it was time to confess what people had suspected all along. The fairies were paper dolls . . . <u>propped</u> up on the grass with pins.
>
> —Kathryn Ann Lindskoog, *Fakes, Frauds, & Other Malarkey*

Instructor: The underlined words are adjectives. In the first sentence of the paragraph, draw arrows from the words *named* and *aged* to the noun *cousins.*

> One Sunday afternoon in 1917, cousins <u>named</u> Frances Griffiths and Elsie Wright, <u>aged</u> nine and fifteen, saw some fairies and took clear snapshots of them with their box . . .

Instructor: Both of those words answer the question *which one*. Which cousins? The ones named Frances and Elsie, aged nine and fifteen. In the last sentence of the paragraph, draw an arrow from *propped* to the noun it describes. What noun is that?

→ Student: Dolls.

> . . . paper dolls . . . <u>propped</u> up on the grass with pins.

Instructor: Which dolls? The dolls propped up on the grass. These three adjectives (*named, aged,* and *propped*) are also frauds, in a way. They are actually verbs, *acting* like adjectives.

Look at the chart. It lists the three principal parts that you learned about in Lesson 46. What are the names of the three principal parts?

→ Student: Present, past, past participle.

Instructor: The first verb in the chart is a regular verb. Read me the principal parts of *plan.*

→ Student: Plan, planned, planned.

Instructor: Regular verbs form the past and the past participle by adding *-ed*. Irregular verbs form the past and past participle in several different ways. Read the principal parts of *burst.*

148

→ *Student: Burst, burst, burst.*

Instructor: Verbs like *burst* use the same form for all three principal parts. Read the principal parts of *catch.*

→ *Student: Catch, caught, caught.*

Instructor: The past and past participle of verbs like *catch* are the same, but they're not formed by adding *-ed.* Read the principal parts of *fall.*

→ *Student: Fall, fell, fallen.*

Instructor: Some verbs, like *fall,* have three different principal parts—but none of them are formed by adding *-ed.* However the principal parts are formed, the third principal part—the past participle—can masquerade as an adjective. In the sentences beneath your chart, you'll see the past participles of *plan, burst, catch,* and *fall* used as adjectives. In these sentences, circle each past participle, and draw an arrow to the noun it modifies.

The (planned) vacation did not go well.

The (burst) balloon fit inside the honey jar.

The (caught) fish wriggled on the hook.

I climbed over the (fallen) tree.

Instructor: Read the rule about past participles out loud.

→ *Student: **The past participle of a verb can act as a descriptive adjective.***

Instructor: Now look back at the paragraph about the cousins. *Named* describes them. It is also a third principal part. What are the first and second principal parts of that verb?

→ *Student: Name, named.*

> **Note to Instructor:** If the student has difficulty, encourage him to say, "Today I name; yesterday I named; I had named before."

Instructor: What are the first and second principal parts that go along with *aged* and *propped?*

→ *Student: Age, aged; prop, propped.*

> **Note to Instructor:** *Age* can also be a noun, but the *-ed* at the end tells you that this is the past participle of the verb *age* rather than the noun.

Instructor: In all three cases, the third principal part is acting as an adjective—just as it is in the next sentences. Listen to the following sentence and tell me the past participle that you hear: *The freshly picked peaches were full of flavor.*

→ *Student: Picked.*

Instructor: What word is modified by *picked?*

→ *Student: Peaches.*

Instructor: There is another verb form which can imitate an adjective. In the next four sentences from *Grimm's Fairy Tales,* circle each word that ends in *-ing.* Then draw an arrow from the circled word to the noun it describes.

As the clock struck twelve, he heard a rustling noise in the air.

By the side of the road, he saw a fox sitting.

Her mother stirred the pot of boiling water.

The snoring guards lay at the doorstep, fast asleep.

Instructor: To find out what kind of verbs these imitators are, you'll need to quickly review the three kinds of verb tenses you have learned about: simple, progressive, and perfect. Read me the definition of a **simple verb**.

→ Student: *A simple verb simply tells whether an action takes place in the past, present, or future.*

Instructor: Read me the three simple forms of the verb *think:* past, present, and future.

→ Student: *I thought, I think, I will think.*

Instructor: Read me the definition of a **perfect verb**.

→ Student: *A perfect verb describes an action which has been completed before another action takes place.*

Instructor: Read me the three perfect forms of the verb *think:* past, present, and future.

→ Student: *I had thought, I have thought, I will have thought.*

Instructor: Notice that each one of the perfect forms uses the third principal part of the verb: *thought.* Now, read me the definition of a **progressive verb**.

→ Student: *A progressive verb describes an ongoing or continuous action.*

Instructor: Finally, read me the three progressive forms of the verb *think:* past, present, and future.

→ Student: *I was thinking, I am thinking, I will be thinking.*

Instructor: All progressive verbs have the same *suffix,* or ending. What is it?

→ Student: *The suffix -ing.*

Instructor: When the -ing form of the verb occurs all by itself, it has a specific name. It is called a *present participle.* A present participle isn't considered to be one of the three *principal parts*—because it never changes. All verbs, no matter how irregular, have a present participle that ends in *-ing.* Read across the chart below, first reading the principal parts and then reading the present participle.

First Principal Part Present	Second Principal Part Past	Third Principal Part Past Participle	Present Participle
rustle	rustled	rustled	rustling
sit	sat	sat	sitting
snore	snored	snored	snoring
am	was	been	being

Instructor: In the four sentences from the Brothers Grimm, the present participles of *stir, rustle, sit,* and *snore* are all acting like adjectives. Read me the next definition.

→ Student: **The present participle of a verb can act as a descriptive adjective.**

Instructor: The past participle (third principal part) and present participle (not a "principal part" at all) of a verb can both act like adjectives. As you look at the next two sentences and diagrams, remember this: When you diagram either a past participle or a present participle, if that participle is acting like an adjective, you put it on a slanted line beneath the noun it modifies, just like a regular adjective. But then the slanted line curves around and becomes straight. Adjectives are usually diagrammed on slanted lines, and verbs are usually diagrammed on straight lines. So when you diagram a participle on a line like this, you're showing that it has both adjective qualities *and* verb qualities.

The burst balloon fit inside the honey jar.

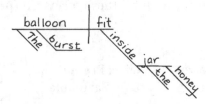

The snoring guards lay at the doorstep, fast asleep.

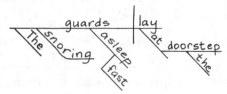

Instructor: Diagram the next two sentences on the frames provided.

Sparkling stars shone.

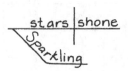

The forgotten cheese molded.

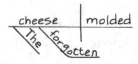

OPTIONAL:

> **Note to Instructor:** This optional section contains additional participle forms used, in more archaic styles, as adjectives. Students who will be reading on a high school level should know this information, but you may want to skip it on the student's first pass through this grammar program, since understanding these additional forms relies on a clear understanding of the past participle/present participle forms as well as regular exposure to classic English literature.

Instructor: One last thing. Past participles and present participles are by far the most common adjective forms you'll see in written English. But occasionally, particularly in older books, you might see other participle forms. The past participle only has one form, but the present participle actually has three more forms. After I read each form, read the corresponding sentence out loud. Present active participle, *rustling.*

→ *Student: The rustling leaves told us that the wind was rising.*

Instructor: Present passive participle, *being rustled*.

→ *Student: The leaves, being rustled, signified the coming of fall.*

Instructor: Perfect present active participle, *having rustled*.

→ *Student: Having rustled the leaves, the wind died down.*

Instructor: Perfect present passive participle, *having been rustled*.

→ *Student: The leaves having been rustled, the wind died down.*

Instructor: Past participle, *rustled*.

→ *Student: The rustled leaves finally stilled.*

Instructor: As you can hear, it's usually much simpler to use a plain present or past participle. But just to give you a little more familiarity with these forms, fill out the rest of the chart before you complete your exercises.

Present (Active) Participle	Present (Passive) Participle	Perfect Present (Active) Participle	Perfect Present (Passive) Participle	Past Participle
add *-ing*	being + past participle	having + past participle	having + been + past participle	add *-ed* (second principal part)
rustling	being rustled	having rustled	having been rustled	rustled
eating	being eaten	having eaten	having been eaten	eaten
reading	being read	having read	having been read	read

Instructor: Complete your exercises now.

— LESSON 62 —

Parts of Speech and Parts of Sentences
Present Participles as Nouns (Gerunds)

Instructor: As you read the paragraph in your book, circle every word that ends in *-ing*.

The cuckoo is one of the great con artists of the animal world. It can trick other birds into (raising) its children by (laying) their eggs in the stranger's nest. When the cuckoo chicks hatch, the youngsters continue their parents' strategy by (killing) any other birds in the nest before they reveal their identity. Scientists have found the imposter cuckoo even fools the foster parent into (thinking) its chicks are still alive by (flapping) yellow patches on its wings. This also creates the illusion there are more mouths to feed and tricks the foster parents into (delivering) more food.

—Augustus Brown, *Why Pandas Do Handstands: And Other Curious Truths About Animals* (Simon and Schuster, 2006), p. 210

Instructor: Like the cuckoo, these words are imposters. They are present participles, but they are acting like nouns. You've already learned that a present participle of a verb can act like a descriptive adjective. In the next sentence, circle the present participle that is acting like a descriptive adjective, and draw a line from it to the noun it modifies.

> **Note to Instructor:** If the student makes mistakes, simply tell him the correct answers.

The (running) rabbit was darting towards the briar patch.

Instructor: *Running* modifies the noun *rabbit*. It answers the question *which one*. There is another present participle in that first sentence—a verb form ending in *-ing*. What is it?

→ *Student: Darting.*

Instructor: The present participle *darting* is part of the progressive verb *was darting*. Remember, the present participle can be used as part of a verb *or* as an adjective. What tense is *was darting*—progressive past, progressive present, or progressive future?

→ *Student: Progressive past.*

Instructor: Now look back at the paragraph about cuckoos.

Present participles can act like verbs, or adjectives,—or even nouns! In the paragraph, each one of the present participles is acting like a noun. Remember, a *noun* is a *part of speech*. What is a part of speech? You can read the definition if necessary.

→ *Student: Part of speech is a term that explains what a word does.*

Instructor: What does a noun do?

→ *Student: A noun names a person, place, thing, or idea.*

Instructor: Nouns can be used as different parts of sentences. What is a part of a sentence? You can read the definition if necessary.

→ *Student: Part of a sentence is a term that explains how a word functions in a sentence.*

Instructor: Nouns can function as at least four different parts of sentences. Read me those parts of sentences.

→ *Student: Subject, direct object, indirect object, object of a preposition.*

Instructor: In the paragraph about cuckoos, all of the present participles acting like nouns fall into one of these categories. Which one is it?

→ *Student: Object of a preposition.*

> **Note to Instructor:** If the student cannot answer, ask him to circle and identify the word that comes right before each *-ing* word in the paragraph. All of the circled words are prepositions.

Instructor: When a present participle is acting like a noun, it is given a particular name; it is called a *gerund*. Read me the definition of a gerund.

→ *Student: **A gerund is a present participle acting as a noun.***

Instructor: Before you complete your exercises, we'll look at examples of gerunds functioning as both subjects and objects. The sentences in your book are all adapted from Alexander Dumas's classic novel *The Count of Monte Cristo*. In the first sentence, what is the verb?

→ *Student: Was.*

Instructor: Underline it twice. What was?

→ *Student: Sailing.*

> **Note to Instructor:** If the student answers *Careful sailing*, say, "Which *single* word answers the question? *Careful* was, or *sailing* was?"

Instructor: The gerund *sailing* is the subject of the sentence. Underline it once. *Sailing* is the present participle of what verb?

→ *Student: Sail.*

Instructor: Write an *S* above *sailing*.

What part of the sentence is *duty*?

→ *Student: Predicate nominative.*

> **Note to Instructor:** If necessary, remind the student that a predicate nominative renames the subject: sailing = duty.

Instructor: Write *PN* above the noun *duty*.

S   PN
Careful <u>sailing</u> <u>was</u> the duty of the captain's mate.

Instructor: In the second sentence, underline the predicate twice. What is it?

→ *Student: Was lost.*

Instructor: Is that an active verb or a passive verb?

→ *Student: Passive.*

> **Note to Instructor:** If necessary, say, "Did the day lose something? If so, the verb is active."

Instructor: What was lost?

→ *Student: This day.*

Instructor: Underline the noun *day* once. It is the subject of the sentence. Which day was lost?

→ *Student: This day.*

Instructor: *This* is a demonstrative adjective. It tells you *which* day. Circle *this* and draw an arrow from it to *day*. Now let's find the gerund. Draw a box around the only word in the sentence that ends with *-ing*. What is it?

→ *Student: Going.*

Instructor: What part of speech is the word that comes right before *going*?

→ *Student: Preposition.*

Instructor: Write *PREP* above the word *of*. *Of going ashore* is a prepositional phrase. *Going* is the object of the preposition *of*. Write *OP* above the gerund *going*. It is the object of the preposition.

PREP OP
(This) <u>day</u> <u>was</u> <u>lost</u> from pure whim, for the pleasure of [going] ashore.

Instructor: So far we've seen a gerund as a subject and a gerund as the object of a preposition. Look at your next sentence and underline the subject once and the predicate twice.

<u>Providence</u> <u>gives</u> the deserving their due.

Instructor: Providence gives something *to* something else. The thing *given* is the direct object. The thing that *receives* it is the indirect object. Can you mark which is which? Use *DO* for direct object and *IO* for indirect object.

       IO   DO

Providence <u>gives</u> the deserving their due.

> **Note to Instructor:** If the student cannot answer, you may need to review the dialogue in Lesson 28.

Instructor: The gerund *deserving* is acting as indirect object. *Deserving* is the present participle of what verb?

→ *Student: Deserve.*

Instructor: Now look at the last sentence. It begins with the prepositional phrase *With the other hand.* You know that the subject and verb will not be in the prepositional phrase. What is the subject and verb?

→ *Student: He repressed.*

Instructor: What did he repress?

→ *Student: Beatings.*

Instructor: *Beatings* is a gerund acting as a direct object. Underline the subject once and the predicate twice. Write *DO* over *beatings.*

                       DO

With the other hand, <u>he</u> <u><u>repressed</u></u> the beatings of his heart.

Instructor: Before you do your exercises, you need to learn how to diagram a gerund. A gerund goes in the same place that any other noun would go on a diagram—on the subject, direct object, indirect object, or object of the preposition line. But you diagram the gerund on a broken line to show that it is part noun and part verb. When you're diagramming the gerund on the main line of the diagram—the subject-predicate line—you draw a little tree and put the broken line on that tree. You do the same thing when you're diagramming a gerund as an object of the preposition or an indirect object, but you put the little tree on the *object of the preposition* or *indirect object* line instead.

Look carefully at the first diagram. Then, diagram the second sentence onto the frame provided.

Running is my favorite exercise.

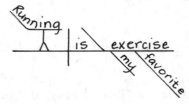

He feared falling.

Instructor: Complete your exercises now.

— LESSON 63 —

Gerunds
Present and Past Participles as Adjectives
Infinitives
Infinitives as Nouns

Instructor: Let's start with a quick review of the imposters we've learned so far. In your book, you will see three sentences adapted from the classic novel *Sense and Sensibility* by Jane Austen. Each sentence has one or more imposters. In the first sentence, underline the two present participles—verbs acting like some other part of speech!

> The <u>comings</u> and <u>goings</u> of her acquaintances <u>provided</u> Mrs. Jennings great entertainment.

Instructor: Underline the action verb *provided* twice. What part of the sentence are *comings* and *goings*?

→ *Student: They are subjects.*

Instructor: These present participles are *gerunds*—verb forms acting like nouns. In this sentence, the gerunds form a compound subject.

In the second sentence, underline the present participle and draw an arrow to the noun it modifies.

> This circumstance was a <u>growing</u> attachment between her eldest girl and the brother of Mrs. John Dashwood.

Instructor: Present participles can also act like adjectives. The adjective *growing* modifies the noun *attachment*.

The third sentence contains a past participle that acts as an adjective. Underline it and then draw a line from it to the noun it modifies.

> The presence of the two Miss Steeles, lately <u>arrived</u>, gave Elinor pain.

Instructor: *Arrived* is the past participle of the verb *arrive*.

Now I'm going to ask you a question, and I want you to answer with an action verb. Answer in a complete sentence. What do you like to do every morning? Start with "I like to . . ."

→ *Student: I like to [activity].*

Instructor: What is something you want to do tomorrow? Start with "I want to . . ."

→ *Student: I want to [activity].*

Instructor: What is something you wish you didn't have to do? Start with "I wish I didn't have to . . ."

→ *Student: I wish I didn't have to [activity].*

Instructor: In each one of your answers, you used an **infinitive**. Read the definition of an infinitive from your workbook.

→ *Student: **An infinitive is formed by combining** to **and the first person singular present form of a verb.***

Instructor: Fill in the blanks with the correct infinitive forms.

	Present Tense		**Infinitive**
	Singular	**Plural**	
First person	I give	we give	
Second person	you give	you give	to give
Third person	he, she, it gives	they give	
First person	I think	we think	
Second person	you think	you think	to think
Third person	he, she, it thinks	they think	
First person	I have	we have	
Second person	you have	you have	to have
Third person	he, she, it has	they have	

Instructor: Like gerunds, infinitives can act like nouns in sentences. Look at the following two sentences and tell me the two infinitives that you see.

→ *Student: To err, to forgive.*

Instructor: *To err* is the subject of the first sentence. *To forgive* is the subject of the second sentence. In both sentences, the subjects are linked (by the linking verb *is*) with a predicate adjective. Now look at the next two sentences. You should be able to find and circle four examples of infinitives. (One is repeated twice.)

(To wish) was (to hope)
(To hope) was (to expect)
—Jane Austen

Instructor: What are the four infinitives?

→ *Student: To wish, to hope, to hope, to expect.*

Instructor: In the first sentence, *To wish* is an infinitive acting as the subject. *To hope* is an infinitive that renames the subject. What kind of word follows a linking verb and renames the subject?

→ *Student: A predicate nominative.*

Instructor: In the second sentence, what is the subject?

→ *Student: To hope.*

Instructor: What is the linking verb?

→ *Student: Was.*

Instructor: What is the predicate nominative?

→ *Student: To expect.*

Instructor: Now look at the diagram in your workbook. Like a gerund, an infinitive is diagrammed on a little tree in the appropriate space on the diagram, topped by a slanted line combined with a straight line. *To* is placed on the slanted line, and the verb form itself is placed on the straight line.

Instructor: Complete your exercises now.

— LESSON 64 —

Gerunds
Present and Past Participles
Infinitives
Gerund, Participle, and Infinitive Phrases

Instructor: What are three of your absolute favorite foods?

→ *Student: [Answers with a short list.]*

Instructor: You could say to me, simply, *I love eating.* But that's not a very informative sentence. Give it a little more meat by adding all of the things you like to eat at the end of the sentence. Write your new sentence on the lines in your workbook.

→ *Student: I love eating [answers will vary: pancakes with maple syrup, yellow cake with chocolate frosting, and grilled ribeye steaks].*

Instructor: In this sentence, the present participle *eating* is acting like a noun—the direct object of the verb *love.* What do we call present participles that act like nouns?

→ *Student: Gerunds.*

Instructor: Here's the funny thing about gerunds: While they're acting like nouns, they can still also act like verbs at the same time. Circle the gerund *eating* and all of the things that you like to eat in one big circle.

I love eating [pancakes with maple syrup, yellow cake with chocolate frosting, and grilled ribeye steaks].

Instructor: The gerund and all of the words that go with it form a *phrase.* What is a phrase?

→ *Student: A phrase is a group of words serving a single grammatical function.*

Instructor: The direct object of the verb *love* is the gerund *eating,* along with all of the words that follow it. But within that phrase itself, *eating* functions as a verb, and all of the things that you eat are the *objects* of that verb. Look at the sample diagram in your workbook.

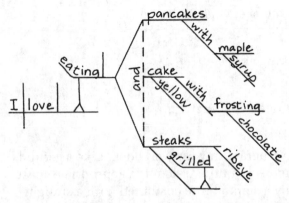

Instructor: The three things that the subject enjoys eating are all objects of the gerund *eating.* And the entire phrase is rooted in the object space on the diagram, because the subject doesn't just love eating, or just love pancakes, cake, and steaks—the subject loves *eating pancakes, cake, and steaks.*

Read the next sentence out loud.

→ *Student: To give without expecting a reward is to receive an even greater gift.*

Instructor: Circle the phrases *To give without expecting a reward* and *to receive an even greater gift.*

(To give without expecting a reward) is (to receive an even greater gift)

Instructor: What part of the sentence is the first phrase?

→ *Student: The subject.*

Instructor: Label the whole phrase with an *S*. What part of the second is the second phrase?

→ *Student: The predicate nominative.*

Instructor: Label the whole phrase with *PN*. Can you find the gerund *within* the first phrase? Remember, gerunds end with *-ing*.

→ *Student: Expecting.*

Instructor: Expecting what?

→ *Student: A reward.*

Instructor: Within the phrase that's serving as the subject of the sentence, the phrase *expecting a reward* serves as the object of the preposition *without*. And within the phrase that's serving as the object of the preposition, *reward* is the direct object of the present participle *expecting*. Underline *expecting a reward*. Write *OP* above the phrase.

S   PN
OP
(To give without expecting a reward) is (to receive an even greater gift)

Instructor: As you can see, writing sentences is a little bit like snapping Legos together. Small pieces fit together into larger pieces, and then those larger pieces connect together to make the whole.

    Look at the diagram of this sentence now. As I describe each part, put your finger on it.

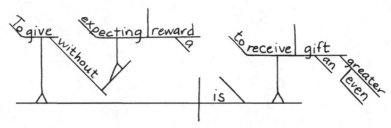

Instructor: *To give without expecting a reward* is an infinitive phrase acting as the subject. Within that phrase, *to give* is the subject. *Without expecting a reward* is a prepositional phrase that modifies the infinitive *to give*. Within that prepositional phrase, *without* is the preposition and *expecting a reward* is a gerund phrase serving as the object of the proposition. Within that gerund phrase, *a reward* is the object of the present participle *expecting*.

    To receive an even greater gift is an infinitive phrase acting as the predicate nominative. The noun phrase *an even greater gift* serves as the object of the infinitive *to receive*. Within that noun phrase, *gift* is the actual object. *An* and *greater* are adjectives describing *gift*, and *even* is an adverb modifying *greater*.

    Past participle phrases are diagrammed the same way. Read me the next sentence.

→ *Student: He saw the priceless antique vase shattered across the floor and scattered on the rug.*

Instructor: Put your finger on the diagrammed phrases *shattered across the floor* and *scattered on the rug*.

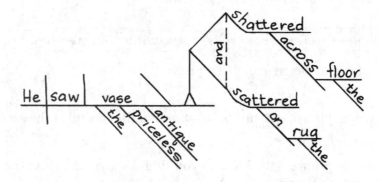

Instructor: What part of the sentence do these phrases serve as?

Note to Instructor: Prompt the student if necessary.

→ *Student: Object complement.*

Instructor: It follows the direct object and describes it. *Shattered* and *scattered* are compound past participles modifying *vase*. *Across the floor* and *on the rug* are prepositional phrases that modify the past participles. Because the participles belong on the main line of the diagram, we put them on a tree.

You've learned that you can simplify your understanding of a sentence by first circling the prepositional phrases. It's also helpful to circle your gerund, infinitive, and past participle phrases so that you can identify what part of the sentence those phrases are filling.

Complete your exercises now.

WEEK 17

Comparatives and Superlatives, Subordinating Conjunctions

— LESSON 65 —

Adjectives
Comparative and Superlative Adjectives

> **Note to Instructor:** For this lesson you will need a quarter, a nickel, and a dime (or any three coins of different sizes).

> **Note to Instructor:** Comparative is pronounced *kuhm PAR uh tiv*. Superlative is pronounced *suh PUR luh tiv*.

Instructor: Look at the three coins in front of you. A quarter is small. One of those coins is even smaller than the quarter, but larger than the other coin. Which is it?

→ *Student: The nickel.*

Instructor: The quarter is small, but the nickel is smaller. The dime is the smallest coin of all. *Small, smaller,* and *smallest* are all adjectives that answer the question *what kind.* Read me the definition of an adjective.

→ *Student: An adjective modifies a noun or pronoun. Adjectives tell what kind, which one, how many, and whose.*

Instructor: *Small, smaller,* and *smallest* are all forms of the adjective *small.* They modify the nouns *quarter, nickel,* and *dime. Small* just tells you the size of the quarter—but *smaller* and *smallest* help you compare the size of the three coins. Today we are going to talk about adjectives that compare. Read me the next three sentences.

→ *Student:* **The positive degree of an adjective describes only one thing. The comparative degree of an adjective compares two things. The superlative degree of an adjective compares three or more things.**

Instructor: *Smaller* is a **comparative adjective**. It is used to compare two things, such as a nickel and a dime. *Smallest* is a **superlative adjective**. It is used to compare three or more things, such as a nickel, a dime, and a quarter. You could compare all the coins you have ever seen with superlative adjectives, since they compare three or more things. No matter how many coins you've seen, you could use the superlative to say that the dime is the *smallest* coin you have ever seen. Now read the next two rules.

→ *Student:* **Most regular adjectives form the comparative by adding -r or -er. Most regular adjectives form the superlative by adding -st or -est.**

Instructor: To see three examples, read the positive, comparative, and superlative forms of the next three adjectives out loud. I'll do the first one for you: Large, larger, largest.

→ *Student: Big, bigger, biggest. Silly, sillier, silliest.*

Instructor: *Large, larger, largest* follows the first spelling rule. Read the rule and examples out loud.

→ *Student:* **If the adjective ends in -e already, add only -r or -st.** *Noble, nobler, noblest; pure, purer, purest.*

Instructor: Write the comparative and superlative forms of the positive adjective *cute* in the blanks, and then read them to me.

→ *Student: Cuter, cutest.*

Instructor: *Big, bigger, biggest* follows the second spelling rule. Read the rule and examples out loud.

→ *Student:* **If the adjective ends in a short vowel sound and a consonant, double the consonant and add -er or -est.** *Red, redder, reddest; thin, thinner, thinnest.*

Instructor: Write the comparative and superlative forms of the positive adjective *flat* in the blanks, and then read them to me.

→ *Student: Flatter, flattest.*

Instructor: *Silly, sillier, silliest* follows the third spelling rule. Read the rule and examples out loud.

→ *Student:* **If the adjective ends in -y, change the y to i and add -er or -est.** *Hazy, hazier, haziest; lovely, lovelier, loveliest.*

Instructor: Write the comparative and superlative forms of the positive adjective *lucky* in the blanks, and then read them to me.

→ *Student: Luckier, luckiest.*

Instructor: Some regular adjectives form the comparative and superlative by adding *more* or *most*, instead of by changing the form of the word. Read the next rule and examples out loud.

→ *Student:* **Many adjectives form their comparative and superlative forms by adding the word more or most before the adjective instead of using -er or -est.** *Unusual, more unusual, most unusual; fascinating, more fascinating, most fascinating; fun, more fun, most fun.*

Instructor: Generally, if the positive form of the adjective has two or more syllables, then we use *more* or *most*. There are exceptions to this rule, though, such as the word *fun*. And sometimes an adjective can be formed both ways. The next four sentences are all correct. Read them out loud now.

→ *Student: She is more lovely than the dawn. She is lovelier than the dawn. She is the most lovely of all women. She is the loveliest of all women.*

Instructor: Often, you can use your ear to figure out the correct form. You probably wouldn't say *beautifuller* or *interestingest*—you would say *more beautiful* or *most interesting* because those forms *sound* better. But if you are unsure about the correct form, you can use a dictionary to double check.

Now, look at the diagram of the first sentence.

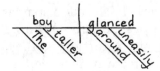

Instructor: Comparative and superlative adjectives that end in *-er* or *-est* are diagrammed as any other descriptive adjective, on a diagonal line underneath the word they modify. Look at the second diagram.

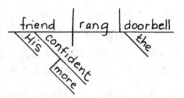

Instructor: In this sentence, the comparative form of the adjective *confident* is *more confident*. When *more* and *most* are used to form comparative and superlative forms, they are acting as adverbs. How confident? More confident. Because *more* is acting as an adverb, it is diagrammed on a diagonal line below the adjective it describes. Read the last rule out loud.

→ *Student:* **In comparative and superlative adjective forms, the words** more **and** most **are used as adverbs.**

Instructor: Complete your exercises now.

— LESSON 66 —

Adverbs
Comparative and Superlative Adverbs
Coordinating Conjunctions
Subordinating Conjunctions

Instructor: Which animal runs faster, a turtle or a rabbit? Answer in a complete sentence.

→ *Student: A rabbit runs faster.*

Instructor: Rabbits run fast. They run faster than turtles. But a cheetah runs the fastest of all three animals. *Fast, faster,* and *fastest* are adverbs that answer the question *how.*

Read me the definition of an adverb.

→ *Student: An adverb describes a verb, an adjective, or another adverb. Adverbs tell how, when, where, how often, and to what extent.*

Instructor: *Fast, faster,* and *fastest* are all forms of the adverb *fast.* They modify the verb *run. Fast* just tells you about how the rabbit runs—but *faster* and *fastest* help you compare how several animals run. Just like adjectives, adverbs have positive, comparative and superlative forms. Read the next three sentences out loud.

→ *Student: The positive degree of an adverb describes only one verb, adjective, or adverb. The comparative degree of an adverb compares two verbs, adjectives, or adverbs. The superlative degree of an adverb compares three or more verbs, adjectives, or adverbs.*

Instructor: *Faster* is a comparative adverb. It is used to compare two actions, such how a rabbit runs and how a turtle runs. *Fastest* is a superlative adverb. It is used to compare three or more actions: the actions taken by the rabbit, the turtle, *and* the cheetah. The adverb *fast* forms the comparative and superlative the same way an adjective does—by adding -*er* and -*est*. But most adverbs that end in -*ly* use *more* and *most* instead of changing form. Read the next rule and examples.

→ Student: **Most adverbs that end in -ly form their comparative and superlative forms by adding the word more or most before the adverb instead of using -er or -est.** *Thoughtfully, more thoughtfully, most thoughtfully; sadly, more sadly, most sadly; angrily, more angrily, most angrily.*

Instructor: A few adverbs, like the common adverb *early*, are exceptions to this rule. The comparative and superlative forms are *earlier* and *earliest* because it follows the same spelling rule as an adjective that ends in -*y*. Read that rule out loud now.

→ Student: **A few adverbs ending in -y change the -y to i and add –er or –est.**

Instructor: You already know how to diagram comparative and superlative adjectives, so diagramming adverbs should be easy. Look at the diagram of the next sentence.

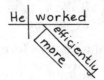

Instructor: But what if that sentence were a little more complicated? Instead of saying "He worked more efficiently," you might want to say, "He worked more efficiently *than his brother*." Circle the word *than*.

He worked more efficiently (than) his brother.

Instructor: You haven't seen this part of speech before. It is called a *subordinating conjunction*. Read me the definition of a conjunction.

→ Student: *A conjunction joins two words or groups of words together.*

Instructor: There are actually two different kinds of conjunctions. Read me the list of the conjunctions you learned in Week Seven.

→ Student: *And, or, nor, for, so, but, yet.*

Instructor: In Week Seven, you learned that these are coordinating conjunctions. Read me the definition of a coordinating conjunction.

→ Student: *A coordinating conjunction joins equal words or groups of words together.*

Instructor: A coordinating conjunction can join two subjects, or two adverbs, or two adjective phrases. In the first sentence, the coordinating conjunction *and* joins two subjects: *sun* and *moon.* In the second sentence, what is the coordinating conjunction?

→ Student: *Yet.*

Instructor: What two words does it join?

→ Student: *Fitfully and brightly.*

Instructor: Those are two adverbs describing how the moon shines. In both sentences, the coordinating conjunction is joining two words that are alike. Subordinating conjunctions do something different. They join together words or groups of words that are unlike. Read me the definition of a **subordinating conjunction**.

→ Student: **A subordinating conjunction joins unequal words or groups of words together.**

Instructor: Your book tells you where the word *subordinate* comes from. When you subordinate something, you make it lower, or less important, than something else. Look again at the sentence *He worked more efficiently than his brother*. There's actually a missing word in that sentence. Read me the next sentence.

→ Student: *He worked more efficiently than his brother [worked].*

Instructor: He worked, and his brother worked. The phrase *than his brother* contains an understood verb: *than his brother worked.*

So you can see that the group of words *than his brother* is *lesser* than the rest of the sentence—because it is missing a verb. We'll come back to subordinating conjunctions in the next week's lesson. Today, you will just learn how to diagram the subordinating conjunction *than* when it introduces a comparison.

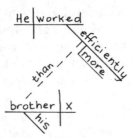

Instructor: Look at each word on the diagram as I explain it. *He* is the subject of the sentence, and *worked* is the verb. He worked efficiently. *Efficiently* is an adverb that shows *how* the boy worked. *More efficiently* is the comparative form of the adverb. You'll remember from the last lesson that *more* is an adverb describing the adverb *efficiently*, so it is diagrammed beneath *efficiently*. A dotted line is drawn from the adverb that compares the two things (*efficiently*) to the second thing being compared (*brother*). The subordinating conjunction *than* is written on the dotted line. *Brother* is the subject of the second, subordinate part of the sentence. The understood verb *worked* is diagrammed as an *x*. *His* is an adjective modifying *brother*.

Here's the principle when you diagram a comparison: Draw a dotted line from the comparative word to the thing or person being compared. We've seen how this works with adverbs; now, let's look at adjectives. Read me the next sentence out loud.

→ Student: *He is older than his brother.*

Instructor: This sentence also has an implied verb. Read me the sentence with the implied verb.

→ Student: *He is older than his brother [is].*

Instructor: Look at each word on the diagram as I explain it.

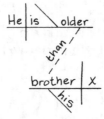

Instructor: *He* is the subject. *Is* is the verb. *Older* is the predicate adjective—but it is also a comparative adjective. A dotted line is drawn from the adjective that compares the two brothers, to the second brother being compared. The subordinating conjunction *than* is written on the dotted line. *Brother* is the subject of the second, subordinate part of the sentence. The understood verb *is* is diagrammed as an *x*.

Complete your exercises now.

— LESSON 67 —

Irregular Comparative and Superlative Adjectives and Adverbs

Instructor: Complete the first exercise in your workbook before we go on.

Instructor: What is the *best* of all?

→ *Student:* [Answers will vary] *is the best.*

Instructor: Which is the *worst*?

→ *Student:* [Answers will vary] *is the worst.*

Instructor: The adjectives *good* and *bad* have irregular comparative and superlative degrees. We say *good, better, best* instead of *good, gooder,* and *goodest.* Many common adjectives and adverbs have irregular comparative and superlative forms. They do not use *-er* or *more* to form the comparative and *-est* or *most* for the superlative. Look at the chart of irregular adjectives. I will read the positive adjective form, and you read the comparative and superlative forms. Let's begin: *Good.*

→ *Student: Better, best . . .*

Irregular Comparative and Superlative Adjectives

Adjective	Comparative Form	Superlative Form
good	better	best
bad	worse	worst
little	less	least
much	more	most
many	more	most

Instructor: Do you remember how many things the comparative form of adjectives and adverbs compares?

→ *Student: Two.*

Instructor: How many things does the superlative form compare?

→ *Student: Three or more.*

Instructor: For example: I have more legs than a snake. An octopus has the most legs of the three. Look at the next chart. Some adverbs have irregular forms too. Let's practice this chart the same way: *Well.*

→ *Student: Better, best . . .*

Irregular Comparative and Superlative Adverbs

Adverb	Comparative Form	Superlative Form
well	better	best
badly	worse	worst
little	less	least
much	more	most
far	farther	farthest

Instructor: There are two common mistakes to avoid when using comparative and superlative forms. The first has to do with using *more* and *most.* Read the next two rules.

→ *Student: **Do not use** more **with an adjective or adverb that is already in the comparative form. Do not use** most **with an adjective or adverb that is already in the superlative form.***

Instructor: It is never correct to say *more faster* or *most highest*. And never use expressions such as *more better* or *most worst!*

The second common mistake has to do with mixing up adjectives and adverbs. The adjectives *good* and *bad* are often confused with the adverbs *well* and *badly*. Read me the first incorrect sentence from your book.

→ Student: *The team played good.*

Instructor: *Good* is an adjective. It can only be used to describe a noun. So you could say that the *team* is good, but you can't say that the team *played* good. To describe *how* they played, you need to use the adverb form. "The team played well" is correct.

Here's something to keep in mind: You can never use the adjective *good* as an adverb, but there's one situation in which you can use the adverb *well* as an adjective. It's when you mean "in good health." Answer me in a complete sentence: Are you well today?

→ Student: *I [am/am not] well.*

Instructor: I am [glad/sorry] to hear it! In that sentence, *well* is a predicate adjective describing *I*.

Now read me the second incorrect sentence.

→ Student: *The tomato smells badly.*

Instructor: *Badly* is an adverb. You can't use it to describe the noun *tomato*. In this sentence, *badly* can only be describing the verb *smells*. That means that the tomato itself must be doing a bad job using its nose to smell. If you want to say that the *tomato* has a bad scent, you must use the adjective *bad* to describe it.

Remember: If you want to describe *how* an action is performed, use an adverb. If you want to describe some aspect of a *noun*, use an adjective. Action verbs take adverbs. Linking verbs have to be followed by an adjective form, *not* an adverb form. What are the linking verbs?

→ Student: *Am, is, are, was, were, be, being, been; taste, feel, smell, sound, look, prove, grow, remain, appear, stay, become, seem.*

Instructor: Which linking verbs can also be used as action verbs?

→ Student: *Taste, feel, smell, sound, look; prove, grow, remain, appear, stay.*

Instructor: Whenever you use these verbs, be careful! Use adverb forms if they are acting as action verbs, and adjective forms if they are behaving like linking verbs. In the next sentence, is *sound* an action verb or a linking verb?

→ Student: *Linking verb.*

Instructor: Cross out the adverb *beautifully. Beautiful* is the correct predicate adjective.

Complete your exercises now.

— LESSON 68 —

Coordinating and Subordinating Conjunctions
Correlative Conjunctions

Instructor: Read the first sentence in your workbook.

→ Student: *When my mother makes tacos al pastor, she uses ancho chilies and pasilla chilies and cumin seed and garlic and pork roast and fresh cilantro.*

Instructor: Ancho chilies and pasilla chilies and cumin seed and garlic and pork roast and fresh cilantro are all *equal*. They are all ingredients that go in *tacos al pastor*. They are joined with *and* because *and* is a coordinating conjunction. What is a coordinating conjunction?

→ *Student: A coordinating conjunction joins equal words or groups of words together.*

Instructor: What are the coordinating conjunctions?

→ *Student: And, but, for, nor, or, so, and yet.*

Instructor: In the first sentence, *and* joins equal words. Read the next sentence.

→ *Student: For dessert, I will have tres leches cake with fresh raspberries or caramel sandwich cookies with ice cream.*

Instructor: In this sentence, the coordinating conjunction *or* joins two *groups* of words: *tres leches cake with fresh raspberries* and *caramel sandwich cookies with ice cream*. Read the next sentence out loud now.

→ *Student: In my opinion, pork without pineapple is much better than pork with pineapple.*

Instructor: In this sentence, the conjunction *than* connects two unequal groups of words. The first group of words is *pork without pineapple is much better*. What is the second group of words?

→ *Student: Pork with pineapple.*

Instructor: The second group of words is unequal, because it is missing a verb and an adjective. *Than* is a subordinating conjunction. What does a subordinating conjunction do?

→ *Student: A subordinating conjunction joins unequal words or groups of words together.*

Instructor: We're not done with conjunctions yet! Read the next two sentences.

→ *Student: We are cooking either pork roasts or goat chops tonight. The patient was neither worse nor better.*

Instructor: Each of these sentences has not *one* conjunction, but *two*. Circle the words *either* and *or*. Those conjunctions, working together, tell you that *pork roasts* or *goat chops* will be on the menu tonight—but not both! Now circle the words *neither* and *nor*. These conjunctions, working together, tell you that *both* options (better and worse) are wrong.

When conjunctions work together in pairs, we call them **correlative conjunctions**. Read me the next two definitions in your workbook.

→ *Student:* **Correlative conjunctions work in pairs to join words or groups of words. Coordinating correlative conjunctions join equal words or groups of words.**

Instructor: In the last two sentences, *pork roast* and *goat chops* are equal groups of words. *Worse* and *better* are both comparative adjectives, so they are also equal words. Read the six pairs of coordinating correlative conjunctions.

→ *Student: Both . . . and; not only . . . but/but also; either . . . or; neither . . . nor; although/though . . . yet/still; if . . . then.*

Instructor: In the next four sentences, circle the correlative conjunctions and underline the equal words or group of words being joined.

In the beginning,(both)the Sun (and)the Moon were dark.

(Not only)the town itself,(but also) the ranches in the neighborhood are built on hilltops.

(Although)he did not remember the way,(still)he pressed on.

(If)we run faster,(then)we will escape.

Instructor: In the first and second sentences, the correlative conjunctions join equal nouns. In the third and fourth, they join equal short sentences.

The last two sets of correlative conjunctions can also be used as *subordinating* conjunctions. In the next two sentences, circle the conjunctions and underline the words or groups of words being connected.

(Though) weary, (still) he presses on.

(If) unseated, (then) he will be unable to continue jousting.

Instructor: The second of those sentences connects a past participle (*unseated*) with a complete sentence. What two types of words or groups of words are connected in the first of those sentences?

→ Student: *An adjective and a sentence.*

Instructor: Those are not equal! Read the definition and list of subordinating correlative conjunctions now.

→ Student: **Subordinating correlative conjunctions join unequal words or groups of words.** *Although/though. . . . yet/still, if . . . then.*

Instructor: We'll talk more about subordinating correlative conjunctions in the next few weeks. But for the rest of this lesson, we'll focus on coordinating correlative conjunctions. First, let's talk about how to diagram them.

When coordinating correlative conjunctions join two words—be they subjects, objects, adjectives, or adverbs—you diagram them just as you would words joined by plain old coordinating conjunctions. Look at the next two sentences and their diagrams.

In the beginning, the Sun and the Moon were dark.
In the beginning, both the Sun and the Moon were dark.

Instructor: There is only one space on this diagram that changes—the space that connects the compound subjects. What is in that space on the first diagram?

→ Student: *And.*

Instructor: What is in on the second diagram?

→ Student: *Both . . . and.*

Instructor: You diagram compound objects, adjectives, or adverbs in the same way—just as if they were simply joined by one conjunction, but writing both conjunctions on the joining line with three dots between them. However, if the conjunctions join two sentences, instead of two parts of a sentence, your diagram will be slightly different. In the next sentence, circle the coordinating correlative conjunctions.

(Although) he did not remember, (still) he pressed on.

Instructor: Now, underline the two sentences that these conjunctions connect: *he did not remember* and *he pressed on.* Examine the diagram that follows, and put your finger on each part of the diagram as I describe it.

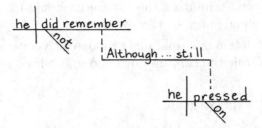

Instructor: The first sentence is diagrammed on top. Then, a dotted line comes down from the predicate. A shelf between the two sentences holds the conjunctions. A second dotted line drops down from the end of that shelf and connects to the predicate of the second sentence.

Before we finish this lesson, let's cover one more important detail about correlative conjunctions. Read me the next sentence in your workbook.

→ *Student: Both the grey foxes and the lion are watching for rabbits.*

Instructor: Is the verb *are watching* singular or plural?

→ *Student: Plural.*

> **Note to Instructor:** If necessary, remind the student that he would say *he is watching* or *they are watching*.

Instructor: Even though *lion* is singular, we use the plural verb because the lion and the grey foxes together make up a plural subject. But now read me the next three sentences.

→ *Student: Not only the grey foxes but also the lion is watching for rabbits. Either the mountain lion or the bears are growling. Neither the butterflies nor the hummingbird was in the garden.*

Instructor: When compound subjects are connected by *not only . . . but/but also, either . . . or,* or *neither . . . nor,* the verb agrees with the subject that is *closest* to the verb. In the first of those sentences, is the verb singular or plural?

→ *Student: Singular.*

Instructor: Is *lion* singular or plural?

→ *Student: Singular.*

Instructor: Even though *foxes* is plural, the verb agrees with *lion* because *lion* is closest. In the next sentence, is the verb singular or plural?

→ *Student: Plural.*

Instructor: Is *bears* singular or plural?

→ *Student: Plural.*

Instructor: Even though *mountain lion* is singular, the verb agrees with *bears* because *bears* is closest. In the final sentence, is the verb singular or plural?

→ *Student: Singular.*

Instructor: Which subject does it agree with?

→ *Student: Hummingbird.*

Instructor: Read me the rule out loud.

→ *Student: **When compound subjects are connected by** not only . . . but/but also, either . . . or, or neither . . . nor, **the verb agrees with the subject that is closest to the verb.***

Instructor: Complete your exercises now.

Clauses

— LESSON 69 —

Phrases

Sentences

Introduction to Clauses

Instructor: Today you'll learn about one of the major building blocks of the English language: the **clause**. Before you learn the definition of a clause, though, we need to review what we know about phrases. Read me the definition of a phrase.

→ *Student: A phrase is a group of words serving a single grammatical function.*

Instructor: So far, you've learned about four kinds of phrases. Read the definition of each kind out loud, and then circle the matching phrase (or phrases) in the sentences that follow.

A verb phrase is the main verb plus any helping verbs.
Four musketeers (were waiting) their turn.

A prepositional phrase begins with a preposition and ends with a noun or pronoun.
The center (of the most animated group) was a musketeer (of great height.)

A prepositional phrase that describes a noun or pronoun is called an adjective phrase.
He wore a long cloak (of crimson velvet.)

A prepositional phrase that describes a verb, adjective, or adverb is called an adverb phrase.
The young man advanced (into the tumult and disorder.)

Instructor: *Of crimson velvet* is an adjective phrase describing the noun *cloak;* draw an arrow from *of crimson velvet* to *cloak. Into the tumult and disorder* is an adverb phrase answering the question *where;* draw an arrow from *into the tumult and disorder* to the verb *advanced.* These groups of words act in different ways, but they all have something in common: None of them contain both a subject *and* a predicate. If a group of words has a subject and a predicate, we call it a *clause.* Repeat this definition after me: **A clause is a group of words that contains a subject and a predicate.**

→ *Student: A clause is a group of words that contains a subject and a predicate.*

Instructor: A phrase, on the other hand, does *not* contain both a subject and a verb. Look at the groups of words that come next in your workbook. Some of them are clauses: they have both subjects and verb. Others are phrases. They might contain verbs, but they don't have a subject *and* a predicate that says something about the subject. Read each group of words aloud, and identify each one as a phrase or a clause.

Note to Instructor: See the Key for the answers.

Instructor: A phrase may have a verb or verb form in it—but phrases don't have subjects *and* predicates. Clauses always have at least one subject and one predicate. To write interesting, complex, gripping sentences, you need to know how to use both phrases and clauses. Imagine that a good sentence is like a building: Phrases are like the bricks that make up the walls. Clauses are like the walls themselves, linked together to form an entire building.

There are two kinds of clauses that can be linked together to make good sentences. When a clause can stand alone as a sentence, it is called an *independent clause*. Read me the definition of an independent clause.

→ *Student: **An independent clause can stand by itself as a sentence.***

Instructor: Not all sentences are independent clauses, because not all sentences have both a subject and predicate, or verb. Most of them do—but not all. Read aloud the final definition of a sentence that you learned back in Lesson 10.

→ *Student: A sentence is a group of words that usually contains a subject and a predicate. A sentence begins with a capital letter and ends with a punctuation mark. A sentence contains a complete thought.*

Instructor: In the excerpt from James Kalat's *Introduction to Psychology*, all of the sentences are complete sentences. All of them convey a complete thought. But only the italicized sentences are also independent clauses. Each one has both a subject *and* a predicate. Underline the subject once and the predicate twice in each italicized sentence.

> *Can we measure intelligence without understanding it? Possibly so. Physicists measured gravity and magnetism long before they understood them theoretically. Maybe psychologists can do the same with intelligence.*
>
> Or maybe not.
>
> —James W. Kalat, *Introduction to Psychology* (Cengage Learning, 2007)

Instructor: When a clause doesn't make sense on its own, it is called a **dependent clause**. Read me the definition of a dependent clause.

→ *Student: **A dependent clause is a fragment that cannot stand by itself as a sentence.***

Instructor: Look at the next five clauses in your workbook. All of them have a subject and a verb, or predicate. But not all of them can stand alone as sentences. Write *I* for independent or *D* for dependent clause next to each.

> **Note to Instructor:** See the Key for the answers.

Instructor: All of these clauses contain a subject and a predicate, but some of them need more words to stand alone as sentences. The clause *Because my grandmother came to visit* has a subject and verb: *grandmother came*. However, it is not a complete sentence by itself. For it to make sense, it would have to be attached to an independent clause. The clause *I cleaned up my room* is a complete thought by itself. Therefore, what kind of clause is it?

→ *Student: Independent.*

Instructor: We can attach the dependent clause *Because my grandmother came to visit* to the independent clause *I cleaned up my room*. Now we have a complete sentence that expresses a complex thought: Read that sentence out loud for me.

→ *Student: Because my grandmother came to visit, I cleaned up my room.*

Instructor: Dependent clauses are *dependent* on independent clauses to become sentences. Independent clauses are already sentences, *independent* of any other words. I want you to notice one last thing about dependent clauses. Each one begins with a word that *makes* it dependent. Circle the first word in each dependent clause. Now read me the three dependent clauses, *without* the circled words.

→ *Student: [Answers will vary.]*

Instructor: Without those first words, the dependent clauses become independent. These words are *subordinating* words. You've already encountered one kind of subordinating word in last week's lessons: subordinating conjunctions. This week we'll study other words that *subordinate* clauses, by making them less grammatically complete.

   Read me the last two rules in your lesson.

→ *Student: **Dependent clauses begin with subordinating words. Dependent clauses are also known as subordinate clauses.***

Instructor: Complete your exercises now.

— LESSON 70 —

Adjective Clauses
Relative Pronouns

Note to Instructor: Have the student complete Intro 70 before beginning the lesson. Remind her that the exercise is for fun; the *correct* answers are based on history and science, not grammar. Consult the Answer Key for solutions.

Instructor: Let's do a quick review. Can you name the two necessary parts of a clause? (It has to have these, or else it's just a phrase.)

→ *Student: Subject and predicate.*

Instructor: Can dependent clauses stand alone as sentences?

→ *Student: No.*

Instructor: What about independent clauses?

→ *Student: Yes.*

Instructor: Look again at your introductory exercise. Are the clauses independent or dependent clauses?

→ *Student: Dependent.*

Instructor: Clauses, just like phrases, can serve different functions in a sentence. Dependent clauses can act as adjectives, adverbs, or nouns. Repeat after me: **Dependent clauses can act as adjectives, adverbs, or nouns.**

→ *Student: Dependent clauses can act as adjectives, adverbs, or nouns.*

Instructor: Today we will talk only about **adjective clauses.** You may remember that adjective phrases are whole prepositional phrases that act as adjectives and modify a noun or pronoun. In the same way, adjective clauses are dependent clauses that act as adjectives, modifying nouns or pronouns. Read the definition in your workbook.

→ *Student: **An adjective clause is a dependent clause that acts as an adjective in a sentence, modifying a noun or pronoun in the independent clause.***

Instructor: Look at the next sentence. (It's from an Irish fairy tale.) It is made up of one independent clause and one dependent clause. The independent clause comes first. Underline the subject once and the predicate twice.

They banded together in small groups that whispered and discussed and disputed.

Instructor: Now circle the dependent clause *that whispered and discussed and disputed. Who* or *what* whispered and discussed and disputed? Answer with a single word.

→ *Student: Groups.*

> **Note to Instructor:** If the student answers *they*, say, "They banded together into what? What did those groups then do?"

Instructor: This dependent clause modifies the noun *groups.* Draw an arrow from the circle back to *groups.* Now do one more thing: Find the elements of the dependent clause. It has to have both a subject and a predicate. What is the predicate—the action in the clause?

→ *Student: Whispered and discussed and disputed.*

Instructor: That's right—there is a compound predicate! Within the dependent clause only, what is the subject? (Who or what whispered and discussed and disputed?)

→ *Student: That.*

Instructor: *That* is correct. *That* is the subject.

> **Note to Instructor:** Emphasize *that* in both sentences above.

Instructor: Underline *that* once and *whispered, discussed,* and *disputed* each twice.

They banded together in small groups that whispered and discussed and disputed.

Instructor: The adjective clause modifies the noun *groups.*

That adjective clause came at the end of the sentence, but often adjective clauses come right in the middle of an independent clause. Look at the next sentence in your workbook. Circle the dependent clause *who passed by.* That clause has both a subject and predicate. What is the predicate—the action in the clause?

→ *Student: Passed.*

Instructor: Underline it twice. What is the subject? (Who or what passed?)

→ *Student: Who.*

Instructor: Underline it once. Now read the independent clause, leaving the dependent clause out.

→ *Student: A man spoke to them.*

Instructor: Underline the subject of the independent clause once and the predicate twice. Now answer the final question: What noun or pronoun in the independent clause does *who passed by* describe?

→ *Student: The man.*

Instructor: Draw an arrow from the circled dependent clause to *man.*

A man who passed by spoke to them.

Instructor: In the first sentence we looked at, what word does the adjective clause start with?

→ Student: That.

Instructor: What about the adjective clause in the second sentence?

→ Student: Who.

Instructor: These are special words called **relative pronouns**. Relative pronouns are used to introduce adjective clauses—and to connect these clauses back to the nouns they modify. Read that definition in your workbook, along with the list of relative pronouns.

→ Student: **Relative pronouns introduce adjective clauses and refer back to an antecedent in the independent clause.** Who, whom, whose, which, that.

Instructor: In the next five sentences, the dependent clauses acting as adjectives are bolded for you. Draw a line from the relative pronoun beginning each dependent clause back to its antecedent—the noun the pronoun refers to.

The men **who had been champions before Finn came** rallied the others against him.

Among the young princes was a boy **whom the High King preferred**.

The Chain of Silence was shaken by the servant **whose duty and honor it was.**

The thing **which was presented to us** is not true.

The people believed in gods **that the king did not accept**.

Instructor: There are a few guidelines for using these relative pronouns. Read those guidelines out loud now.

→ Student: Use who, whom, *and* whose *to refer to persons. Use* which *to refer to animals, places, and things. Use* that and whose *to refer to persons, animals, places, or things.*

Instructor: Notice that you can use either *who* or *whom* for persons. *Who* and *whom* are like *he* and *him,* or *she* and *her.* Back in Week Thirteen, you learned that personal pronouns have subject and object forms. Read the next sentence out loud.

→ Student: *She saw him, and he saw her.*

Instructor: Write *S* over each subject and *DO* over each direct object.

    S   DO   S   DO
    She saw him, and he saw her.

Instructor: In the same way, *who* is the subject form of the relative pronoun referring to persons, and *whom* is the object form.

To find out whether the pronoun is acting as a subject or an object, first circle the dependent clause. Forget about the rest of the sentence. Find the predicate of the dependent clause and then ask: Who or what is performing the predicate? Then look for direct objects, indirect objects, and prepositional phrases. Try this with the sentences in your workbook now. Circle each dependent clause; underline the subject of the clause once and the predicate twice; then label any parts of the dependent clause.

               P OP
I who speak to you have seen many evils.

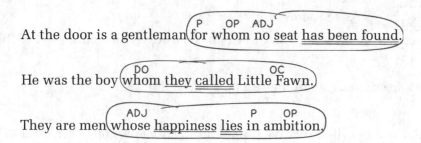

At the door is a gentleman for whom no seat has been found.

He was the boy whom they called Little Fawn.

They are men whose happiness lies in ambition.

Instructor: As you can see, one of the challenges with adjective clauses is that the words can be all out of order! Objects and prepositional phrases often come *before* the subject and predicate. We'll continue to practice identifying and analyzing adjective clauses (and other clauses) in future lessons.

Before we finish today, examine the diagrams in your workbook. Follow along as I describe each one.

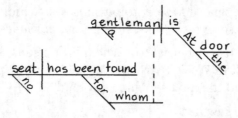

Instructor: In the first sentence, *I* is the subject of the independent clause. *Have seen* is the predicate. *Evils* is the direct object. *Many* is an adjective modifying *evils*. A dotted line connects the relative pronoun in the dependent clause to its antecedent in the independent clause—you'll see this in every diagram of an adjective clause. A dotted line always connects the relative pronoun to the noun or pronoun that it refers back to. Within the dependent clause, *who* is the subject, *speak* is the predicate, and *to you* is a prepositional phrase acting as an adverb and answering the question *how*.

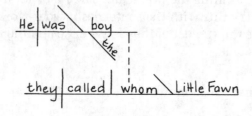

Instructor: In the second sentence, *gentleman* is the subject of the independent clause, modified by *a*. *Is* is the predicate, and *at the door* is an adverb phrase answering the question *where*. In the dependent clause, *seat* is the subject, *has been found* is the predicate, and *no* modifies *seat*. *For whom* is a prepositional phrase acting as an adverb and answering the question *how*. (This is a tricky one—you could also argue that it modifies *seat* and answers the question *which one*. English grammar is not always straightforward! If you had diagrammed this under *seat* instead, it would not be wrong.) Notice that the dotted line still connects the relative pronoun *whom* with the antecedent *gentleman*, even though placing the line got a little tricky!

Instructor: In the third sentence, *He* is the subject of the main independent clause, *was* is the predicate (a linking verb), and *boy* is the predicate nominative that renames *boy*. *The* modifies *boy*. The dotted line connects *boy* with the relative pronoun *whom*. (Notice that it isn't connected to *He*. Normally, you'll connect an adjective clause to the word it immediately follows—we'll learn more about that shortly.) Within the dependent clause, *whom* is the direct object, *They* is the subject and *called* is the predicate. *Little Fawn* renames the direct object, so it is diagrammed as an object complement.

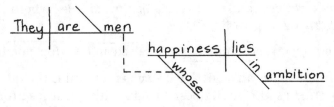

Instructor: Finally, in the last sentence, *They* is the subject; *are*, the predicate; and *men*, the predicate nominative. *Men* is connected to the relative pronoun that refers back to it, *whose*, by the dotted line. Within the dependent clause, *whose* acts as a possessive adjective modifying *happiness*. *Happiness* is the subject, *lies* is the predicate, and *in ambition* is an adverb phrase that answers the question *where*.

That's enough for one lesson! Complete your exercises now.

— LESSON 71 —

Adjective Clauses
Relative Adverbs
Adjective Clauses with Understood Relatives

Instructor: What is the difference between a phrase and a clause? You can look at the definitions in your workbook, but tell me in your own words.

→ *Student: A clause has a subject and a predicate; a phrase doesn't.*

Instructor: In your own words, what is the difference between an independent clause and a dependent clause?

→ *Student: An independent clause can stand on its own and a dependent clause can't [or An independent clause is a sentence and a dependent clause is a fragment].*

Instructor: Dependent clauses begin with a word that turns them into a fragment and makes them rely on the independent clause for meaning. What is that word called?

→ *Student: A subordinating word.*

Instructor: What kind of subordinating word begins an adjective clause?

→ *Student: A relative pronoun.*

Instructor: We've been calling dependent clauses that modify a noun or pronoun in the independent clause *adjective clauses,* but sometimes you'll also see them called *relative clauses,* because they *relate* back to another word. And they begin with a **relative pronoun**. Read me the definition and list of relative pronouns.

→ Student: **Relative pronouns introduce adjective clauses and refer back to an antecedent in the independent clause.** *Who, whom, whose, which, that.*

Instructor: There's another kind of relative word that a relative clause can begin with. Read the next sentence out loud.

→ Student: *This was the very spot where a proud tyrant raised an undying monument to his own vanity.*

Instructor: Underline the word *spot* and circle the adjective clause "where a proud tyrant raised an undying monument to his own vanity."

This was the very spot <u>where</u> a proud tyrant raised an undying monument to his own vanity.

Instructor: This clause functions as an adjective because it modifies the noun *spot* and answers the question, *Which spot?* But it doesn't begin with a relative pronoun. What part of speech is *where?*

→ Student: *An adverb.*

Instructor: There are three cases in which an adjective clause can actually begin with an adverb—but the clause as a whole still works like an adjective. The first case is when the adjective clause refers back to and describes a *place*—like the *spot* in your sentence. The second case is when the adjective clause refers back to and describes a *time.* Read your second sentence now.

→ Student: *He was going back to serve his country at a time when death was the usual reward for such devotion.*

Instructor: Underline the word *time* and circle the adjective clause *when death was the usual reward for such devotion.*

He was going back to serve his country at a <u>time</u>
<u>when</u> death was the usual reward for such devotion

Instructor: What part of speech is *when?*

→ Student: *An adverb.*

Instructor: The clause begins with an adverb, but as a whole it acts like an adjective because it modifies the noun *time* and answers the question, *Which time?* Read the third sentence now.

→ Student: *The reasons why he vented his ill humor on the soldiers were many.*

Instructor: The third case is when a clause describes the *reason* for something. Underline the word *reasons* and circle the adjective clause *why he vented his ill humor on the soldiers.*

The <u>reasons</u> <u>why</u> he vented his ill humor on the soldiers were many.

Instructor: What question does this clause answer?

→ Student: *It answers the question "Which kind of reasons?"*

Instructor: Read the rule and the list of **relative adverbs** in your workbook.

→ Student: **Relative adverbs introduce adjective clauses and refer back to a place, time, or reason in the independent clause.** *Where, when, why.*

Instructor: When you diagram an adjective clause that's introduced by an adverb, you follow the same principle you've learned—connect the relative word to the noun or pronoun it refers to with a dotted line. Just remember that within the relative clause, the adverb is functioning like . . . an adverb! Examine the diagram of the first sentence in your workbook.

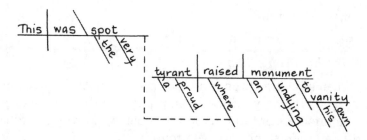

Instructor: You can see that the dotted line connects *spot* to the relative adverb that refers to it, *where*—even though *where* is diagrammed down below the predicate of the dependent clause. All you have to keep in mind is: Connect the relative word, whatever it is, to the noun or pronoun that the entire clause describes. You just might have to get a little creative with your dotted lines!

Fill out the frames for the next two sentences now.

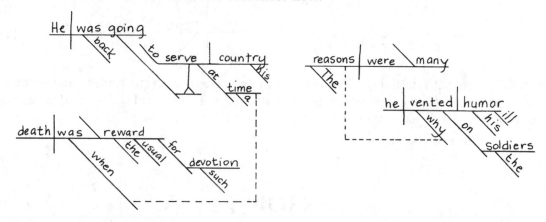

Instructor: Now let's talk about a strange version of adjective clauses—the version where the relative word itself disappears. Read the next sentence (from Shakespeare's play *Julius Caesar*) out loud.

→ *Student: The evil men do lives after them.*

Instructor: Circle the words *men do,* and read the sentence out loud without the circled words.

→ *Student: The evil lives after them.*

Instructor: That is the independent clause in the sentence. *Men do* is a dependent clause—but it's missing a word. Draw a caret (a little wedge with the sharp end pointing up) between the words *evil* and *men,* and write the relative pronoun *that* above it.

      that
   The evil ^(men do) lives after them.

Instructor: Now read the sentence again, including the inserted word.

→ *Student: The evil that men do lives after them.*

Instructor: Look at the next sentence in your workbook. Underline the subject once, the predicate twice, and write *DO* above the direct object.

       DO
   I read the book you sent me.

Instructor: The remaining words are a dependent clause—missing a relative pronoun. Draw a caret between *book* and *you* and write the word *which* above it.

I read the book^you sent me.
^{DO which}

Instructor: Then, read the sentence out loud.

→ *Student: I read the book which you sent me.*

Instructor: In English, when a relative pronoun is the direct object in its dependent clause, we often just leave it out. If you're analyzing a sentence and you find two sets of subjects and predicates, with no conjunctions or punctuation between them, you're probably looking at a dependent clause with an understood relative pronoun.

When you diagram these sentences, put the pronoun back in, but place it in parentheses to show that it's understood. Examine the diagrams of these two sentences in your workbook.

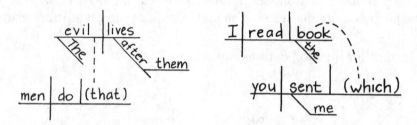

Instructor: Notice that the dotted line connects each antecedent with the understood relative pronoun serving as a direct object of its dependent clause. The second sentence also has an indirect object in the dependent clause.

Complete your exercises now.

— LESSON 72 —

Adverb Clauses

Instructor: What is a clause?

→ *Student: A clause is a group of words that contains a subject and a predicate.*

Instructor: Read me the next three related statements about dependent clauses.

→ *Student: A dependent clause is a fragment that cannot stand by itself as a sentence. Dependent clauses begin with subordinating words. Dependent clauses are also known as subordinate clauses.*

Instructor: So far, we've looked at dependent clauses that act as adjectives. But what other two parts of speech can a dependent clause stand in for?

→ *Student: Adverbs and nouns.*

Instructor: We'll finish out today's work by looking at **adverb clauses**. Adjective clauses describe nouns or pronouns in the independent clause. What kinds of words do you think adverb clauses will describe? Answer without looking at your workbook.

→ *Student: Verbs, adjectives, and other adverbs.*

Instructor: What questions do you think adverb clauses will answer?

→ *Student: Where, when, how, how often, to what extent.*

Instructor: Exactly! Instead of referring back to an antecedent, adverb clauses tell you more about a verb, or an adjective, or another adverb. They aren't introduced by pronouns—instead, they are connected to independent clauses by adverbs.

Most often, adverb clauses modify verbs. Read me the first sentence in your workbook.

→ Student: *When the supper was finished, the king expressed a wish.*

Instructor: Circle the dependent clause *When the supper was finished*. Underline the subject of the clause once and the predicate twice.

When the <u>supper</u> <u>was finished,</u> the king expressed a wish.

Instructor: The introductory word, *when,* doesn't play a part in the clause *the supper was finished*. Instead, it tells you more about the time that the king expressed a wish. It answers the question *when.*

Look at the diagram in your workbook now. Notice that the introductory adverb *when* connects the predicate of the dependent clause to the predicate of the independent clause, because it describes the relationship between the finishing of the supper and the expressing of the wish.

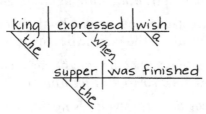

Instructor: *When* is an adverb. When an adverb clause modifies a verb, it is often introduced by an adverb. Read me the next rule in your workbook and the list of adverbs that follows it.

→ Student: **Adverb clauses can be introduced by adverbs.** *Common adverbs that introduce clauses: as and its compounds (as if, as soon as, as though); as if; how and its compound (however); when and its compound (whenever); whence; where and its compounds (whereat, whereby, wherein, wherefore, whereon); while; whither.*

Instructor: But adverb clauses can also be introduced by a part of speech we talked about last week: a subordinating conjunction. What is a subordinating conjunction?

→ Student: *A subordinating conjunction joins unequal words or groups of words together.*

Instructor: You have already studied one kind of subordinating conjunction: the kind that joins words in a comparison. Read me the next sentence in your workbook.

→ Student: *An honest enemy is better than an agreeable coward.*

Instructor: You learned that the second part of a comparison is *unequal* because it is missing a verb: An honest enemy is better than an agreeable coward [is]. Now that you've studied clauses, you should be able to recognize the second part of this comparison. Circle the words *than an agreeable coward [is].*

An honest enemy is better than an agreeable coward [is].

Instructor: That is a dependent clause with one word omitted. Look at the diagram of this comparison.

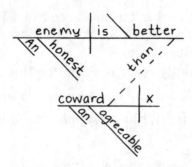

Instructor: In the diagram, the dotted line connects the comparative adjective with the subject of the dependent clause (the thing being compared), and the subordinating conjunction *than* goes on the dotted line.

But there are many other subordinating conjunctions! Read the next rule and the list of conjunctions now.

→ Student: **Subordinating conjunctions and subordinating correlative conjunctions often join an adverb clause to an independent clause.** *After, although, as, as soon as, because, before, if, in order that, lest, since, though, till, unless, until, although/though. . . . yet/still, if . . . then.*

Instructor: Most of the time, adverb clauses introduced by these conjunctions will modify the verb of the independent clause. Read me the next two sentences.

→ Student: *Because she loves Korean food, my aunt taught me to cook kimchi. I will put six plates on the table unless our neighbors are also coming for dinner.*

Instructor: Circle the adverb clauses *Because she loves Korean food* and *unless our neighbors are also coming for dinner.*

(Because she loves Korean food,) my aunt taught me to cook kimchi.

I will put six plates on the table (unless our neighbors are also coming for dinner.)

Instructor: Both of these clauses tell you more about the main verbs. Your aunt's teaching you is related to her love for Korean food. Your putting plates on the table is affected by how many people are coming to dinner.

Look carefully at the diagram of the first sentence. Notice that the dotted line with the subordinating conjunction on it connects the verb of the subordinate clause with the word being modified—the verb of the independent clause. Then, diagram the second sentence onto the frame provided.

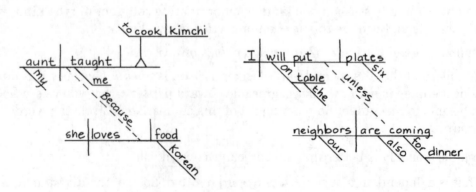

Instructor: Sometimes, an adverb clause will modify an adjective—usually, a predicate adjective. Read me the next two sentences in your workbook.

→ *Student: The task is difficult if you do not take care. She was confident that she could reach the top of the mountain.*

Instructor: Circle the adverb clauses *if you do not take care* and *that she could reach the top of the mountain.*

The task is difficult (if you do not take care.)

She was confident (that she could reach the top of the mountain)

Instructor: These clauses tell you more about the difficulty and the confidence. Look carefully at the first diagram. Notice that the dotted line connects the verb of the adverb clause to the predicate adjective being modified. Then, diagram the second sentence onto the frame provided.

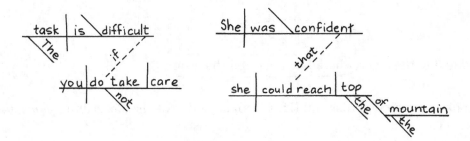

Instructor: Finally, adverb clauses occasionally modify adverbs. Read the next two sentences now.

→ *Student: He sprinted quickly as though he were being chased by monsters. The judge spoke severely because the attorney was not paying attention.*

Instructor: Find and circle the dependent clauses.

He sprinted quickly (as though he were being chased by monsters)

The judge spoke severely (because the attorney was not paying attention)

Instructor: The dependent clauses tell you more about the quickness of the sprinting and the severity with which the judge spoke! Examine the first diagram and then complete the second.

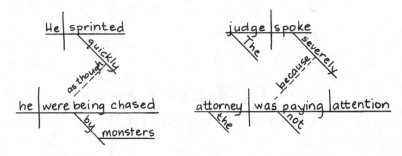

Instructor: Just one last thing! Remember that some clauses introduced by adverbs are actually adjective clauses. Read the last two sentences now.

→ *Student: I will wait where I am. I waited at the place where I had marked the ground.*

Instructor: Circle the adverb clause *where I am* in the first sentence and draw an arrow back to the verb *will wait.*

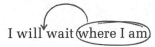

I will wait (where I am)

Instructor: Now look at the first diagram. This is an adverb clause answering the question *where* about the verb *will wait*.

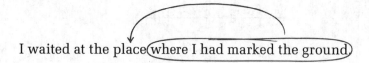

Instructor: In the second sentence, circle the adjective clause *where I had marked the ground* and draw an arrow back to the noun *place*.

I waited at the place where I had marked the ground

Instructor: Look at the second diagram. This is an adjective clause describing *place*, introduced by a relative adverb.

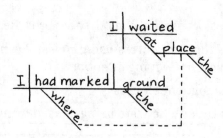

Remember: adjective clauses describing a place, time, or reason can be introduced by a relative adverb rather than a relative pronoun.

Complete your exercises now.

— REVIEW 6 —

The review exercises and answers are found in the Student Workbook and accompanying Key.

WEEK 19

More Clauses

— LESSON 73 —

Adjective and Adverb Clauses
Introduction to Noun Clauses

Instructor: Last week you learned about clauses that act like adjectives, and clauses that act like adverbs. What is a clause?

→ *Student: A clause is a group of words that contains a subject and a predicate.*

Instructor: There's an even more important part of speech that clauses can stand in for. Read me the first sentence in your workbook.

→ *Student: I know that a noun is the name of a person, place, thing, or idea.*

Instructor: Circle the dependent clause *that a noun is the name of a person, place, thing, or idea.* That leaves you with a very short independent clause: *I know!* Underline the subject once and the predicate twice.

I know (that a noun is the name of a person, place, thing, or idea.)

Instructor: Now read me the next sentence.

→ *Student: I know an old lady who swallowed a fly while she was sitting on the front porch.*

Instructor: Underline the subject once and the predicate twice. What part of the sentence is *lady*?

→ *Student: Direct object.*

Instructor: Write *DO* above the word *lady*. The old lady and the idea that a noun is the name of a person, place, thing, or idea are both *known* by you. Both the noun and the dependent clause are acting as *direct objects* of the verb *know*. When a dependent clause functions as the subject, object, or direct object of a sentence, or as the object of a preposition, it is called a **noun clause**. Read the next two definitions in your workbook.

→ *Student: Dependent clauses can act as adjective clauses, adverb clauses, or noun clauses. An adjective clause is a dependent clause that acts as an adjective in a sentence, modifying a noun or pronoun in the independent clause. Relative pronouns introduce adjective clauses and refer back to an antecedent in the independent clause.*

Instructor: In the sentence "I know an old lady who swallowed a fly while she was sitting on the front porch," circle the adjective clause *who swallowed a fly.* Draw a line from the relative pronoun *who* back to the word *lady*.

                                   DO
I know an old lady (who swallowed a fly) while she was sitting on the front porch.

Instructor: Now read the next definition in your workbook.

185

→*Student: Adverb clauses modify verbs, adjectives, and other adverbs in the independent clause. They answer the questions where, when, how, how often, and to what extent. Adverb clauses can be introduced by adverbs. Subordinating conjunctions and subordinating correlative conjunctions often join an adverb clause to an independent clause.*

Instructor: In the same sentence, circle the adverb clause *while she was sitting on the front porch.* Draw a line from the adverb *while* back to the verb *swallowed.*

I <u>know</u> an old lady who swallowed a fly while she was sitting on the front porch

Instructor: The adverb clause answers the question, "When did she swallow the fly?" and modifies the verb in the first adverb clause. As you can see, the English language uses lots of clauses—because we often need to talk about ideas or situations that are more complicated than one-word modifiers allow us to express.

Look at the two diagrams in your workbook now. Put your finger on each part of the diagram as I describe it.

Instructor: In the first diagram, the adjective clause *who swallowed a fly* is diagrammed below the dependent clause, and the dotted line connects the relative pronoun *who* to its antecedent, *lady.* The adverb clause is connected to the verb it modifies with a dotted line that has the connecting adverb *while* written on it.

Instructor: In the second diagram, the noun clause is diagrammed on a tree that sits in the object space. In the dependent clause, *noun* is the subject, *is* is the predicate, and *name* is the predicate nominative. *Of a person, place, thing, or idea* is a prepositional phrase acting like an adjective and modifying *name* (*What kind of name?*). Where is the subordinating word *that*?

→*Student: On a line above the verb.*

Instructor: *That* doesn't play any important part in the noun clause itself. It just connects the clause to the rest of the sentence. So we place it above the verb on its own line, and draw a dotted line to the verb *is*, just to anchor it to the most central part of the clause—the predicate.

That seems simple enough—but of course, it isn't quite that easy! Noun clauses can take many different forms. Read the definition in your workbook now.

→ *Student:* **A noun clause takes the place of a noun. Noun clauses can be introduced by relative pronouns, relative adverbs, subordinating conjunctions, or understood subordinating words.**

Instructor: In each of the next sentences, we will find and circle the noun clause, label it with the part of the sentence it's standing in for, and underline its subordinating word. Then you'll diagram each sentence onto the frame provided

> **Note to Instructor:** Give the student a chance to find each noun clause for herself, but provide all help necessary.

Instructor: In the first sentence, what is the noun clause?

→ *Student: Where your lost keys are.*

Instructor: Circle it. What part of the sentence is this noun clause?

→ *Student: Direct object.*

Instructor: Write *DO* above the circle. What part of speech is *where*?

→ *Student: An adverb.*

Instructor: Write *ADV* above the word *where*, inside the circle. Then place each word on the frame provided.

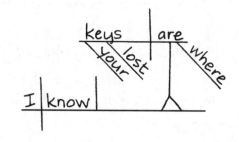

Instructor: In the second sentence, what is the noun clause?

→ *Student: Whoever runs fastest.*

Instructor: Circle it. What part of the sentence is this noun clause?

→ *Student: Subject.*

Instructor: Write *S* above the circle. The word *whoever* is a pronoun—but not a relative pronoun, because it doesn't *relate* to any noun in the independent clause. It's simply a pronoun. Write *PRO* above the word *Whoever,* inside the circle. Then place each word on the frame provided.

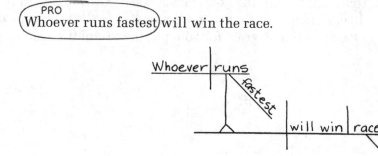

Instructor: In the third sentence, what is the noun clause?

→ *Student: I had more chocolate.*

Instructor: Circle it. What part of the sentence is this noun clause?

→ *Student: Direct object.*

Instructor: Write *DO* above the circle. This noun clause has an understood subordinating word: *that.* Draw a caret between *wish* and *I* and insert the word *that* in brackets.

DO

I really wish ∧ (that I had more chocolate)

Instructor: Now place each word on the frame of the diagram. *That* has been indicated for you by the *x.*

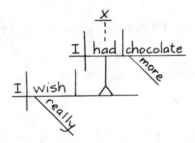

Instructor: Just two more examples. In the fourth sentence, what is the noun clause?

→ *Student: As it should be.*

Instructor: Circle it. What part of the sentence is this noun clause?

→ *Student: Predicate nominative.*

Instructor: Write *PN* above the circle. What part of speech is the introductory word *as?*

→ *Student: A subordinating conjunction.*

Instructor: Write *SC* above it.

PN

SC

Nothing was (as it should be)

> **Note to Instructor:** Since this is a noun clause, it has to stand in for a noun—not an adjective; therefore this is labeled predicate nominative rather than predicate adjective (although this distinction makes little difference to the function or diagram of the sentence).

Instructor: This subordinating conjunction simply connects the noun clause to the rest of the sentence; it doesn't play an important part within the noun clause itself. So, like *that* in the first sentence of this lesson, it is diagrammed on its own line, connected to the predicate with a dotted line. *As* has already been placed on the diagram for you; put the rest of the sentence on the diagram now.

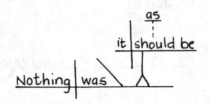

Instructor: Let's look at one last sentence. This has *two* noun clauses in it! What are they?

→ *Student: "What matters most in this situation" and "how you feel about it."*

Instructor: Circle both of them. What part of the sentence is the first noun clause?

→ *Student: The subject.*

Instructor: Write *S* above the circle. This noun clause is introduced by the pronoun *what.* Like *whoever,* it isn't a relative pronoun because it doesn't have an antecedent in the sentence—it is simply standing in for *the thing that matters.* Write *P* above *what.* What part of the sentence is the second noun clause?

→ *Student: Predicate nominative.*

Instructor: Label it *PN.* The introductory word, *how,* is an adverb. It modifies the verb *feel.* Write *ADV* above it.

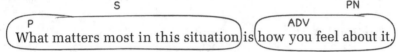

Instructor: Place the sentence on the frame provided.

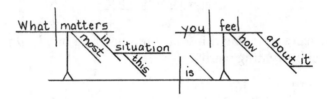

Instructor: Notice that in each diagram, the straight line of the tree connects with the noun clause it supports by touching the predicate space.

Complete your exercises now.

— LESSON 74 —

Clauses Beginning with Prepositions

Instructor: In the last few lessons, you've seen that clauses can act as adjectives, adverbs, and nouns. Let's review quickly with these sentences, adapted from the works of the 17th-century poet John Donne. The first sentence has an adjective clause beginning with a relative pronoun. Circle the relative clause and draw a line from the relative pronoun back to its antecedent.

The sun itself, which makes time, is elder by a year now.

Instructor: The second sentence contains an adverb clause that answers the question *how.* Circle the adverb clause, and draw a line from the subordinating conjunction back to the word modified.

Any man's death diminishes me, because I am involved in mankind.

Instructor: The third sentence has a noun clause that serves as the subject of the sentence. Circle that noun clause and write *S* above it.

$\overset{\text{S}}{(\text{What we call fortune here})}$ has another name above.

Instructor: Place these three sentences on the diagram frames below. Be careful, though—the diagrams are out of order! You'll have to find the correct frame for each sentence.

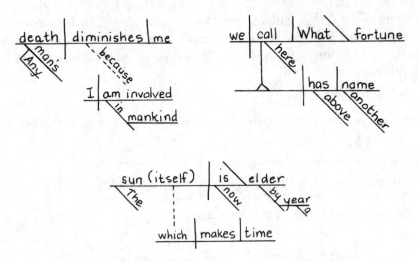

Instructor: All of these clauses have one thing in common: each one *begins* with its subordinating word. What are those subordinating words?

→ *Student: Which, because, what.*

Instructor: The next three sentences (also taken from John Donne's writings) have dependent clauses too. In the first sentence, the carrack is what ship?

→ *Student: The ship in which they are to sail.*

Instructor: Circle the adjective clause *in which they are to sail* and draw a line from the relative pronoun *which* back to the antecedent *ship*. Write *ADJ* above the circle.

That carrack is the ship (in which they are to sail)

Instructor: Look at the next sentence. Which friends?

→ *Student: The friends of whom he took a solemn farewell.*

Instructor: Circle the adjective clause *of whom he took a solemn farewell* and draw a line from the relative pronoun *whom* back to the antecedent *friends*. Write *ADJ* above the circle.

He sent for his friends, (of whom he took a solemn farewell)

Instructor: Now look at the last sentence. Whom are we *not* asking for?

→ *Student: For whom the bell tolls.*

Instructor: Circle the noun clause *for whom the bell tolls*. This serves as the direct object of the verb *to ask*. Write *DO* just above the circle.

Do not ask (for whom the bell tolls)

Instructor: Each of these dependent clauses begins with the same part of speech. What are the words *in*, *of*, and *for*?

→ *Student: Prepositions.*

Instructor: When the relative pronoun (in an adjective clause) or pronoun (in a noun clause) serves as the object of a preposition, the preposition often *begins* the dependent clause. Look at the diagram of the first sentence.

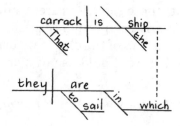

Instructor: What two words does the dotted line connect?

→ *Student: Ship and which.*

Instructor: In an adjective clause, when the relative pronoun is the object of the preposition, you might have to get a little creative with the dotted line that connects the pronoun to its antecedent in the main clause. Look at the second diagram carefully. Draw a dotted line connecting the relative pronoun to its antecedent.

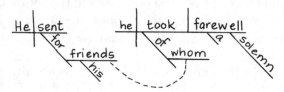

Note to Instructor: Any dotted line connecting *friends* with *whom* is acceptable.

Instructor: When the prepositional phrase is in a noun clause, you simply diagram it like any other prepositional phrase. Place the third sentence on the frame provided.

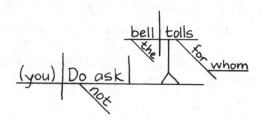

Instructor: Now that you've seen examples of dependent clauses that begin with prepositions, there are two related issues to discuss! First, look back at the second and third sentences above. In the second sentence, what is the direct object of the preposition *of?*

→ *Student: Whom.*

Instructor: What is the direct object of the preposition *for?*

→ *Student: Whom.*

Instructor: It's time to review a rule you learned about 20 lessons ago. Read the rule from your workbook now.

→ *Student:* Who *always acts as a subject or predicate nominative within a sentence.* Whom *always acts as an object.*

Instructor: You should never use *who* in a dependent clause when the pronoun is the object of a preposition! Read the next two incorrect sentences out loud now.

→ *Student: He sent for his friends, of who he took a solemn farewell. Do not ask for who the bell tolls.*

Instructor: You can probably hear that those sentences aren't quite right! But that brings us to the second related issue. Often, particularly in informal English, we tend to put the preposition that introduces a relative clause at the end of the clause instead of the beginning. And then it becomes much harder to *hear* whether we should use *who* or *whom*. Read the next two incorrect sentences now.

→ *Student: He sent for his friends, who he took a solemn farewell of. Do not ask who the bell tolls for.*

Instructor: Even though each preposition is now at the end of its dependent clause, the pronoun is still the object—so you should use the object form *whom*. Read the correct informal sentences now.

→ *Student: He sent for his friends, whom he took a solemn farewell of. Do not ask whom the bell tolls for.*

Instructor: If you don't know whether to use *whom* or *who* in a dependent clause, look for a preposition at the end of the clause. If you see one, rewrite the sentence with the preposition coming directly before its object. Use *whom* for an object pronoun and *who* for a subject pronoun. Try this now. Circle the adjective clause that describes *person*.

She is growing angry at the person (who/whom she is arguing with.)

Instructor: Now rewrite the adjective clause with the preposition at the beginning of the clause, choosing the correct form of the pronoun to be the object of the preposition.

with whom she is arguing

Instructor: Read the original sentence out loud, using the correct pronoun form.

→ *Student: She is growing angry at the person whom she is arguing with.*

Instructor: That is a correct sentence! You'll notice that it ends with a preposition. Some grammar books will tell you never to end a sentence with a preposition. That's an unnecessary rule. In formal writing, it's probably better to put prepositions in front of their objects, but sometimes this makes your sentence extremely convoluted—as you can see from the examples! Read the next sentence out loud.

→ *Student: Rude behavior is something I won't put up with!*

Instructor: *I won't put up with* is an adjective clause with an understood relative pronoun in it. To get rid of the preposition phrase *up with* at the end, you'd have to put the relative pronoun back in *and* move the preposition phrase to the front of the clause—as in the next sentence. Read it out loud.

→ *Student: Rude behavior is something up with which I will not put!*

Instructor: That's just silly. So remember: it's acceptable to end a sentence with a preposition if rephrasing it makes it sound clunky and awkward.

Complete your exercises now.

— LESSON 75 —

Clauses and Phrases
Misplaced Adjective Phrases
Misplaced Adjective Clauses

Instructor: Let's talk about birthdays—and review the difference between clauses and phrases. Read me the first two sentences in your workbook.

→ *Student: In many East Asian countries, the day a baby is born is considered its first birthday. The first birthday after a baby is born is considered its second birthday.*

Instructor: In the first sentence, the phrase *In many East Asian countries* is a prepositional phrase acting as an adverb—it tells you *where* the birthday is counted. Circle the phrase, write *ADV* above it, and draw an arrow to the verb.

ADV
(In many East Asian countries) the day a baby is born is considered its first birthday.

Instructor: Let's review a couple of definitions. What is a phrase?

→ *Student: A phrase is a group of words serving a single grammatical function.*

Instructor: There are many different kinds of phrases, but all of them have one thing in common— they do *not* contain both a subject and a predicate. How is this different from a *clause?*

→ *Student: A clause is a group of words that contains a subject and a predicate.*

> **Note to Instructor:** If the student does not answer with the full definition, follow her answer up with the question, "What is the definition of a clause?"

Instructor: The second sentence that you read to me does contain a clause—a dependent clause introduced by a subordinating word. Can you find and circle it?

> **Note to Instructor:** The student should circle *after a baby is born*. If necessary, tell the student that *birthday/is considered* is the subject/predicate pair of the main clause, and then ask the student to find the other verb in the sentence. This is the predicate of the dependent clause.

Instructor: This dependent clause is also acting as an adverb. It modifies the adjective *first* and tells you *when*. It isn't just a birthday after the baby is born—it is the *first* after a baby is born. Circle the dependent clause, write *ADV* above it, and draw an arrow to the word *first*. Then underline the subject of the clause once and the predicate twice.

ADV
The first birthday (after a baby is born) is considered its second birthday.

Instructor: In the next two pairs of sentences, you will see both phrases and clauses. Look at the next pair now. In the first sentence, what is the adjective phrase that modifies *cake?*

> **Note to Instructor:** During the remainder of this dialogue, prompt the student as necessary.

→ *Student: Made especially for the occasion.*

Instructor: This isn't a prepositional phrase. What part of speech is *made?* HINT: Its principal parts are *make, made, made.*

→ *Student: Past participle.*

Instructor: This is a past participle phrase acting as an adjective. Circle it, write *ADJ* above it, and draw a line back to the word it modifies.

                                                                        ADJ
            Western birthdays are often celebrated with a cake (made especially for the occasion)

Instructor: The second sentence contains a clause that acts as an adjective. What is it?

→ *Student: When the Oxford Dictionary listed the phrase for the first time.*

Instructor: Remember, a clause introduced by an adverb like *when* can serve as an adjective, often when it follows an expression of time. This clause describes the noun 1785—a *year,* which is a *thing.* Circle the clause, write *ADJ* above it, and draw a line back to the word it modifies.

                                                                        ADJ
        The first reference to a "birthday cake" dates from 1785, (when the Oxford Dictionary
    listed the phrase for the first time.)

Instructor: The phrase in the first sentence and the clause in the second sentence both contain verb forms—the past participles *made* and *listed.* A phrase may have a verb in it—but remember that it has to have a subject *and* a predicate in order to be a clause! What is the subject and predicate of the clause in the second sentence?

→ *Student: Oxford Dictionary listed.*

Instructor: Underline the subject once and the predicate twice.

When you studied modifying phrases, you learned that adjective phrases should come right after the nouns they modify. Let's review that now. The next two sentences have misplaced adjective phrases. Read me the next sentence in your workbook.

→ *Student: The young woman went to the awards ceremony with her father in a gorgeous ball gown.*

Instructor: The closest noun to that adjective phrase is *father.* But who was actually wearing the ball gown? (Probably.)

→ *Student: The young woman.*

Instructor: In the next sentence, does the past participle phrase *made of gingerbread* describe the little girl?

→ *Student: No.*

Instructor: Not unless we're telling a fairy tale! Circle each one of those misplaced modifying phrases, and draw an arrow to the correct place in each sentence.

            The young woman went to the awards ceremony with her father (in a gorgeous ball gown).

> **Note to Instructor:** It would not be incorrect for the prepositional phrase to come right after the verb *went,* since it is still closer to *woman* than any other noun, but it is a little smoother to place it directly after the noun.

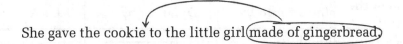

She gave the cookie to the little girl made of gingerbread.

Instructor: Now read me the next sentence in your workbook.

→ *Student: Paige gave a birthday cake to her cousin which she had baked herself.*

Instructor: *Which she had baked herself* is a clause because it has a subject (she) and a predicate (*had baked*). But, like the adjective phrases, it's in the wrong place—it sounds like Paige baked her cousin! Let's fix it now. Underline the clause and circle the relative pronoun *which*. What is the *antecedent* of this pronoun?

→ *Student: Birthday cake.*

Instructor: Draw an arrow from the <u>circle</u> back to *cake.*

Paige gave a birthday cake to her cousin which she had baked herself.

Instructor: Generally speaking, adjective clauses, like phrases, should go right after the word they modify—not somewhere else in the sentence! Read that rule out loud from your workbook.

→ *Student:* **Adjective clauses and phrases should usually go immediately before or after the noun or pronoun they modify.**

Instructor: If we follow this rule, where should the phrase *which she had baked herself* go in this sentence?

→ *Student: After the word* cake.

Instructor: Say the whole sentence, putting the clause in the correct place.

→ *Student: Paige gave a birthday cake which she had baked herself to her cousin.*

Instructor: That sounds much better! Remember: To correct a misplaced adjective clause, find the word modified and place the clause after it.

Finish your exercises now.

— LESSON 76 —

Noun, Adjective, and Adverb Clauses
Restrictive and Non-Restrictive Modifying Clauses

Instructor: Over the last few lessons, you've learned about clauses that function as adverbs, clauses that function as adjectives, and clauses that function as nouns. Everything that you've learned is summed up in the chart in your workbook.

Take a few minutes now to read through this chart. To make sure that you're paying careful attention, I want you to read it out loud, beginning with the name of the type of clause and then reading across about the function, introductory words, diagram, and alternate names of each kind of clause.

> **Note to Instructor:** Insist that the student read each column in the chart out loud; this will improve both understanding and retention.

Type of clause	Function in the sentence	Introduced by . . .	Diagram by . . .	Also known as
Adjective clause	Modifies a noun or pronoun in the main clause. Answers the questions *Which one? What kind? How many? Whose?*	. . . a relative pronoun, relative adjective, or relative adverb that refers back to a noun or pronoun in the main clause. The most common are *who, whom, whose, that, which, where, when, why.*	. . . placing every word of the dependent clause on a separate diagram below the diagram of the main clause. Connect the relative pronoun, adjective, or adverb to the word it refers to in the main clause with a dotted line.	Relative clause, dependent clause, subordinate clause
Adverb clause	Modifies a verb, adjective, or adverb in the main clause. Answers the questions *Where? When? How? How often? To what extent?*	. . . subordinating conjunctions, such as *when, until, before, after, as, while, where, although, unless, because, since, though, so that, even though.* (NOTE: There are many other subordinating conjunctions.)	. . . placing every word of the dependent clause EXCEPT for the subordinating word on a separate diagram below the diagram of the main clause. Draw a dotted line connecting the predicate of the dependent clause to the word modified in the independent clause, and write the subordinating word on the dotted line.	Subordinate clause, dependent clause
Noun clause	Stands in as any part of the sentence that a noun can fill: subject, direct object, indirect object, predicate nominative, object of the preposition, appositive [see Lesson 94], object complement.	. . . most commonly, *that.* Can also be introduced by *who, whom, which, what, whether, why, when, where, how,* or other subordinating words.	. . . drawing a tree in the appropriate "noun" space on the diagram and placing each word in the noun clause on a diagram that sits on top of the tree. If the subordinating word only connects the dependent clause to the rest of the sentence and doesn't have a grammatical function *within* the dependent clause, diagram it on a line that floats above the predicate of the clause and is attached to the predicate by a dotted line.	Nominal clause, subordinate clause, dependent clause

Instructor: Now that you've read through the chart carefully, complete the first exercise in your workbook. *[Give the student time to complete Exercise 76A.]*

We're going to finish up this week's work by looking at one more rule about clauses. This rule only applies to adjective and adverb clauses, not noun clauses. Read the next two sets of rules out of your workbook, and then we'll discuss them.

→ *Student: **A restrictive modifying clause defines the word that it modifies. Removing the clause changes the essential meaning of the sentence. A non-restrictive modifying clause describes the word that it modifies. Removing the clause doesn't change the essential meaning of the sentence.***

Instructor: That sounds more complicated than it actually is! Read the next sentence out loud.

→ *Student: In much of Asia, the day that a baby is born is considered to be its first birthday.*

Instructor: Circle the relative clause *that a baby is born.*

In much of Asia, the day(that a baby is born)is considered to be its first birthday.

Instructor: This clause describes *day.* Now, read the sentence without the relative clause.

→ *Student: In much of Asia, the day is considered to be its first birthday.*

Instructor: That sentence no longer makes sense. The first birthday isn't just a day—it's *the day that a baby is born.* The relative clause *defines* the subject. Now read the second sentence.

→ *Student: Wei's second birthday, which would have been considered his first in North America, was celebrated with a feast of long noodles and red-dyed eggs.*

Instructor: Circle the relative clause describing the second birthday.

Wei's second birthday,(which would have been considered his first in North America)
was celebrated with a feast of long noodles and red-dyed eggs.

Instructor: Now read the sentence without the relative clause.

→ *Student: Wei's second birthday was celebrated with a feast of long noodles and red-dyed eggs.*

Instructor: That makes perfect sense! If you can take out a clause without ruining the sentence or changing its meaning, it is a *non-restrictive* clause—a non-essential clause. But if the clause is *essential,* it's *restrictive.* You're *restricted* from removing it.

> **Note to Instructor**: Actually, *restrictive* means that the clause *restricts* or *constrains* the meaning of the word modified, but the explanation for this is technical and fairly convoluted; the suggested explanation above is more helpful to grammar students.

Instructor: Look at the next four sentences. In the first, what is the adjective clause?

→ *Student: Which lasted far too long.*

Instructor: What does it modify?

→ *Student: Movie.*

Instructor: Does the sentence make sense without it?

→ *Student: Yes.*

Instructor: Removing it doesn't change the meaning of the sentence. The movie, no matter what its length, is still boring. So that is a non-restrictive clause. What is the adjective clause in the second sentence?

→ *Student: Who talk during a movie.*

Instructor: What does it modify?

→ *Student: People.*

Instructor: Read the sentence without the clause.

→ *Student: I get very angry at people.*

Instructor: That actually makes sense, but it has a different meaning than the original sentence. It says that you get mad at *all* people—not just those who talk during movies. Taking away the clause changes the meaning of the sentence, so *who talk during a movie* is a *restrictive* clause. What is the adjective clause in the third sentence?

→ *Student: Who enjoys ballet and* muay thai *fighting.*

Instructor: What does it modify?

→ *Student: Sister.*

Instructor: Is it restrictive or non-restrictive?

> **Note to Instructor:** If necessary, say, "Restrictive clauses can't be removed. Non-restrictive clauses can."

→ *Student: Non-restrictive.*

Instructor: Whether or not your sister likes ballet and *muay thai* fighting, she'll still be climbing Denali. This clause can be taken out, so it's non-restrictive. What is the adverb clause in the last sentence?

→ *Student: Because there was a mountain lion behind her.*

Instructor: This clause explains the reason behind the verb—*why* she was running—so it modifies the verb. If you remove the clause, the sentence loses most of its meaning. You just know that she is running—not the cause. The clause is essential. So is it restrictive or non-restrictive?

→ *Student: Restrictive.*

Instructor: Now look back at those five sentences. The three sentences with non-restrictive clauses have something in them that the other two don't. What do they have?

→ *Student: Commas.*

Instructor: Knowing the difference between a restrictive and a non-restrictive clause will help you use commas properly. If a clause can be taken out, it's non-restrictive, and you should put commas around it. If it's essential to the sentence, it's restrictive, and no commas should be used. Read me the rule in your workbook.

→ *Student: **Only non-restrictive clauses should be set off by commas.***

Instructor: If you don't understand the difference, your sentences may be afflicted by random commas! Look at the first pair of sentences after the rule. Because the adjective clause *who spent much of his life at war* is non-restrictive, commas should be placed on either side of it. Without commas, the sentence is hard to read.

In the second pair of sentences, why is the first sentence correct and the second incorrect?

→ *Student: The adjective clause is restrictive.*

Instructor: If you put commas around a restrictive clause, the sentence will look awkward and read in a stilted, jerky fashion. In the final pair of sentences, which is correct and which is incorrect? Write the answers in the blanks.

The king had no firm foundation on which to build. <u>CORRECT</u>
The king had no firm foundation, on which to build. <u>INCORRECT</u>

Instructor: Without the clause *on which to build*, the foundation could be *anything:* rock for his palace, good laws for his country, or the support of the people for his crown.

We'll come back to restrictive and non-restrictive clauses in later lessons. But now you know enough about both kinds of clauses to complete your exercises.

Constructing Sentences

— LESSON 77 —
Constructing Sentences

Instructor: You're going to start this week's work by taking the grab bag of clauses and phrases in your workbook and putting them together to form sentences.

Here's your challenge: Make up complete sentences, without repeating any of the clauses and phrases or leaving any of them out!

This is your only assignment today. Take your time, and ask for help if you need it.

> **Note to Instructor:** Give the student as much time as needed to complete Exercise 77. If the student asks for help, encourage him once or twice to try again before giving assistance; however, if he's still frustrated, help him by writing out the next sentence from the Answer Key and crossing out the clauses and phrases used from his list. As necessary, repeat in order to narrow down the choices available.

— LESSON 78 —
Simple Sentences
Complex Sentences

(The sentences in this lesson are from *The Cricket in Times Square* by George Selden.)

Instructor: In the last lesson, you practiced constructing sentences. And many, many lessons ago, you learned a three-part definition of a sentence. Read it to me now.

→ *Student: A sentence is a group of words that usually contains a subject and a predicate. A sentence begins with a capital letter and ends with a punctuation mark. A sentence contains a complete thought.*

Instructor: In the last lesson, you assembled a lot of sentences with subjects and predicates that contained complete thoughts. But not all of the sentences were the same. Some had clauses and some didn't. Some had prepositional phrases and some had gerund or infinitive phrases. This week, we're going to classify sentences. Let's start with the simplest kind. Read me the first sentence in your workbook.

→ *Student: A mouse was looking at Mario.*

Instructor: Underline the subject once and the predicate twice.

A <u>mouse</u> <u>was looking</u> at Mario.

Instructor: This is a **simple sentence**. It has only one subject-predicate set. Let's compare it to a more complex sentence. Read me the next sentence.

→ *Student: Gradually the dirt that had collected on the insect fell away.*

Instructor: Underline the main subject once and the main predicate twice. Circle the adjective clause *that had collected on the insect.* It modifies the noun *dirt.* Then, underline the subject of the adjective clause once and the predicate of the adjective clause twice.

Gradually the <u>dirt</u> (that <u>had collected</u> on the insect) <u>fell</u> away.

Instructor: This sentence has two different subject-predicate sets! In fact, any sentence with a dependent clause in it has more than one subject-predicate set, because all clauses have both *subjects* and *predicates.* That's definitely more complex than the first sentence. Read me the two definitions in your workbook.

→ *Student: **A complex sentence contains at least one subordinate clause. A simple sentence contains one independent clause and no subordinate clauses.***

Instructor: Simple sentences aren't *complex,* but they can be very *complicated.* The next three sentences from *The Cricket in Times Square* are all *simple sentences.* Underline the subject and predicate in the first one, and then circle each prepositional phrase.

But (in all his days) and (on all his journeys) (through the greatest city) (in the world) <u>Tucker</u> <u>had</u> never <u>heard</u> a sound quite (like this one)

Instructor: A sentence can be filled with prepositional phrases—or gerund phrases or infinitive phrases—and still be *simple* if it does not contain a subordinate clause. Here's another way to put this: **No matter what else is in a simple sentence, it will only have one subject-predicate set in it.** That doesn't mean only one subject, or only one predicate. A simple sentence can have a compound predicate. In the next sentence, underline the subject once and the predicates twice.

Then <u>he</u> <u>folded</u> a sheet of Kleenex, <u>tucked</u> it in the box, and <u>put</u> the cricket in it.

Instructor: Although there are three predicates, there is still only one independent clause, because all three predicates have the same subject. A simple sentence can also have a compound subject. In the third sentence, underline each subject once and the predicate twice.

The <u>thrumming</u> of the rubber tires of automobiles, and the <u>hooting</u> of their horns, and the <u>howling</u> of their brakes <u>made</u> a great din.

Instructor: This sentence has three subjects—but all three subjects have the same predicate, so there's *still* only one independent clause.

Diagramming a sentence can tell you whether it's simple or complex. Place the subjects and predicates of all five sentences on the frames in your workbook.

```
                                                  dirt | fell
         mouse | was looking              ─────────────────────
                                              that | had collected

                                                         folded
         Tucker | had heard               he  ┌───  tucked
                                              └──  put
```

```
         thrumming
              ┬
                  ╲
                   ╲ and
         hooting    ╲
              ┬       ├──── made
                   ╱ and
                  ╱
         howling ╱
              ┬
```

Instructor: No matter how many subjects and predicates a sentence has, if there's only *one* vertical line separating the subjects and predicates, it's a simple sentence. Which diagram has *two* vertical lines separating subjects and predicates?

→ *Student: The second.*

Instructor: You know that this is the only complex sentence of the five—because it is the *only* one with two vertical lines separating two sets of subjects and predicates. Now look at the last sentence and underline the subjects and predicates.

My closest <u>friend</u> and my greatest <u>enemy</u> <u>met</u> on the battlefield and <u>fought</u> bitterly.

Instructor: Is this a simple or complex sentence? If you're not sure, diagram the subjects and predicates on your own paper.

```
    friend              met
        ╲              ╱
      and│    │    and│
         ╲    │      ╱
    enemy      fought
```

→ *Student: Simple.*

Instructor: It has two subjects and two predicates, but *both* subjects perform *both* predicates. There's no subordinate clause. So this is a simple sentence.

Now that you've learned these two basic categories for sentences, complete your exercises.

— LESSON 79 —

Compound Sentences
Run-on Sentences
Comma Splice

Instructor: You've learned about two different sentence categories—simple and complex. There's one more major sentence category left. Once you've learned about it, you'll be able to put every sentence in the English language into one of these three categories.

Read the first sentence in your workbook (from Jane Austen's classic novel *Pride and Prejudice*) out loud.

→ Student: *Bingley had never met with more pleasant people or prettier girls in his life; everybody had been most kind and attentive to him; there had been no formality, no stiffness; he had soon felt acquainted with all the room.*

Instructor: Take a minute to underline the subjects once, and the predicates twice.

Note to Instructor: Give all necessary help if the student is confused.

Bingley had never met with more pleasant people or prettier girls in his life; everybody had been most kind and attentive to him; there had been no formality, no stiffness; he had soon felt acquainted with all the room.

Instructor: How many subject-predicate pairs are in this sentence?

→ Student: *Four.*

Instructor: That's more than a simple sentence should have. But are there any subordinating words in this sentence?

→ Student: *No.*

Instructor: Read the first clause, before the first semicolon.

→ Student: *Bingley had never met with more pleasant people or prettier girls in his life.*

Instructor: Is that an independent clause or a dependent clause? (Can it stand on its own as a sentence, or not?)

→ Student: *Independent.*

Instructor: Read the second clause. Is it independent or dependent?

→ Student: *Everybody had been most kind and attentive to him. Independent.*

Instructor: Read the third clause. Independent or dependent?

→ Student: *There had been no formality, no stiffness. Independent.*

Instructor: The fourth?

→ Student: *He had soon felt acquainted with all the room. Independent.*

Instructor: Each one of these clauses can stand alone as its own sentence. But Jane Austen links them all together into *one* sentence. This is the third category of sentence: the **compound sentence**. A compound sentence is formed when you link other complete sentences together into one. Read me the definition of a compound sentence out loud.

→ *Student:* ***A compound sentence is a sentence with two or more independent clauses.***

Instructor: Read the next two independent clauses (both of them are simple sentences).

→ *Student: Everybody was surprised. Darcy, after looking at her for a moment, turned silently away.*

Instructor: Now read the compound sentence Jane Austen actually wrote.

→ *Student: Everybody was surprised, and Darcy, after looking at her for a moment, turned silently away.*

Instructor: Circle the connectors between the two sentences—a punctuation mark and a part of speech. What are they?

> Everybody was surprised, and Darcy, after looking at her for a moment, turned silently away.

→ *Student: A comma and a coordinating conjunction.*

> **Note to Instructor:** If the student says "conjunction," say, "Is it a subordinating or a coordinating conjunction?"

Instructor: Quick review: what is a coordinating conjunction?

→ *Student: A coordinating conjunction joins similar or equal words or groups of words together.*

Instructor: Independent clauses are equal groups of words, so they are joined by coordinating conjunctions. What are the coordinating conjunctions?

→ *Student: And, or, nor, for, so, but, yet.*

Instructor: When you use a comma to link independent clauses together into a compound sentence, you *must also use* a coordinating conjunction. If you put two sentences together with *only* a comma, you've written a **run-on sentence**. The sentence doesn't have enough of a *pause* in the middle—it just keeps on tumbling forward, like a runner sprinting along at top speed.

Instructor: Look at the next four sentences in your workbook. Both of the incorrect sentences are run-on sentences. What has been added, in the correct versions of the sentences?

→ *Student: Conjunctions.*

Instructor: Sometimes, this mistake is called a **comma splice**. When you splice two trees together, you jam them into each other so that will become *one* thing. But we don't want the two independent clauses to grow into each other—we want them to remain separate, but be connected by a comma and conjunction link.

Read the next set of simple sentences.

→ *Student: Mr. Bennet, you are wanted immediately. We are all in an uproar.*

Instructor: Now look at the compound sentence that Jane Austen actually wrote. Circle the connector that links the two sentences.

> Mr. Bennet, you are wanted immediately; we are all in an uproar.

Instructor: This is a **semicolon**. A full **colon** is made up of two periods, one on top of the other; a semicolon is made up of a period on top of a comma. In future lessons, we'll study the various uses of both colons and semicolons, but here is the first use of a semicolon: It can go between the independent clauses of a compound sentence.

When you read, you should pause at a semicolon longer than at a comma. Try reading the compound sentence now. Pause at the comma for the count of one, and the semicolon for a count of two.

→ *Student: Mr. Bennet, you are wanted immediately; we are all in an uproar.*

Instructor: Now listen to me read it.

> **Note to Instructor:** The student is developing a sense of what grammatical sentences *sound* like. Count silently to one at the comma, and two at the semicolon.

Mr. Bennet, you are wanted immediately; we are all in an uproar.

Instructor: Does this sentence have a coordinating conjunction?

→ *Student: No.*

Instructor: When you use a comma, you *must also use* a coordinating conjunction. If you use a semicolon, you can use the punctuation mark alone, with no conjunction. But you can *choose* to use a conjunction after the semicolon, if it makes the sentence sound better. Read the next two sentences out loud, and then read the compound sentence, pausing slightly at the semicolon.

→ *Student: The envelope contained a sheet of elegant, little, hot-pressed paper, well covered with a lady's fair, flowing hand. Elizabeth saw her sister's countenance change as she read it.*

> *The envelope contained a sheet of elegant, little, hot-pressed paper, well covered with a lady's fair, flowing hand; and Elizabeth saw her sister's countenance change as she read it.*

Instructor: By putting the conjunction after the semicolon, Jane Austen throws extra emphasis on that last independent clause. You'll learn more grammar and style in future lessons; right now, just be aware of the rule. Read it from your workbook now.

→ *Student:* **The independent clauses of a compound sentence must be joined by a comma and a coordinating conjunction, a semicolon, or a semicolon and a coordinating conjunction. They cannot be joined by a comma alone.**

Instructor: Diagramming a compound sentence is simple. Diagram each independent clause separately, and then link the two sentences together by drawing a dotted line that connects the main predicates of the clauses. In the middle of the dotted line, draw a shelf. The coordinating conjunction goes on this shelf. If there's no coordinating conjunction, just a semicolon, put an *x* on the shelf. Read me the next sentence.

→ *Student: Mr. Collins was not agreeable; his society was irksome, and his attachment to her must be imaginary.*

Instructor: Underline each subject once and each predicate twice.

> Mr. Collins <u>was</u> not agreeable; his <u>society</u> <u>was</u> irksome, and his <u>attachment</u> to her <u>must be</u> imaginary.

Instructor: How many independent clauses are in this compound sentence? (Count the subject-predicate pairs.)

→ *Student: Three.*

Instructor: Look carefully at the diagram.

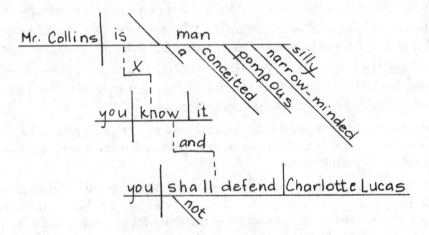

Instructor: Then, place every word of the next sentence on the frame in your workbook.
Mr. Collins is a conceited, pompous, narrow-minded, silly man; you know it, and you
shall not defend Charlotte Lucas.

Instructor: Before you complete your exercises, look at the chart at the end of your lesson. Each
coordinating conjunction has a slightly different meaning. The chart is an introduction to
these shades of meaning. The only way to develop a really good sense of which conjunction to
use is to read, and read, and read, so that you can see the choices that good writers make. But
this chart is an introduction to those shades of meaning. Read each line across from left to
right out loud.

Note to Instructor: Reading aloud is important for understanding and memory; don't let the
student sweep her eyes silently over the chart instead!

Coordinating Conjunction	Meaning/Function	Example
and	simply *in addition to*	I ran and he ran.
or	presents alternatives	He can teach or his assistant can teach.
nor	presents negative alternatives	He did not work, nor did he sleep.
for	*because*	I sang loudly, for I was happy.
so	showing results	He ate too much, so his stomach hurt.
but	*despite that*	I ran ten miles, but I wasn't tired.
yet	*nevertheless*	I had little money, yet I was content.

Instructor: Complete your exercises now.

— LESSON 80 —

Compound Sentences
Compound-Complex Sentences
Clauses with Understood Elements

Instructor: Putting together independent clauses to form compound sentences is a little bit like hooking train cars together. What's the difference between the train cars on the left and the train cars on the right?

→ *Student: The ones on the left are all the same [or equivalent answer].*

Instructor: The compound sentences you studied in the last lesson were all made up of simple sentences—independent clauses with no dependent clauses attached, like the **compound sentence** below the train cars on the left. Read that sentence out loud.

→ *Student: The rabbit jumped, and the lion roared, and the giraffe ambled.*

Instructor: But you can also use coordinating conjunctions to hitch together complex sentences, or a combination of simple and complex sentences. The sentence beneath the train cars on the right is made up of a complex sentence, a simple sentence, and another complex sentence.

When a compound sentence has at least one complex sentence as one of its independent clauses, we call it a ***compound-complex sentence***. Read me the definition from your workbook.

→ *Student: **A compound-complex sentence is made up of two or more independent clauses, at least one of which is a complex sentence.***

Instructor: In the first sentence from *Pride and Prejudice*, find the subordinating word and circle the dependent clause. What is it?

→ *Student: That he would never come there again.*

He was the proudest, most disagreeable man in the world, and everybody hoped that he would never come there again.

Instructor: Look carefully at the diagram.

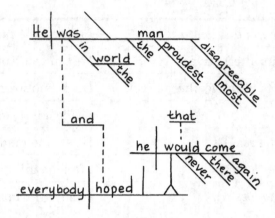

Instructor: Notice that the first part of the compound-complex sentence is a simple
   sentence. What is it?

→ *Student: He was the proudest, most disagreeable man in the world.*

Instructor: The second part is a complex sentence with a dependent clause. What part of the
   sentence is the dependent clause?

→ *Student: The direct object.*

Instructor: To diagram compound-complex sentences, simply diagram each individual sentence
   by the rules you've already learned, and then connect them with the compound sentence dotted
   line. Place every word of the second sentence on the frame in your workbook.

Instructor: How many total clauses are in this sentence? Remember: you can count the number of subject-predicate pairs by counting how many vertical lines separating subject from predicate (those are the lines that go all the way through the horizontal line) are in the diagram.

→ *Student: Four.*

Instructor: How many are independent clauses?

→ *Student: Three.*

Instructor: This compound-complex sentence is made up of two simple sentences and one complex sentence. Read me the complex sentence.

→ *Student: She could not recover from the surprise of what had happened.*

Instructor: What part of the sentence is the dependent clause *what had happened*?

→ *Student: Object of the preposition.*

Instructor: Compound-complex sentences allow us to express complicated ideas and situations. We use compound-complex sentences in English all the time. In fact, we use them *so* much that parts of them sometimes fall out.

Back in Lesson 71, you learned that in English, when a relative pronoun is the direct object in its dependent clause, we often just leave it out. This happens most often when the dependent clause is an adjective clause. The next three complex sentences in your workbook are all missing the relative pronoun "that." Can you insert it into each one?

That was the weirdest thing ^*that* I have ever seen.

The apples ^*that* I bought yesterday had just been picked.

The speech ^*that* he made was short and powerful.

Instructor: Adjective clauses aren't the only parts of sentences that lose words, though. The next three complex-compound sentences are all missing words! Read me the first sentence.

→ *Student: He is vain, and you know he is not a sensible man.*

Instructor: Underline the subject and predicate of the first part, which is a simple sentence. Circle the comma and coordinating conjunction.

He is vain(, and)you know he is not a sensible man.

Instructor: The second part is a complex sentence. Underline the subject *you* once and the predicate *know* twice. What do you know?

→ *Student: He is not a sensible man.*

Instructor: *He is not a sensible man* is a noun clause acting as the direct object of the verb *know*. It's just lost its relative pronoun! Insert *that* between *know* and *he* and write *DO* above the completed noun clause.

He is vain(, and)you know ^*that* ᴰᴼ he is not a sensible man.

Instructor: Read me the second sentence.

→ *Student: He was at the same time haughty, reserved, and fastidious, and his manners, although well-bred, were not inviting.*

Instructor: Underline each subject once and each predicate twice.

> He <u>was</u> at the same time haughty, reserved, and fastidious, and his <u>manners</u>, although well-bred, <u>were</u> not <u>inviting</u>.

Instructor: Read me the first independent clause in this complex-compound sentence.

→ *Student: He was at the same time haughty, reserved, and fastidious.*

Instructor: The second sentence is "His manners, although well-bred, were not inviting." Look more closely at the phrase *although well-bred*. It looks like a prepositional phrase. But is *although* on your list of prepositions? (Look back at page 128 if you can't remember.)

→ *Student: No.*

Instructor: Look at the list of subordinating conjunctions on pages 230-231. Now can you find it?

→ *Student: Yes.*

Instructor: In your workbook, insert the words *they were* after *although*. "They were well-bred" is the adjective clause, describing *manners* and made dependent by the subordinating word *although*.

> He <u>was</u> at the same time haughty, reserved, and fastidious, and his <u>manners</u>, although ^they were^ well-bred, <u>were</u> not <u>inviting</u>.

Instructor: Read the third sentence out loud.

→ *Student: The situation that troubled her remained the same, her peace equally disturbed by the circumstances.*

Instructor: Circle the relative clause that describes the noun *situation*. Then, underline the subjects of both independent clauses once and the predicates twice.

> The <u>situation</u> (that troubled her) <u>remained</u> the same, her <u>peace</u> equally <u>disturbed</u> by the circumstances.

Instructor: Read me the two subject-predicate pairs.

→ *Student: Situation remained, peace disturbed.*

Instructor: Situations can remain, but peace doesn't disturb things! Peace *is disturbed* by other things. This is a passive verb with an understood helping verb—you are supposed to supply "was" in your mind, so that the sentence means, "Situations remained, peace was disturbed."

Jane Austen (the author) also left out the coordinating conjunction. Insert *and* after the comma, and the helping verb *was* just after the noun *peace*.

> The <u>situation</u> (that troubled her) <u>remained</u> the same, ^and^ her <u>peace</u> ^was^ equally <u>disturbed</u> by the circumstances.

Instructor: Read both versions of the sentence out loud now, and listen to yourself carefully.

→ *Student: The situation that troubled her remained the same, her peace equally disturbed. The situation that troubled her remained the same, and her peace was equally disturbed.*

Instructor: How is the original sentence different from your version?

Note to Instructor: This question is intended to help the student start to think more critically about the stylistic choices writers make. Any reasonable answer is acceptable; sample answers might be, "The original sentence is more poetic" or "Jane Austen's sentence makes *remained* and *disturbed* parallel" or "The first sentence ends more quickly."

Instructor: Whenever you are diagramming or working with a sentence and you come across a sentence part that you just can't identify, always ask yourself whether a clause has been contracted and try to provide the missing words. In a diagram, put the missing words in parentheses, as illustrated in the diagram in your workbook.

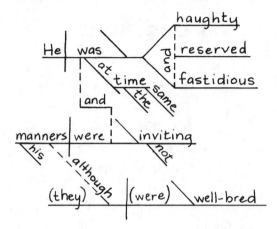

Instructor: You'll study this again in future lessons. Now, complete the exercises at the end of your lesson.

Conditions

— LESSON 81 —

Helping Verbs
Tense and Voice
Modal Verbs

Instructor: Many lessons ago, you learned a list of all the helping verbs. Can you repeat it without looking at the chart in your workbook?

→ *Student: Am, is, are, was, were; be, being, been; have, has, had; do, does, did; shall, will, should, would, may, might, must, can, could.*

Instructor: You also learned that helping verbs help main verbs form their *tense:* the time a verb is showing. What are the three basic tenses?

> **Note to Instructor:** If necessary, help the student by saying, "You learn today, you learned yesterday, you will learn tomorrow."

→ *Student: Past, present, and future.*

Instructor: Those are *simple* tenses. They tell you when something happened, but nothing more. There are two other types of tenses besides simple. What are they?

> **Note to Instructor:** If necessary, help the student by saying, "You learn, you are learning, you have learned."

→ *Student: Progressive and perfect.*

Instructor: Past, present, and future tenses can be simple, progressive, or perfect. That's three tenses that can be expressed three ways. What is three times three?

→ *Student: Nine.*

Instructor: So there are nine tenses in all. You also learned about two different *voices* that each verb has. Do you remember what they are called?

> **Note to Instructor:** If necessary, help the student by saying, "I call, I have been called."

→ *Student: Active and passive.*

Instructor: In a sentence with an active verb, what does the subject do?

→ *Student: The subject performs the action.*

Instructor: In a sentence with a passive verb, what happens to the subject?

→ *Student: The subject receives the action.*

Instructor: Verbs form tense and voice by adding *helping verbs.* In your workbook, you'll see the list of rules explaining how helping verbs form the progressive and perfect tenses. Read through the rules. As you do so, go back up and cross out every verb in your helping verbs list that is mentioned in the rules.

> **Helping Verbs**
> ~~am, is, are, was, were~~
> ~~be, being, been~~
> ~~have, has, had~~
> do, does, did
> ~~shall, will,~~ should, would, may, might, must
> can, could

Instructor: That leaves ten helping verbs unaccounted for. Today, we're going to talk about those helping verbs.

Let's start with *do, does,* and *did.* These helping verbs have three different uses. Read me the next three sentences.

→ *Student: I do not believe in aliens. He does not believe in aliens. We did not believe in aliens (until they landed).*

Instructor: All three of those sentences are *negatives.* This is the first use of *do, does,* and *did:* we use it to say that something is *not* so. *Do not, does not,* and *did not* can also be contracted. Cross out each of those phrases and write the contraction above it.

> **Note to Instructor:** Provide help if necessary.

> I ~~do not~~ believe in aliens.
>   don't

> He ~~does not~~ believe in aliens.
>   doesn't

> We ~~did not~~ believe in aliens (until they landed).
>   didn't

Instructor: Read the next three sentences.

→ *Student: Do you believe in aliens? Does he believe in aliens? Did we believe in aliens (after they landed)?*

Instructor: The second use of *do, does,* and *did* is to form questions. Read the last three sentences.

→ *Student: I do too believe in aliens! He does believe in aliens! We did believe in aliens (once they had landed)!*

Instructor: The third use is simply to add emphasis. Read the rule from your workbook.

→ *Student:* **Use the helping verbs** do, does, **and** did **to form negatives, ask questions, and provide emphasis.**

Instructor: Notice that when you use the helping verb *did,* it changes the way the main verb acts! Instead of changing, the main verb stays the same—and the helping verb changes instead! In the regular simple present, the verb *believe* changes in the third person singular. But in the emphatic simple present, the verb stays the same all the way through—and the *helping verb* changes in the third person singular. In the conjugation of *believe,* circle the form that changes in the simple present and in the simple present emphatic.

	SIMPLE PRESENT		**SIMPLE PRESENT EMPHATIC**	
First person	I believe	we believe	I do believe	we do believe
Second person	you believe	you believe	you do believe	you do believe
Third person	he, she, it believes	they believe	he, she, it does believe	they do believe

Instructor: Look at the simple past conjugation of this same verb. The simple past is formed by adding a -*d* to the simple present form of the verb. How is the simple past emphatic formed?

→ *Student: With the helping verb* did *and the simple present of the verb.*

> **Note to Instructor:** Some grammar texts call this "simple present" form the *infinitive*, since it is also found by removing *to* from an infinitive (such as *to believe*). This can be unnecessarily confusing, so we will continue to use the term *infinitive* only for the full *to [verb]* form.

Instructor: Fortunately, you'll usually only see these emphatic forms in the simple present and simple past—so there's no need to look at more conjugations!

Now let's look at the rest of the helping verbs. The next seven sentences in your workbook all have something in common—and it's not aliens! What is it?

> **Note to Instructor:** Let the student think about the question and offer suggestions. If necessary, prompt by saying, "Have any of these things actually happened?"

→ *Student: [None of these things have actually happened OR equivalent answer].*

Instructor: The helping verbs *should, would, may, might, must, can* and *could* are most often used to help other verbs express situations that haven't actually happened—situations that are uncertain, or possible, or probable, or hypothetical. We call these **modal verbs. Modal verbs express situations that have not actually happened,** and we can divide them into four kinds of situations. The first kind has to do with *possibility*. Read the next five sentences out loud.

→ *Student: I would love to go eat a huge cheeseburger. I can either sleep or eat. I could probably finish my work by supper. I may go down to the hamburger stand on the boardwalk. I might get a burger with onions and Swiss cheese.*

Instructor: All of those sentences have to do with *possible* and *probable* actions—they might or might not happen. The second kind of modal verb has to do with *obligation*—things that you *ought* to do (but haven't done yet!). Read the next two sentences.

→ *Student: I must stop eating this cheeseburger! I really should eat more vegetables.*

Instructor: *Must* and *should* express obligation. The third and fourth groups of modal verbs only have one helping verb each! Read the next sentence.

→ *Student: Yes, you may eat that burger!*

Instructor: You have permission to eat—but you haven't eaten it yet! Read the final sentence.

→ *Student: I can exercise self-control!*

Instructor: *Can* has to do with your *ability* to do something. What four things do modal verbs express?

→ *Student: Possibility, obligation, permission, and ability.*

Instructor: Modal verbs do not have as many tenses as other verbs! Today, we'll look at the two most common tenses: the simple present and the perfect present. You use the simple present for situations in the present, and the perfect present for situations in the past. The simple present is formed with the helping verb and the first person singular form of the main verb. The perfect past is formed with the helping verb, the additional helping verb *have,* and the past participle. That never changes, no matter what the person and number of the verb is! Read the simple present conjugation of the modal verb *could eat.*

→ *Student: I could eat, you could eat, he could eat, we could eat, you could eat, they could eat.*

Instructor: Notice that the only thing changing is the personal pronoun! The verb stays the same. The same is true in the perfect present conjugation; read it out loud.

→ *Student: I should have eaten, you should have eaten, she should have eaten, we should have eaten, you should have eaten, they should have eaten.*

Instructor: Just one more thing. The perfect present forms *should have, could have,* and *would have* can all be contracted. Read the next sentence out loud.

→ *Student: I should've finished my work early; I could've finished it, if I'd had peace and quiet; I would've finished it, if everyone hadn't kept interrupting me.*

Instructor: Write the full form above each contraction in that sentence.

        should have   could have   I had

I should've finished my work early; I could've finished it, if I'd had peace and quiet; I

        would have   had not

would've finished it, if everyone hadn't kept interrupting me.

Instructor: It's fine to contract *should have, could have,* and *would have* in speech, but you should avoid these contractions in formal writing.

Complete your exercises now.

— LESSON 82 —

Conditional Sentences
The Condition Clause
The Consequence Clause

Instructor: The first three sentences in your workbook are from Norton Juster's novel *The Phantom Tollbooth.* Read them out loud.

→ *Student: If you have any more questions, please ask the giant. If one is right, then ten are ten times as right. If you are not perfectly satisfied, your wasted time will be refunded.*

Instructor: Just like modal verbs, each one of these sentences describes something that hasn't actually happened. But these sentences have something extra in them—conditions. What is a **condition**? The definition is in your workbook.

→ *Student: **A condition is a circumstance that restricts, limits, or modifies.***

Instructor: It won't snow unless there are three special *circumstances,* or *conditions.* What are they?

→ *Student: Freezing temperatures up high, freezing temperatures on the ground, and water droplets in the air.*

Instructor: In a conditional sentence, a special circumstance has to occur so that something else can happen. In the first sentence, the special circumstance is *having more questions*. Only *then* can you *ask the giant*. In the second sentence, the special circumstance is that *one is right*. Only then can *ten be ten times as right*. What is the circumstance that has to occur before wasted time is refunded?

→ *Student: You are not perfectly satisfied.*

Instructor: In a conditional sentence, the clause describing the special circumstance is called the **condition clause**. The clause describing what will happen if that circumstance comes to pass is called the **consequence clause**. Read those two definitions from your workbook.

→ *Student: **A condition clause describes a circumstance that has not yet happened. A consequence clause describes the results that will take place if the condition clause happens.***

Instructor: Write *CONDITION* or *CONSEQUENCE* above each clause in the three sentences from *The Phantom Tollbooth*.

        CONDITION   CONSEQUENCE
    If you have any more questions, please ask the giant.

        CONDITION   CONSEQUENCE
    If one is right, then ten are ten times as right.

        CONDITION   CONSEQUENCE
    If you are not perfectly satisfied, your wasted time will be refunded.

Instructor: Most condition clauses are dependent clauses that start with a subordinating word. Circle the subordinating words in the next three sentences, and label each clause as *CONDITION* or *CONSEQUENCE*.

          CONDITION   CONSEQUENCE
  (Unless) it gets warmer, I will stay inside.

     CONSEQUENCE   CONDITION
  I will not go for a walk (if) it remains this cold.

       CONDITION   CONSEQUENCE
  (When) the temperature reaches 70 degrees, I will go outside.

Instructor: But not every condition clause starts with a subordinating word—and occasionally a condition clause can be independent. Label each clause in the next three sentences as *condition* or *consequence*.

        CONDITION   CONSEQUENCE
    Should it rain, I will not come.

        CONDITION   CONSEQUENCE
    Had he been fired, he could have left immediately.

       CONDITION   CONSEQUENCE
    Refuse my conditions, and I will become your enemy!

Instructor: Which condition clause is an independent clause?

→ *Student: Refuse my conditions.*

Instructor: Read me the definition of a conditional sentence now.

→ *Student: **A conditional sentence expresses the conditions under which an action may take place. It contains a condition clause and a consequence clause.***

Instructor: If you don't understand how conditional sentences work, you might use the wrong tenses.

Note to Instructor: Pause for a moment to see if the student realizes that you've used a conditional sentence. If the student doesn't respond, say, "Did you hear that condition? *If you don't understand, you might use the wrong tenses?*

Instructor: So today, you'll be learning about the three groups of conditional sentences. The first kind express circumstances that might actually happen. Look again at the three sentences that began this lesson. Each one of those is a first conditional. There might actually be questions! One might *actually* be right! And there could really be a lack of satisfaction!

Underline the predicate in each condition clause. All three are in the same tense. What is it?

→ *Student: Present.*

Note to Instructor: If the student answers, *Simple present*, say, "That's correct. Condition clauses in first conditional sentences can also be in the progressive present." Then continue with the dialogue.

Instructor: Write *present* in the first blank beneath the description of first conditional sentences.

Now underline the predicate in each consequence clause of those three sentences. There are three different tenses represented! Write each tense in the blank at the end of the sentence.

       CONDITION   CONSEQUENCE
If you <u>have</u> any more questions, please <u>ask</u> the giant.   <u>imperative</u>

       CONDITION   CONSEQUENCE
If one <u>is</u> right, then ten <u>are</u> ten times as right.   <u>simple present OR present</u>

       CONDITION   CONSEQUENCE
If you <u>are</u> not perfectly satisfied, your wasted time <u>will be</u> refunded.   <u>simple future</u>
   <u>OR future</u>

Instructor: In a first conditional sentence, the predicate of the condition clause is in the present tense. The predicate of the consequence clause is often an imperative verb—a command. In the definition of first conditional sentences, write *imperative* in the blank that follows "The predicate of the consequence clause is an…" That predicate can also be in a present or future tense. Write *present* and *future* in the next two blanks.

First conditional sentences express circumstances that might actually happen.
The predicate of the condition clause is in a <u>present</u> **tense.**
The predicate of the consequence clause is an <u>imperative</u> **or is in a** <u>present</u> **or** <u>future</u> **tense.**

Instructor: The next two sentences belong to the second group of conditional sentences— sentences expressing circumstances that are contrary to reality. Label each clause in those two sentences as *condition* or *consequence,* and underline the predicate in each clause.

        CONDITION   CONSEQUENCE
If only Rhyme and Reason <u>were</u> here, things <u>would improve</u>.

           CONDITION   CONSEQUENCE
If you <u>walked</u> as fast as possible and <u>looked</u> at nothing but your shoes, you <u>would arrive</u> at your destination more quickly.

Instructor: The predicates in the condition clauses are both in the same tense. What is it?

→ *Student: Past [OR Simple past].*

Instructor: In a second conditional sentence, the predicate of the condition clause is in a past tense. This can be a progressive or simple past sentence, or even a perfect past. Write *past* in the first blank of the definition of second conditional clauses after the definition. What kind of verb is the predicate in the consequence clause?

Hint: the helping verb *would* should tip you off.

Second hint: look back at Lesson 81.

→ *Student: A modal verb.*

Instructor: A modal verb expresses a situation that has not actually happened—and neither of these consequence clauses have happened, because the conditions haven't come to pass! In the last lesson, you learned that modal verbs are usually in the simple present and perfect present. What tense are *would improve* and *would arrive* in? (The conjugations in your workbook should help you answer.)

→ *Student: Simple present.*

Instructor: In a second conditional sentence, the predicate of the consequence clause is a modal verb in the *simple present* tense. Write *simple present modal* in the last blank of the second conditional sentence definition.

> **Second conditional sentences express circumstances that are contrary to reality.**
> **The predicate of the condition clause is in a** <u>past</u> **tense.**
> **The predicate of the consequence clause is in the** <u>simple present modal</u> **tense.**

Instructor: The last group of conditional sentences expresses past circumstances that never happened. Read the two sentences that follow the definition.

→ *Student: If we had told you then, you might not have gone. If the kingdom had been divided equally, both sons would now be ruling as kings.*

Instructor: For the last time, label each clause as *condition* or *consequence,* and underline the predicate of each clause.

> CONDITION   CONSEQUENCE
> If we <u>had told</u> you then, you <u>might</u> not <u>have gone</u>.

>   CONDITION   CONSEQUENCE
> If the kingdom <u>had been divided</u> equally, both sons <u>would</u> now <u>rule</u> as kings.

Instructor: In both condition clauses, what tense are the predicates?

→ *Student: Perfect past.*

Instructor: Write *perfect past* in the first blank beneath the definition. Each consequence clause has a modal verb—but are they in the same tense?

→ *Student: No.*

Instructor: In the first sentence, the past condition didn't happen, so the past consequence didn't happen either. That's the perfect present. In the second sentence, the past condition didn't happen—and as a result, a present consequence hasn't come about. That's a simple present. Write *perfect present modal* and *present modal* in the last two blanks.

> **Third conditional sentences express past circumstances that never happened.**
> **The predicate of the condition clause is in the** <u>perfect past</u> **tense.**
> **The predicate of the consequence clause is in the** <u>perfect present modal OR</u>
>   <u>simple present modal</u> **tense.**

Instructor: Now you have learned about all three groups of conditional sentences! Use the completed definitions in your workbook to help you complete the exercises now.

— LESSON 83 —

Conditional Sentences
The Subjunctive

Instructor: <u>If you understand conditional sentences, you will become a better writer</u>! That's a conditional sentence. Look at the definitions in your workbook. What kind of conditional sentence did I just use?

→ *Student: First conditional.*

Instructor: Yes, because understanding conditional sentences is a circumstance that might actually happen! On the other hand, <u>if you had never studied any grammar in your entire life, you *could possibly* become a good writer</u>—but the odds are against it. What kind of conditional sentence is that?

→ *Student: Third conditional.*

Instructor: That is a past circumstance that never happened—you *have* studied grammar! Here's one last scenario: <u>If you were an iguana, you wouldn't have to study grammar at all</u>. What kind of conditional sentence is that?

→ *Student: Second conditional.*

Instructor: Exactly. You being an iguana is a circumstance that is contrary to reality.

Look in your workbook now. Read each set of rules out loud. Then, underline the main predicate of each condition clause and each consequence clause in the sentences that follow. Write the tense of each predicate above it. Just use *present, past,* and *future*—you don't have to indicate *simple.*

First conditional sentences express circumstances that might actually happen.
The predicate of the condition clause is in a present tense.
The predicate of the consequence clause is in an imperative, present, or future tense.

present   present   future
If we <u>surrender</u> and I <u>return</u> with you, <u>will</u> you <u>promise</u> not to hurt this man?

imperative   present imperative
So <u>bow</u> down to her if you <u>want</u>, <u>bow</u> to her.

present   future
If she <u>is</u> otherwise when I find her, I <u>shall be</u> very put out.

present   present
Unless I <u>am</u> wrong (and I am never wrong), they <u>are headed</u> dead into the fire swamp.

Second conditional sentences express circumstances that are contrary to reality.
The predicate of the condition clause is in a past tense.
The predicate of the consequence clause is in the simple present modal tense.

present modal   past
I <u>would</u> not <u>say</u> such things if I <u>were</u> you!

    past   present modal
If I <u>had</u> a month to plan, maybe I <u>could come</u> up with something.

        past   present modal
If we only <u>had</u> a wheelbarrow, that <u>would be</u> something.

Third conditional sentences express past circumstances that never happened.
The predicate of the condition clause is in the perfect past tense.
The predicate of the consequence clause is in the perfect present modal or simple present modal tense.

         perfect present modal   perfect past
But they <u>would have killed</u> Westley, if I <u>hadn't</u> <u>done</u> it.

Instructor: Each one of these conditional clauses has a predicate expressing something that is contrary to fact. Five of those subjects and predicates are listed in your workbook, under the heading *contrary to fact*. Read that left-hand column out loud.

→ Student: *If we surrender; if you want; if she is; if I were; if we had.*

Instructor: In the right-hand column, all of those subjects and predicates have been turned into statements of fact. Read them out loud.

→ Student: *We surrender; we want; she is; I was; we had.*

Instructor: Verbs that express unreal situations, like all of those in the *contrary to fact* column, are said to be **subjunctive verbs**. Read me the definition from your workbook.

→ Student: **Subjunctive verbs express situations that are unreal, wished for, or uncertain.**

Instructor: *Sub-* is Latin for "under, beneath," and *junctive* means "joining." Subjunctive verbs usually occur in a dependent clause, so their meaning is joined (in a subordinate, *beneath* way) to the meaning of the predicate in the main clause. Write *subjunctive* on the blank beneath *contrary to fact*.

Read me the definition of an indicative verb.

→ Student: **Indicative verbs affirm or declare what actually is.**

Instructor: Write *indicative* on the blank beneath *fact*. Most of the verbs you've studied so far are indicative verbs. (We'll talk more about this in the next lesson.) But any time a verb expresses an unreal, wished for, or uncertain action, it's a subjunctive verb.

You might notice that the subjunctive and indicative verbs look almost exactly the same! There's only one verb in that list that has a different form in the subjunctive than in the indicative. Find and circle that verb in both columns.

CONTRARY TO FACT	FACT
<u>subjunctive</u>	<u>indicative</u>
If we surrender	We surrender.
If you want	We want.
If she is	She is.
(If I were)	(I was)
If we had	We had.

Instructor: Long, long ago, the English language had different forms for subjunctive verbs. But over time, most of those subjunctives forms fell out of use. In English today, subjunctive verbs usually look just like the regular present tense. In the next two pairs of sentences, underline all of the predicates, and then circle the subjunctive verbs.

> I <u>eat</u> gingerbread men.
> If I (eat) too many gingerbread men, I <u>will</u> not <u>want</u> any dinner.
>
> The three little pigs <u>build</u> houses.
> If the three little pigs (build) straw houses, the wolf <u>will blow</u> them all down.

Instructor: In the first pair of sentences, the first *eat* is indicative, and the second *eat* is subjunctive. In the second pair, which verb is indicative in the first sentence and subjunctive in the second?

→ *Student: Build.*

Instructor: Usually, you only know that a verb is subjunctive because it is in a condition clause. But there are two situations in which subjunctive verbs actually take different forms. The first is when you're using a state-of-being verb in a condition clause to express a circumstance contrary to reality. Look back up at the definition of a second conditional sentence. What tense should you use in the condition clause?

→ *Student: The past tense.*

Instructor: Now look at the chart in your workbook. Normally, the past tense of state-of-being verbs takes the forms *was* and *were,* depending on whether it's first, second, or third person. But in the subjunctive, it *always* takes the form *were.* That's why Prince Humperdinck says, "I would not say such things if I *were* you!"

Look at the next set of three sentences. Each one talks about you being cold. Circle the state-of-being verb in each sentence.

> CORRECT   I (was) cold.
>
> CORRECT   If I (were) cold, I would put on a hat.
>
> INCORRECT   If I (was) cold, I would put on a hat.

Instructor: The first sentence is a statement of fact; it uses the past indicative. The next sentence is a second conditional—it's a state contrary to reality. You're not actually cold! So it uses the subjunctive form *were* instead of *was.* Many people incorrectly use an indicative verb instead of a subjunctive verb in this kind of sentence.

Look at the next two sentences, and write the correct subjunctive verb in the blank.

> He was smart.
> If he <u>were</u> smart, he would go immediately.

Instructor: The second situation in which the subjunctive takes a different form than the indicative is in a dependent clause expressing something that has been suggested, or recommended, or asked for—but hasn't happened yet. Usually these clauses begin with *that* and serve as the direct object of the sentence. In the next three sentences, the dependent clause is underlined. Circle the predicate in each underlined clause.

> I insist <u>that she (leave) the door open</u>.
> I recommend <u>that he (arrive) early</u>.
> The professor asked <u>that the student (read) out loud</u>.

Instructor: All three of those verbs are in the present subjunctive. The present subjunctive is exactly like the indicative present—except in the third person singular. Look at the chart in your workbook. Notice that in the subjunctive, instead of adding an *-s*, the verb just stays the same.

	INDICATIVE SIMPLE PRESENT		SUBJUNCTIVE SIMPLE PRESENT	
First person	I leave	we leave	I leave	we leave
Second person	you leave	you leave	you leave	you leave
Third person	he, she, it leaves	they leave	he, she, it leave	they leave

Instructor: In the next three pairs of sentences, fill in the blanks with the correct form of the verb in brackets.

It is vital that a life guard <u>watch</u> the children swim. [subjunctive present of *watch*]
The life guard <u>watches</u> the children swim. [indicative present of *watch*]

The woman demanded that the mechanic <u>fix</u> her car. [subjunctive present of *fix*]
The mechanic <u>fixes</u> her car. [indicative present of *fix*]

My mother suggested that my sister <u>go</u> to bed early. [subjunctive present of *go*]
My sister <u>goes</u> to bed early. [indicative present of *go*]

Instructor: Complete the exercises in your workbook now.

— LESSON 84 —

Conditional Sentences
The Subjunctive
Moods of Verbs
Subjunctive Forms Using *Be*

Note to Instructor: Grammarians differ on the exact classifications of *mood*. Some consider infinitives to be a separate mood, some consider modality to be an *aspect* rather than a mood, and there are other ways to categorize verbs as well. I have chosen to ignore aspect and to classify verbs according to tense, voice, and mood, with four moods (indicative, subjunctive, imperative, and modal). The purpose of studying grammar is to improve written English, and in my opinion these classifications give students the best tools for composition.

Instructor: Let's talk about verbs. You've learned nine different tenses—forms that tell you *when* a verb happened. Review the definitions of simple, progressive, and perfect tenses by reading them out loud to me.

→ Student: *A simple verb simply tells whether an action takes place in the past, present, or future. A progressive verb describes an ongoing or continuous action. A perfect verb describes an action which has been completed before another action takes place.*

Instructor: In your workbook, you'll see three sentences from Lloyd Alexander's novel *The Book of Three*. We're going to look at the verbs in each one. Read the first sentence out loud.

→ *Student: The air was bracing, yet with a cold edge which made the travelers grateful for the cloaks Medwyn had given them.*

Instructor: What tense are the verbs *was* and *made*?

> **Note to Instructor:** Throughout this initial dialogue, prompt the student as needed.

→ *Student: Simple past.*

Instructor: Write *simple past* on the top line above each verb. The third verb, *had given*, happens in the past *before* the other verbs. What tense is it?

→ *Student: Perfect past.*

Instructor: Write *perfect past* on the top line. You've also learned two different *voices.* Voice tells you something about the relationship between the subject and the verb. Read me the definitions of *voice.*

→ *Student: In a sentence with an active verb, the subject performs the action. In a sentence with a passive verb, the subject receives the action.*

Instructor: Are the verbs in the first sentence active or passive?

→ *Student: Active.*

Instructor: Write *active* on the second line above each verb. Read me the next sentence.

→ *Student: It is not given to men to know the ends of their journeys.*

Instructor: What is the tense and voice of the verb *is given*?

→ *Student: Simple present, passive.*

Instructor: Write the tense and voice on the first and second lines above the verb.

Every verb has tense and voice, but you have *three* lines to fill. Verbs also have mood. *Mood* is hard to define simply, but most grammar books tell you that *mood* has to do with the likelihood, or possibility, of the verb. You've actually learned all four *moods* already. Read me the definitions in your workbook.

→ *Student: Indicative verbs express real actions. Subjunctive verbs express unreal actions. Imperative verbs express intended actions. Modal verbs express possible actions.*

Instructor: Read me the remaining sentences.

→ *Student: "Drink," the stranger said again, while Taran took the flask dubiously. "You look as though I were trying to poison you." There can be no victory over the Cauldron-Born, but with luck, we can hold.*

Instructor: What tense, voice, and mood is the verb *drink*?

→ *Student: Simple present, active, imperative.*

Instructor: Write the tense on the top line, the voice on the second line, and the mood on the third line. Now, fill in all of the remaining blanks.

simple past	simple past
active	active
modal	modal

The air <u>was</u> bracing, yet with a cold edge which <u>made</u> the travelers grateful for the cloaks

perfect past
_____
active
_____
indicative

Medwyn <u>had given</u> them.

simple present
_____
passive
_____
indicative

It <u>is</u> not <u>given</u> to men to know the ends of their journeys.

simple present   simple present
_____   _____
active   active
_____   _____
imperative   indicative

"<u>Drink</u>," the stranger said again, while Taran took the flask dubiously. "You <u>look</u> as

progressive pas
_____
active
_____
subjunctive

though I <u>were trying</u> to poison you."

simple present   simple present
_____   _____
active   active
_____   _____
modal   modal

There <u>can be</u> no victory over the Cauldron-Born, but with luck, we <u>can hold</u>.

Instructor: Now you know how to **parse** a verb. Parsing a verb means finding its tense, voice, and mood.

We'll finish up this lesson by paying a little more attention to the subjunctive mood. First, let's review. In the last lesson, you learned that the subjunctive expresses situations that aren't real. Sometimes, those unreal situations are expressed in conditional sentences. Let's review the definitions by reading them out loud. I'll read the first definition, and you read the example sentence. First conditional sentences express circumstances that might actually happen. The predicate of the condition clause is in a present tense. The predicate of the consequence clause is an imperative, present or future tense.

→ *Student: Unless I am wrong (and I am never wrong), they are headed dead into the fire swamp.*

Instructor: Now, you read the second definition, and I'll read the example sentence.

→ *Student: Second conditional sentences express circumstances that are contrary to reality. The predicate of the condition clause is in the past tense. The predicate of the consequence clause is in the simple present modal tense.*

Instructor: If we only had a wheelbarrow, that would be something. I'll read the last definition; you read the example sentence. Third conditional sentences express past circumstances that never happened. The predicate of the condition clause is in the perfect past tense. The predicate of the consequence clause is in the perfect present modal or simple present modal tense.

→ *Student: But they would have killed Westley, if I hadn't done it.*

Instructor: The verbs in all of those condition clauses are subjunctive—but remember that the subjunctive often looks just like the indicative. In the two sentences that follow, circle the past indicative and past subjective forms of the verb *leave.*

> simple past indicative
> He (left) me behind.

> simple past subjunctive   simple present modal
> If he (left) me behind, I would feel quite upset.

Instructor: For most regular verbs, the simple past subjunctive and indicative look the same. The simple present subjunctive and infintive *almost* look the same. The only difference is in the third person singular form that is bolded in your workbook.

	INDICATIVE PRESENT (SIMPLE)		SUBJUNCTIVE PRESENT (SIMPLE)	
First person	I leave	we leave	I leave	we leave
Second person	you leave	you leave	you leave	you leave
Third person	he, she, it leaves	they leave	he, she, it **leave**	they leave

Instructor: In the two sentences that follow, underline the indicative verb and circle the subjunctive verb.

> INDICATIVE   He <u>leaves</u> at noon.
> SUBJUNCTIVE: It's important that he (leave) at noon.

Instructor: You also learned that the past subjunctive of the state-of-being verb *is* different from the indicative. It is *were,* no matter what the person of the verb is. In the next chart, circle the two forms of the subjunctive that are different from the indicative.

	INDICATIVE PAST (SIMPLE)		SUBJUNCTIVE PAST (SIMPLE)	
First person	I (was)	we were	I were	we were
Second person	you were	you were	you were	you were
Third person	he, she, it (was)	they were	he, she, it were	they were

Instructor: Read Prince Humperdinck's second conditional sentence out loud!

→ *Student: I would not say such things if I were you!*

Instructor: Not all sentences with subjunctive verbs in them are conditionals. Let's look at a few examples. Read the sentence from *The Book of Three* out loud.

→ *Student: You look as though I were trying to poison you.*

Instructor: The main clause is *You look.* Underline the dependent clause *as though I were trying to poison you.* This dependent clause is functioning as a predicate adjective, describing *you.* Label the clause *PA* and draw a line back to the subject *you.*

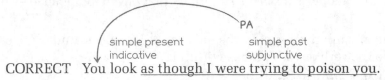

> PA
>   simple present   simple past
>   indicative   subjunctive
> CORRECT   You look <u>as though I were trying to poison you.</u>

Instructor: Because this dependent clause is describing something that isn't actually happening (there's no poisoning going on), the verb is in the subjunctive. In the incorrect sentence, both verbs are in the indicative.

In the next two sentences, underline each dependent clause, label its function in the sentence, and then circle the subjunctive verb that expresses an unreal situation.

                          DO
I wish he (were) here.

> **Note to Instructor:** This is a dependent clause with an understood subordinating word (that).

                                                  ADV
A trace of a smile appeared on his face, <u>as though he (were) savoring something pleasant</u>.

> **Note to Instructor:** The clause modifies the verb because it describes how the smile appeared—the manner of its appearance.

Instructor: Now that we've reviewed subjunctive forms, it's time to learn a new one. The subjunctive *present* of the state-of-being verb is just as irregular as the past! Look at the conjugation in your workbook.

	INDICATIVE PRESENT (SIMPLE)		**SUBJUNCTIVE PRESENT (SIMPLE)**	
First person	I am	we are	I be	we be
Second person	you are	you are	you be	you be
Third person	he, she, it is	they are	he, she, it be	they be

Instructor: Which subjunctive forms are different from the indicative?

→ *Student: All of them.*

Instructor: Look at the first pair of sentences. Underline the state-of-being verb in each one.

    INDICATIVE   I <u>am</u> well-organized.
    SUBJUNCTIVE   My job requires that I <u>be</u> well-organized.

Instructor: Does the first sentence state a fact?

→ *Student: Yes.*

Instructor: Does the second sentence claim that the speaker *is* well-organized?

→ *Student: No.*

Instructor: She *might* be, but all we know for sure is that the job requires it. So the subjunctive reflects uncertainty.

Sometimes the present subjunctive can be combined with a modal helping verb. Look at the next three sentences and underline the verb or verb phrase in each.

    INDICATIVE   You <u>are</u> on time.
    SUBJUNCTIVE   I strongly suggest that you <u>be</u> on time.
    SUBJUNCTIVE/MODAL   Tomorrow, you <u>should be</u> on time.

Instructor: The second and third sentences describe situations that haven't happened—so both use the subjunctive form.

Let's look at one last odd subjunctive form. In the next three sentences, underline each dependent clause and circle the verb or verb phrase within it.

He suggested <u>that she (be given) a new task</u>.

The captain ordered <u>that the anchor (be lifted)</u>.

It is vital <u>that we all (be) properly (prepared)</u>.

Instructor: All of these verbs are in the present *tense* and the subjunctive *mood*. What *voice*?

→ *Student: The passive voice.*

Instructor: The present passive subjunctive is formed by pairing *be* with the *past participle* of a verb. Read that rule out loud.

→ *Student: The present passive subjunctive is formed by pairing* be *with the* past participle *of a verb.*

Instructor: Write the present passive subjunctive form of each verb on the blank to its right.

enjoy	be enjoyed
juggle	be juggled
plan	be planned
roast	be roasted

Instructor: These can also be combined with modal verbs—for example, *should be roasted* or *might be enjoyed.*

This has been a long lesson. If you were not such a good student, you'd be confused now! Go ahead and finish your exercises.

— REVIEW 7 —

The review exercises and answers are found in the Student Workbook and accompanying Key.

Parenthetical Elements

— LESSON 85 —
Verb Review

Instructor: Before we move on to this week's new topic, you'll get a day to review what you've learned about verbs.

In your workbook, you'll see three charts containing all of the verb tenses, voices, and moods you've learned up until now—nine indicative tenses, two modal tenses, and two subjunctive tenses. As you might guess from the charts, there are more tenses to come, and there are also more passive forms still to be learned. But take a few minutes now to go over the forms we've already covered.

Today's assignment is simple. The charts show you the third person singular forms of the regular verb *follow,* along with the active forms of the state-of-being verb *am.* First, read each one of the charts out loud, from left to right. I'll read the first line for you. "Indicative. Simple past. Active: he followed, he was. Passive: he was followed." Go on from there.

→ *Student: Indicative. Simple present. Active: he follows, he is. Passive: he is followed. Indicative. Simple future. Active: he will follow, he will be. Passive: he will be followed . . .*

> **Note to Instructor:** Follow along on the chart below as the student reads the remaining lines. Insist that the student continue to read out loud. This will train the ear to hear correct verb forms and improve the student's verb choice when he writes.

INDICATIVE TENSES

SIMPLE		Active	Passive
	Past	he followed he was	he was followed
	Present	he follows he is	he is followed
	Future	he will follow he will be	he will be followed

PROGRESSIVE

		Active	Passive
	Past	he was following he was being	he was being followed
	Present	he is following he is being	he is being followed
	Future	he will be following he will be being	he will be being followed

PERFECT

		Active	Passive
	Past	he had followed he had been	he had been followed
	Present	he has followed he has been	he has been followed
	Future	he will have followed he will have been	he will have been followed

MODAL TENSES
(would OR should, may, might, must, can, could)

SIMPLE

		Active	Passive
	Present	he would follow he would be	

PERFECT

		Active	Passive
	Past	he would have followed he would have been	

SUBJUNCTIVE TENSES

SIMPLE

		Active	Passive
	Past	he followed he were	
	Present	he follow he be	

Instructor: You only have one other assignment today. First, fill out the empty charts in your workbook with the correct forms of the verbs indicated. Second, write sentences that contain all of these forms. You can write one sentence for each form, or write compound or complex sentences so that each sentence has more than one predicate. If you need help or ideas, ask me.

— LESSON 86 —

Restrictive and Non-Restrictive Modifying Clauses
Parenthetical Expressions

(The first sentence in this lesson is from A. A. Milne's *Winnie-the-Pooh*.)

Instructor: The paragraph in your workbook is one single very long sentence! Read it out loud.

→ *Student: In after-years Piglet liked to think that he had been in Very Great Danger during the Terrible Flood, but the only danger he had really been in was in the last half-hour of his imprisonment, when Owl, who had just flown up, sat on a branch of his tree to comfort him, and told him a very long story about an aunt who had once laid a seagull's egg by mistake, and the story went on and on, rather like this sentence, until Piglet, who was listening out of his window without much hope, went to sleep quietly and naturally, slipping slowly out of the window towards the water until he was only hanging on by his toes, at which moment luckily a sudden loud squawk from Owl, which was really part of the story, woke Piglet up and just gave him time to jerk himself back into safety and say, "How interesting, and did she?" when—well, you can imagine his joy when at last he saw the good ship The Brain of Pooh (Captain, C. Robin; 1st Mate, P. Bear) coming over the sea to rescue him.*

Instructor: That sentence is filled with clauses, but we're only going to look at a few of the the *modifying clauses*—the dependent clauses that act like adjectives or adverbs. Underline the clause *he had really been in*. That clause has an understood relative pronoun: *the only danger [that] he had really been in*. What does the clause modify?

→ *Student: Danger.*

Instructor: Draw an arrow from the clause back to *danger*. Underline the clause *who had just flown up*. What does it modify?

→ *Student: Owl.*

Instructor: Draw an arrow from the clause back to *Owl*. Underline the clause *who had once laid a seagull's egg by mistake*. What does it modify?

→ *Student: Aunt.*

Instructor: Draw an arrow from the clause back to *aunt*. Underline the clause *who was listening out of his window without much hope*. What does it modify?

→ *Student: Piglet.*

Instructor: Draw an arrow from the clause back to *Piglet*. Underline the clause *until he was only hanging on by his toes*. This is an adverb clause; do you know what it modifies? Hint: It answers the question "to what extent."

→ *Student: Slipping.*

Instructor: Draw an arrow from the clause back to the present participle *slipping*. Underline the clause *which was really part of the story*. What does it modify?

→ *Student: Squawk.*

Instructor: Some of those adjective clauses are **restrictive** and some are **non-restrictive**. Review the definitions of both in your workbook, and then label each adjective clause with an *R* for restrictive and an *N* for non-restrictive.

In after-years Piglet liked to think that he had been in Very Great Danger during the
Terrible Flood, but the only danger he had really been in was in the last half-hour of his
imprisonment, when Owl, who had just flown up, sat on a branch of his tree to comfort
him, and told him a very long story about an aunt who had once laid a seagull's egg by
mistake, and the story went on and on, rather like this sentence, until Piglet, who was
listening out of his window without much hope, went to sleep quietly and naturally,
slipping slowly out of the window towards the water until he was only hanging on by
his toes, at which moment luckily a sudden loud squawk from Owl, which was really
part of the story, woke Piglet up and just gave him time to jerk himself back into safety
and say, "How interesting, and did she?" when—well, you can imagine his joy when at
last he saw the good ship *The Brain of Pooh* (Captain, C. Robin; 1st Mate, P. Bear) coming
over the sea to rescue him.

Instructor: Read the sentence one more time, but this time leave out the non-restrictive adjective
clauses. Notice that the sentence still sounds just fine!

→ *Student: In after-years Piglet liked to think that he had been in Very Great Danger during
the Terrible Flood, but the only danger he had really been in was in the last half-hour of his
imprisonment, when Owl sat on a branch of his tree to comfort him, and told him a very long
story about an aunt who had once laid a seagull's egg by mistake, and the story went on and on,
rather like this sentence, until Piglet went to sleep quietly and naturally, slipping slowly out of
the window towards the water until he was only hanging on by his toes, at which moment luckily
a sudden loud squawk from Owl woke Piglet up and just gave him time to jerk himself back into
safety and say, "How interesting, and did she?" when—well, you can imagine his joy when at last
he saw the good ship* The Brain of Pooh *(Captain, C. Robin; 1st Mate, P. Bear) coming over the
sea to rescue him.*

Instructor: The commas on each side of the non-restrictive adjective clauses tell you that they're
not *necessary* to the meaning of the sentence—they just add additional description. But
there's another kind of punctuation that A. A. Milne could have used—**parentheses**. Read the
definition in your workbook.

→ *Student: **Parentheses ( ) can enclose words that are not essential to the sentence.***

Instructor: Parentheses usually occur in pairs on either side of the nonessential words, so we
usually use the plural form of the word to refer to them. The singular is *parenthesis*. One
parenthesis, a pair of parentheses. Put a parenthesis on either side of the non-restrictive clauses
in the A. A. Milne sentences that come next in your workbook.

when Owl (who had just flown up) sat on a branch of his tree to comfort him

until Piglet (who was listening out of his window without much hope) went to sleep quietly

a sudden loud squawk from Owl (which was really part of the story) woke Piglet up

Instructor: Non-restrictive modifying clauses can be set off with either commas *or* parentheses, because they aren't essential to the meaning of the sentence. Writers tend to use commas in order to connect the clause more tightly to the rest of the sentence, and parentheses when they want to separate the clause or make it less important. Look back at the long beginning sentence one more time. What expression did Milne actually put into parentheses?

→ *Student: (Captain, C. Robin; 1st Mate, P. Bear.)*

Instructor: Notice that those words don't have much to do with the rest of the sentence! Read me the next rule about parenthetical expressions.

→ *Student:* **Parenthetical expressions often interrupt or are irrelevant to the rest of the sentence.**

Instructor: Parenthetical expressions are useful because they allow writers to put in observations or ideas that don't fit neatly into the grammatical structure of a sentence. The words inside the parentheses can be dependent clauses, phrases, complete sentences, or even just a word or two, as long as they follow two rules. Read the next two rules out loud.

→ *Student:* **Punctuation goes inside the parentheses if it applies to the parenthetical material; all other punctuation goes outside the parentheses. Parenthetical material only begins with a capital letter if it is a complete sentence with ending punctuation.**

Instructor: The next eight sentences in your workbook, taken from *The Chronicles of Narnia* by C. S. Lewis, show several different ways that parenthetical expressions can be used. The first two parenthetical expressions are non-restrictive modifying clauses.

> As soon as he saw his companion fall, the other soldier, with a loud cry, jumped out of the boat on the far side, and he also floundered through the water (which was apparently just in his depth) and disappeared into the woods of the mainland.

> If you can swim (as Jill could) a giant bath is a lovely thing.

Instructor: What does *which was apparently just in his depth* modify?

→ *Student: Water.*

Instructor: How about *as Jill could*?

→ *Student: Swim.*

Instructor: The first dependent clause is adjectival, and the second is adverbial. C. S. Lewis could just as easily have set off each one with commas on either side, but he chose to make the clauses less important by separating them off with parentheses.

> The next two expressions are just phrases—they don't contain subjects and predicates.

>> He had only once been in a ship (and then only as far as the Isle of Wight) and had been horribly seasick.

>> The cabin was very tiny but bright with painted panels (all birds and beasts and crimson dragons and vines) and spotlessly clean.

Instructor: The first parenthetical expression tells you more about how long Eustace had been in a ship, so it's acting as an adverb. What does the second phrase describe?

→ *Student: The painted panels.*

Instructor: So the parenthetical expression itself is acting as an adjective. But what part of speech is *birds*? And *beasts*? And *dragons*? And *vines*?

→ *Student: They are all nouns.*

Instructor: The parentheses allow Lewis to use all of these nouns as if they were adjectives. The next four parenthetical expressions are all complete sentences, but each one is used slightly differently.

> From the waist upward he was like a man, but his legs were shaped like a goat's (the hair on them was glossy black) and instead of feet he had goat's hoofs.

> Get me a score of men-at-arms, all well mounted, and a score of Talking Dogs, and ten Dwarfs (let them all be fell archers), and a Leopard or so, and Stonefoot the Giant.

> Edmund had had no gift, because he was not with them at the time. (This was his own fault, and you can read about it in the other book.)

> Because it was such an important occasion they took a candle each (Polly had a good store of these in her cave).

Instructor: Read me the first parenthetical expression, which tells you more about Mr. Tumnus's legs.

→ *Student: The hair on them was glossy black.*

Instructor: This is a complete sentence, but it doesn't have either a capital letter at the beginning or a punctuation mark at the end. What kind of sentence is it—statement, question, exclamation, or command?

→ *Student: Statement.*

Instructor: What kind of a sentence is the next parenthetical expression?

→ *Student: Command.*

Instructor: It isn't capitalized or punctuated either. When you put a complete sentence inside parentheses and then place it in the middle of another sentence, you normally don't capitalize it and give it ending punctuation. The third parenthetical expression *does* have both a capital letter *and* an ending sentence. What's the difference?

→ *Student: It isn't in the middle of another sentence.*

Instructor: Now look at the last parenthetical expression. Why does it begin with a capital letter?

→ *Student: Polly is a proper name.*

Instructor: Look at the period at the end. Is it inside or outside the parentheses?

→ *Student: Outside.*

Instructor: The period ends the entire sentence, not just the parenthetical expression, so it is placed outside the closing parenthesis.

> The last three sentences illustrate the correct ways to punctuate parenthetical expressions.

> > I read the *Chronicles of Narnia* (all seven of them!) in three days.
> > Did you know that C. S. Lewis wrote the *Chronicles of Narnia* (all seven of them)?
> > C. S. Lewis and J. R. R. Tolkien were good friends (amazing, isn't it?).

Instructor: In the first sentence, what is the exclamation?

→ *Student: All seven of them!*

Instructor: The exclamation point applies only to the exclamation, not the rest of the sentence, so it goes inside the closing parenthesis. In the second sentence, what is the question?

→ *Student: Did you know that C. S. Lewis wrote* The Chronicles of Narnia?

Instructor: The parenthetical expression *all seven of them* just describes the Chronicles—it isn't a question. It's part of the whole sentence, so the question mark goes at the very end of the whole sentence, not inside the parentheses. In the third sentence, what is the question?

→ *Student: Amazing, isn't it?*

Instructor: The question mark only applies to those words, not to the whole sentence. There's no question that Lewis and Tolkien were good friends! So the question mark goes inside the parentheses. But the entire sentence as a whole still needs an ending punctuation mark, so the period goes outside the closing parenthesis.

Complete your exercises now.

— LESSON 87 —

Parenthetical Expressions
Dashes

Instructor: In your workbook, you'll see five sentences from Lewis Carroll's novel *Through the Looking-glass.* Read me the first sentence.

→ *Student: A little provoked, she drew back, and after looking everywhere for the queen (whom she spied out at last, a long way off), she thought she would try the plan, this time, of walking in the opposite direction.*

Instructor: What is the parenthetical element?

→ *Student: Whom she spied out at last, a long way off.*

Instructor: Is that a phrase, a dependent clause, or a sentence?

→ *Student: A dependent clause.*

Instructor: Does it act as an adjective or an adverb?

→ *Student: An adjective.*

Instructor: What does it modify?

→ *Student: Queen.*

Instructor: Underline the clause, label it as *ADJ*, circle the relative pronoun, and draw a line from the relative pronoun back to *queen*.

> A little provoked, she drew back, and after looking everywhere for the queen (whom) <u>she spied out at last, a long way off</u>), she thought she would try the plan, this time, of walking in the opposite direction.

Instructor: Lewis Carroll could simply have put commas around that dependent clause, but instead he decided to make it less important to the sentence by putting it into parentheses. Now read me the next sentence.

→ *Student: There was a Beetle sitting next to the Goat (it was a very queer carriage-full of passengers altogether).*

Instructor: What is the parenthetical element?

→ *Student: It was a very queer carriage-full of passengers altogether.*

Instructor: Is that a phrase, a dependent clause, or a sentence?

→ *Student: A sentence.*

Instructor: Carroll could have made that an entirely separate sentence, but he made it less important to the story by putting it into parentheses. Label the parenthetical element as *SENTENCE*.

> SENTENCE
> There was a Beetle sitting next to the Goat (it was a very queer carriage-full of passengers altogether).

Instructor: There is also a compound noun in that parenthetical element, made up of a noun attached to an adjective with a hyphen. Circle the compound noun.

> Read the next sentence out loud.

→ *Student: Or—let me see—suppose each punishment was to be going without a dinner; then, when the miserable day came, I should have to go without fifty dinners at once!*

Instructor: This sentence also has a parenthetical element—but it's set off with different punctuation marks. What is the parenthetical element?

→ *Student: Let me see.*

Instructor: Is it a phrase, a dependent clause, or a sentence?

→ *Student: A sentence.*

Instructor: Go ahead and label it.

> SENTENCE
> Or—let me see—suppose each punishment was to be going without a dinner; then, when the miserable day came, I should have to go without fifty dinners at once!

Instructor: This parenthetical element is set off with *dashes.* Put one finger on one of the dashes, and the other on the hyphen in the compound noun ("carriage-full") above. A dash is twice as long as a hyphen. When you write a dash, make it a little longer than a hyphen. When you type a dash, use two hyphens for each dash.

> In pairs, dashes can replace parentheses to set off parenthetical elements. But although parentheses always occur in twos, dashes can also be used alone. Read the next sentence out loud.

→ *Student: I can see all of it when I get upon a chair—all but the bit behind the fireplace.*

Instructor: A dash can also be used in place of a comma to give emphasis to a certain part of a sentence. Look at the version of the sentence written with the comma instead of the dash. The original draws your attention to *the bit behind the fireplace*. In the last sentence, you'll see a dash acting in place of a comma to introduce a dependent clause. The clause itself also contains a parenthetical element. Read the last sentence out loud. As you do, notice that you pause a little longer at a dash than at a comma.

→ *Student: But the beard seemed to melt away as she touched it, and she found herself sitting quietly under a tree—while the Gnat (for that was the insect she had been talking to) was balancing itself on a twig just over her head, and fanning her with its wings.*

Instructor: Review the rules about parentheses by reading them out loud now.

→ *Student: **Parentheses ( ) can enclose words that are not essential to the sentence. Parenthetical expressions often interrupt or are irrelevant to the rest of the sentence. Punctuation goes inside the parentheses if it applies to the parenthetical material; all other punctuation goes outside the parentheses. Parenthetical material only begins with a capital letter if it is a complete sentence with ending punctuation.***

Instructor: Now read the two-sentence rule about dashes.

→ *Student:* **Dashes — — can enclose words that are not essential to the sentence. Dashes can also be used singly to separate parts of a sentence.**

Instructor: Notice that there aren't any rules about punctuation. Normally, parenthetical sentences or expressions with ending punctuation will be placed within parentheses, not dashes.

Now listen to me read the next three sentences out loud.

Note to Instructor: Follow the instructions in brackets as you read.

[Pause briefly at each comma] I read Lewis Carroll's poem "Jabberwocky" which, I thought, was very weird.

[Pause slightly longer at each dash] I read Lewis Carroll's poem "Jabberwocky" which—I thought—was very weird.

[Pause for the same length of time at the parentheses, but lower your voice slightly to indicate an *aside* comment] I read Lewis Carroll's poem "Jabberwocky" which (I thought) was very weird.

Instructor: Do you hear the differences? The way I read these sentences reflects the three rules in your workbook. Read them out loud.

→ *Student:* **Commas make a parenthetical element a part of the sentence. Dashes emphasize a parenthetical element. Parentheses minimize a parenthetical element.**

Instructor: Read the first sentence, pausing at each comma.

→ *Student: I read Lewis Carroll's poem "Jabberwocky" which, I thought, was very weird.*

Instructor: Read the second sentence, pausing for a slightly longer time at each dash.

→ *Student: I read Lewis Carroll's poem "Jabberwocky" which—I thought—was very weird.*

Instructor: Read the third sentence and pause for the same length of time at each parenthesis, but lower your voice slightly to indicate an *aside* comment.

→ *Student: I read Lewis Carroll's poem "Jabberwocky" which (I thought) was very weird.*

Instructor: Now you've learned three important things. First, you can set off parenthetical elements in three different ways. Second, you can turn a dependent clause into a parenthetical element just by putting it inside dashes or parentheses. And third, you can use a dash in place of a comma to emphasize the part of the sentence that follows. There's just one more thing to remember. You can use commas instead of parentheses or dashes around a parenthetical element—but *not* if that turns the sentence into a run-on sentence! Review the definition of a run-on sentence by reading it out loud.

→ *Student:* **The independent clauses of a compound sentence must be joined by a comma and a coordinating conjunction, a semicolon, or a semicolon and a coordinating conjunction. They cannot be joined by a comma alone.**

Instructor: The last two sentences in your lesson show the difference between an independent sentence serving as a parenthetical expression within another sentence, and a run-on sentence. Circle the commas that should be parentheses in the incorrect sentence.

Alice ventured to taste it, and finding it very nice(,)it had, in fact, a sort of mixed flavour of cherry tart, custard, pineapple, roast turkey, toffee, and hot buttered toast(,)she very soon finished it off.

Instructor: Complete your exercises now.

— LESSON 88 —

Parenthetical Expressions

Dashes

Diagramming Parenthetical Expressions

Instructor: Look at the next four sentences in your workbook. Three of them contain parenthetical expressions. One of them doesn't. Which sentence does *not* contain a parenthetical expression?

→ *Student: The third* OR *The chef decided to put liver, which was one of his favorites, on the dinner menu.*

Instructor: Underline the parenthetical elements in the other three sentences.

> We met the new neighbors today, who, <u>we think</u>, are very pleasant people.
> It was a glorious morning—<u>a cool, sunny, sweet-scented morning</u>.
> The chef decided to put liver, which was one of his favorites, on the dinner menu.
> The liver (<u>which most diners didn't order</u>) was cooked with onions and red wine.

Instructor: You can recognize a parenthetical element in a sentence in one of two ways. First, dashes and parentheses always turn a clause or phrase into a parenthetical element—even if there's actually a grammatical relationship between the clause or phrase and the rest of the sentence. Second, if a clause or phrase is set off by commas, but doesn't have a clear grammatical relationship to the rest of the sentence, it's actually parenthetical. What do dashes and parentheses always do?

→ *Student: Turn a clause or phrase into a parenthetical element.*

Instructor: Which two sentences fall into this category?

→ *Student: The second and fourth* OR *It was a glorious morning—a cool, sunny, sweet-scented morning AND The liver (which most diners didn't order) was cooked with onions and red wine.*

Instructor: How do you know that a clause or phrase set off by commas is actually parenthetical?

→ *Student: It doesn't have a clear grammatical relationship to the rest of the sentence.*

Instructor: Which sentence falls into this category?

→ *Student: The first* OR *We met the new neighbors today, who, we think, are very pleasant people.*

Instructor: Today, we're going to look at how to diagram parenthetical elements. Examine the first diagram in your workbook.

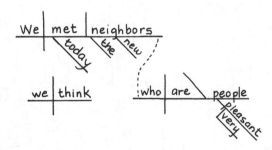

Instructor: What is the main clause?

→ *Student: We met the new neighbors today.*

Instructor: What is the dependent clause?

→ *Student: Who are very pleasant people.*

Instructor: To what word in the main clause does the relative pronoun *who* refer?

→ *Student: Neighbors.*

Instructor: You have learned to diagram a dependent clause introduced by a relative pronoun by diagramming the clause as a separate sentence and connecting the pronoun to its antecedent with a dotted line. Now look at how *we think* is diagrammed. Is this a phrase or a clause?

→ *Student: A clause.*

Instructor: It has a subject and a predicate. However, it isn't linked to the rest of the sentence by a relative pronoun (even an understood one!), a subordinating word, or a conjunction. So it has no grammatical relationship to the sentence. We place it over to the left, on its own, to show that while it *belongs* to the sentence, it doesn't have a grammatical *connection* to the sentence.

Now try to diagram the second sentence onto the frame provided.

> **Note to Instructor:** If the student asks for help, encourage him to make at least one more try before showing him the answer below.

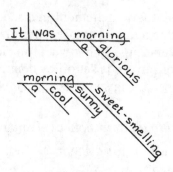

Instructor: The most important word in the parenthetical expression is *morning*, so that noun goes on its own line, with the adjectives that describe it diagrammed beneath it.

Now diagram the third and fourth sentences onto the frames provided.

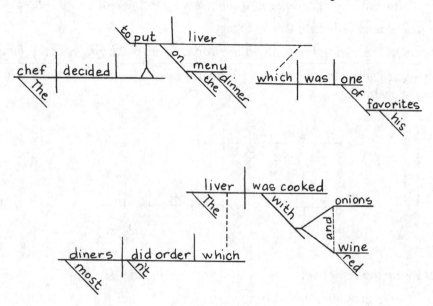

Instructor: Remember, a diagram shows the logical relationship between parts of a sentence—it isn't intended to show the writer's punctuation choices! So if the parenthetical element has a grammatical connection to the rest of the sentence, diagram it just as you would if it *didn't* have dashes or parentheses around it, and don't worry about putting the punctuation somewhere on the diagram.

If it *doesn't* have a grammatical connection, diagram it near the main sentence, but separately.

When a parenthetical expression has *no* grammatical relationship to anything else in the sentence, you may have to get creative in how you diagram it! How would you diagram the following sentence? Do your best on your own paper, and then we'll compare answers.

The train—can you believe it?—was on time (a rare and happy occurrence!).

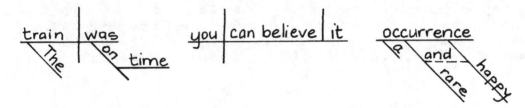

Instructor: There are so many different kinds of parenthetical elements that no grammar book could describe exactly how to diagram each one! So the rest of this lesson is just one diagramming exercise. Do your best to create diagrams that make sense, and then compare your answers with the diagrams in the Answer Key.

Dialogue and Quotations

> **Note to Instructor:** This week's work deals with the technical and grammatical aspects (punctuation and capitalization) of dialogue and quotations. Further study in the effective use of both, as well as the study of proper documentation (footnotes and endnotes), belongs to writing instruction rather than to grammar.
>
> If your writing program does not deal with dialogue and/or the use of direction quotation, consider supplementing with James Scott Bell's *How to Write Dazzling Dialogue: The Fastest Way to Improve Any Manuscript* (Compendium Press, 2014) and *They Say / I Say: The Moves That Matter in Academic Writing*, 3rd ed., by Gerald Graff and Cathy Birkenstein (W. W. Norton, 2014).

— LESSON 89 —
Dialogue

Instructor: Your lesson today begins with an excerpt from the classic science fiction novel *Ender's Game,* by Orson Scott Card. Three characters—Ender, his brother Peter, and his sister Valentine—are talking. There are two different kinds of sentences in these paragraphs: the actual words that the characters speak, and the story itself. The words that the characters speak are called **dialogue** and are set off with quotation marks. The rest of the story is called the **narrative**.

I will read the narrative out loud; you read the dialogue. Try to use a different voice for each character.

→ *Student: I'm sorry, Ender.*

Instructor: Valentine whispered. She was looking at the band-aid on his neck. Ender touched the wall and the door closed behind him.

→ *Student: I don't care. I'm glad it's gone.*

> **Note to Instructor:** Make sure that the student realizes this is Ender's dialogue, not Valentine's, and that the following speech is Peter's.

→ *Student: What's gone?*

Instructor: Peter walked into the parlor, chewing on a mouthful of bread and peanut butter. Ender did not see Peter as the beautiful ten-year-old boy that grown-ups saw, with dark, thick, tousled hair and a face that could have belonged to Alexander the Great. Ender looked at Peter only to detect anger or boredom, the dangerous moods that almost always led to pain. Now as Peter's eyes discovered the band-aid on his neck, the telltale flicker of anger appeared. Valentine saw it too.

→ *Student: Now he's like us.*

Instructor: She said, trying to soothe him before he had time to strike.

We'll use these paragraphs to go over the rules for writing dialogue correctly. First, underline the words *Valentine whispered* and *she said*. These are called **dialogue tags**.

"I'm sorry, Ender⊙" <u>Valentine whispered</u>. She was looking at the band-aid on his neck.

Valentine saw it too. "Now he's like us⊙" <u>she said</u>, trying to soothe him before he had time to strike.

Instructor: Read the definition of a dialogue tag from your workbook.

→ *Student: **A dialogue tag identifies the person making the speech.***

Instructor: Circle the punctuation mark that comes at the end of each one of Valentine's speeches. What is it?

→ *Student: A comma.*

Instructor: Read the next rule in your workbook.

→ *Student: **When a dialogue tag comes after a speech, place a comma, exclamation point, or question mark inside the closing quotation marks.***

Instructor: You'll see this rule illustrated in the next three sentences. Read them out loud, using the correct tone of voice for each one.

→ *Student: "I ate the cookie," my brother said. "I ate seventeen cookies!" my brother exclaimed. "Do you think I'll be sick?" my brother asked.*

Instructor: Do not use a period! Cross out the incorrect version below.

        INCORRECT: ~~"I ate the cookie." My brother said~~.

Instructor: Dialogue tags can also come *before* speeches. Read me the next rule.

→ *Student: **When a dialogue tag comes before a speech, place a comma after the tag. Put the dialogue's final punctuation mark inside the closing quotation marks.***

Instructor: In the sentences that follow, underline each dialogue tag, circle each comma, and draw a box around each final punctuation mark.

    <u>My brother said</u>⊙"I ate the cookie[.]"

    <u>My brother exclaimed</u>⊙"I ate seventeen cookies[!]"

    <u>My brother asked</u>⊙"Do you think I'll be sick[?]"

Instructor: Now look back at the excerpt from *Ender's Game*. Two of the speeches have dialogue tags—but two don't. Draw a box around the two speeches without dialogue tags.

"I'm sorry, Ender⊙" <u>Valentine whispered.</u> She was looking at the band-aid on his neck.

Ender touched the wall and the door closed behind him. ⌈"I don't care. I'm glad it's gone."⌉

⌈"What's gone?"⌉ Peter walked into the parlor, chewing on a mouthful of bread and peanut butter. . . .

Valentine saw it too. "Now he's like us⊙" <u>she said</u>, trying to soothe him before he had time to strike.

    —From *Ender's Game* by Orson Scott Card

Instructor: When you write dialogue, you can place the speeches into the text without a tag—as long as the text makes clear who's speaking. What sentence tells you that Ender says, "I don't care. I'm glad it's gone"?

→ *Student: Ender touched the wall and the door closed behind him.*

Instructor: What sentence tells you that Peter says, "What's gone?"

→ *Student: Peter walked into the parlor, chewing on a mouthful of bread and peanut butter.*

Instructor: Like dialogue tags, the sentence explaining who is speaking can come before or after the dialogue itself. Read the next rule.

→ *Student: **Speeches do not need to be attached to a dialogue tag as long as the text clearly indicates the speaker.***

Instructor: There are two more important rules about dialogue. Usually, you should begin a new paragraph each time a different speaker starts to talk. The next set of speeches are also from *Ender's Game*. Although there are no dialogue tags, it's clear that two different people are speaking to each other, because whenever the speaker changes, a new paragraph begins. Let's read this dialogue together. You begin, and I'll be the second speaker.

→ *Student: I've watched through his eyes, I've listened through his ears, and I tell you he's the one. Or at least as close as we're going to get.*

Instructor: That's what you said about the brother.

→ *Student: The brother tested out impossible. For other reasons. Nothing to do with his ability.*

Instructor: Same with the sister. And there are doubts about him. He's too malleable. Too willing to submerge himself in someone else's will.

→ *Student: Not if the other person is his enemy.*

Instructor: So what do we do? Surround him with enemies all the time?

→ *Student: If we have to.*

Instructor: Read the next rule out loud.

→ *Student: **Usually, a new paragraph begins with each new speaker.***

Instructor: Dialogue can also come in the middle of a speech. Look at the next two sentences. In both of them, the dialogue tag *George retorted* comes in the middle of George's dialogue. In both sentences, what punctuation mark comes after *think*?

→ *Student: A comma.*

Instructor: It is a comma because of the rule you learned above: When a dialogue tag comes after a speech, place a comma, exclamation point, or question mark—but *not* a period—inside the closing quotation marks. What punctuation mark comes after the first *retorted*?

→ *Student: A period.*

Instructor: A period follows the dialogue tag because the next part of George's speech is a complete sentence: "I wish you could be honest too." If a comma followed *retorted*, you would have a run-on sentence, because the complete sentence *George retorted* and the complete sentence *I wish you could be honest too* would be connected *only* by a comma. What punctuation mark follows the second *retorted*?

→ *Student: A comma.*

Instructor: *Whether or not you like it* is a dependent clause, not a complete sentence. So if a period came after *retorted* you would have a sentence fragment. Look at the two incorrect examples and cross each one through.

> INCORRECT (Run-on sentence): ~~"I'm not afraid to say what I think," George retorted, "I wish you could be honest too."~~

INCORRECT (Ends with a sentence fragment): ~~"I'm not afraid to say what I think,"~~ ~~George retorted. "Whether or not you like it."~~

Instructor: Read the last rule out loud now.

→ *Student: When a dialogue tag comes in the middle of a speech, follow it with a comma if the following dialogue is an incomplete sentence. Follow it with a period if the following dialogue is a complete sentence.*

> **Note to Instructor:** Accomplished writers often break this rule for effect, but students should learn to follow it until they reach a higher level of composition.

Instructor: Complete your exercises now.

— LESSON 90 —

Dialogue
Direct Quotations

Instructor: Your lesson today starts with two excerpts from books about the medieval kingdom of Mali, in West Africa. The first book is based on the real story of the king known as Mansa Musa of Mali, but the book itself is fiction. The author has made up dialogue for her characters. Underline the dialogue, and circle the dialogue tags.

> (The stranger said) "I have come far seeking Mali and have found great wealth here. But I must tell your king that great wealth that the world has not seen is worth less to your children's children than a rumor of water to a people dying of thirst."
>
> The elders wondered silently about this stranger who presumed to lecture the king of Mali, but they were much too polite to say anything that might make a guest feel less than welcome.
>
> "You will have to go to Niani, the capital city, to speak with the *mansa*—that is, the king—of Mali," (said Musa Weree) with a smile that seemed to mask a secret.
>
> But the stranger showed no interest in Niani. "The king has heard me!" (he said)
>
> —From *Mansa Musa: The Lion of Mali,* by Khephra Burns

Instructor: Let's quickly review the rules you learned about punctuating dialogue. If necessary, you can look back at the last lesson. When a dialogue tag comes before a speech, what punctuation mark goes after the tag?

→ *Student: A comma.*

Instructor: Which dialogue tag illustrates this rule?

→ *Student: The first OR The stranger said.*

Instructor: When a dialogue tags follows a speech, what three punctuation marks can end the speech?

→ *Student: A comma, an exclamation point, or a question mark.*

Instructor: Do they go inside or outside the closing quotation marks?

→ *Student: Inside.*

Instructor: What two speeches illustrate this rule?

→ *Student: The second and the third* OR *You will have to go to Niani, the capital city, to speak with the* mansa—*that is, the king—of Mali* and *The king has heard me!*

Instructor: Take a minute now to read through the second excerpt. This is from the nonfiction history book *The History of the Renaissance World.*

When you are finished, underline the two sentences that are surrounded by quotation marks.

> During the two months he remained in Mali, Ibn Battuta paid grudging respect to the safety and justice of the kingdom: "<u>A traveler may proceed alone among them, without the least fear of a thief or robber,</u>" he noted.

> They were required to keep solemn and attentive in his presence: "<u>Whoever sneezes while the king is holding court,</u>" al-'Umari explains, "<u>is severely beaten.</u>"

Instructor: What is the first sentence surrounded by quotation marks?

→ *Student: A traveller may proceed alone among them, without the least fear of a thief or robber.*

Instructor: Those are the exact words of the medieval traveller Ibn Battuta, but he didn't *speak* them. Instead, he wrote them. What is the second sentence?

→ *Student: Whoever sneezes while the king is holding court is severely beaten.*

Instructor: This sentence comes from the writings of the 14th-century Arab historian al-'Umari [al oo MAR ee].

When you use the exact words of another writer, you are using a *direct quotation*. Direct quotations are set off with quotation marks—just like the exact words of a *speaker*. Read the two definitions in your workbook.

→ *Student: **Dialogue: the exact words of a speaker. Direct quotation: the exact words of a writer.***

Instructor: Dialogue tags attach dialogue to a speaker. Direct quotations are attached to the person who wrote them with an **attribution tag**. Read the next two definitions out loud.

→ *Student: **Dialogue tags attach dialogue to a speaker. Attribution tags attach direct quotations to a writer.***

Instructor: Attribution tags have the same punctuation rules as dialogue tags. Read each one of the following rules out loud. In the sentences that illustrate each rule, circle the punctuation mark that the rule affects.

→ *Student: **When an attribution tag comes after a direct quote, place a comma, exclamation point, or question mark inside the closing quotation marks.***

> "Many ships sank that day$_\bigodot$" the chronicler wrote.

> "Seventeen ships sank that day$\bigodot$" the chronicler lamented.

> "Who can say how many lives were lost$\bigodot$" the chronicler mourned.

> INCORRECT: "Many ships sank that day$_\bigodot$" The chronicler wrote.

→ *Student: **When an attribution tag comes before a direct quote, place a comma after the tag. Put the dialogue's final punctuation mark inside the closing quotation marks.***

> According to the chronicler$_\bigodot$ "Many ships sank that day$_\bigodot$"

> The chronicler tells us$_\bigodot$ "Seventeen ships sank that day$\bigodot$"

> One witness asked$_\bigodot$ "Who can say how many lives were lost$\bigodot$"

→ *Student: When an attribution tag comes in the middle of a direct quotation, follow it with a comma if the remaining quote is an incomplete sentence. Follow it with a period if the remaining quote is a complete sentence.*

> "Many ships," the chronicler tells us⊙"sank that day."
> "Seventeen ships sank that day," the chronicler tells us⊙"Who can say how many lives were lost?"

Instructor: Look back up at the excerpt from *The History of the Renaissance World*. What is the attribution tag for the first direct quotation?

→ *Student: He noted.*

Instructor: Circle that attribution tag. What punctuation mark comes at the end of the first direct quotation and before the attribution tag?

→ *Student: A comma.*

Instructor: Is it outside or inside the closing quotation marks?

→ *Student: Inside.*

Instructor: What is the attribution tag for the second direct quotation?

→ *Student: Al-'Umari explains.*

Instructor: Circle that attribution tag. What punctuation mark comes before the attribution tag?

→ *Student: A comma.*

Instructor: Is it outside or inside the closing quotation marks?

→ *Student: Inside.*

Instructor: What part of the direct quotation comes after the attribution tag?

→ *Student: Is severely beaten.*

Instructor: Is that a complete sentence?

→ *Student: No.*

Instructor: Because it is not a complete sentence, a comma comes after the attribution tag—not a period.

> During the two months he remained in Mali, Ibn Battuta paid grudging respect to the safety and justice of the kingdom: "A traveller may proceed alone among them, without the least fear of a thief or robber," he noted
> In Sulayman's twenty-four years on the throne, Mali remained firmly under his authority. Sulayman surrounded himself with the trappings of an emperor: gold arms and armor; ranks of courtiers and Turkish mamluks, warrior slaves bought from Egypt, surrounding him. They were required to keep solemn and attentive in his presence: "Whoever sneezes while the king is holding court," al-'Umari explains "is severely beaten."
>
> —From *The History of the Renaissance World* by Susan Wise Bauer

Instructor: There is one rule that makes direct quotations different from dialogue. A speech doesn't have to have a dialogue tag. Review the next rule, which you learned in the last lesson, by reading it out loud.

→ *Student: Speeches do not need to be attached to a dialogue tag as long as the text clearly indicates the speaker.*

Instructor: **Every direct quote *must* have an attribution tag!** You can never drop a direct quote into your writing without telling the reader exactly who said it. Look at the two examples in your workbook, taken from *The History of the Medieval World.*

In the correct paragraph, circle the attribution tag.

CORRECT:

The soldiers chased Yazdegerd north into the province of Kirman, but the Arab army was caught in a blizzard and froze. "The snow reached the height of a lance," al-Tabari says Only the commander, one soldier, and a slave girl survived, the latter because her owner slit open the stomach of a camel and packed her inside it to keep her warm.

—*The History of the Medieval World,* by Susan Wise Bauer

Instructor: In the incorrect paragraph, cross out the direct quote that has no attribution tag.

INCORRECT:

The soldiers chased Yazdegerd north into the province of Kirman, but the Arab army was caught in a blizzard and froze. "The snow reached the height of a lance." Only the commander, one soldier, and a slave girl survived, the latter because her owner slit open the stomach of a camel and packed her inside it to keep her warm.

Instructor: Many beginning writers make this mistake. Don't forget: Every direct quote must have an attribution tag! Read that rule out loud three times.

→ *Student: Every direct quote must have an attribution tag. Every direct quote must have an attribution tag. Every direct quote must have an attribution tag.*

Instructor: Complete your exercises now.

— LESSON 91 —

Direct Quotations
Ellipses
Partial Quotations

> **Note to Instructor:** "Sun" is pronounced with a vowel halfway between "oo" and "uh." "Tzu" is pronounced like a "dz" followed by a very brief schwa (the neutral sound that English speakers use in the word "the").

Instructor: In the 5th century B.C., in the country that is now China, a general named Sun Tzu fought in vicious civil wars between powerful noble families. Afterwards, he wrote a guide to conquering your enemies—while avoiding as much actual fighting as possible. It is called *The Art of War,* and it has been used by generals from ancient times up until the present day. Take a minute now to read (either silently or out loud) the short excerpt from *The Art of War* in your workbook.

Instructor: The next excerpt in your workbook is from a history of ancient times that quotes *The Art of War.* Take another minute to read it (again, silently or out loud).

Instructor: Now compare the quote in the second excerpt to the selection from *The Art of War.* The author has used some of the selection—but not all of it. Cross out everything in the first selection that is *not* used in the second.

~~A few clouds of dust moving to and fro signify that the army is encamping.~~ Humble words and increased preparations are signs that the enemy is about to advance. Violent language and driving forward as if to the attack are signs that he will retreat. ~~When the light chariots come out first and take up a position on the wings, it is a sign that the enemy is forming for battle.~~ Peace proposals unaccompanied by a sworn covenant indicate a plot. ~~When there is much running about and the soldiers fall into rank, it means that the critical moment has come. When some are seen advancing and some retreating, it is a lure.~~

   —Sun Tzu, *The Art of War,* trans. Lionel Giles

The good general not only deceives the enemy himself, but assumes that his enemy is always deceiving him: "Humble words and increased preparations are signs that the enemy is about to advance," Sun Tzu explains. "Violent language and driving forward as if to the attack are signs that he will retreat . . . Peace proposals unaccompanied by a sworn covenant indicate a plot." Both Confucius and Sun-Tzu, roughly contemporary as they are, offer a philosophy of order, a way of dealing with a disunified country; stability through the proper performance of social duties, or stability through intimidation.

   —Susan Wise Bauer, *The History of the Ancient World*

Instructor: In the second excerpt, the sentence beginning *When the light chariots come out first* is left out. But the author has left you a clue that something's been eliminated: three periods in a row. Leaving something out is called an **ellipsis**. And these three dots are called *ellipses*. (That's the plural of "ellipsis.") Read the definition in your workbook.

→ *Student: **Ellipses show where something has been cut out of a sentence.***

Instructor: *Ellipses* comes from the Greek word meaning "omission." Whenever you see three periods, you know that something has been *omitted*. And when you're writing, if you cut something out of the middle of your quote, you should indicate it with three periods.

 Do ellipses show that that the first sentence from *The Art of War* has been left out?

→ *Student: No.*

Instructor: Do ellipses show that the last two sentences have been left out?

→ *Student: No.*

Instructor: Usually, you only use ellipses to show that the omission comes in the middle of whatever you're quoting.

 So far, we've only looked at direct quotes that are whole sentences taken from other writers. But when you're writing, you'll often want to quote just part of a sentence: a clause, a phrase, or even just a word. The next five sentences from *The History of the Ancient World* all show correct ways of quoting *part* of a sentence. Read me the first sentence.

→ *Student: The Roman historian Varro mentions an early division of Rome's people into three "tribes" of some kind.*

Instructor: The word *tribes* is a direct quote. The author wants you to know that the Roman historian Varro uses the exact word *tribes*, so she puts it in quotation marks to show that this is the same word that Varro uses. Now read me the second sentence.

→ *Student: The attackers were thoroughly thrashed, since the army of debtors that came charging out to meet them was, as Livy puts it, "spoiling for a fight."*

Instructor: What is the direct quote from the writings of the Roman historian Livy?

→ *Student: Spoiling for a fight.*

Instructor: *Spoiling* is a particular form of the verb *spoil*. What form is it?

→ *Student: A present participle.*

Instructor: Review the rule by reading it out loud.

→ *Student: The present participle of a verb can act as a descriptive adjective.*

Instructor: *Spoiling* is a present participle acting as a descriptive adjective. *Spoiling for a fight* is an entire participle phrase, acting as an adjective. Circle it, and draw an arrow back to the noun it modifies.

> The attackers were thoroughly thrashed, since the army of debtors that came charging out to meet them was, as Livy puts it, "spoiling for a fight."

Instructor: Whenever you use just part of a direct quote, you have to make it a correct, grammatical part of your own sentence. In this sentence, the author uses Livy's participle phrase as an adjective phrase describing one of her own nouns. In the next sentence she uses another direct quote from Livy as part of her sentence. Read me the sentence.

→ *Student: The city needed laws "which every individual citizen could feel that he had . . . consented to accept."*

Instructor: Before we talk about this sentence, review the first rule that comes beneath it.

→ *Student: Every direct quote must have an attribution tag.*

Instructor: Two of the remaining sentences in this exercise may not seem to have an attribution tag—but the attribution of the direct quotes to the historian Livy comes earlier in the paragraph, when Livy is first quoted. When you clearly attribute a direct quote to a source, you can quote from it a second or third time without another attribution tag, as long as the context makes the source of the quote very clear. Read that rule out loud.

→ *Student: **A second or third quote from the same source does not need another attribution tag, as long as context makes the source of the quote clear.***

Instructor: Now, underline the subject of the sentence once. Underline the predicate twice. Label the direct object with *DO*.

> The <u>city</u> <u><u>needed</u></u> laws^DO "which every individual citizen could feel that he had . . . consented to accept."

Instructor: The direct quote "which every individual citizen could feel that he had consented to accept" is a dependent clause. Review the next four rules in your workbook by reading them out loud.

→ *Student: A clause is a group of words that contains a subject and a predicate. A dependent clause is a fragment that cannot stand by itself as a sentence. Dependent clauses begin with subordinating words. Dependent clauses are also known as subordinate clauses.*

Instructor: In the dependent clause, underline the subject once and the predicate twice.

> The <u>city</u> <u><u>needed</u></u> laws^DO "which every individual <u>citizen</u> <u><u>could feel</u></u> that he had . . . consented to accept."

Instructor: What is the subordinating word that begins the dependent clause?

→ *Student: Which.*

Instructor: Read the next two rules out loud.

→ *Student: Adjective clauses are also known as relative clauses because they relate to another word in the independent clause. Relative pronouns introduce adjective clauses and refer back to an antecedent in the independent clause.*

Instructor: What kind of subordinating word is *which*?

→ *Student: A relative pronoun.*

Instructor: What is its antecedent?

→ *Student: Laws.*

Instructor: The entire direct quote is an adjective clause, or relative clause, describing *laws*. Circle *which* and draw an arrow back to *laws*.

$$\text{DO}$$

The city needed laws "which every individual citizen could feel that he had . . . consented to accept."

Instructor: Let's use this dependent clause to review a couple of other grammatical forms you've learned about. This is quite a complicated dependent clause! Look at the last part of the quote and underline *that he had . . . consented to accept*. Part of the quote has been omitted. What do we call the three periods showing where words have been left out?

→ *Student: Ellipses.*

Instructor: Without the missing words, *that he had consented to accept* forms another dependent clause—a clause within a clause! Read me the next definition.

→ *Student: **A noun clause takes the place of a noun.***

Instructor: This noun clause is introduced by the subordinating word *that*. The whole clause "that he had consented to accept" is actually the *direct object* of the predicate *could feel*. It is the thing being felt by the citizens. So this is a clause standing in for a direct object. Underline it three times and write *DO* above the clause.

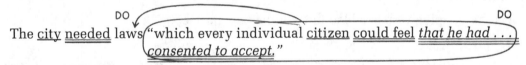

The city needed laws "which every individual citizen could feel *that he had . . . consented to accept.*"

Instructor: Within that direct-object noun clause, what is the subject?

→ *Student: He.*

Instructor: What is the predicate?

→ *Student: Had consented.*

Instructor: What had he consented?

→ *Student: To accept.*

Instructor: *To accept* is an infinitive serving as the direct object of the predicate *had consented*. So far, this sentence has *three* types of direct object: a noun, a noun clause, and an infinitive acting as a noun! But we're not done yet. What exactly were the citizens accepting?

→ *Student: The laws.*

Instructor: They (subject) were accepting (predicate) the laws (direct object). Within the dependent clause, the relative pronoun *which* stands in for *laws* and serves as the direct object of the infinitive *to accept*. So there are actually *four* different kinds of direct objects in the sentence! This will be clearer to you once you place each word of the sentence on the diagram frame provided.

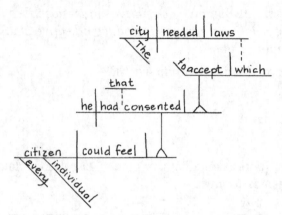

Instructor: Now put your finger on each object space on the diagram. You should find four.

> **Note to Instructor:** Each space following a vertical line that does *not* go all the way through the horizontal line is an object space.

Instructor: Let's look at two more examples of making a quote a grammatical part of another sentence. Read me the next sentence.

→ *Student: The city of Veii, Livy writes, had "inflicted worse losses than she suffered," which means that the siege had significantly weakened the Roman army.*

Instructor: Underline the subject of the main clause once, the predicate twice, and write *DO* above the direct object.

> The <u>city</u> of Veii, Livy writes, <u>had "inflicted</u> worse lo^{DO}sses than she suffered," which means that the siege had significantly weakened the Roman army.

Instructor: What tense is *had inflicted*? (If you need help, look back at the charts in Lesson 18.)

→ *Student: Past perfect.*

Instructor: What helping verb is added to form the past perfect?

→ *Student: Had.*

Instructor: This sentence quotes Livy's *Early History of Rome*. In the excerpt from the *Early History* below, underline the words quoted.

> Such was the fall of Veii, the wealthiest city of Etruria. Even her final destruction witnessed to her greatness, for after a siege of ten summers and ten winters, during which she <u>inflicted worse losses than she suffered</u>, even when her destined hour had come she fell by a stratagem and not by direct assault.
>
> —Livy, *The Early History of Rome*

Instructor: In Livy's sentence, what tense is the verb *inflicted?*

→ *Student: Simple past.*

Instructor: When you quote, you can add helping verbs to change the tense of the original predicate—as long as the final sentence makes sense as a whole. Read the last sentence out loud now.

→ *Student: He had heard, "in the silence of the night," an inhuman voice saying, "Tell the magistrates that the Gauls are coming."*

Instructor: This sentence uses two different exact quotes. What kind of phrase is *in the silence of the night*?

→ *Student: A prepositional phrase.*

Instructor: What part of speech is it acting as?

→ *Student: An adverb.*

Instructor: This quote is an adverbial prepositional phrase, describing the verb *had heard* and answering the question *when*. What is the second direct quote?

→ *Student: Tell the magistrates that the Gauls are coming.*

Instructor: The author has chosen to insert this direct quote as a line of dialogue. What is the dialogue tag?

→ *Student: An inhuman voice saying.*

Instructor: What punctuation mark comes after it?

→ *Student: A comma.*

Instructor: Where does the final period come?

→ *Student: Inside the closing quotation marks.*

Instructor: All of these examples are illustrations of the final rule. Read it out loud.

→ *Student: **Direct quotes can be words, phrases, clauses, or sentences, as long as they are set off by quotation marks and form part of a grammatically correct original sentence.***

Instructor: Complete your exercises now.

— LESSON 92 —

Partial Quotations
Ellipses
Block Quotes
Colons
Brackets

Instructor: We'll finish up this week's work by looking at two more rules about using direct quotes. For a change, you'll read the rules first, and then examine illustrations of how they work. Read me the first rule out loud.

→ *Student: **If a direct quotation is longer than three lines, indent the entire quote one inch from the margin in a separate block of text and omit quotation marks.***

Instructor: Read the second rule.

→ *Student: **If you change or make additions to a direct quotation, use brackets.***

Instructor: The two excerpts in your workbook will illustrate how these rules work. Start off by reading the first excerpt (either silently or out loud). This comes from a 1661 essay with the wonderful title *Scepsis* [Skepsis] *Scientifica: Or, Confest Ignorance, The Way to Science; In an Essay of the Vanity of Dogmatizing and Confident Opinion.* The writer, Joseph Glanvill, is predicting air travel, a flight to the moon, and the telephone—over 200 years before any of those things even began to happen!

Now, read the second excerpt. This is part of a paper that *quotes* Glanvill's essay. How many different times does the paper quote from Glanvill?

→ *Student: Three times.*

Instructor: The first and third quotations, in the first sentence and the last sentence, are short partial quotations. Underline the first quote. Now, go back up and find *many things* in Glanvill's original essay. What part of the sentence is *things*?

→ *Student: Direct object.*

Instructor: In the second essay, what part of speech has *things* become?

→ *Student: The object of the preposition of.*

Instructor: As you learned in the last lesson, a partial quote has to become part of a new sentence—which means that some of the words in the quote might have to serve a new function. Now, underline the third quote, in the last sentence. What part of the sentence does this quote serve as?

→ *Student: A parenthetical expression.*

Instructor: Both of these quotes also have an attribution tag. Circle each attribution tag.

> In 1661, the English philosopher Joseph Glanvill predicted the invention of "many things, that are now but Rumors." Among them were space travel, airplanes, and conversation over long distances. In his essay *Scepsis Scientifica,* Glanvill admits that these inventions seem farfetched, but he argues that the discovery of a new continent must have seemed just as unlikely:
>
> > It may be some ages hence, a voyage to the Southern unknown Tracts, yea possibly the Moon, will not be more strange than one to America. To them, that come after us, it may be as ordinary to buy a pair of wings to fly into remotest Regions; as now a pair of Boots to ride a Journey. And to confer at the distance of the Indies by Sympathetick conveyances, may be as usual to future times, as to us in a litterary correspondence. . . [T]hose great Inventions that have in these later Ages altered the face of all things . . . were to former times as *ridiculous.* To have talk'd of a *new Earth* [the North and South American continents] to have been discovered, had been a Romance [Glanvill means a "fairy tale"] to Antiquity.
>
> Glanvill goes on to point out that navigating a ship by compass ("the guidance of a Mineral," as he puts it) instead of by the stars must have seemed just as impossible to ancient sailors as moon travel does to people of his own day.

Instructor: Now take a look at the long quote in the middle. Notice that it has been indented one inch from the margin. There is also an extra line space both before and after the quote. When you are using a word processing program, you should leave this extra space on either side of a block quote. Read me that rule now.

→ *Student:* **When using a word processing program, leave an additional line space before and after a block quote.**

Instructor: Now put your finger on the punctuation mark that *precedes* this block quote. This is a *colon.* You've studied semicolons, which look like a period sitting above a comma. This is a *full* colon, which looks like a period sitting above another period.

Full colons have several different uses. This is the first one: colons often come before block quotes. Read me the next rule.

→ Student: **Block quotes should be introduced by a colon (if preceded by a complete sentence) or a comma (if preceded by a partial sentence).**

Instructor: Read the complete sentence that precedes the block quote.

→ Student: *In his essay* Scepsis Scientifica, *Glanvill admits that these inventions seem farfetched, but he argues that the discovery of a new continent must have seemed just as unlikely.*

Instructor: Since a block quote comes next, that sentence ends with a colon instead of a period. But if the block quote were introduced by a partial or incomplete sentence, you would use a comma instead. In your workbook, you'll now see an example of this punctuation. Read the incomplete sentence that introduces the next block quote.

→ Student: *As the English philosopher Joseph Glanvill predicted in 1661.*

Instructor: That is a dependent clause, not an independent clause, so it is an incomplete sentence. So a comma comes between that incomplete sentence and the block quote.

Now look back up at the first version of the essay. How do you know that two different chunks of Glanvill's original text have been left out of the middle of the direct quote?

→ Student: *By the ellipses.*

Instructor: In the second example, text has been left out at the beginning and end. But you don't need to use ellipses in either place—you only use them to show what's been omitted in the middle.

Go back up to now to the first version of the essay. Circle the phrase *those great Inventions* in the block quote. Then, go all the way back up to the original excerpt from Joseph Glanvill and circle the phrase there. What's the difference between the two quotes?

→ Student: *The second quote is capitalized.*

> Now those, that judge by the narrowness of former Principles, will smile at these Paradoxical expectations: But questionless those great Inventions that have in these later Ages altered the face of all things; in their naked proposals, and meer suppositions, were to former times as *ridiculous*. To have talk'd of a *new Earth* to have been discovered, had been a Romance to Antiquity. And to say without sight of Stars or shoars by the guidance of a Mineral, a story more absurd, than the flight of Daedalus.
> —Joseph Glanvill, *Scepsis Scientifica: Or, Confest Ignorance, The Way to Science; In an Essay of the Vanity of Dogmatizing and Confident Opinion*

Instructor: When the writer shortened the direct quote, she left out the first two words of the original sentence, *But questionless*, because they weren't necessary. The next word, *those,* became the first word of the sentence—and the first word of a sentence always begins with a capital letter. So she changed the small t into a capital T. Read the rule one more time.

→ Student: *If you change or make additions to a direct quotation, use brackets.*

Instructor: Brackets look like parentheses, but they're square instead of round. Whenever condensing a quote means that you have to make a change in order for it to be grammatically correct, put the change in brackets to show the reader that you've altered the original.

In that first version of the essay, there are two more sets of brackets in the direct quote. Both contain explanations. What is the *new Earth* that Glanvill mentions?

→ Student: *The North and South American continents.*

Instructor: What does Glanvill mean by *Romance*?

→ *Student: A fairy tale.*

Instructor: The writer knows that readers who aren't familiar with Glanvill's work might not know what he means by these two terms. So she provides a short explanation. Because those aren't in the original, they too have brackets around them.

Complete your exercises now.

WEEK 24

Floating Elements

— LESSON 93 —

Interjections
Nouns of Direct Address
Parenthetical Expressions

Instructor: Hurrah, it's time to do grammar! Come what may, [student name], we will learn about interjections and words of direct address. And, as it happens, we'll also review parenthetical expressions.

I just used all three of the sentence parts we'll be discussing today. Read me the first set of sentences in your workbook out loud. Use some emotion!

→ Student: *Oh dear, I've dropped my keys. Oops! The keys fell through the grate into the sewer. Alas, I will not be able to unlock my door. Whew! That was a close one. Whoa, let's just slow down here for a minute. Hush, I'm on the phone.*

Instructor: Each one of those sentences begins with an **interjection**. An interjection is a word that shows sudden feeling or emotion. But it doesn't have a grammatical connection with the rest of the sentence—it just floats there, unattached. The word *interjection* comes from Latin. Literally, interjection means "to throw between." You throw interjections into sentences! Read me the definition in your workbook now.

→ Student: **Interjections express sudden feeling or emotion. They are set off with commas or stand alone with a closing punctuation mark.**

Instructor: Read the second set of sentences out loud.

→ Student: *Friends, Romans, countrymen, lend me your ears! Stars, hide your fire! I am afraid, my dear, that you are too late. Run, baby, run. Get down, dog!*

Instructor: Each one of those sentences contains a noun of direct address—the name of the person or thing to whom the sentence is being said. The first sentence contains three nouns of direct address! Read me all of the nouns of direct address in those five sentences.

→ Student: *Friends, Romans, countrymen, stars, my dear [or just "dear"], baby, dog.*

Instructor: Now read the definition of nouns of direct address.

→ Student: **Nouns of direct address name a person or thing who is being spoken to. They are set off with commas. They are capitalized only if they are proper names or titles.**

Instructor: Like interjections, nouns of direct address just float somewhere in the sentence, unattached.

Back in Lesson 86, you learned that parenthetical elements can also float in a sentence. Review the rules about parenthetical elements by reading them out loud now.

→ *Student: Parentheses ( ) can enclose words that are not essential to the sentence. Parenthetical expressions often interrupt or are irrelevant to the rest of the sentence. Punctuation goes inside the parentheses if it applies to the parenthetical material; all other punctuation goes outside the parentheses. Parenthetical material only begins with a capital letter if it is a complete sentence with ending punctuation. Parenthetical expressions can also be set off by commas.*

Instructor: In English, we have a whole set of two- and three-word parenthetical expressions that we use *all* the time. In the next six sentences, circle each short parenthetical expression.

The doctor was so late, (in fact,) that the baby was born before he arrived.

(To be sure,) she will tell a very plausible story.

When Marco Polo travelled to China he crossed, (as it were,) the horizon of European knowledge.

Fear was, (no doubt,) the greatest enemy the army had.

(In a word,) he supported the other candidate.

These things are always difficult, (you know.)

Instructor: As you also learned in Lesson 86, some parenthetical expressions do have a grammatical relationship to the rest of the sentence. But other parenthetical expressions, like these, are just as free-floating as an interjection or a noun of direct address.

Most free-floating parenthetical expressions could be set off with parentheses instead of commas. But very short expressions like the ones above are usually set off with commas. Read the next rule out loud.

→ *Student: Short parenthetical expressions such as the following are usually set off by commas: in short, in fact, in reality, as it were, as it happens, no doubt, in a word, to be sure, to be brief, after all, you know, of course.*

Instructor: You've now learned about three elements of sentences that are *free floating* and don't have a clear grammatical connection to the rest of the sentence: interjections, nouns of direct address, and some parenthetical expressions. When you diagram these parts of sentences, you place interjections and nouns of direct address on a separate line above the diagram, and parenthetical expressions on a separate line below. Examine all three diagrams in your workbook, and then diagram the next three sentences onto the frames provided.

Whew! That was a close one.

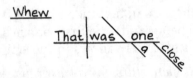

Friends, Romans, countrymen, lend me your ears!

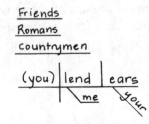

In a word, he supported the other candidate.

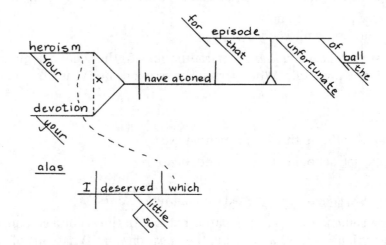

(The following sentences are taken from *The Scarlet Pimpernel*, by Baroness Emmuska Orczy.)

Your heroism, your devotion, which I, alas, so little deserved, have atoned for that unfortunate episode of the ball.

> **Note to Instructor:** The interjection *alas* is placed above the dependent adjective clause in which it occurs, rather than above the main clause (to which it has no relation). The phrase "for that episode . . ." could also be diagrammed as an adverb modifier, since "atone" can be either transitive or intransitive.

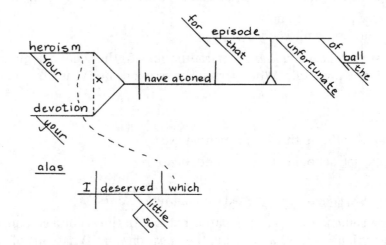

Do you impugn my bravery, Madame?

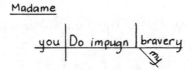

This restriction, of course, did not apply to her, and Frank would, of course, not dare to oppose her.

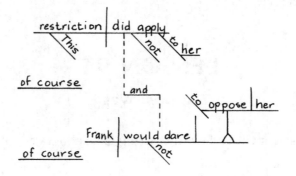

> **Note to Instructor:** Although "of" is a preposition, "of course" is not a prepositional phrase ("course" is not the object of the preposition); it is an idiomatic expression that needs to be diagrammed as though it were a single word.

Instructor: One caution, before you do your exercises. The parenthetical expressions listed in your workbook can also function as actual, essential, parts of a sentence. In this case, they probably won't have commas around them. Let's look at three examples. In the first pair of sentences, underline the subject once and the predicate twice.

> The storm will, no doubt, snarl the traffic.
> There is no doubt that the storm is coming.

Instructor: *No doubt* is parenthetical in the first sentence. In the second sentence, though, *doubt* is the subject, the linking verb *is* serves as the predicate, and *There* is an adverb. *That the storm is coming* is a noun clause, renaming *doubt*. What part of the sentence does the noun clause serve as?

→ *Student: Predicate nominative.*

Instructor: Underline the subjects and predicates in the second set of sentences.

> We aren't ready yet, you know.
> You know that we aren't ready yet.

Instructor: In the first sentence, *you know* is parenthetical. In the second sentence, *you* is the subject and *know* is the predicate. What part of the sentence does the noun clause *that we aren't ready yet* serve as?

→ *Student: Direct object.*

Instructor: Do the same with the third set of sentences.

> The snow caused school to be cancelled, of course.
>
> In case of snow, school is cancelled as a matter (of course)

Instructor: In the first sentence, *of course* is parenthetical. In the second sentence, *as a matter of course* is a prepositional phrase answering the question *how*. What part of speech does the prepositional phrase serve as?

→ *Student: Adverb.*

Instructor: Circle the phrase *of course*. Within the prepositional phrase *as a matter of course*, what does the shorter phrase *of course* modify?

→ *Student: Matter.*

Instructor: Instead of being a parenthetical expression, it is a prepositional phrase serving as an adjective. Draw a line from *of course* back to *matter*.

> Finish your exercises now.

— LESSON 94 —

Appositives

Instructor: Today's lesson starts with a few interesting facts about great cities. Take a minute to read those facts now.

When you are finished, underline the nickname for each city.

> Rome, <u>the Eternal City</u>, is built on seven hills that lie on both sides of the Tiber River.
> Dubrovnik, <u>the Pearl of the Adriatic</u>, is a walled seaside fortress in Croatia.
> Helsinki, <u>the White City of the North</u>, gets no sunshine at all for about fifty days every winter.
> In Mumbai, <u>the City of Dreams</u>, almost seven million people ride the trains every day.
> Chinese tin miners founded the Malaysian city Kuala Lumpur, <u>the Golden Triangle,</u> in 1857.
> The people of Sydney, <u>the Harbour City</u>, celebrate Harbour Day, a commemoration of the first convict ships landing in Sydney Cove, on January 26.

Instructor: Each one of these nicknames *renames* one of these great cities—but instead of following a linking verb, like a predicate nominative, these nicknames simply come right after the nouns they rename. We call names like this **appositives**. Read the definition from your workbook.

→ *Student: **An appositive is a noun, pronoun, or noun phrase that usually follows another noun and renames or explains it.***

Instructor: The simplest appositives are just single nouns. Read me the three examples that come next in your workbook.

→ *Student: Rome's first ruler, Romulus, killed his brother and seized power. In the Middle Ages, many Spanish Jews, Conversos, migrated to Dubrovnik. A 1981 movie about the USSR, Reds, was actually filmed in Helsinki.*

Instructor: What is another name for Rome's first ruler?

→ *Student: Romulus.*

Instructor: For Spanish Jews?

→ *Student: Conversos.*

Instructor: For the 1981 movie?

→ *Student: Reds.*

Instructor: *Romulus, Conversos,* and *Reds* are all single noun appositives. But an appositive can also be a noun phrase—a noun along with its modifiers—like *The White City of the North.* In that appositive phrase, what is the central noun that renames *Helsinki*?

→ *Student: City.*

Instructor: *White* is an adjective that describes *City,* and *the* is an article that describes *City.* What is *of the North*?

→ *Student: A prepositional phrase acting as an adjective* OR *A prepositional phrase describing City.*

Instructor: Appositives "float," like interjections, nouns of direct address, and parenthetical expressions. There's no grammatical element that connects them to the rest of the sentence. In fact, if you delete them completely, it makes no difference to the sentence's meaning. Read the next three sentences out loud.

→ *Student: Rome is built on seven hills that lie on both sides of the Tiber River. Dubrovnik is a walled seaside fortress in Croatia. Helsinki gets no sunshine at all for about 50 days every winter.*

Instructor: Without the appositive phrases *the Eternal City, the Pearl of the Adriatic,* and *the White City of the North,* these sentences still make perfect sense.

When you diagram an appositive noun, place it in parentheses after the noun it renames or explains. The parentheses show that the appositive isn't necessary. Examine the diagram in your workbook. *Romulus*, the appositive, follows the noun *ruler* on the subject line. But notice where the adjectives *Rome's* and *first* are diagrammed. They modify *ruler*. Where are they placed?

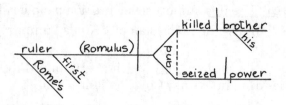

→ *Student: Under the noun* ruler.

Instructor: When you diagram an appositive, make sure that any modifiers describing the original noun are attached to the diagram space where that noun sits—and place modifiers that describe the appositive beneath the appositive's space.

In the next two sentences, the nouns that take appositives aren't subjects—they are playing other parts in the sentences. Diagram each sentence onto the frame provided.

In Mumbai, the City of Dreams, almost seven million people ride the trains every day.

> **Note to Instructor:** *Seven million* is a single compound adjective, since removing either *seven* or *million* completely changes the meaning of the adjective.

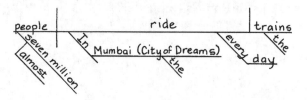

Chinese tin miners founded the Malaysian city Kuala Lumpur, the Golden Triangle, in 1857.

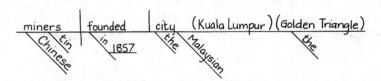

Instructor: In the first sentence, what part of the sentence is *Mumbai*?

→ *Student: Object of the preposition.*

Instructor: The prepositional phrase *in Mumbai* as a whole functions as an adverb, answering the question *where*. Where is the article *the* diagrammed?

→ *Student: Beneath* City of Dreams.

Instructor: In the second sentence, what part of the sentence is *Kuala Lumpur*?

→ *Student: Direct object.*

Instructor: Where is the article *the* diagrammed?

→ *Student: Beneath* Golden Triangle.

Instructor: Read me the rule about appositives one more time.

→ Student: *An appositive is a noun, pronoun, or noun phrase that usually follows another noun and renames or explains it.*

Instructor: Let's talk briefly about that adverb *usually*. Almost all the time, an appositive will follow the noun it renames or explains—particularly when the appositive is just one noun, or a noun and one article. But when an appositive is a noun phrase, it *can* come first.

In the following three sentences, the whole first phrase, set off by a comma, is an appositive. Circle the appositive phrases and write *A* (for appositive) above the central noun that renames the subject. Then, in the main clauses, underline each subject once and predicate twice.

(The wisest philosopher of the ancients,) Socrates wrote nothing.

(A better-known destination,) Marseilles is less picturesque than the surrounding villages.

(An ancient breed,) the Kuvasz protects helpless livestock.

Instructor: This can be a little tricky—because in all three of these sentences, the subject *could* easily become the appositive! Read me the next rule.

→ Student: **Appositives are set off by commas.**

Instructor: In the next three sentences, the appositives are set off by commas. Underline the subject once and the predicate twice.

The wisest philosopher of the ancients, Socrates, wrote nothing.

A better-known destination, Marseilles, is less picturesque than the surrounding villages.

An ancient breed, the Kuvasz, protects helpless livestock.

Instructor: In these versions of the sentences, what are the three appositives?

→ Student: *Socrates, Marseilles, and Kuvasz.*

Instructor: Putting commas on *both* sides of these nouns turns them from subjects into appositives! Read the explanation of how appositives are set off by commas from your workbook.

→ Student: *An appositive that occurs within a sentence has commas both before and after it. An appositive at the beginning of a sentence has one comma that follows it. An appositive at the end of a sentence has one comma that precedes it.*

Instructor: You will see examples of all three kinds of punctuation in the three sentences that follow. Underline each appositive or appositive phrase, and circle the comma or commas that set it off.

My grandfather, Aquilino Ramos, makes the best pork adobo I've ever eaten.
The best supper ever, pineapple chicken adobo waited for us on the table.
My grandfather prepared a fantastic meal, squid adobo with tomatoes.

Instructor: Now read me the full rule governing appositives from your workbook.

→ Student: **An appositive is a noun, pronoun, or noun phrase that usually follows another noun and renames or explains it. Appositives are set off by commas.**

Instructor: Complete your exercises now.

Note to Instructor: Just to complicate matters, one-word appositives in very short sentences are occasionally written without commas (My friend Jane is a gymnast). However, it is never incorrect to write appositives with commas (My friend, Jane, is a gymnast.) And it can often be incorrect to write even a short appositive without commas.

INCORRECT: The secretary Jim was late to the meeting.

CORRECT: The secretary, Jim, was late to the meeting.

So I suggest that you teach the student to always use commas around appositives. She will learn exceptions during her high school study of rhetoric.

— LESSON 95 —

Appositives
Intensive and Reflexive Pronouns
Noun Clauses in Apposition
Object Complements

Instructor: All the way back in Lesson 57, you learned about the eight pronouns listed in your workbook. Read that list to me.

→ Student: *Myself, himself, herself, itself, yourself, yourselves, ourselves, themselves.*

Instructor: You learned that these pronouns can function in two ways. They can be either *reflexive* or *intensive.* Read those two definitions out loud.

→ Student: *Reflexive pronouns refer back to the subject. Intensive pronouns emphasize a noun or another pronoun.*

Instructor: A reflexive pronoun refers back to the subject—but it also acts as an essential part of the sentence. Look at the next sentences in your workbook. (They come from the novel *The Idiot,* by Fyodor Dostoyevsky.) In the first sentence, underline the subject once and the predicate twice.

                               R DO
      I <u>may have expressed</u> myself badly.

Instructor: What did *I* express?

→ Student: *Myself.*

Instructor: *Myself* is a reflexive pronoun acting as the direct object of the sentence. Label it with an *R* and a *DO.*

    Now read me the second sentence.

→ Student: *I myself was never top in anything!*

Instructor: Underline the subject once and the predicate twice.

      I myself <u>was</u> never top in anything!

Instructor: In this sentence, *myself* isn't reflexive. In fact, it's not functioning as an essential part of the sentence. It's simply renaming the subject *I* in order to emphasize it. So what kind of pronoun is this?

→ Student: *An intensive pronoun.*

Instructor: Intensive pronouns function exactly like appositives—except that they're pronouns instead of nouns! Review the definition of an appositive by reading it out loud.

→ Student: *An appositive is a noun, pronoun, or noun phrase that usually follows another noun and renames or explains it. Appositives are set off by commas.*

Instructor: Just like appositives, intensive pronouns follow nouns and rename them, but without commas. They are even diagrammed just like appositives. Look at the three diagrams in your workbook. In the first sentence, where is the reflexive pronoun *myself* diagrammed?

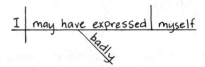

→ Student: *In the direct object space OR After the verb.*

Instructor: In the second sentence, where is the intensive pronoun *myself* diagrammed?

→ Student: *In parentheses after the subject.*

Instructor: In the third sentence, where is the appositive *Fyodor Dostoyevsky* diagrammed?

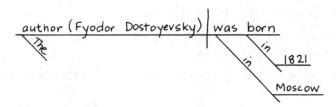

→ Student: *In parentheses after the subject.*

Instructor: Before we go on, complete Exercise 95A in your workbook.

Instructor: An appositive can be a noun or a noun phrase—but sometimes a dependent clause can also stand in for an appositive. Read me the rule in your workbook.

→ Student: **A dependent clause can act as an appositive if it renames the noun that it follows.**

Instructor: The next sentence in your workbook illustrates this rule. What is the argument in the article?

→ Student: *That studying grammar is good for your brain.*

Instructor: *That studying grammar is good for your brain* doesn't *describe* the argument—it *is* the argument. The dependent clause renames the argument, so it is acting like an appositive.

Look carefully at the diagram in your workbook.

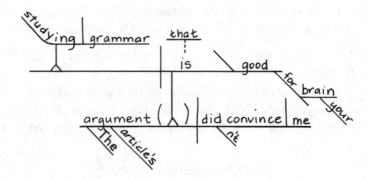

Instructor: You can see that the entire dependent clause is placed in a tree that's in the appositive space, between the parentheses. What is the subject of the dependent clause?

→ Student: *Studying grammar.*

Instructor: What kind of phrase is that?

→ Student: *A participle phrase.*

Instructor: Since the participle phrase is acting like a noun and serving as the subject, it is diagrammed on a tree that goes in the subject space of the dependent clause. *That* is diagrammed on a separate line because it only makes the clause subordinate—it doesn't serve a grammatical role within the clause itself.

In the second sentence, what is the dependent clause?

→ Student: *That we left early and didn't stop on the way.*

Instructor: "That we left early and didn't stop on the way" *is* the story. The clause is acting as an appositive because it *renames* the noun *story.*

Take a minute now and diagram the second sentence onto the frame provided.

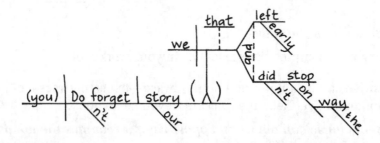

Instructor: A dependent clause that acts as an appositive is a *noun clause,* because it takes the place of a noun. It's easy to confuse a noun clause acting as an appositive with an adjective clause! Review the three definitions in your workbook by reading them out loud.

→ Student: *Dependent clauses can act as adjective clauses, adverb clauses, or noun clauses. An adjective clause is a dependent clause that acts as an adjective in a sentence, modifying a noun or pronoun in the independent clause. Relative pronouns introduce adjective clauses and refer back to an antecedent in the independent clause. A noun clause takes the place of a noun. Noun clauses can be introduced by relative pronouns, relative adverbs, or subordinating conjunctions.*

Instructor: The next sentence contains an adjective clause, not a noun clause acting as an appositive. Circle the adjective clause and draw a line back to the noun it modifies.

Reread the story that made you happy.

Instructor: You can tell that this is an adjective clause, not a noun clause acting as an appositive, in two ways. First, the clause *that made you happy* could refer to the story—or to a song, or to a chocolate-frosted piece of cake! The clause doesn't *rename* the story—it *describes* it, in the same way that it might describe something *else* that makes you happy. An appositive is *equal* to the noun it renames, so it can't be paired with other nouns as well.

Second, you can tell that this is an adjective clause because *that* isn't just a subordinating conjunction—it's a relative pronoun that refers back to *story* AND has an important grammatical function in the clause. Take a minute now and diagram the sentence onto the frame provided.

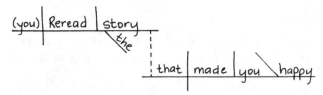

Instructor: Within the adjective clause *that made you happy*, what part of the clause is the relative pronoun *that*?

→ *Student: The subject.*

Instructor: *That* refers back to *story,* but also acts as the subject of the clause. *Made* is the predicate, and *you* is the direct object. *Happy* is the object complement. Review the definition of an object complement by reading it out loud.

→ *Student: An object complement follows the direct object and renames or describes it.*

Instructor: *Happy* follows the direct object *you* and describes it, so it is placed on the same line as the direct object, with a slanted line pointing back towards the noun it describes.

There's one more wrinkle you might see with appositives. An appositive can be a noun or noun phrase, or it can be a noun clause. But sometimes, an appositive will be a noun or noun phrase—which is then followed by an *adjective* clause! Look carefully at the next sentence in your workbook. Underline the subject once and the predicate twice.

The <u>story</u>, a long boring tale that seemed to go on forever, <u>took</u> up most of the evening.

Instructor: In this sentence, a four-word noun phrase renames, or explains, the *story.* What is the story? (Answer in four words.)

→ *Student: A long boring tale.*

Instructor: The dependent clause *that seemed to go on forever* tells you *what kind* of long boring tale it is. So this clause acts as an adjective modifying the *appositive,* and the appositive itself renames the subject. Diagram this sentence onto the frame provided, and notice where the dotted line connecting the relative pronoun *that* to its antecedent is placed.

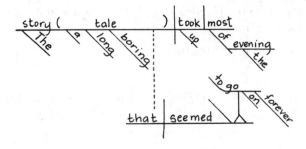

Instructor: Complete the remaining two exercises now.

— LESSON 96 —

Appositives
Noun Clauses in Apposition
Absolute Constructions

Instructor: The five sentences in your workbook are all from Agatha Christie's classic mystery novel *The Mysterious Affair at Styles.* One word (in two different forms) appears in every single one of those sentences. What is that word?

→ *Student: Absolute [absolutely].*

Instructor: Take a few minutes to look at those sentences. In each one, cross out the word *absolute* or *absolutely* and write a synonym above it. You may use a thesaurus if necessary.

> **Note to Instructor:** Suggested answers are in brackets below; accept any reasonable answers.

[completely, truly, definitely, honestly, very, unequivocally, definitely, utterly, entirely, totally]
I am absolutely serious, my friend.

[completely, truly, definitely, honestly, very, unequivocally, definitely, utterly, entirely, totally]
The whole story is absolutely untrue.

[completely, truly, definitely, honestly, very, unequivocally, definitely, utterly, entirely, totally]
There is absolutely no question as to the alibi!

[complete, outright, pure, utter, thorough, definite, out-and-out, total]
He appeared to be in an absolute frenzy.

[completely, truly, definitely, honestly, very, unequivocally, definitely, utterly, entirely, totally]
Her face and voice were absolutely cold and expressionless.

Instructor: When we use the word *absolutely* or *absolute,* we mean "total, complete, definitive, entire." The last floating element we're going to examine this week is called an *absolute construction.* It's a group of words that doesn't stand by itself as a complete sentence—but also isn't connected, grammatically, to the rest of the sentence. It is *totally, completely, definitively* separate.

Compare the next two sentences. In the first sentence, underline the subject once and the predicate twice. Then, circle the participle phrase "having no near relations or friends."

(Having no near relations or friends) I was trying to make up my mind what to do, when I ran across John Cavendish.

Instructor: Who has no near relations or friends?

→ *Student: I OR The subject.*

Instructor: Draw a line from the circle to *I.* The participle phrase is acting as an adjective describing *I.* But now look at the second sentence. Again, underline the subject once and the predicate twice. Circle the beginning participle phrase.

(Our efforts having been in vain) we had abandoned the matter.

Instructor: This sentence makes perfect sense. *Our efforts having been in vain* is the *cause* of *we had abandoned the matter.* But the participle phrase isn't an adjective—it doesn't modify *we* or *matter.* It isn't an adverb—it doesn't modify *had abandoned.* It doesn't modify *anything* in the main sentence! It is an **absolute construction**.

We say that an absolute construction has a *semantic* relationship, rather than a *grammatical* relationship, to the rest of the sentence. *Semantic* comes from the Greek word for *having meaning.* Read me the definition of *semantic* in your workbook.

→ Student: *Semantic: having to do with meaning.*

Instructor: Now read the definition of an absolute construction.

→ Student: **An absolute construction has a strong semantic relationship but no grammatical connection to the rest of the sentence.**

Instructor: Other kinds of phrases can also serve as absolute constructions. The next three sentences, also from *The Mysterious Affair at Styles,* have four different kinds of absolute constructions. In the first, circle the absolute construction *to tell the truth.* What kind of phrase is this?

(To tell the truth,) an idea, wild and extravagant in itself, had once or twice that morning flashed through my brain.

→ Student: *An infinitive phrase.*

Instructor: This phrase is semantically connected to the entire rest of the sentence—all the rest of the sentence is *the truth,* but it isn't grammatically connected to any particular word. Notice that *wild and extravagant in itself* is *not* an absolute construction. What does it modify?

→ Student: *The idea.*

Instructor: It is an adjective phrase answering the question *what kind. Once or twice* is also not an absolute construction. It is an adverb phrase answering the question *when.* What does it modify?

→ Student: *Flashed.*

Instructor: In the next sentence, circle the absolute construction *his grave bearded face unchanged.* This construction is almost acting like an adjective—it's describing something about Dr. Bauerstein—but *face* can't be an adjective. It can only be a noun. And this can't be a dependent clause acting as an adjective, because there's no subordinating word, and there's no predicate—*unchanged* is a past participle acting as an adjective and describing *face.* So this too is an absolute construction.

Dr. Bauerstein remained in the background, (his grave bearded face unchanged)

Instructor: Let's look at the third sentence. Circle the words *as the saying goes.*

He has lived by his wits (as the <u>saying goes</u>).

Instructor: This is another abstract construction, but unlike the last one, it *is* a dependent clause! It just doesn't modify any particular word in the main clause. Underline the subject of the dependent clause once and the predicate twice. Write *S* above the subordinating word.

Now, examine the first diagram.

To tell the truth, an idea, wild and extravagant in itself, had once or twice that morning flashed through my brain.

Instructor: Where is the absolute construction *to tell the truth* diagrammed?

→ *Student: Above the sentence.*

Instructor: Just like parenthetical expressions, absolute constructions are diagrammed separately from the main sentence—but usually parenthetical expressions go below the sentence, while absolute constructions go above. That's supposed to remind you that absolute constructions are *more* important to the sentence than parenthetical expressions.

Place the next two sentences on to the frames provided.

Dr. Bauerstein remained in the background, his grave bearded face unchanged.

He has lived by his wits, as the saying goes.

Instructor: You'll see more absolute constructions in the weeks to come! For now, finish your exercises.

— REVIEW 8 —

The review exercises and answers are found in the Student Workbook and accompanying Key.

Complex Verb Tenses

— LESSON 97 —

Verb Tense, Voice, and Mood
Tense Review (Indicative)
Progressive Perfect Tenses (Indicative)

Instructor: A few weeks ago, you learned that verbs have three different qualities, or aspects, or attributes: they have tense, they have voice, and they have mood. Mood is the trickiest of the qualities. It doesn't mean that verbs are grumpy, cheerful, or depressed; it means that they are indicative, subjunctive, imperative, or modal.

Each one of the four sentences in your workbook illustrates one of these moods. Without looking ahead at the definitions, see if you can identify the *mood* of each underlined verb.

> **Note to Instructor:** If the student has difficulty, allow her to look ahead at the definitions.

(The following sentences are from Beverly Cleary's novel *Fifteen*.)

He spoke rapidly, as if he <u>were</u> anxious to get the words out of the way.
Mood: ___subjunctive___

And <u>be</u> home by ten thirty.
Mood: ___imperative___

To hide her discomfort she <u>took</u> small bites of ice cream.
Mood: ___indicative___

<u>Should</u> they <u>talk</u> awhile, or <u>should</u> she <u>suggest</u> that they leave, or <u>should</u> she <u>wait</u> for him to suggest it?
Mood: ___modal___

Instructor: Now read the definitions of each mood out loud.

→ Student: **Indicative verbs express real actions. Subjunctive verbs express unreal actions. Imperative verbs express intended actions. Modal verbs express possible actions.**

Instructor: Verbs have *mood*, but they also have *voice*: active and passive. The next sentences in your workbook illustrate both voices. In the blanks, identify the mood and voice of the underlined verbs.

Here everything looked brand-new, as if the furniture <u>had been delivered</u> only the day before.
Mood: ___subjunctive___
Voice: ___passive___

> Now the fat pug dog <u>rose</u> and <u>shook</u> himself, scattering his hair over the carpet.
> Mood: <u>indicative</u>
> Voice: <u>active</u>

Instructor: Read the definition of each voice out loud.

→ *Student: In a sentence with an active verb, the subject performs the action. In a sentence with a passive verb, the subject receives the action.*

Instructor: And now for the final piece of the verb puzzle—tense! You've learned nine different tenses—forms that tell you *when* a verb happened. Review the definitions of simple, progressive, and perfect tenses by reading them out loud to me.

→ *Student: A simple verb simply tells whether an action takes place in the past, present, or future. A progressive verb describes an ongoing or continuous action. A perfect verb describes an action which has been completed before another action takes place.*

Instructor: Each one of these three kinds of tenses can be put into the past, the present, or the future—which means that you've learned *nine* different tenses so far. Today, we're just going to focus on the indicative tenses. Complete Exercise 97A in order to review the nine tenses you already know.

Instructor: There are actually 12 tenses in English. The last three tenses are a combination of the perfect and progressive tenses. Read the definition in your workbook out loud.

→ *Student: **A progressive perfect verb describes an ongoing or continuous action that has a definite end.***

Instructor: Imagine that, early this morning, you ran three miles and then you came in for breakfast. If you wanted to put this in the perfect past, you would say, "I had run three miles at dawn." That just describes the completed action. If you wanted to put this in the progressive past, you would say, "I was running for half an hour before breakfast." That describes the ongoing action of your running. But if you wanted to describe the ongoing action *and* the point at which the action ended, you would use the progressive perfect past. You would say, "I had been running for half an hour before I decided to stop."

Look at the three sentences about running in your workbook. I just read you the past of the progressive perfect—it expresses that an action went on in the past for some time, and then stopped in the past. Read me the progressive perfect present sentence about your running.

→ *Student: I have been running all morning.*

Instructor: This expresses that an action began in the past (before the present moment) and is continuing on into the present. Read me the progressive perfect future sentence.

→ *Student: I will have been running for an hour by the time you arrive.*

Instructor: This expresses that an action will go on for some time in the future, *before* another action happens!

Progressive perfect is a complicated tense! The next three sets of sentences illustrate the past, present, and future of all four tense types: simple, progressive, perfect, and progressive perfect. Read me all four past sentences.

→ *Student: I rejoiced over my grammar! I was rejoicing over my grammar. I had rejoiced over my grammar. I had been rejoicing over my grammar, until I realized I had done the wrong exercises.*

Instructor: Notice that in the progressive perfect past, the rejoicing went on for some time—and then stopped at a definite point in the past! Read me all four present sentences.

→ *Student: I enjoy this schoolwork! I am enjoying this schoolwork. I have enjoyed this schoolwork. I have been enjoying this schoolwork, but unfortunately I have to stop now and go play Minecraft.*

Instructor: Notice that in the progressive perfect present, the enjoying has been going on for some time—and is still going on, but is now stopping at a definite point in the present! Read me all four future sentences.

→ *Student: I will expect to receive a prize! All afternoon, I will be expecting to receive a prize. By dinner time, I will have expected to receive my prize. By dinner time, I will have been expecting to receive a prize for at least four hours.*

Instructor: Notice that in the progressive perfect future, the expecting goes on for a continuous time in the future—and then stops at a definite point in the future (dinner time).

All of these are in the indicative mood and in the active voice. Just for your information— there *is* such a thing as a progressive perfect passive verb, but you won't see it very often. To form a passive, you use the past participle of the verb and add the helping verb *being*. Underline the complete verb phrase in each of the following sentences.

> PROGRESSIVE PERFECT PAST
> *Active*   The house <u>had been showing</u> signs of wear.
> *Passive*   The house <u>had been being shown</u> to prospective buyers for months.
>
> PROGRESSIVE PERFECT PRESENT
> *Active*   I <u>have been sending</u> letters out every day.
> *Passive*   I <u>have been being sent</u> to the post office by my mother every day.
>
> PROGRESSIVE PERFECT FUTURE
> *Active*   Come June, the professors <u>will have been teaching</u> Latin for two years.
> *Passive*   Come June, the students <u>will have been being taught</u> Latin for two years.

Instructor: The chart in your workbook shows how the progressive perfect tenses are formed.

Instructor: Use the chart for reference as you complete your exercises.

Here's one quick note: In modern English, the progressive perfect future passive is disappearing. We tend to drop *being* from the passive form of the progressive perfect future tense, so that it just sounds like a plain old perfect future. It probably sounds more natural for you to say, "Come June, the students will have been taught Latin for two years." The context tells you that the teaching was progressive, not the verb. You'll see examples in your workbook.

It isn't incorrect to drop *being*, but in your exercises, be sure to use the complete progressive perfect future passive form, including *being*.

Complete your exercises now.

— LESSON 98 —

Simple Present and Perfect Present Modal Verbs
Progressive Present and Progressive Perfect Present Modal Verbs

Instructor: You have studied all 12 tenses in both voices—active *and* passive—in the indicative mood. But in the other moods, you've only studied a few tenses. Over the next three days, we're going to review the remaining moods—and look at all of the tenses and both voices in each one.

Today, we'll work on the modal voice. Read me the definition of a modal verb.

→ *Student: Modal verbs express situations that have not actually happened.*

Instructor: There are seven helping verbs that we combine with other verbs to create *modal verbs.* Read me the list of those verbs.

→ *Student: Should, would, may, might, must, can, could.*

Instructor: You have already learned that modal verbs can express *possibility, obligation, permission,* and *ability.* Take a moment now to go through the list in your workbook. Fill in the sentences in the blanks with the appropriate helping verbs.

> **Note to Instructor:** Within each kind of situation, the student may choose different helping verbs than the originals, as long as the sentences make sense. Encourage the student not to use the same verb repeatedly.

Would, may, might, can, could: **possibility**

He was afraid that, in a little while, death _would_ meet him.

I fear that we _may_ never see him in this life again.

Oh, that I _might_ strike a blow for him before I die!

Only a knight of true valor _could_ hope to win.

Madam, how then _can_ I help you?

Must, should: **obligation**

I _must_ find a man whom I can truly love.

You _should_ do homage to King Arthur for your kingdom.

May: **permission**

May I go to Camelot, to see the jousting?

Can: **ability**

Nothing _can_ heal his wound on this side of the water.

Instructor: You have already learned *two* modal tenses: the simple present and the perfect present, both in the active voice. The modal simple present is formed with one of the seven helping verbs and the first person singular form of the main verb. Read me the simple present conjugation, active, of the modal verb *help.*

→ *Student: I could help; you could help; he could help; we could help; you could help; they could help.*

Instructor: The modal perfect present, active, is formed with one of the seven helping verbs, the additional helping verb *have,* and the past participle of the main verb. Read me the perfect present conjugation of the modal verb *help.*

→ *Student: I should have helped; you should have helped; she should have helped; we should have helped; you should have helped; they should have helped.*

Instructor: Modal verbs only have two more tenses—the progressive present, and the progressive perfect present. So modal verbs don't have 12 tenses. How many do they have?

→ *Student: Four.*

Instructor: Look at the chart in your workbook. What are the two simple present forms, active and passive?

→ *Student: I should help. I should be helped.*

Instructor: What are the two progressive present forms?

→ *Student: I could be helping. I could be being helped.*

Instructor: What are the two perfect present forms?

→ *Student: I would have helped. I would have been helped.*

Instructor: What are the two progressive perfect present forms?

→ *Student: I might have been helping. I might have been being helped.*

Instructor: All modal verbs are in some form of the *present:* whether that's simple, progressive, perfect, or progressive perfect. That's because modal verbs really don't have any past or future. They express actions that *haven't happened.* And if you talk about something that's happened in the simple past, or progressive past, or perfect past, it has already happened. It can't be modal. If you talk about something that will happen in the future, it hasn't happened by definition. So there's no such thing as a future modal verb either.

Read me the rule about when to use the simple present or progressive present.

→ *Student: **Use the simple present or progressive present when the situation isn't happening in the present.***

Instructor: The next two sentences have both indicative and modal verbs in them. Fill in the tense and voice of each verb.

Since I <u>slept</u> badly last night, I <u>might go</u> take a nap.

mood	indicative		modal
tense	simple present		simple present
voice	active		actice

People <u>are being left</u> in the hospital when they <u>could be being nursed</u> at home.

mood	indicative		modal
tense	progressive present		progressive present
voice	passive		actice

Instructor: Read me the rule about when to use the perfect present or progressive perfect present.

→ *Student: **Use the perfect present or the progressive perfect present when the situation didn't happen in the past.***

Instructor: The next two sentences have both indicative and modal verbs in them. Fill in the mood, tense, and voice of each modal verb.

I <u>was eating</u> cheese and crackers when I <u>could have been sitting</u> down to a big juicy steak.

mood	indicative		modal
tense	progressive past		progressive perfect present
voice	active		active

While the floors <u>were being scrubbed</u>, I <u>could have vacuumed</u> the rugs.

mood	indicative		modal
tense	progressive past		perfect present
voice	passive		active

Instructor: Your workbook has two simple formulas for you to remember. Read them to me now.

→ *Student: Modal Present: Simple or Progressive. Modal Past: Perfect or Progressive Perfect.*

Instructor: The chart in your workbook shows how each modal tense is formed. Use the chart to complete your exercises now.

— LESSON 99 —

Modal Verb Tenses
The Imperative Mood
The Subjunctive Mood
More Subjunctive Tenses

Instructor: Now you've learned 12 indicative tenses and four modal tenses. There are only two moods left: imperative and subjunctive. Review the four tenses by reading the definitions in your workbook out loud.

→ *Student: Indicative verbs express real actions. Subjunctive verbs express unreal actions. Imperative verbs express intended actions. Modal verbs express possible actions.*

Instructor: We'll start with the imperative mood, since it's simpler. The imperative mode only has one tense: the present. But that active tense has two voices: active and passive. Read the next three sentences out loud.

→ *Student: Turn to the end of your book. Eat more vegetables! Go away.*

Instructor: *Turn, eat,* and *go* are all present, active, imperative verbs. The understood subject, *you,* is being commanded, in the present, to perform each action. But in the next sentence, the present imperative verb is passive. Read me the next sentence.

→ *Student: Be checked by a doctor before you come back to work.*

Instructor: Is the understood subject, *you,* doing the checking?

→ *Student: No.*

Instructor: The doctor is doing the checking; the subject, *you,* is receiving the action. So this is a passive imperative. Read the rule about forming the present passive imperative.

→ *Student: **The present passive imperative is formed by adding the helping verb** be **to the past participle of the verb.***

Instructor: You won't see present passive imperatives very often, but you should know that they exist.

Now you've studied, in the active *and* passive voices, eight modal tenses, 12 indicative tenses, and one imperative tense. Let's finish up by looking at the subjunctive. Read me the full definition of the subjunctive mood.

→ *Student: **Subjunctive verbs express situations that are unreal, wished for, or uncertain.***

Instructor: When you first studied subjunctive verbs, you learned that present subjunctive verbs often look just like the present indicative forms. You know that they are subjunctive only from context.

Look at the two sentences in your book. The first is taken from the autobiography of the Apache leader Geronimo. Circle the subjunctive verb and underline the indicative verb.

If we kept our ponies up in the winter time, we gave them fodder to eat.

Instructor: Now look at the second version of the sentence. Underline both verbs.

We kept our ponies up in the winter time, and we gave them fodder to eat.

Instructor: Both of them are indicative. Notice that there is no difference between the simple past subjunctive of the verb *keep,* and the simple past indicative of the same verb.

But state-of-being verbs don't behave in the same way. In the present and past subjunctive tenses, they are different from their indicative forms. You've already learned the simple present and simple past subjunctive tenses for state-of-being verbs. Read the simple present conjugation in your workbook.

→ *Student: I be; you be; he, she, it be; we be; you be; they be.*

Instructor: Underline the simple present subjunctive verb in the sentence that follows.

Should you <u>be</u> in town, come by and see me.

Instructor: Now read the simple past subjunctive conjugation.

→ *Student: I were; you were; he, she, it, were; we were; you were; they were.*

Instructor: Underline the simple past subjunctive verb in the sentence that follows.

If I <u>were</u> a bird, I would fly across the water.

Instructor: Now let's review the subjunctive forms of active verbs. You have already learned the simple present active and passive. Read me the simple present active conjugation.

→ *Student: I leave; you leave; he, she, it leave; we leave; you leave; they leave.*

Instructor: This is different from the indicative only in the third person singular form. Read the first sentence below the conjugation.

→ *Student: He leaves early to avoid traffic.*

Instructor: *He leaves* is indicative. Read the second sentence.

→ *Student: I suggest that he leave early to avoid traffic.*

Instructor: *He leave* is subjunctive. Now read me the rule that governs the simple present *passive* subjunctive.

→ *Student: **The present passive subjunctive is formed by pairing** be **with the past participle of a verb.***

Instructor: Read the simple present subjunctive passive conjugation out loud.

→ *Student: I be left; you be left; he, she, it be left; we be left; you be left, they be left.*

Instructor: In the sentence *The tent was left behind*, what mood is the simple present passive verb *was left*?

→ *Student: Indicative.*

Instructor: In the sentence *The guide recommended that the tent be left behind*, what mood is the simple present passive verb *be left*?

→ *Student: Subjunctive.*

Instructor: Let's take a few minutes now to look at the remaining subjunctive tenses. We've done simple present, so we'll move on to simple past. The simple past subjunctive, active, is identical to the indicative. Read me the first sentence below the conjugations.

→ *Student: If I left early, I might be able to pick up the milk.*

Instructor: *Left* is subjunctive. Read the second sentence.

→ *Student: I left early to pick up the milk.*

Instructor: *Left* is indicative. However, the simple past subjunctive is different in the passive voice. Read me the simple past subjunctive, passive.

→ *Student: I were left; you were left; he, she, it were left; we were left; you were left; they were left.*

Instructor: If this were an indicative verb, the bolded helping verbs would be *was* instead of *were.* In the next pair of sentences, read me the sentence with two indicative verbs in it.

→ *Student: I was left behind, which made me very upset.*

Instructor: Now read me the sentence with one subjunctive and one modal verb in it.

→ *Student: If I were left behind, I would be very upset.*

Instructor: There is no future subjunctive in English. If you want to talk about something unreal in the future, you don't use a future subjunctive—instead, you use an infinitive along with the simple past subjunctive state-of-being verb. Read me that rule and the sentence that follows.

→ *Student:* **Use the simple past subjunctive state-of-being verb, plus an infinitive, to express a future unreal action.** *If I were to die tomorrow, I would have no regrets.*

Instructor: Now let's look at the progressive tenses. Technically speaking, the progressive present subjunctive should be *I be leaving, you be leaving, he be leaving,* and so on. But that form is dying out. You will only see it in books written at least 50 (or more) years ago, where you might read things like, *If I be running late, I must throw myself upon your kind mercies.* Today, we just use the indicative forms for both the active and passive forms of the progressive present. Underline the subjunctive verbs in the next three sentences.

> If I <u>be running</u> late, I must throw myself upon your kind mercies.
> If I <u>am running</u> late, I will call you.
> It is unlikely that I <u>am being penalized</u>.

Instructor: *I am running* and *I am being penalized* are identical to the indicative forms.

The rest of the subjunctive tenses are the same as the indicative—EXCEPT for tenses that use the helping verb *was* in the indicative. In the subjunctive, *was* always becomes *were.* Read me both progressive past conjugations.

→ *Student: I were leaving; you were leaving; he, she, it were leaving; we were leaving; you were leaving; they were leaving. I were being left; you were being left; he, she, it were being left; we were being left; you were being left; they were being left.*

Instructor: The bolded forms would be *was* in the indicative. In the next two pairs of sentences, underline each subjunctive verb.

> If I <u>were running</u> in the race, I would certainly win.
> I was running in the race.

> If I <u>were being left</u> behind, I would make a huge fuss.
> I was being left behind.

Instructor: The perfect and progressive perfect subjunctive forms are just the same as the indicative—and none of the subjunctive tenses have a future. The conjugations of the verb *leave* in your workbook show this for your reference.

Now you have studied all 12 indicative tenses, all four modal tenses, the one imperative tense, and all eight subjunctive tenses. How many tenses is that in all?

→ *Student: Twenty-five.*

Instructor: And each tense has both an active and passive voice—so how many different verb forms is that?

→ *Student: Fifty.*

Instructor: That's probably why you feel so tired right now. But you still have to do your exercises.

—LESSON 100—

Review of Moods and Tenses
Conditional Sentences

Instructor: Now that you've learned 25 tenses, in two voices, in all four moods, let's review a kind of statement that makes use of all of them: conditional statements. Take a minute to read back through the three types of conditional statements that you studied in Lesson 83.

> **Note to Instructor:** If the student already understands conditional statements, you may allow him to review the following material silently. If he is still struggling with the concept, ask him to read all three definitions and all three sets of sentences aloud (even though this takes additional time).

First conditional sentences express circumstances that might actually happen. The predicate of the condition clause is in a present tense. The predicate of the consequence clause is an imperative or is in a present or future tense.

> If we surrender and I return with you, will you promise not to hurt this man?
> So bow down to her if you want, bow to her.
> If she is otherwise when I find her, I shall be very put out.
> Unless I am wrong (and I am never wrong), they are headed dead into the fire swamp.

Second conditional sentences express circumstances that are contrary to reality. The predicate of the condition clause is in a past tense. The predicate of the consequence clause is in the simple present modal tense.

> I would not say such things if I were you!
> If I had a month to plan, maybe I could come up with something.
> If we only had a wheelbarrow, that would be something.

Third conditional sentences express past circumstances that never happened. The predicate of the condition clause is in the perfect past tense. The predicate of the consequence clause is in the perfect present modal or simple present modal tense.

> But they would have killed Westley, if I hadn't done it.

Instructor: Now that you know all four modal tenses, we can make those last two definitions a little sharper. Look carefully at the definition of a second conditional sentence. In the final sentence, what is the predicate of the consequence clause in?

→ *Student: The simple present modal.*

Instructor: When you learned this definition, the simple present was the only modal present tense that you knew. But now you know that there is also a progressive present modal tense. And the predicate of the consequence clause can be in the simple present *or* the progressive present. Draw an insertion arrow and add *or progressive* after *the simple*.

Second conditional sentences express circumstances that are contrary to reality. The predicate of the condition clause is in a past tense.
                                                            or progressive
The predicate of the consequence clause is in the simple^present modal tense.

Instructor: Now read the entire definition out loud.

→ *Student: Second conditional sentences express circumstances that are contrary to reality. The predicate of the condition clause is in a past tense. The predicate of the consequence clause is in the simple or progressive present modal tense.*

Instructor: In the first pair of sentences that follow the definitions, underline the modal verb in each sentence.

> If I were you, I <u>would go</u> home.
> If I were you, I <u>would be dancing</u> with joy.

Instructor: Write *simple present modal* over the first verb, and *progressive present modal* over the second.

> simple present modal
> If I were you, I <u>would go</u> home.

> progressive present modal
> If I were you, I <u>would be dancing</u> with joy.

Instructor: We can also simplify the definition of a third conditional sentence. In your original definition, what two tenses could the predicate of the consequence clause be in?

→ *Student: The perfect present modal or simple present modal.*

Instructor: When you learned that definition, you hadn't learned about the progressive present or progressive perfect present modal tenses. Look down at the next set of four example sentences. Underline the modal verbs in each sentence.

> If I had been wrong, I <u>would say</u> so now.
> If I had been wrong, I <u>would be apologizing</u> with sincerity.
> If I had been wrong, I <u>would have said</u> so.
> If I had been wrong, I <u>would have been running</u> for my life.

Instructor: What tense is the first modal verb?

→ *Student: Simple present.*

Instructor: The second?

→ *Student: Progressive present.*

Instructor: The third?

→ *Student: Perfect present.*

Instructor: The fourth?

→ *Student: Progressive perfect present.*

Instructor: Those are all four of the modal tenses you've learned. In the last sentence of the third conditional sentence definition, cross out t*he perfect present modal or simple present* and write *any* above it.

> **The predicate of the consequence clause is in** ~~**the perfect present modal or simple present**~~ **modal tense.**
>   any

Instructor: Read the simplified definition out loud.

→ *Student: The predicate of the consequence clause is in any modal tense.*

Instructor: Now you've fine-tuned the definitions of the three types of conditional sentences. In your workbook, you'll see all three definitions, each one followed by examples. Take a minute now and parse each underlined verb by writing the mood, tense, and voice above it.

Note to Instructor: Since the indicative and subjunctive forms are identical in many cases, you may need to remind students that a verb expressing an unreal situation is in the subjunctive mood, even if it appears in form to be indicative.

Instructor: The examples in this lesson are adapted from Mary Shelley's *Frankenstein*.

First conditional sentences express circumstances that might actually happen.
The predicate of the condition clause is in a present tense.
The predicate of the consequence clause is an imperative or is in a present or future tense.

subjunctive simple   indicative simple
  present active   future active

If I <u>fail</u>, you <u>will see</u> me again soon, or never.

    subjunctive simple   imperative
      present active   present active

If you <u>believe</u> that she is innocent, <u>rely</u> on the justice of our laws.

     modal simple   modal simple
     present active   present active

If I <u>could bestow</u> animation upon lifeless matter, I <u>might renew</u> life.

Second conditional sentences express circumstances that are contrary to reality.
The predicate of the condition clause is in a past tense.
The predicate of the consequence clause is in the simple or progressive present modal tense.

         subjunctive   modal simple
       past perfect passive   present active

Unless such symptoms <u>had been shown</u> early, a sister or brother <u>could</u> never <u>suspect</u> the other of fraud.

    subjunctive simple   modal progressive
     past active   present active

If you <u>cherished</u> a desire of revenge against me, you <u>would be rejoicing</u> in my destruction

Third conditional sentences express past circumstances that never happened.
The predicate of the condition clause is in the perfect past tense.
The predicate of the consequence clause is in any modal tense.

    subjunctive perfect   modal perfect
     past active   present active

If she <u>had</u> earnestly <u>desired</u> it, I <u>should have</u> willingly <u>given</u> it to her.

    subjunctive perfect   modal simple
     past active   present active

If you <u>had known</u> me as I once was, you <u>would</u> not <u>recognize</u> me in this state of degradation.

     subjunctive perfect   modal perfect
      past passive   present active

If the voice of conscience <u>had been heeded</u>, Frankenstein <u>would</u> yet <u>have lived</u>.

Instructor: In your exercises, you'll continue to review conditional sentences—and you'll also work on identifying all of the indicative, subjunctive, imperative, and modal tenses you've learned. Complete those exercises now.

More Modifiers

—LESSON 101—

Adjective Review
Adjectives in the Appositive Position
Correct Comma Usage

Instructor: The first sentence in your workbook is one of the most famous in the English language. It is the opening of a novel by the English writer Edward Bulwer-Lytton. Read the sentence out loud.

→ Student: *It was a dark and stormy night; the rain fell in torrents, except at occasional intervals, when it was checked by a violent gust of wind which swept up the streets (for it is in London that our scene lies), rattling along the house-tops, and fiercely agitating the scanty flame of the lamps that struggled against the darkness.*

Instructor: Edward Bulwer-Lytton was famous for his flowery sentences filled with adjectives—like *dark, stormy, occasional, violent,* and *scanty.* Today, with Mr. Bulwer-Lytton's help, we'll review what you already know about adjectives—and learn a few new things as well.

Let's start with definitions. Read me the first five definitions.

→ Student: *An adjective modifies a noun or pronoun. Adjectives tell what kind, which one, how many, and whose. Descriptive adjectives tell what kind. A descriptive adjective becomes an abstract noun when you add -ness to it. Possessive adjectives tell whose.*

Instructor: *Dark, stormy, occasional, violent,* and *scanty* are all descriptive adjectives, answering the question *what kind.* Possessive adjectives answer the question *whose.* There are two kinds of possessive adjectives—adjectives formed from nouns and adjectives formed from pronouns. Let's start with nouns. Read me the next sentence.

→ Student: *Hastings kissed the duke's hand in silence.*

Instructor: Whose hand?

→ Student: *The duke's.*

Instructor: The noun *duke* (the name of a person) becomes an adjective modifying *hand.* Nouns become adjectives when they are made possessive. Take a minute to review the rules about forming possessives of nouns. Fill in the blank next to each noun with its correct possessive form.

> **Form the possessive of a singular noun by adding an apostrophe and the letter *s*.**
> duchess _____duchess's_____

> **Form the possessive of a plural noun ending in *-s* by adding an apostrophe only.**
> emperors _____emperors'_____

Form the possessive of a plural noun that does not end in -s as if it were a singular noun.

noblemen   <u>noblemen's</u>

Instructor: Now let's look at possessive adjectives formed from pronouns. Read me the next sentence. Don't giggle.

→ Student: *Since choice was mine, I chose the man love could not choose, and took this sad comfort to my heart.*

Instructor: Circle the possessive pronouns *mine* and *my*.

Since choice was (mine), I chose the man love could not choose, and took this sad comfort to (my) heart.

—From *The Last of the Barons*, by Edward Bulwer-Lytton

Instructor: Both of these pronouns refer back to the speaker. *Choice* and *heart* both belong to her. But the adjectives have different forms. Does *mine* come before or after the noun that it modifies?

→ Student: *After.*

Instructor: Does *my* come before or after the noun that it modifies?

→ Student: *Before.*

Instructor: All the way back in Lesson 4, you learned that when an adjective comes right before the noun it modifies, we say that it is in the *attributive position*. When it follows the noun, it is in the *predicative position*. You had to know the difference, because when a descriptive compound adjective is in the attributive position, it is usually hyphenated—and when it is in the predicative position, it usually isn't. In the next two sentences, identify the compound adjective *well known* as either attributive or predicative.

attributive

On the floor is the image of a dog in mosaic, with the well-known motto "Cave canem" upon it.

predicative

My name is well known, methinks, in Pompeii.

—From *The Last Days of Pompeii*, by Edward Bulwer-Lytton

Instructor: Compound adjectives change in form, depending on whether they come before or after the noun they modify—and so do the possessive pronouns that act as adjectives. Read the chart below out loud, reading first the attributive, and then the predicative version of each adjective.

→ Student: *My, mine; your, yours; his, her, its, his, hers, its; our, ours; your, yours; their, theirs.*

Instructor: In the next sentence, underline all of the descriptive adjectives, circle the abstract noun formed from a descriptive adjective, and draw a box around the possessive adjective.

The eyes were <u>soft</u>, <u>dark</u>, and <u>brilliant</u>, but <u>dreamlike</u> and <u>vague</u>; the features in youth must have been <u>regular</u> and <u>beautiful</u>, but [their] contour was now sharpened by the (hollowness) of the cheeks and temples.

—From *The Last of the Barons*, by Edward Bulwer-Lytton

Instructor: Let's talk a little more about adjectives in the attributive and predicative position. Go back up to the two sentences from *The Last Days of Pompeii*. In the second sentence, the one with the adjective in the predicative position, underline the *predicate* twice.

predicative
My name is well known, methinks, in Pompeii.
—From *The Last Days of Pompeii,* by Edward Bulwer-Lytton

Instructor: An adjective in the predicative position doesn't just come after the noun it modifies—it also comes after the predicate! Now look at the next sentence in your workbook. Underline every descriptive adjective in it.

His face was far less handsome than Marmaduke Nevile's, but infinitely more expressive, both of intelligence and command,—the features straight and sharp, the complexion clear and pale, and under the bright grey eyes a dark shade spoke either of dissipation or of thought.
—From *The Last of the Barons,* by Edward Bulwer-Lytton

Instructor: What position are the adjectives *bright, grey,* and *dark* in?

→ *Student: Attributive.*

Instructor: How about *handsome* and *expressive?*

→ *Student: Predicative.*

Instructor: *Handsome* and *expressive* are predicate adjectives, linked to the subject *face* by the predicate *was.* But now look at *straight* and *sharp* and *clear* and *pale.* These adjectives come *after* the nouns they modify—but there are no predicates to link them together. When adjectives follow directly after a noun in this way, we call them **appositive adjectives**. Read me the rule about appositive adjectives.

→ *Student: **Appositive adjectives directly follow the word they modify.***

Instructor: In the next two sentences, underline the appositive adjectives that follow the nouns *sea* and *wife.* As you do so, notice that compound adjectives in the appositive position follow the same rule as compounds in the attribute position—they are hyphenated.

The sea, blue and tranquil, bounded the view.

To add to the attractions of his house, his wife, simple and good-tempered, could talk with anybody, take off the bores, and leave people to be comfortable in their own way.
—From *Alice: or, The Mysteries* by Edward Bulwer-Lytton

Instructor: How many appositive adjectives modify each noun?

→ *Student: Two.*

Instructor: What kind of word connects them?

→ *Student: A coordinating conjunction.*

Instructor: Now underline the appositive adjectives that modify *spot* and *girl* in the next two sentences. Again, notice that the appositive adjective *self-possessed* is hyphenated. It would only lose the hyphen if it were in the *predicate* position. Appositive adjectives follow the same rules as attributive adjectives.

It was a spot remote, sequestered, cloistered from the business and pleasures of the world.

The latter was a fine dark-eyed girl, tall, self-possessed, and dressed plainly indeed, but after the approved fashion.
—From *Alice: Or, The Mysteries,* by Edward Bulwer-Lytton

Instructor: How many appositive adjectives modify each noun?

→ *Student: Three.*

Instructor: What punctuation mark separates them?

→ *Student: A comma.*

Instructor: Read the rule now.

→ *Student: **When three or more nouns, adjectives, verbs, or adverbs appear in a series, they should be separated by commas.***

Instructor: Although this seems like a simple rule, it has a few wrinkles in it. Read me the first "wrinkle."

→ *Student: When three or more items are in a list, a coordinating conjunction before the last term is usual but not necessary.*

Instructor: Choosing to leave the last coordinating conjunction out changes the sound and rhythm of a sentence. The first three pairs of sentences contain lists of verbs, nouns, and adverbs. Read all six sentences out loud and listen carefully to the difference in rhythm.

→ *Student: The horse spun, bucked, kicked with abandon. The horse spun, bucked, and kicked with abandon. Chickens, roosters, ducks filled the yard. Chickens, roosters, and ducks filled the yard. I ran quickly, efficiently, easily. I ran quickly, efficiently, and easily.*

Instructor: The last two pairs of sentences contain lists of adjectives, first in the predicate position, and then in the attributive position. Read all four sentences and listen to the rhythms.

→ *Student: It was a spot remote, sequestered, cloistered. It was a spot remote, sequestered, and cloistered. It was a dark, stormy, frightening night. It was a dark, stormy, and frightening night.*

Instructor: Read me the second "wrinkle" now.

→ *Student: When three or more items are in a list and a coordinating conjunction is used, a comma should still follow the next-to-last item in the list.*

Instructor: In the first sentence about the fourteen-year-old, it is clear that she loves three different things. What are they?

→ *Student: Her sisters, Taylor Swift, and Jennifer Lawrence.*

Instructor: In the second sentence, which doesn't have the comma after Taylor Swift, it sounds as if the fourteen-year-old loves her sisters, who are Taylor Swift and Jennifer Lawrence. The last comma prevents misunderstanding.

Not everyone agrees about this rule, because this kind of confusion isn't usually a problem. Read the next two sentences out loud.

→ *Student: Oranges, apples, and plums filled the fruit bowl. Oranges, apples and plums filled the fruit bowl.*

Instructor: Both of those sentences are perfectly clear, so some style guides and grammar books will tell you that it's OK to leave out the final comma. However, it's always good to avoid even the possibility of misunderstanding, so please use the comma!

> **Note to Instructor:** This final comma before the coordinating conjunction is called the *Oxford comma* because the style guidelines for Oxford University Press recommend it. You can explain this to the student if it seems helpful.

Instructor: Now read me the final "wrinkle."

→ *Student: When two or more adjectives are in the attributive position, they are only separated by commas if they are equally important in meaning.*

Instructor: If you can put *and* between the adjectives, or reverse their position, and the sentence still sounds fine, the adjectives are equally important in meaning and you should put commas between them. Read the three sentences about Monday.

→ Student: *Monday was a tiring, difficult day. Monday was a tiring and difficult day. Monday was a difficult, tiring day.*

Instructor: Monday was difficult. Monday was tiring. Both are equally true, so a comma goes between them. But now read the next three sentences.

→ Student: *The old man was wearing a grey wool overcoat. The old man was wearing a grey and wool overcoat. The old man was wearing a wool grey overcoat.*

Instructor: Wool describes the overcoat—but grey describes both the wool *and* the overcoat. But wool doesn't describe grey. So wool only describes one term, and grey describes two. They are not equal, so you don't put a comma between them.

Complete your exercises now.

—LESSON 102—

Adjective Review
Pronoun Review
Limiting Adjectives

(All sentences in this lesson are taken from *The Two Towers*, by J. R. R. Tolkien.)

Instructor: The first sentence in your workbook contains both types of adjectives studied in the last lesson—in all three positions! Five adjectives are underlined once. What sort of adjectives are they?

→ Student: *Descriptive.*

Instructor: What position are *lasting* and *dark* in?

→ Student: *Attributive.*

Instructor: What position is *void* in?

→ Student: *Predicative.*

Instructor: In this sentence, *made* is acting as a linking verb. What position are *defiled* and *diseased* in?

→ Student: *Appositive.*

Instructor: Two adjectives are underlined twice. What sort of adjectives are they?

→ Student: *Possessive.*

Instructor: Descriptive and possessive adjectives are very different. Descriptive adjectives give you much more information about the nouns they describe—while possessive adjectives just define who, or what, the noun belongs to. Look at the first column in your workbook. The descriptive adjectives *brown, curling, long, black,* and *snowy* all give you a mental picture of what the hair is *like*. But the possessive adjective *his* doesn't tell you *anything* about the hair—except that it belongs to *him*, not to anyone else. *His* hair is limited to *him*, only.

Look at the second column. What descriptive adjectives modify *horse?*

→ *Student: Old, tired, white, running.*

Instructor: The possessive adjective *king's* tells you that the horse belongs to the king—but do you know anything else about the horse?

→ *Student: No.*

Instructor: It could be old, tired, white, running, or none of the above. All you know about the horse is that it doesn't belong to anyone else. Anything you say about the horse will only apply to the *king's* horse.

Possessive adjectives belong to a larger category called *limiting adjectives.* **Descriptive adjectives *describe* by giving additional details. Limiting adjectives *define* by setting limits.** The horse is not Aragorn's horse, or Boromir's horse, or Gollum's horse. It is *only* the king's horse.

Read the two definitions out loud.

→ *Student: Descriptive adjectives* describe *by giving additional details. Limiting adjectives* define *by setting limits.*

Instructor: There are three kinds of descriptive adjectives. What are they?

→ *Student: Regular, present participles, past participles.*

Instructor: There are *six* kinds of limiting adjectives—but you've already studied all of them! We'll take the rest of this lesson to review them.

We've already talked about possessives. Let's review articles. What are the articles?

→ *Student: The articles are* a, an, *and* the.

Instructor: I don't think we need to spend any more time on that! Let's review demonstratives. First, read the definition of a demonstrative pronoun and the list of pronouns that follows.

→ *Student:* **Demonstrative pronouns demonstrate or point out something. They take the place of a single word or a group of words.** *This, that, these, those.*

Instructor: Demonstrative pronouns can be used on their own—or they can modify a noun, which turns them into adjectives. Read the definition of a demonstrative adjective.

→ *Student:* **Demonstrative adjectives modify nouns and answer the question** which one.

Instructor: In the next two sentences, label the demonstratives as *PRO* for pronoun or *ADJ* for adjective.

> ADJ
> If those unhappy hobbits are astray in the woods, it might draw them hither.

> PRO
> The prisoners are NOT to be searched or plundered; those are my orders.

Instructor: Now read the definition of indefinite pronouns.

→ *Student:* **Indefinite pronouns are pronouns without antecedents.**

Instructor: Since indefinite pronouns don't have antecedents, it can be difficult to tell whether they are singular or plural. Read the list of singular indefinite pronouns out loud, reading each line from left to right.

→ *Student: Anybody, anyone, anything; everybody, everyone, everything; nobody, no one, nothing; somebody, someone, something; another, other, one; either, neither, each.*

Instructor: Read the plural indefinite pronouns.

→ *Student: Both, few, many, several.*

Instructor: Read the indefinite pronouns that can be either singular or plural.

→ *Student: All, any, most, none, some.*

Instructor: In the next two sentences, identify the indefinite pronouns as *S* for singular or *P* for plural.

S
I do not understand all that goes on myself, so I cannot explain it to you. Some of us are

P
still true Ents, and lively enough in our fashion, but many are growing sleepy, going tree-ish, as you might say.

Instructor: Like demonstrative pronouns, indefinite pronouns can also serve as adjectives. Read the definition in your workbook.

→ *Student:* **Indefinite adjectives modify nouns and answer the questions** which one **and** how many.

Instructor: In the next four sentences, identify each indefinite as *PRO* for pronoun or *ADJ* for adjective.

ADJ
We will ride for a few hours, gently, until we come to the end of the valley.

PRO
The cord hurts us, yes it does, it hurts us, and we've done nothing.

PRO   PRO
Some are quite wide awake, and a few are, well, ah, well, getting Entish.

ADJ   PRO   ADJ
Each Palantir replied to each, but all those in Gondor were ever open to the view of Osgiliath.

Instructor: Now for interrogatives! Once again, we see words that can act either as pronouns or as limiting adjectives. Read the first definition, the list of pronouns, and the second definition.

→ *Student:* **Interrogative pronouns take the place of nouns in questions.** *Who, whom, whose, what, which.* **Interrogative adjectives modify nouns.**

Instructor: Identify the interrogatives in the next sentences as *PRO* for pronoun or *ADJ* for adjective.

PRO
Then if not yours, whose is the wizardry?

ADJ
At whose command do you hunt Orcs in our land?

ADJ
Which way do we go from here?

PRO
How far back his treachery goes, who can guess?

Instructor: Only one kind of limiting adjective left: numbers!

In your math studies, you may have learned that there are two different kinds of numbers: cardinal and ordinal. Cardinal numbers (like one, two, three, four) represent quantities. Ordinal numbers (like first, second, third, fourth) represent the order in which things are put.

Both kinds of numbers can serve as limiting adjectives—or, they can stand alone and function as nouns. In the next four sentences, label each number as *N* for noun or *ADJ* for adjective.

                                                 ADJ
Treebeard was at their head, and some fifty followers were behind him.

      N   ADJ
Fifteen of my men I lost, and twelve horses, alas!

                          N
"Not Elves," said the fourth, the tallest, and as it appeared, the chief among them.

             ADJ
Gollum was the first to get up.

Instructor: One last caution: When numbers answer the question *when*, they are functioning as adverbs, not adjectives. In the sentence in your workbook, *first* modifies the verb *was,* just as *soon* modifies the second *was.*

It was his turn to sleep (first) and he was (soon) deep in a dream.

Instructor: Finish your exercises now.

—LESSON 103—

Misplaced Modifiers
Squinting Modifiers
Dangling Modifiers

Instructor: All the way back in Lesson 43, you learned that if you put an adjective or adverb phrase in the wrong place, you'll confuse your readers! Read the first sentence in your workbook.

→ Student: *The party organizer passed around stuffed mushrooms to the guests on tiny bamboo mats.*

Instructor: The guests *might* have been sitting on tiny bamboo mats—but it's more likely that the mushrooms were on the tiny mats and the guests were standing around chatting, like people at a party usually do! Circle the adjective phrase *on tiny mats*. It sounds as if it modifies *guests,* but what noun does it actually modify?

→ Student: *Mushrooms.*

Instructor: The adjective phrase should come immediately after the noun it modifies. Draw an arrow from the circle back the space right after *mushrooms* and then read the sentence again.

The party organizer passed around stuffed mushrooms to the guests (on tiny bamboo mats)

→ Student: *The party organizer passed around stuffed mushrooms on tiny bamboo mats to the guests.*

Instructor: Read the next sentence out loud.

→ Student: *Churning inexorably towards the coast, we breathlessly watched the weather reports about the hurricane.*

Instructor: That sounds as if *we* are *churning inexorably towards the coast*. But what's actually churning?

→ *Student: The hurricane.*

Instructor: Circle the adjectival participle phrase, draw an arrow to the space after *hurricane*, and read the sentence again.

(Churning inexorably towards the coast) we breathlessly watched the weather reports about the hurricane.

→ *Student: We breathlessly watched the weather reports about the hurricane churning inexorably towards the coast.*

Instructor: You can also misplace an adverb phrase. Read the next sentence in your workbook.

→ *Student: Miranda spotted a blue heron on the way home.*

Instructor: Who's on the way home—Miranda or the blue heron?

→ *Student: Miranda.*

Instructor: *On the way home* should be an adverb phrase, describing *where* Miranda did the *spotting* of the blue heron. But because it's placed right after the noun *heron*, it has become an adjective phrase describing the heron.

Circle the phrase *on the way home*, draw an arrow from the circle to the space right before *Miranda*, and read the sentence again.

Miranda spotted a blue heron (on the way home.)

→ *Student: On the way home, Miranda spotted a blue heron.*

Instructor: In the next sentence, are the crowds of fans actually in a limousine?

→ *Student: No.*

Instructor: The adverb phrase *in a limousine* describes *where* and *how* the movie star was riding, so it should come directly after the verb *rode*. Circle the phrase, draw an arrow from the circle to the space right after *rode*, and read the sentence again.

The movie star rode through the crowds of fans (in a limousine.)

→ *Student: The movie star rode in a limousine through the crowds of fans.*

Instructor: Misplaced adjective modifiers are more likely to be phrases than single adjectives—because when you put a single adjective in the wrong place, you can immediately hear it. Read the next two sentences and you'll see what I mean.

→ *Student: The inconsiderate child was kicking the back of the airplane seat. The child was kicking the inconsiderate back of the airplane seat.*

Instructor: You probably wouldn't write that second sentence without realizing that the sentence has a problem! But it's easy to misplace a single adverb—particularly very simple adverbs such as *nearly, almost, often, barely*. The next two sentences mean very different things because of a slight change in the position of the adverb *almost*. In the first sentence, how many colleagues did Mari upset?

→ *Student: Almost all of them.*

Instructor: In the second sentence, how many did she upset?

→ *Student: [Answers will vary.]*

Instructor: Actually, she didn't upset any. She *almost upset* all of them. The sentences mean two different things, depending on the placement of the adverb. Look at the next two sentences. Can you explain the difference between them?

→ *Student: [Answers will vary.]*

> **Note to Instructor:** Prompt the student as necessary to explain that in the first sentence, the speaker slept, but for a little less than an hour; in the second, the speaker didn't really sleep, but that state lasted for a full hour.

Instructor: Read the full definition of a misplaced modifier now.

→ *Student: **A misplaced modifier is an adjective, adjective phrase, adverb, or adverb phrase in the wrong place.***

Instructor: One particularly tricky kind of misplaced modifier is called a **squinting modifier**. Squinting modifiers are words or phrases that are placed between two parts of a sentence so that you can't tell exactly which part they're supposed to be modifying. Underline the adverb in the first sentence.

> The chocolate fudge cake that I baked <u>recently</u> fell off the table onto the dirty floor.

Instructor: Did the speaker bake the cake recently, or did it fall off the table recently?

→ *Student: [Answers will vary but should be some form of We can't tell.]*

Instructor: Underline the adverb in the second sentence.

> Doing fifty chin-ups <u>quickly</u> strengthens your biceps.

Instructor: Where is the confusion in this sentence?

→ *Student: [Answers will vary, but should be some form of We can't tell whether the chin-ups are done quickly, or whether doing them makes your biceps strong quickly.]*

Instructor: Squinting modifiers can also be phrases. In the third sentence, underline the adverb phrase *on Monday*. It's impossible to tell whether the friend said, on Monday, that they would go camping on some unspecified day—or whether the friend said, at some time in the past, that a camping trip would happen on Monday.

Draw an arrow-headed line from each underlined modifier to a place in the sentence that will clear up the confusion. Then, read each sentence out loud again.

> **Note to Instructor:** Each adverb has several different possible placements; see the options beneath each sentence.

> The chocolate fudge cake that I baked <u>recently</u> fell off the table onto the dirty floor.
> ***Recently**, the chocolate fudge cake that I baked fell off the table onto the dirty floor.*
> *The chocolate fudge cake that I **recently** baked fell off the table onto the dirty floor.*
> *The chocolate fudge cake that I baked fell off the table **recently** onto the dirty floor.*
> *The chocolate fudge cake that I baked fell off the table onto the dirty floor **recently**.*

> Doing fifty chin-ups <u>quickly</u> strengthens your biceps.
> ***Quickly** doing fifty chin-ups strengthens your biceps.*
> *Doing fifty chin-ups strengthens your biceps **quickly**.*

> My friend said <u>on Monday</u> we would go camping.
> ***On Monday**, my friend said we would go camping.*
> *My friend said we would go camping **on Monday**.*

Instructor: Now read the definition of the squinting modifier.

→ Student: **A squinting modifier can belong either to the sentence element preceding or the element following.**

Instructor: You should be aware of one more modifier problem. Sometimes, a modifying phrase isn't just misplaced—it doesn't refer to anything in the sentence at all! Read the next sentence out loud.

→ Student: *After reading more on the subject, the article turned out to be incorrect.*

Instructor: The participle phrase *After reading more on the subject* is acting as an adjective—but what does it modify?

→ Student: *Nothing.*

Instructor: The only noun in the main is *article*—and the article certainly isn't doing the reading! In this sentence, the word modified by the adjective phrase is completely missing. When this happens, we say that the modifier is **dangling**. Sometimes the modifier dangles off the beginning of the sentence; other times, off the end. What is the main clause in the next sentence?

→ Student: *The experiment failed.*

Instructor: Who do you think *not having procured the correct ingredients* describes?

→ Student: *The people doing the experiment [or, No one].*

Instructor: Again, the noun modified by the phrase is just missing from the sentence.

Sometimes the noun is present in the sentence—but it can't be modified because it's been turned into something else! In the next sentence, who is exhausted by long days at work?

→ Student: *The secretary.*

Instructor: What part of speech is *secretary's*? (You just studied it in the last lesson!)

→ Student: *A possessive adjective.*

Instructor: An adjective phrase has to modify a noun—not another adjective! So although the secretary is *kind* of present in the main clause, the adjective phrase is dangling because there is no noun for it to modify.

Read the definition of a dangling modifier now.

→ Student: **A dangling modifier has no noun or verb to modify.**

Instructor: Fixing a dangling modifier isn't a simple matter of moving it to a different place. Instead, you have to rewrite the sentence to provide the missing noun or verb! And that will force you to change other parts of the sentence as well. Read me the first strategy in your workbook.

→ Student: *Provide the missing word in the main clause.*

Instructor: In the sentence "After reading more on the subject, I discovered that the article was incorrect," *I* is now modified by the previously dangling modifier—but the verb had to change, and *article* had to become the direct object. Read the second strategy.

→ Student: *Turn the dangling phrase into a clause by putting the missing word(s) into the phrase itself.*

Instructor: *I* has become the subject of the dependent clause *after I read more on the subject,* and the participle has been turned into the predicate of the clause.

Take a minute now to rewrite the incorrect sentence in your workbook twice, using each strategy.

Note to Instructor: Answers may vary, as long as they follow the strategies below.

INCORRECT: Having been delayed by traffic, the bride's frustration was easily understood.

1. Provide the missing noun or verb in the main clause.
   Having been delayed by traffic, the bride was understandably frustrated.

2. Turn the dangling phrase into a clause by putting the missing noun or verb into the phrase itself.
   Because the bride was delayed by traffic, her frustration was easily understood.

Instructor: Complete your exercises now.

—LESSON 104—

Degrees of Adjectives
Comparisons Using *More*, *Fewer*, and *Less*

Instructor: The first poem in your workbook is a popular dictation exercise used by writing teachers over a hundred years ago. Read it out loud.

→ Student: *Good, better, best,/ Never let it rest,/ Till your good is better,/ And your better, best.*

Instructor: That poem contains three different forms of the adjective *good*. Do you remember what those three forms are called?

Note to Instructor: If the student can't remember, tell him to look a little further down the lesson.

→ Student: *Positive, comparative, superlative.*

Instructor: Good, better, and best are the positive, comparative, and superlative forms of the adjective *good*. In the next lines, from the poet John Greenleaf Whittier, you'll see the same three forms of another adjective. Read all five lines out loud.

→ Student: *And summer days were sad and long,/ And sad the uncompanioned eyes,/ And sadder sunset-tinted leaves./ Of all sad words of tongue or pen,/ The saddest are these: "It might have been!"*

Instructor: What are the positive, comparative, and superlative forms in those lines?

→ Student: *Sad, sadder, saddest.*

Instructor: Read the next three definitions out loud.

→ Student: *The positive degree of an adjective describes only one thing. The comparative degree of an adjective compares two things. The superlative degree of an adjective compares three or more things.*

Instructor: *Sad* is a regular adjective. Read the two lines describing the formation of regular adjective, and then write the three correct forms of *sad* on the lines provided.

→ *Student: Most regular adjectives form the comparative by adding -r or -er. Most regular adjectives form the superlative by adding -st or -est.*

positive	comparative	superlative
sad	sadder	saddest

Instructor: Read the line about irregular adjectives, and then write the three correct forms of *good* on the lines provided.

→ *Student: Irregular adjectives may change form completely.*

positive	comparative	superlative
good	better	best

Instructor: The excerpt from Richard Connell's classic short story "The Most Dangerous Game" shows one more way that adjectives can form the positive, comparative, and superlative degrees—through adding adverbs. Circle the two forms of the adjective *dangerous* in the excerpt.

> For a moment the general did not reply; he was smiling his curious red-lipped smile. Then he said slowly, "No. You are wrong, sir. The Cape buffalo is not the most dangerous game." He sipped his wine. "Here in my preserve on this island," he said in the same slow tone, "I hunt more dangerous game."
> —Richard Connell, "The Most Dangerous Game" (1924)

Instructor: Read me the rule that follows.

→ *Student: Many adjectives form their comparative and superlative forms by adding the word* more *or* most *before the adjective instead of using -er or -est. In comparative and superlative adjective forms, the words* more *and* most *are used as adverbs.*

Instructor: Write the three forms of the verb *dangerous* on the lines provided.

positive	comparative	superlative
dangerous	more dangerous	most dangerous

Instructor: Now that you've reviewed these adjective forms, let's look at two more ways that the English language forms comparisons. The first is illustrated in the next quote in your workbook—an excerpt from an essay in a Canadian magazine called *The Grip*. In the late 19th century, Canadian temperance activists were arguing for prohibition—outlawing the sale of all alcohol in the entire country. What does *The Grip* say about this argument? Read it out loud.

→ *Student: So long as people will drink, drink will be made; and so long as drink is made, there will be those to sell it. Well, the more the restrictions, the fewer to sell; the fewer to sell, the less sold; the less sold, the less made; the less made, the less drunk; the less drunk, the fewer the inebriates—and that's what the temperance people are after.*

Instructor: English often uses *more* along with *less* or *fewer* to form comparisons. But *more, less,* and *fewer* are tricky words—they can change from one part of speech to another, depending on how the comparison is formed. And there are, of course, other things to keep in mind as well!

Let's start with the next two sentences. Read them aloud.

→ *Student: The more thoroughly we searched, the fewer treasures we found. The more love I offered, the less enthusiasm he showed.*

Instructor: Here's the first rule to keep in mind: Use *fewer* when you're talking about concrete items—things that can be counted. Use *less* when you're talking about abstractions. Are *treasures* concrete or abstract?

→ *Student: Concrete.*

Instructor: You can touch, count, and handle treasures, so you would say *fewer treasures*. But you can't touch, count, or handle *enthusiasm,* so you would say *less enthusiasm.* Read the rule out loud.

→ *Student:* **Use** fewer *for concrete items and* less *for abstractions.*

Instructor: Whether you're actually making a comparison or not, this rule still holds. In the next two sentences (from the novel *Jane Eyre*), what concrete items are modified by *fewer*?

→ *Student: Cakes and sweetmeats.*

Instructor: What abstraction is modified by *less*?

→ *Student: Sad.*

Instructor: Read me the second rule.

→ *Student:* **In comparisons using** more . . . fewer *and* more . . . less, more *and* less *can act as either adverbs or adjectives and* the *can act as an adverb.*

Instructor: *Fewer* is always an adjective—but *more, less,* and *the* can change back and forth between adverb and adjective. To understand this, let's look more carefully at *The more thoroughly we searched, the fewer treasures we found* and *The more love I offered, the less enthusiasm he showed.*

Instructor: To understand how this comparison works, we'll rearrange the sentences. First, realize that each of these sentences actually comprises two independent clauses. Read them without the article (which makes them sound awkward).

→ *Student: We searched more thoroughly. We found fewer treasures. I offered more love. He showed less enthusiasm.*

Instructor: Examine the diagram of the first sentence, and then place every word of the second diagram on the frame.

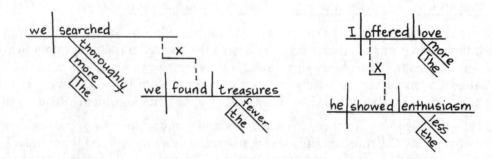

Instructor: In the first sentence, what part of speech is *more*?

→ *Student: An adverb.*

Instructor: In the second sentence, *more* and *less* are both what part of speech?

→ *Student: They are adjectives.*

Instructor: In both sentences, *the* is an adverb because it modifies a modifier.

Now put every word of the next sentence on the frame.

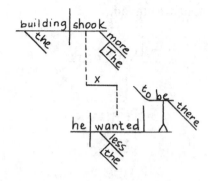

Instructor: In this sentence, *more* and *less* are both what part of speech?

→ *Student: They are adverbs.*

Instructor: These comparisons all use some combination of *more* and *fewer* or *less*. But comparisons using this basic form—and following these rules—can take other patterns as well. Read me the next two sentences.

→ *Student: The more the building shook, the more we held on. The less we saw, the less we knew.*

Instructor: What word is repeated twice in the first sentence?

→ *Student: More.*

Instructor: In the second?

→ *Student: Less.*

Instructor: So you can repeat *more*, or repeat *less* (or *fewer*), or use a combination of the two.

Look at the next four sentences. Each one follows the same pattern. Can you identify it?

→ *Student:* [Phrasing may vary.] *Each sentence has a comparative adverb or adjective along with* more, less, *or* fewer.

> **Note to Instructor:** Each sentence combines *more, less,* or *fewer* with the comparative form of an adjective:

The more the wave rose, the faster we ran.	*more/faster*
The less we worried, the better we felt.	*less/better*
The happier we were, the more we rejoiced.	*happier/more*
The louder the wind, the fewer words we were able to exchange.	*louder/fewer*

> **Note to Instructor:** If the student is unable to identify the pattern, use the following questions: 1) Does each sentence contain *more, less,* or *fewer*? and 2) *Faster, better, happier,* and *louder* are all the same degree of modifier. What is it?

Instructor: Finally, look at the last two sentences. Does they contain *more, less,* or *fewer*?

→ *Student: No.*

Instructor: You can also form a comparison by using two comparative forms in the place of *more* and *less* or *more* and *fewer*. Underline the comparative forms in each sentence.

> The <u>better</u> we felt, the <u>longer</u> we stayed.
> The <u>longer</u> the tail grew, the <u>better</u> the horse could swat flies.

Instructor: When you form a comparison in this way, the comparative forms—like *more* and *less*—can serve as either adjectives or adverbs. Put each sentence on the frame provided.

The better we felt, the longer we stayed.

The longer the tail grew, the better the horse could swat flies.

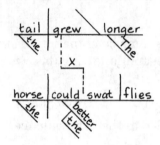

Instructor: In the first sentence, what part of speech is *better*?

→ *Student: Adjective* OR *Predicate adjective.*

Instructor: What part of speech is it in the second sentence?

→ *Student: Adverb.*

Instructor: In the first sentence, what part of speech is *longer*?

→ *Student: Adverb.*

Instructor: In the second sentence, what part of speech is it?

→ *Student: Adjective* OR *Predicate adjective.*

Instructor: Before you complete your exercises, review the complete rules you've learned today by reading them out loud.

→ *Student: Use* fewer *for concrete items and* less *for abstractions. Comparisons can be formed using a combination of* more *and* fewer *or* less; *a combination of* more *and* more *or* fewer/less *and* fewer/less; *a combination of* more *or* fewer/less *with a comparative form; or simply two comparative forms. In comparisons using* more, fewer *and* less, more *and* less *can act as either adverbs or adjectives, and* the *can act as an adverb. In comparisons using two comparative forms, the forms may act as either adverbs or adjectives, and* the *can act as an adverb.*

Instructor: Complete your exercises now.

Double Identities

—LESSON 105—

Clauses with Understood Elements
Than as Conjunction, Preposition, and Adverb
Quasi-Coordinators

Instructor: This week, we'll be working with words that can serve as two or three different parts of speech—or even more.

Today, we're going to talk about the tricky little word *than.* Read the next four sentences out loud.

→ *Student: I like chocolate better than vanilla. Other than pistachio, I'll eat any flavor of ice cream. I am more than satisfied with chocolate, but less than happy with pistachio. I will starve rather than eat pistachio.*

Instructor: *Than* plays a different part in each one of these sentences. Let's start with the first. You've actually studied this one already! Back in Lesson 66, you learned that *than* is a subordinating conjunction when it introduces a comparison. Read the two definitions in your workbook.

→ *Student: A coordinating conjunction joins equal words or groups of words together. A subordinating conjunction joins unequal words or groups of words together.*

Instructor: The example from Lesson 66 is "He worked more efficiently than his brother." The first clause in that sentence is *He worked more efficiently.* There's an understood word that's been eliminated from the second clause in the sentence. What is it?

→ *Student: Worked.*

Instructor: The two clauses are unequal because one of them is missing a word! You also learned that to diagram a comparison, you write the subordinating conjunction *than* on the dotted line joining the two clauses. The line is drawn from the comparative word to the thing or person being compared, and an *x* replaces the missing word or words.

In the sentence "I like chocolate better than vanilla," what words have been left out of the second clause?

> **Note to Instructor:** Supply the answer if necessary.

→ *Student: I like.*

Instructor: Insert the words *I like* into the sentence, using a caret (the little wedge with the sharp end pointing up).

I like chocolate better than ^ vanilla.

Instructor: Now place the words of the sentence on the diagram frame.

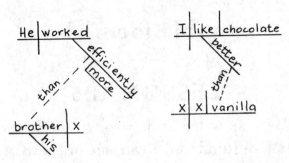

Instructor: When *than* acts like a subordinating conjunction and introduces a comparison, make sure you know what words have actually been left out! Read me the next four sentences beneath the diagram out loud, adding in the words you think have been eliminated.

> **Note to Instructor:** Prompt the student as needed. The student does not necessarily need to add the words in brackets.

→ *Student: Tomorrow should be sunnier than today is [sunny]. A new broom sweeps better than an old one sweeps [OR does]. The cook added more salt than he should have added [salt]. I love him more than I love you OR I love him more than you love him.*

> **Note to Instructor:** If the student does not recognize the ambiguity of the last sentence and gives you one of the options above, say, "What about . . ." and read the other sentence.

Instructor: That last sentence has two possible meanings! It isn't clear whether the writer means, "I love him more than you love him," or "I love him more than I love you." When you write comparisons, be sure that the reader can only interpret them in one way! Using a caret, modify that last sentence now so that it isn't ambiguous (capable of two different meanings).

love him

I love him more than you ^.

OR

I love

I love him more than ^ you.

Instructor: Remembering those left-out words can also keep you from using the wrong pronoun form in your comparisons. Read me the next sentence, adding in the understood words.

→ *Student: He is stronger than I am [strong].*

Instructor: Add the missing words, using a caret.

am [strong]

He is stronger than I ^.

Instructor: In the clause *I am [strong]*, what part of the sentence is *I*?

→ *Student: The subject.*

Instructor: So you should use the subject pronoun *I*, not the object pronoun *me*, in a comparison like this! *He is stronger than me* is not correct. You can use it in casual speech—but not in formal writing!

Read the definition in your workbook now.

→ *Student:* **When than *is used in a comparison and introduces a clause with understood elements, it is acting as a subordinating conjunction.***

Instructor: Now let's look at the next sentence. Examine the diagram carefully. What part of speech do you think *than* is playing?

Other than pistachio, I'll eat any flavor of ice cream.

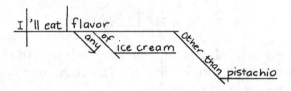

→ *Student:* [Answers will vary.]

Instructor: In English, when *than* is paired with *other* it creates a compound preposition that means "besides" or "except." *Other than pistachio* is a prepositional phrase modifying *flavor*.

Read the definition in your workbook out loud.

→ *Student:* **Other than *is a compound preposition that means "besides" or "except."***

Instructor: Put every word of the third sentence on the diagram frame provided.

> **Note to Instructor:** Give all necessary help.

I am more than satisfied with chocolate, but less than happy with pistachio.

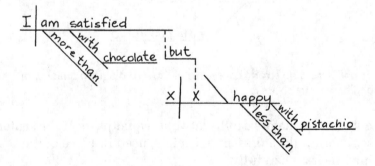

Instructor: What words are missing from the second clause?

→ *Student: I am.*

Instructor: *More than* and *less than* serve as what part of speech?

→ *Student: An adverb.*

Instructor: *More than* is a compound adverb modifying the verb *am satisfied*. *Less than* is a compound adverb modifying the adjective *happy*. Read the definition in your workbook now.

→ *Student:* **More than *and* less than *are compound modifiers.***

Instructor: In these sentences, they modify verbs, so they are acting as adverbs.

Now let's look at that very last sentence! So far, you've seen *than* act as a subordinating conjunction, and as part of a compound preposition and as a compound adverb. In this sentence, it's playing yet another role. Begin by underlining the subject once and the verbs twice.

I will starve rather than eat pistachio.

Instructor: In this sentence, the subject is followed by a compound predicate—two verbs. You've learned about compound predicates connected by coordinating conjunctions such as *and*. But in this case, it doesn't make sense to join the verbs with *and*.

I will starve *and* eat pistachio.

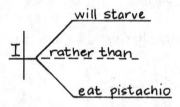

Instructor: Only one of the verbs is going to happen. One verb is in the future tense and the other is present. One has an object and one doesn't. The verbs are not equal—and coordinating conjunctions only join equal parts of a sentence.

Instead, these verbs are connected by *rather than*. In this sentence, *rather than* is called a **quasi-coordinator.** Read the definition out loud.

→ Student: **Quasi-coordinators link compound parts of a sentence that are unequal.** *Quasi-coordinators include* rather than, sooner than, let alone, *and* not to mention.

Instructor: We diagram quasi-coordinators on a horizontal dotted line between the words they connect.

I will starve rather than eat pistachio.

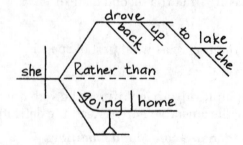

> **Note to Instructor:** There is no strong consensus on how to diagram quasi-coordinators; the method described here is the clearest.

Instructor: Because quasi-coordinators can link two unequal parts of the sentence, sometimes you'll see another verb form, like a present participle, used in place of the second verb. Examine the next sentence and diagram carefully.

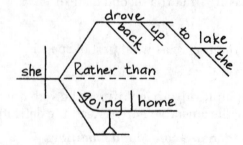

Instructor: What word is taking the place of the second verb?

→ Student: *Going.*

Instructor: The next three sentences illustrate the use of the quasi-coordinators *let alone, not to mention,* and *sooner than*. Diagram each one onto the frame provided.

He could not keep up with Patel, let alone Krishna.

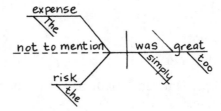

The expense, not to mention the risk, was simply too great.

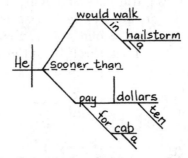

He would walk in a hailstorm sooner than pay ten dollars for a cab.

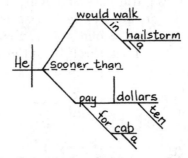

Note to Instructor: "ten dollars" could also be diagrammed as a single compound noun.

Instructor: Before completing your exercises, review everything you've learned about the word *than* by reading all four rules and definitions out loud.

→ *Student: When* than *is used in a comparison and introduces a clause with understood elements, it is acting as a subordinating conjunction. Other than is a compound preposition that means "besides" or "except." More than and less than are compound modifiers. Quasi-coordinators link compound parts of a sentence that are unequal. Quasi-coordinators include* rather than, sooner than, let alone, *and* not to mention.

—LESSON 106—
The Word *As*
Quasi-Coordinators

Note to Instructor: While it is impossible to cover every single permutation of *as* and its various combinations—let alone all of the other words in the English language that can serve as more than one part of a sentence—the next three lessons will help the student learn how to look more carefully at the function of any given word.

When you read the next sentence, emphasize each *as* slightly.

Instructor: As soon as you read the title of the lesson, we'll see if you're as excited as I am to learn about *as*—as that is the topic we'll be studying today.

As is an even trickier word than *than!* It comes from the Middle English word *alswa*, which means "similarly," and *as* is similar to a lot of different parts of speech.

Since we've been talking about comparisons, let's start with *as* when it introduces a comparison. Look at the next sentence in your workbook, from John R. Gribbin's book *The Scientists: A History of Science Told Through the Lives of Its Greatest Inventors.* What is the twenty-fourth object as big as?

→ *Student: A sugar cube.*

Instructor: How about the fifty-seventh?

→ *Student: The sun.*

Instructor: In this sentence, the first occurrence of *as* modifies the adjective *big.* How big? What kind of word modifies an adjective?

→ *Student: An adverb.*

Instructor: The second occurrence of *as* introduces a comparison with a missing word. The twenty-fourth object is as big *as a sugar cube is.* The fifty-seventh object is about as big *as the Sun is.* Just like *than* in the last lesson, the second *as* is a subordinating conjunction introducing a dependent clause with a missing verb. Look carefully at the diagram.

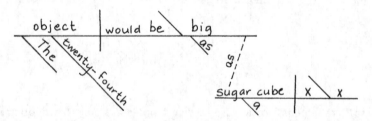

Instructor: Where is the adverb *as* diagrammed?

→ *Student: Beneath the adjective* big.

Instructor: Where is the subordinating conjunction *as* diagrammed?

→ *Student: Connecting* big *and* sugar cube.

Instructor: *As* can also act like a subordinating conjunction on its own. Read me the next sentence.

→ *Student: An equally important factor, as many people have argued, was the depopulation of Europe by the Black Death.*

Instructor: Look carefully at the diagram.

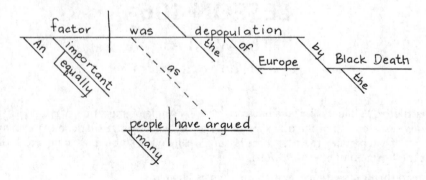

Instructor: What is the main clause of the sentence?

→ *Student: An equally important factor was the depopulation of Europe by the Black Death.*

Instructor: What is the subordinate clause?

→ *Student: As many people have argued.*

Instructor: In the next sentence, *as* is an adverb *and* a subordinating conjunction—twice! Do your best to put every word of the sentence on the frame provided.

As long as Frederick remained on the throne, Tycho was able to enjoy an unprecedented amount of freedom to run his observatory just as he liked.

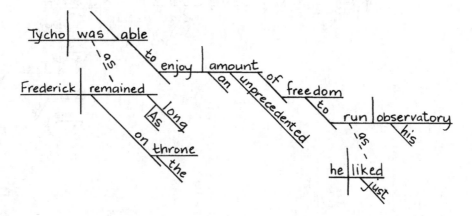

> **Note to Instructor:** Some manuals would prefer to diagram *as long as* and *just as* on the dotted lines, as compound subordinating conjunctions. Since *long* and *just* are both adverbs, however, I find it more accurate to diagram them as shown above.

Instructor: Now you've seen *as* behaving like an adverb and like a subordinating conjunction. But that's not all it can do! Read me the next sentence.

→ *Student: There were many translations and new editions of the book, which laid the foundations for chemistry as a genuinely scientific discipline.*

Instructor: Is *as a genuinely scientific discipline* a phrase or a clause?

→ *Student: A phrase.*

Instructor: So *as* can't be a subordinating conjunction. And it isn't an adverb. Instead, it's a preposition, and *as a genuinely scientific discipline* is a prepositional phrase acting as an adjective and modifying *chemistry*.

In the next sentence, *as* appears three times: once as an adverb and twice as a preposition. Try to put every word of the sentence on the frame provided.

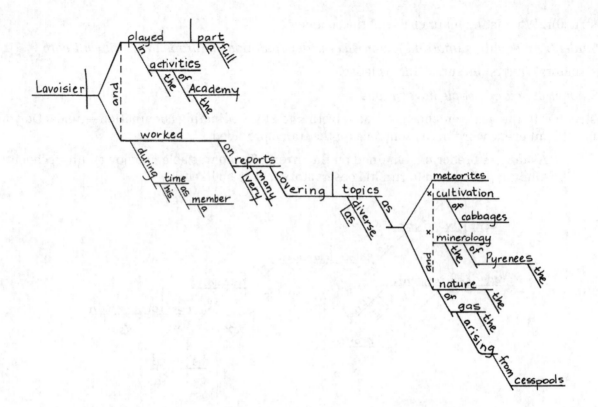

Instructor: *As* can be an adverb, a subordinating conjunction, or a preposition. But it has at *least* one more identity! Read me the next sentence.

→ Student: *At the time of his marriage, as well as considerable property, Charles Cavendish had a disposable annual income of at least £2000, which grew as time passed.*

Instructor: Charles Cavendish had two things at the time of his marriage. What were they?

→ Student: *Considerable property and a disposable annual income [of at least £2000].*

Instructor: Even though *considerable property* comes before the verb and *income* comes after, both are direct objects. What three words link those two direct objects?

> **Note to Instructor:** Prompt the student if necessary.

→ Student: *As well as.*

Instructor: In combination with *well*, *as* serves as a quasi-coordinator. *As well as* links *property* to *income.* Review the definition of a quasi-coordinator by reading it out loud.

→ Student: *Quasi-coordinators link compound parts of a sentence that are unequal. Quasi-coordinators include* rather than, sooner than, let alone, as well as, *and* not to mention.

Instructor: Your next sentence also uses the quasi-coordinator *as well as*. Diagram it onto the frame provided.

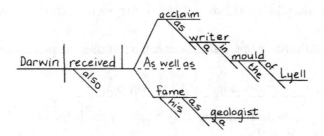

Instructor: *As* appears *four* times in that sentence! It appears twice in the quasi-coordinator *as well as*. What part of the sentence does it play the other two times?

→ Student: *A preposition.*

Instructor: Complete your exercises now.

—LESSON 107—
Words That Can Be Multiple Parts of Speech

Instructor: The English novelist Charles Dickens was a master of words—especially words that can be more than one part of speech. Today we're going to use these sentences from his novel *Bleak House* to examine words that can be conjunctions, adverbs, adjectives, prepositions—and sometimes even more.

Let's start with the simple word *but*. Read me the first sentence from *Bleak House*.

→ Student: *I had an illness, but it was not a long one.*

Instructor: Circle the word *but*. It connects the two independent clauses, *I had an illness* and *it was not a long one*. What part of speech is *but* in this sentence?

→ Student: *A coordinating conjunction.*

Instructor: Write *coordinating conjunction* on the first line after *but*. Read me the second sentence.

→ Student: *He has never hurt anybody but himself.*

Instructor: Diagram this sentence onto the frame provided.

But   coordinating conjunction   preposition

I had an illness,(but)it was not a long one.

He has never hurt anybody but himself.

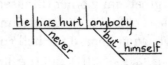

Instructor: What part of speech is *but* in the second sentence?

→ Student: *Preposition.*

Instructor: *But himself* is an adjectival prepositional phrase modifying *anybody*. Write *preposition* on the second line.

    For can also act as either a coordinating conjunction or a preposition. Write those words on the lines next to *for*.

    For   <u>coordinating conjunction</u>   <u>preposition</u>

Instructor: Read the next two sentences carefully. Identify each *for* as *CC* for coordinating conjunction or *PREP* for preposition.

                   PREP   PREP
    I can answer for him as little as for you.

                                                 CC
    I should have been ashamed to come here to-day, for I know what a figure I must seem to you two.

Instructor: What are the two objects of the two occurrences of the preposition *for* in the first sentence?

→ *Student: Him and you.*

Instructor: In the second sentence, what type of clauses do the coordinating conjunction link?

→ *Student: Two independent clauses.*

Instructor: The word *about* also has two different functions—but not the same two as *for* and *but*. Circle *about* in the two sentences that follow the blanks.

    In the first sentence, how did the horses slip?

→ *Student: About.*

Instructor: What part of speech is *about*?

→ *Student: An adverb.*

Instructor: Write that on the first line.

    In the second sentence, what were the notes about?

→ *Student: Jams, pickles, preserves, bottles, glass, china, and a great many other things.*

Instructor: Those are seven *objects* of the word *about*. What part of speech is it?

→ *Student: A preposition.*

Instructor: Write that on the second line.

    About   <u>adverb</u>   <u>preposition</u>

    You could hear the horses being rubbed down outside the stable and being told to "Hold up!" and "Get over," as they slipped (about) very much on the uneven stones.

    What with making notes on a slate (about) jams, and pickles, and preserves, and bottles, and glass, and china, and a great many other things; and what with being generally a methodical, old-maidish sort of foolish little person, I was so busy that I could not believe it was breakfast-time when I heard the bell ring.

Instructor: The word *yet* has two identities as well. Read the next three sentences, find the right diagram frame for each one, and place each word onto the correct frame.

    Is he here yet?
    At this time, Jo has not yet died.
    It is good, yet it could be improved.

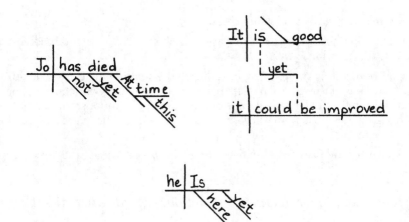

Instructor: What part of speech is *yet* in *Is he here yet?*

→ *Student: An adverb.*

Instructor: What part of speech is *yet* in "At this time, Jo has not yet died"?

→ *Student: An adverb.*

Instructor: What part of speech is *yet* in "It is good, yet it could be improved"?

→ *Student: A coordinating conjunction.*

Instructor: Write *adverb* and *coordinating conjunction* on the lines next to the word.

Yet ___adverb___   ___coordinating conjunction___

Instructor: You have already learned that *any* is an indefinite pronoun. Do you remember whether it is singular or plural?

→ *Student: It can be either.*

Instructor: And you have learned that indefinite pronouns can also serve as adjectives. But *any* can also be an adverb. In the next five sentences, find and circle each occurrence of *any*. Label each as *ADV* for adverb, *ADJ* for adjective, or *PRO* for pronoun.

Any ___pronoun___   ___adjective___   ___adverb___

ADV
I could not reproach myself (any) less. [Modifies the adjective *less*.]

ADJ
It would be an insult to the discernment of (any) man with half an eye to tell him so. [Modifies the noun *man*.]

PRO
I wonder whether (any) of the gentlemen remembered him.

ADJ
I then asked Richard whether he had thought of (any) more congenial pursuit. [Modifies the noun *pursuit*, NOT the adverb *more*.]

ADV
I thought it was impossible that you could have loved me (any) better. [Modifies the adjective *better*.]

Instructor: The next four words also have three uses each.

Can you tell me the three different parts of speech that *before* serves as in the next three sentences?

> **Note to Instructor:** Prompt the student if necessary.
>
> The first is a preposition; the prepositional phrase *before her* modifies *lies* and functions as an adverb answering the question *where*.
>
> The second is a subordinating conjunction, introducing the subordinate clause "he took his candle and his radiant face out of the room." Notice that it is subordinating, not coordinating, because "before he took his candle and his radiant face out of the room" cannot stand on its own (while "for I know what a figure I must seem to you two" and "yet it could be improved" can both stand on their own as sentences).
>
> The third is an adverb, modifying the infinitive form *to have been exhausted* and answering the question *when*.

Instructor: Write *preposition, subordinating conjunction,* and *adverb* on the three lines next to *before.*

Before __preposition__   __subordinating conjunction__   __adverb__

Instructor: You already know that *above* is a preposition. In the first sentence, circle the prepositional phrase that functions as an adverb. What is the object of the preposition *above?*

→ *Student: Gate.*

Instructor: What question does the phrase answer?

→ *Student: Where?*

Instructor: Circle *above* in the second sentence. It also answers the question *where.* What word does it modify?

→ *Student: Fixed.*

Instructor: What part of speech is it?

→ *Student: An adverb.*

Instructor: Write that on the second line. Circle *above* in the third sentence. It also seems to answer the question *where,* but what word does it actually describe?

→ *Student: Darkness.*

Instructor: Here, *above* is a descriptive adjective, telling you *what* darkness. Write *adjective* on the third line.

Above __preposition__   __adverb__   __adjective__

The flame of gas was burning so sullenly (above) the iron gate.
His eyes were fixed high (above)
But it is all blank, blank as the darkness (above)

Instructor: Like *above,* the word *after* can be both a preposition and an adverb. It can also be one more part of speech—*not* an adjective! In the sentences below, circle each occurrence of *after.* Label the preposition as *PREP* and the adverb as *ADV.* Then, decide what part of speech the third *after* plays, and tell me what it is.

> **Note to Instructor:** Use the bracketed information below to prompt the student if necessary.

After __preposition__   __adverb__   __subordinating conjunction__

                    PREP
In half an hour (after) our arrival, Mrs. Jellyby appeared.

> [*After our arrival* is a prepositional phrase modifying *half an hour,* which is a compound noun and the object of the preposition *in,* so the phrase is acting as an adjective.]

SC
I once more saw him looking at me (after) he had passed the door.

> [*He had passed the door* is a clause with a subject and predicate, and *after* is the conjunction that subordinates it to the main clause *I once more saw him looking at me.*]

ADV
He presented himself soon (after)

> [*After* modifies the verb *presented*, and *soon* is an additional adverb modifying the adverb *after.*]

Instructor: Let's look at another word that has three different functions. Can you identify the part of speech that *otherwise* plays in the next three sentences? Tell me each one.

> **Note to Instructor:** Use the bracketed information below to prompt the student if necessary.

Otherwise ____adjective____   ____adverb____   ____coordinating conjunction____

We are not so prejudiced as to suppose that in private life you are otherwise than a very estimable man.

> [Predicate adjective modifying *you.*]

How could you do otherwise?

> [Adverb modifying *could do.*]

Love her and all will go well; otherwise, all will go ill.

> [Coordinating conjunction linking two independent clauses.]

Instructor: Write *adjective, adverb,* and *coordinating conjunction* on the lines next to *otherwise.*

Now for one last word. In the next five sentences, the word *still* serves as *five* different parts of speech! Identify each one and write it on the line to the right.

> *Note to Instructor:* If necessary, use the information in brackets to prompt the student.

Still

It is quite still and silent.   ____adjective____

> [Predicate adjective following the linking verb *is* and describing *it.*]

She remained perfectly still until the carriage turned into the drive.   ____adverb____

> [Adverb modifying *remained* and answering the question *how.*]

The cause was hopeless; still, they fought.   ____coordinating conjunction____

> [Conjunction links the equal independent clauses.]

Still yourself, my dear, and wait in patience.   ____verb____

> [Imperative verb.]

In the still, the woods seemed massively hushed in sleep.   ____noun____

> [The *still* is an abstract noun representing the state in which the woods are.]

Instructor: Unlike the other words you studied in this lesson, *still* can *also* be a verb or a noun! In the last lesson this week, we'll look at a few other nouns that play multiple roles as different parts of speech. But before we do, go ahead and complete your exercises.

—LESSON 108—

Nouns Acting as Other Parts of Speech
Adverbial Noun Phrases

Instructor: Today, we'll finish up by talking about nouns (like *still*) that can also act as other parts of speech.

Begin by completing Exercises 108A and B now.

> **Note to Instructor:** The answers to all exercises are found in the corresponding Answer Key to the student workbook.

Instructor: As you've seen from your exercises, adjectives, adverbs, conjunctions, and prepositions aren't the only words that can change from one part of speech to another. Nouns can also act as other parts of speech.

One particular kind of noun can change into another part of speech—while still remaining a noun! Read me the next sentence in your workbook.

→ *Student: Mary and her lamb went into the school.*

Instructor: Where did they go?

→ *Student: Into the school.*

Instructor: What kind of phrase is *into the school*?

→ *Student: Prepositional.*

Instructor: What does it modify?

→ *Student: Went.*

Instructor: Circle the phrase and draw an arrow back to *went*. The prepositional phrase *into the school* is acting as an adverb, answering the question *where*. Now read the next sentence.

→ *Student: Mary and her lamb went home.*

Instructor: *Home* is a noun. But it's also answering the question *where*, which means it's behaving like an adverb. Circle *home* and draw an arrow back to *went*.

Mary and her lamb went (into the school)

Mary and her lamb went (home)

Instructor: We call *home* an **adverbial noun**. It's behaving like an adverb—but it doesn't stop being a noun. It answers the question *where*, like an adverb does, but *home* is still the name of the place Mary and her lamb went.

Adverbial nouns show up most often to express where, when, how far, or how much. Look at the next two sentences. Which sentence contains the adverbial noun?

→ *Student: He followed her to school one day.*

Instructor: The prepositional phrase *on Monday* and the adverbial noun *day* both answer what question?

→ *Student: When.*

Instructor: In this sentence, the adverbial noun *day* is modified by the adjective *one.* Together, they form an adverbial noun phrase. Circle both adverbial phrases, and draw a line back to the verb modified, *followed.*

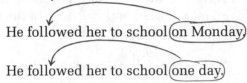

He followed her to school (on Monday.)

He followed her to school (one day.)

Instructor: Read the definition out loud now.

→ *Student: **An adverbial noun tells the time or place of an action, or explains how long, how far, how deep, how thick, or how much. It can modify a verb, adjective, or adverb. An adverbial noun plus its modifiers is an adverbial noun phrase.***

Instructor: Each one of the next four sentences has an adverbial noun or noun phrase in it. As we go through them, circle each adverbial noun or noun phrase and draw a line from the circle to the word modified. In the next sentence, what question does *a mile* answer?

→ *Student: How far.*

Before the lamb had travelled (a mile,) Mary turned around.

> **Note to Instructor:** "Travelled" is an intransitive verb, so "mile" cannot be a direct object.

Instructor: In *The road to school was two miles long,* what is the subject?

→ *Student: Road.*

Instructor: What is the verb?

→ *Student: Was.*

Instructor: What part of the sentence is *long?*

→ *Student: Predicate adjective.*

Instructor: In this sentence, the adverbial noun phrase *two miles* modifies the predicate adjective *long* and answers the question *how long.*

The road to school was (two miles) long.

Instructor: Read me the next sentence.

→ *Student: The mud puddle in the road was three inches deep.*

Instructor: What word does the adverbial noun phrase *three inches* modify?

→ *Student: Deep.*

The mud puddle in the road was (three inches) deep.

Instructor: Read me the next sentence.

→ *Student: The lamb splashed in the puddle until he was covered with inch-thick mud.*

Instructor: What adjective does the adverbial noun *inch* modify?

→ *Student: Thick.*

Instructor: It answers the question *how thick*. Here's something to keep in mind: In English, we often put the adverbial noun and the adjective it modifies *after* the noun described. Read me the second version of the sentence.

→ *Student: The lamb splashed in the puddle until he was covered with mud an inch thick.*

Instructor: Both sentences are correct, but when the adverbial noun and adjective come after the word modified, we usually add an article to the adverbial noun. In both versions of the sentence, circle the adverbial noun or noun phrase, and draw a line to the word modified.

The lamb splashed in the puddle until he was covered with (inch)-thick mud.

The lamb splashed in the puddle until he was covered with mud (an inch) thick.

Instructor: Diagramming adverbial nouns or noun phrases is easy. The noun goes underneath the word it modifies, like an adverb—but because you want to remember that it is actually a *noun*, you diagram it on a straight *noun* line rather than on a slanting *modifier* line. Examine the two diagrams in your workbook, and then place every word of the following two sentences on the frames provided.

The storm continued all night.

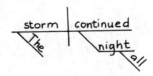

The earth's mantle is roughly 1,800 miles thick.

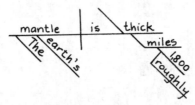

He slept eight hours and then woke up early the next morning.

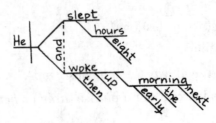

After our delicious picnic lunch, we walked the two miles to the battlefield.

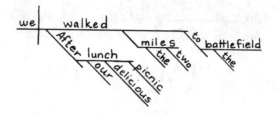

Instructor: Complete your exercises now.

WEEK 28

— REVIEW 9 —

The review exercises and answers are found in the Student Workbook and accompanying Key.

Still More Verbs

—LESSON 109—

Hortative Verbs
Subjunctive Verbs

Note to Instructor: Hortative verbs can be classified in multiple ways. For example, some grammar books divide hortative verbs into seven types—adhortative, exhortative, suprahortative, cohortative, dehortative, inhortative, and infrahortative. This is unnecessarily complicated (and these types overlap with regular imperative and subjunctive verbs), so we are going to simply use the single term *hortative* to cover the types of verbs in this lesson.

Note to Instructor: Repeat the three sentences below as necessary.

Instructor: You've now completed 28 weeks of grammar. Be happy! Now, let's begin on Week Twenty-Nine.

What statement of fact did I just make?

→ *Student: You've now completed 28 weeks of grammar.*

Instructor: What command did I give you?

→ *Student: Be happy!*

Instructor: I also said something that's neither a command nor a statement. And it isn't a question or explanation either. *Let's begin on Week Twenty-Nine* is a sentence with a very odd kind of verb: a **hortative** verb. Read me the definition of a hortative verb.

→ *Student:* **A hortative verb encourages or recommends an action.**

Instructor: We get the word *hortative* from the Latin verb *hortari* [hor-TARR-ee]. What does that verb mean?

→ *Student: To encourage or urge.*

Instructor: The two most common English words related to *hortari* are *exhort* and *hortative.* Read me the definition of *exhort.*

→ *Student: To urge, or to give urgent recommendations.*

Instructor: "I exhorted him to keep running despite his weariness" means "I urged him." What is the definition of *hortative*?

→ *Student: Encouraging or urging on.*

Instructor: If you name your child Patience, Charity, or Praise-God (that was a popular Puritan name in the 17th century!), you are *encouraging* them to be a certain way! These are *hortative* names.

The next three sets of sentences all have hortative verbs, encouraging three different kinds of actions. Read the first set of sentences out loud.

→ *Student: Let's be more careful next time. Let's run faster. Let's be finished now.*

Instructor: What two words is the contraction *let's* made up of?

→ *Student: Let us.*

Instructor: In these sentences, the speaker is encouraging both herself and another person at the same time. Usually, this sort of hortative verb combines the main verb with the subject *us* and the helping verb *let*. Underline the helping verb and circle the main verb in each sentence.

> Let's (be) more careful next time.
> Let's (run) faster.
> Let's (be finished) now.

Instructor: The first verb is a state-of-being verb. The second and third are action verbs. Label them as *active* or *passive*.

> Let's (be) more careful next time.
>
> active
> Let's (run) faster.
>
> passive
> Let's (be finished) now.

Instructor: In first person plural hortative verbs, the state-of-being verb takes the form *be*. The active verb is the same form as the present active indicative. The passive verb combines *be* with the past participle. Read that out loud for me now.

→ *Student: **In first person plural hortative verbs, the helping verb** let **is used. The state-of-being verb takes the form** be**. The active verb is the same form as the present active indicative. The passive verb combines** be **with the past participle.***

Instructor: Now read the second set of sentences.

→ *Student: May you be happy. May you walk in joy. May you be saved from your own foolishness.*

Instructor: In these sentences, the helping verb *may* is used, and the speaker is addressing *just* the other person—not herself. Underline the helping verb and circle the main verb in each sentence. Label the verbs as *active, passive,* or *state-of-being.*

> state-of-being
> May you (be) happy.
>
> active
> May you (walk) in joy.
>
> passive
> May you (be saved) from your own foolishness.

Instructor: Except for the different helping verb, these verbs are formed in the same way as the first person plural hortative. Read the next set of rules out loud.

→ *Student: **In second person hortative verbs, the helping verb** may **is used. The state-of-being verb takes the form** be**. The active verb is the same form as the present active indicative. The passive verb combines** be **with the past participle.***

Instructor: Now read the last set of sentences.

→ *Student: Let the trumpets be sounded. May no creature on earth be silent. Let the Lord of the Black Lands come forth.*

Instructor: In these third person hortative statements, the speaker is encouraging someone or something else to do something—not herself, or someone she is speaking to, but a third party. These kinds of hortative verbs can take either *let* or *may*. In each sentence, underline the helping verb *let* or *may*, circle each main verb, and label the verbs as *state-of-being*, *active*, or *passive*.

> passive
> Let the trumpets be sounded
>
> state-of-being
> May no creature on earth be silent.
>
> active
> Let the Lord of the Black Lands come forth.

Instructor: These third person verbs are *almost* the same as the first person hortative verbs. Read the final set of rules out loud.

→ *Student: **Third person hortative verbs use the helping verbs** let or may. **The state-of-being verb takes the form** be. **The active verb is the same form as the present active subjunctive. The passive verb combines** be **with the past participle.***

Instructor: When third person hortative verbs are active, they use the subjunctive form. Look at the next chart in your workbook. Notice that for the first and second person hortative statements, the verb is the same as the active indicative: We sing, you sing, let us sing, may you sing. But look at the third person statements. What is the indicative form of the verb *sing*?

→ *Student: Sings.*

Instructor: What is the subjunctive form?

→ *Student: Sing.*

Instructor: What is the hortative form?

→ *Student: Sing.*

Instructor: There's one more thing to keep in mind when you're using hortative verbs. Look carefully at the next two sentences. In the first sentence, *you* is the subject, and *May travel* is the hortative verb. But in the second sentence, *us* cannot be the subject. Why not?

> **Note to Instructor:** If the student does not know the answer, tell him to turn back to Lesson 50 and examine the definitions and lists carefully.

→ *Student: Us is an object pronoun.*

Instructor: Hortative sentences that use *let* instead of *may* are actually assigning the action to an unknown subject—maybe one that exists, maybe an impersonal force of some kind. There's no way to know what the subject actually is.

Look at the diagram of *May you travel safely*.

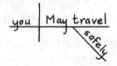

Instructor: It's a simple diagram. But to diagram *Let us travel safely,* you have to mark the subject space with an *x* for *unknown.*

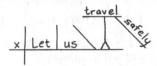

Instructor: Then, instead of diagramming *Let* as a helping verb, you place it on the main verb space, followed by the object pronoun *us. Travel safely* then sits in the object complement space on the diagram. You studied object complements back in Lesson 40. Review the definition by reading it out loud, and then examine the sentence and diagram that follows it.

→ *Student: An object complement follows the direct object and renames or describes it.*

Instructor: In a hortative sentence that uses *let,* the main verb isn't actually an object complement, even though it follows the object and completes it. So even though it sits in the object complement spot, we put it up on a tree to remind ourselves that it is actually a verb.

Put the next two diagrams on the diagram frames provided.

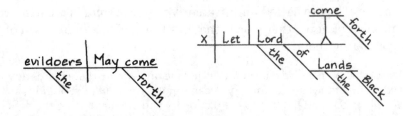

> **Note to Instructor:** Black Lands can also be diagrammed as a single compound noun.

Instructor: Complete your exercises now.

—LESSON 110—

Transitive Verbs
Intransitive Verbs
Sit/Set, Lie/Lay, Rise/Raise
Ambitransitive Verbs

Instructor: The first two sentences in your workbook come from traditional Inuit folk tales. Underline the verb in each sentence, and parse each verb by writing the tense, mood, and voice above it.

simple past,
indicative, active
The reindeer <u>broke</u> the first house apart.

simple past,
indicative, active
The ice between the two floes <u>broke</u> apart.

Instructor: Those two verbs look exactly the same—but they're not. Read me the next two definitions. You first learned them back in Lesson 56.

→ *Student: Transitive verbs express action that is received by some person or thing. Intransitive verbs express action that is not received by any person or thing.*

Instructor: Here's another way to put it: Transitive verbs can have direct objects, but intransitive verbs can't. Label the direct object in the first sentence.

simple past,
indicative, active   DO

The reindeer <u>broke</u> the first house apart.

simple past,
indicative, active

The ice between the two floes <u>broke</u> apart.

Instructor: What did the reindeer break?

→ *Student: The first house.*

Instructor: In the second sentence, the ice broke—but it didn't *break* anything! English has many verbs that are transitive, many that are intransitive—and many that can be both! These verbs have an interesting name. They're called **ambitransitive** verbs. *Ambi* is a Latin prefix that means "both." You probably know other words that use the preface *ambi-*. Two of them are shown below. Can you define them?

> **Note to Instructor:** You can spend as much or as little time on defining these words as you choose. If the student isn't familiar with them, you can simply give him the definitions and allow him to write them in, or you can send him to the dictionary and ask him to find the definitions; you could also decide to ask him to find the root of each word. Use the information below to complete the assignment in the way that you choose.

ambidextrous   <u>both right- and left-handed; able to use both hands equally</u>
                   dexter: Latin for "right-handed"
                   ambi-dextrous: literally "right-handed with both [hands]"

ambiguous   <u>having several possible meanings; meaning both one thing and another</u>
                   agere: Latin for "to drive, to lead"
                   ambi-[a]guous: literally "driving both [ways]"

ambitransitive   **both transitive and intransitive**

Instructor: Before we look at more ambitransitive verbs, let's review a few important details. First, only transitive verbs can be passive. Circle the transitive verbs in the next two sentences.

When I (hear) my voice on a record I absolutely (loathe) my voice. I (cannot stand) my voice.
    —Roger Daltrey

Music in the soul (can be heard) by the universe.
    —Laozi

Instructor: The action of each transitive verb is received by something else. In the first sentence, the three actions are received by three direct objects. What are they?

→ *Student: Voice, voice, voice.*

Instructor: In the second sentence, the action is received by what word?

→ *Student: Music.*

Instructor: In a sentence with a passive transitive verb, the subject receives the action, rather than the action affecting a direct object. So remember: transitive verbs either have objects, or are passive, but *something* has to receive the action!

Read me the next two definitions.

→ *Student: Transitive verbs can be active or passive. Intransitive verbs can only be active.*

Instructor: Rephrase the sentence *I hate thunderstorms* with a passive transitive verb.

→ *Student: Thunderstorms are hated by me.*

Instructor: Is there any way to rephrase *The goat bleated* with a passive verb instead of an active one?

> **Note to Instructor:** You can offer the student silly options such as *The goat was bleated*, if you choose.

→ *Student: No.*

Instructor: So you know that *bleated* is an intransitive verb.

Knowing the difference between transitive and intransitive verbs can keep you from misusing words that are commonly confused—like *sit* and *set, lie* and *lay,* and *rise* and *raise.* Read the next two rules.

→ *Student:* **Sit, lie,** *and* **rise are intransitive. Set, lay,** *and* **raise** *are transitive.*

Instructor: Fill in the blanks in the following sentences with the active indicative form of one of these six verbs, in the tense indicated.

(simple present)	Strong women __rise__ above adverse circumstances.
(simple present)	The waiter __sets__ the coffee carefully on the table.
(progressive past)	The hen __was laying__ four or five eggs every week.
(simple present)	She __sits__ primly on the elaborate throne.
(simple past)	The farmer __raised__ corn, wheat, and rye.
(progressive present)	The horse __is lying__ peacefully on its side in the pasture.

Instructor: In those sentences, *set, lay,* and *raise* are transitive. *Raise* and *lay* are *always* transitive. But *set* can be ambitransitive. Put every word of the sentences on the diagram frames that follow.

The cook tied on his apron and set to work.
The travellers set off first thing in the morning.
As we reached the ocean, the sun was setting.

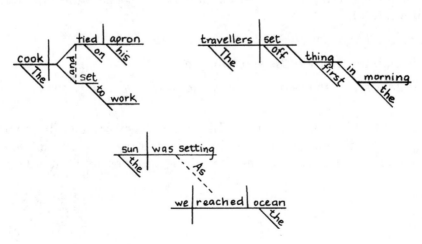

Instructor: Which two verbs in those sentences are transitive?

→ *Student: Tied and reached.*

Instructor: In all three sentences, *set* acts like an intransitive action verb. Before you complete your exercises, review all five definitions from this lesson by reading them out loud.

→ *Student: Transitive verbs can be active or passive. Intransitive verbs can only be active. Ambitransitive verbs can be either transitive or intransitive. Transitive verbs express action that is received by some person or thing. Intransitive verbs express action that is not received by any person or thing.*

Instructor: Complete your exercises now.

— LESSON 111 —

Ambitransitive Verbs
Gerunds and Infinitives
Infinitive Phrases as Direct Objects
Infinitive Phrases with Understood *To*

Instructor: In your workbook, you'll see four sentences that use the ambitransitive verb *try*. What does ambitransitive mean? You can look back at the definition if necessary.

→ *Student: Ambitransitive means that the verb can be either transitive or intransitive.*

Instructor: In which sentence is *try* intransitive?

→ *Student: The first sentence.*

Instructor: In the next three sentences, circle the direct object of the transitive verb *try*.

> I may not succeed, but I will try.
>
> Try the chocolate (cake.)
>
> The concert-goers tried (arriving) early.
>
> Every night, he tries (to go) to bed by ten.

Instructor: *Cake, arriving,* and *to go* are all different parts of speech. *Cake* is a noun. *Arriving* is a gerund. What is a gerund?

→ *Student: A gerund is a present participle acting as a noun.*

Instructor: *To go* is an infinitive. What is an infinitive?

→ *Student: An infinitive is formed by combining* to *and the first person singular present form of a verb.*

Instructor: Just like gerunds, infinitives can act like nouns. They can be subjects or objects. You've already learned how to diagram gerunds and infinitives acting as nouns. Review that now by putting each sentence onto the correct frame below. (The frames aren't in order.)

Instructor: In the sentence "Every night, he tries to go to bed by ten," *to go* is the infinitive acting as the direct object of the transitive verb *tries*. What kind of phrase is *to bed*?

→ Student: A prepositional phrase.

Instructor: Be sure not to confuse infinitives with prepositional phrases that use *to*! An infinitive phrase will always have a verb following the *to*. A prepositional phrase will have a noun or pronoun as the object of the preposition.

For the rest of today, we'll examine infinitive phrases that are a little bit more complicated. Read me the next sentence out loud.

→ Student: Mother told me to clean my room.

Instructor: Underline the subject once and the predicate twice.

<u>Mother</u> <u><u>told</u></u> me to clean my room.

Instructor: What command did the mother actually issue?

→ Student: Clean your room.

Instructor: *To clean my room* is the direct object of the transitive verb *told*. Put the subject, verb, and direct object on the diagram frame in your workbook.

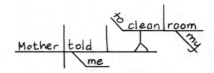

Instructor: That just leaves one word: *me*. What part of the sentence is *me*?

> **Note to Instructor:** If the student cannot identify it, say, "Think about a similar sentence. *Mother gave me cake. Cake* is the direct object. What is *me*?"

→ Student: Indirect object.

Instructor: Certain verbs, such as *told, ordered,* and *made*, take both an infinitive phrase as a direct object and a noun or pronoun as an indirect object. You know that *me* has to be *some* kind of object. How do you know that?

→ Student: Me *is an object pronoun.*

> **Note to Instructor:** If the student cannot answer, say, "Turn back to Lesson 50, Pronoun Case, and look at the list of pronouns."

Instructor: Add *me* to the diagram in your workbook.

Let's look at a sentence where the indirect object is a noun instead of a pronoun. Read me the next sentence.

→ *Student: The duchess ordered the maid to arrange the flowers.*

Instructor: Circle the direct object and label it *DO*. Underline the indirect object and label it *IO*.

IO   DO

The duchess ordered the <u>maid</u> (to arrange the flowers)

Instructor: Sometimes, infinitive phrases acting as direct objects lose the *to* when they're paired with indirect objects. Read me the next sentence.

→ *Student: His mistake made me lose money.*

Instructor: What's the subject?

→ *Student: Mistake.*

Instructor: What's the predicate?

→ *Student: Made.*

Instructor: The direct object is *to lose money*, but the infinitive *lose* has lost its *to*. Draw a caret between *me* and *lose*, and insert the word *to*. Then circle the direct object and label it *DO*. Underline the indirect object and label it *IO*.

IO   DO
     to

His mistake made <u>me</u> ^ (lose money)

Instructor: Examine the diagram of this sentence carefully.

Instructor: Then, place every word of the next sentence on the diagram frame provided.

Instructor: Remember, infinitive phrases can also act like adverbs. In the next three sentences, the infinitive phrase is *not* a direct object. Read me the first sentence.

→ *Student: I was made to love you.*

Instructor: *To love you* can't be a direct object—because the verb is passive! The subject *I* is already receiving the action of the verb—it can't also have a direct object! Put the sentence on the frame provided.

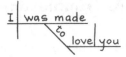

Instructor: In that sentence, the infinitive phrase *to love you* is an adverb, describing *how* the speaker was made. Read me the next sentence.

→ *Student: He was good enough to sing.*

Instructor: What kind of verb is *was*?

→ *Student: A linking verb [OR A state-of-being verb].*

Instructor: Only action verbs can take direct objects. *To sing* describes the predicate adjective *good* and answers the question *how*. How good was he? Good enough to sing. Put the sentence on the frame provided.

Instructor: The next sentence has a very peculiar verb in it. Read the sentence to me.

→ *Student: You ought to go home.*

Instructor: *Ought* is a very old form of the verb *owe*—in fact, it comes from Old English, which was spoken over a thousand years ago. Like *should* or *need*, it expresses obligation. The sentence would mean the same thing if you said, *You need to go home* or *You should go home*. But now look at the three diagrams in your *workbook*.

Instructor: In the first sentence, *to go home* is an infinitive phrase acting as a direct object. *Need* is a transitive verb that takes a direct object—think about the sentences *I need chocolate* or *The dog needs water*. *Home* is an adverbial noun answering the question *where*.

In the second sentence, *should* is a helping verb accompanying *go*, and *home* is still an adverbial noun answering the question *where*.

And in the third sentence, the verb phrase *ought to* actually acts as a helping verb—just like the helping verb *should*! In the next two sentences, circle *ought to* and *should* and underline the entire verb phrase.

The politician (ought to) have been thrown in jail.

The politician (should) have been thrown in jail.

Instructor: Both of those verbs are perfect present tense, passive voice, and modal mood—expressing obligation. *Ought to* and *should* are both helping verbs that are used to form the modal mood. So remember—when you see *ought*, the *to* that follows isn't the start of an infinitive. It belongs to *ought*. Old words don't always follow the rules of modern English!

Finish your exercises now.

— LESSON 112 —

Principal Parts
Yet More Troublesome Verbs

Instructor: Over the last weeks, you have learned a tremendous amount about verbs! Take a few minutes now to review by completing the first exercise in your workbook, Exercise 112A.

Instructor: Let's take some time to focus in on just *three* of those definitions: first principal part, second principal part, and third principal part. All the way back in Lesson 46, you learned about principal parts. How many principal parts do English verbs have?

→ *Student: Three.*

Instructor: You also learned what those parts are—present, past, and past participle—and how to form them—the first person singular forms of the simple present, simple past, and perfect past, minus helping verbs. What are the three principal parts of the verb *pontificate*?

> **Note to Instructor:** Make sure that the student knows that *pontificate* means "to speak in a lecturing, dogmatic manner." If he's unfamiliar with the word, you can choose to define it for him—or send him to the dictionary.

→ *Student: Pontificate, pontificated, pontificated.*

Instructor: What are the three principal parts of the verb *sing*?

→ *Student: Sing, sang, sung.*

Instructor: What are the three principal parts of the verb *cut*?

→ *Student: Cut, cut, cut.*

Instructor: What are the three principal parts of the verb *become*?

→ *Student: Become, became, become.*

Instructor: Each one of these verbs has a slightly different pattern of principal parts. *Sing* changes three times. *Pontificate* has one form for the present and another form for the past and past participle. *Become* has the same form for the present and the past participle, but changes for the past only. *Cut* doesn't change at all!

Knowing the principal parts of a few tricky verbs can help you to use them properly. So let's take a look at our old friends *sit/set*, *lie/lay*, and *rise/raise*. Two lessons ago, you learned how to tell them apart. What is the difference?

→ *Student: Sit, lie, and rise are intransitive. Set, lay, and raise are transitive.*

Instructor: Of course, it's not quite that easy! For one thing, the simple past of *lie* looks almost exactly like the simple present of *lay*—with the except of the third person singular form. Examine the conjugations in your workbook, and then fill in the blanks in the sentences with the correct form.

(simple past)   The child <u>laid</u> out her clothes for the birthday party the night before.
(simple past)   She got sunburned because she <u>lay</u> out in the sun too long.
(simple present)   <u>Lie</u> down and go to sleep now.
(simple present)   <u>Lay</u> your head down and close your eyes.

Instructor: The principal parts of these six common verbs can point you towards the correct forms to use. Reading left to right on the chart, say the principal parts out loud now.

→ *Student: Lie, lay, lain. Lay, laid, laid. Sit, sat, sat. Set, set, set, Rise, rose, risen. Raise, raised, raised.*

Instructor: Complete your second exercise now.

Instructor: Those verbs in your last lesson are probably the most likely to be misused, no matter where you are in the country. But in different parts of the U.S., other verbs are commonly used incorrectly in casual speech. You may not make any of the mistakes associated with *give, come, write, go,* and *eat,* but some people do! Read the principal parts of each verb, from left to right.

→ *Student: Give, gave, given. Come, came, come. Write, wrote, written. go, went, gone. Eat, ate, eaten.*

Instructor: In the five sentences that follow, cross out the incorrect form and replace it with the correct principal part from the chart above.

She had ~~gave~~ her outgrown shoes to her sister.
_{given}

Has she ~~came~~ home from the movies yet?
_{come}

The policeman had ~~wrote~~ her a speeding ticket.
_{written}

When Mom got home, I had already ~~went~~ to bed.
_{gone}

He has ~~ate~~ his dinner too fast.
_{eaten}

Instructor: Complete your final exercise now.

Still More About Clauses

—LESSON 113—
Clauses and Phrases

Instructor: In the first paragraph in your workbook, Father Abbot from Redwall is enjoying a feast. Father Abbot, in case you've never read *Redwall,* is a mouse. Read the paragraph out loud.

→ *Student: All eyes were on the Father Abbot. He took a dainty fork loaded precariously with steaming fish. Carefully he transferred it from plate to mouth. Chewing delicately, he turned his eyes upwards then closed them, whiskers atwitch, jaws working steadily, munching away, his tail curled up holding a napkin which neatly wiped his mouth.*

Instructor: The author, Brian Jacques, is a master at using the building blocks of sentences: phrases, independent clauses, and dependent clauses. Today we're going to review what you've learned about clauses and phrases over the past few months.

Let's start with that very first sentence: *All eyes were on the Father Abbot.* Underline the subject once and the predicate twice.

All <u>eyes</u> <u>were</u> on the Father Abbot.

Instructor: Now, read me the next three definitions in your workbook.

→ *Student: A clause is a group of words that contains a subject and a predicate. An independent clause can stand by itself as a sentence. A sentence is a group of words that usually contains a subject and a predicate. A sentence begins with a capital letter and ends with a punctuation mark. A sentence contains a complete thought.*

Instructor: Is *All eyes were on the Father Abbot* a sentence?

→ *Student: Yes.*

Instructor: It is an independent clause—which means that yes, it is a sentence! Read me the next sentence in the excerpt.

→ *Student: He took a dainty fork loaded precariously with steaming fish.*

Instructor: Underline the subject once and the predicate twice.

<u>He</u> <u>took</u> a dainty fork loaded precariously with steaming fish.

Instructor: There are two verb forms in that sentence that are not acting as predicates—a past participle and a gerund. What is the past participle?

→ *Student: Loaded.*

Instructor: What is the gerund?

→ *Student: Steaming.*

Instructor: Both of those verb forms are part of phrases. What is a phrase?

→ *Student: A phrase is a group of words serving a single grammatical function.*

Instructor: What is the difference between a clause and a phrase?

→ *Student: A clause has a subject and predicate, and a phrase doesn't.*

Instructor: Circle the phrase *loaded precariously* and the phrase *with steaming fish*. What word does the past participle phrase *loaded precariously* describe?

→ *Student: Fork.*

Instructor: This is an adjective phrase describing the noun *fork*. What word does the prepositional phrase *with steaming fish* describe?

→ *Student: Loaded.*

> **Note to Instructor:** If necessary, prompt the student by saying, "How was the fork loaded?"

Instructor: Draw arrows from each circle back to the word modified.

He took a dainty fork (loaded precariously) (with steaming fish)

Instructor: In the third sentence, circle the two prepositional phrases that are acting as adverbs, and draw arrows back to the word modified.

Carefully he transferred it (from plate) (to mouth)

> **Note to Instructor:** These are adverb phrases because they answer the question *where*: Where did he transfer it?

Instructor: Now you've reviewed independent clauses, and phrases acting as adjectives and adverbs. But, of course, clauses can also act as adjectives and adverbs—as long as they are dependent clauses. Begin your review of dependent clauses by reading the next four rules out loud.

→ *Student: A dependent clause is a fragment that cannot stand by itself as a sentence. Dependent clauses can act as adjective clauses, adverb clauses, or noun clauses. An adjective clause is a dependent clause that acts as an adjective in a sentence, modifying a noun or pronoun in the independent clause. Relative pronouns* (who, whom, whose, which, that) *introduce adjective clauses and refer back to an antecedent in the independent clause.*

Instructor: Circle the adjective clause in the last sentence, underline the subject and predicate of the clause, and draw an arrow back to the word modified.

Chewing delicately, he turned his eyes upwards then closed them, whiskers atwitch,

jaws working steadily, munching away, his tail curled up holding a napkin

(which neatly wiped his mouth)

> **Note to Instructor:** If the student identifies *his tail curled up* as a clause, point out that *curled* is a past participle acting as an adjective, not a verb acting as a predicate.

Instructor: Adjective clauses are usually introduced by relative pronouns—but in some circumstances, they can be introduced by a relative adverb. Read me the next rule.

→ *Student: Relative adverbs (where, when, why) introduce adjective clauses when they refer back to a place, time, or reason in the independent clause.*

Instructor: If an adjective clause describes a time (an hour, or year, or minute), a reason (why something happened), or a place (a mountain, a kitchen, a field), it often begins with an adverb—even though the clause itself acts like an adjective. In the next sentence, what clause describes *which* side of the wall Matthias starts to slide down?

→ *Student: Where the woods came close up to the Abbey.*

Instructor: Circle that adjective clause, draw an arrow back to the place noun *side*, and then underline the subject of the dependent clause once and the predicate twice. Then, draw a box around the relative adverb.

Matthias started to slide down the rope on the Mossflower side of the wall, (where) the <u>woods</u> <u>came</u> close up to the Abbey.

Instructor: Whether an adjective clause is introduced by a relative pronoun or a relative adverb, remember that a dotted line connects the relative word to the noun or pronoun it describes. Examine the first diagram in your workbook. The adjective clause *on which hung a long tapestry* describes what word?

→ *Student: Wall.*

Instructor: The relative pronoun *which* refers back to the antecedent *wall*, and a dotted line connects them. Within the dependent clause itself, what part of the sentence is *which*?

→ *Student: The object of the preposition.*

The Father Abbot halted in front of the wall on which hung a long tapestry.

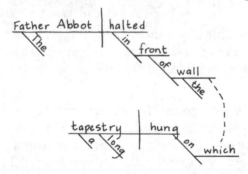

Instructor: Examine the second diagram. What word does the adjective clause *when the Founders were under attack from many foxes, vermin, and a great wildcat* describe?

→ *Student: Winter.*

Instructor: The clause tells you *which* winter. The relative adverb *when* refers back to the antecedent *winter*, and a dotted line connects them. Within the dependent clause itself, what part of the sentence is *when*?

→ *Student: An adverb.*

He arrived here in the deep winter when the Founders were under attack from many foxes, vermin, and a great wildcat.

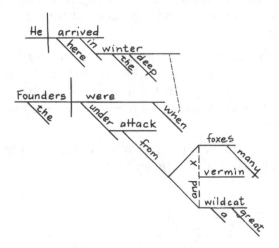

Instructor: Except for clauses that describe times, reasons, and places, dependent clauses beginning with adverbs are usually . . . acting as adverbs! Read me the next rule, including the list of common adverbs that introduce dependent clauses.

→ *Student: Adverb clauses can be introduced by adverbs. Common adverbs that introduce adverbial clauses are:*

> *as and its compounds (as if, as soon as, as though)*
> *how and its compound (however)*
> *when and its compound (whenever)*
> *whence*
> *where and its compounds (whereat, whereby, wherein, wherefore, whereon)*
> *while*
> *whither*

Instructor: Circle the adverb clauses in the next sentence and draw an arrow from each to the word it modifies. In each dependent clause, underline the subjects once and the predicate twice, and draw a box around the adverb that subordinates the clause.

> **Note to Instructor:** This is a tricky sentence; the clause *where she dug her paws in, holding the cart still and secure* is an adjective clause beginning with an adverb and describing a place (the slope of the ditch). Watch the student as she completes her work, and if she begins to circle the adjective clause, stop and ask her to look at the clause again.

Her blunt claws churned the roadside soil as she propelled the cart through a gap in the hawthorn hedge down to the slope of the ditch where she dug her paws in, holding the cart still and secure while John Churchmouse and Cornflower's father jumped out and wedged the wheels firmly with stones.

Instructor: Adverb clauses can also be introduced by subordinating conjunctions. Read the next two rules and the list of subordinating conjunctions now.

→ *Student: A subordinating conjunction joins unequal words or groups of words together. Subordinating conjunctions and subordinating correlative conjunctions often join an adverb clause to an independent clause. Common subordinating conjunctions are: After, although, as (as soon as), because, before, if, in order that, lest, since, though, till, unless, until, although/ though… yet/still, if… then.*

Instructor: Whether an adverb clause is introduced by an adverb or by a subordinating conjunction, it is diagrammed the same way—the verb of the adverb clause is attached to the word it modifies in the main clause by a dotted line, and the subordinating word is written on the dotted line. The next sentence has one adverb clause and one adjective clause. Put each word on the frame provided.

> All the mice took a solemn vow never to harm another living creature, unless it was an enemy that sought to harm our Order by violence.

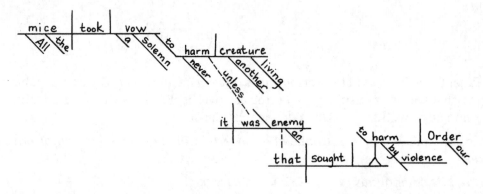

Instructor: We are almost at the end of our clause review. Clauses can act like adjectives; clauses can act like adverbs; and clauses can also act like one more part of speech. Read me the next rule.

→ *Student: A noun clause takes the place of a noun. Noun clauses can be introduced by relative pronouns, relative adverbs, or subordinating conjunctions.*

Instructor: A noun clause can be a subject, predicate nominative, object, direct object, indirect object, or object of a preposition—just like a noun. In the next three sentences, noun clauses act as three different sentence parts, and are introduced by three different kinds of words. Read me the first sentence.

→ *Student: Somewhere there had to be a clue, a single lead that might tell him where the resting place of Martin the Warrior could be found, or where he could regain possession of the ancient sword for his Abbey.*

Instructor: There are *two* noun clauses in this sentence. Both of them lie *inside* the adjective clause describing *lead*. What is that entire adjective clause? It tells you *which* lead.

→ *Student: That might tell him where the resting place of Martin the Warrior could be found, or where he could regain possession of the ancient sword for his Abbey.*

Instructor: Underline the subject of that clause once and the predicate twice. *Him* is the indirect object of the verb. It has *two* direct objects. Each direct object is a noun clause. What are the two things that the lead might tell?

→ *Student: "Where the resting place of Martin the Warrior could be found," "Where he could regain possession of the ancient sword for his Abbey."*

Instructor: Circle each noun clause and label it *DO*. Then, draw a box around the word that introduces each clause. Is this a relative pronoun, relative adverb, or subordinating conjunction?

→ *Student: Relative adverb.*

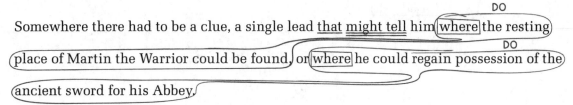

Somewhere there had to be a clue, a single lead <u>that</u> <u>might tell</u> him where the resting place of Martin the Warrior could be found, or where he could regain possession of the ancient sword for his Abbey.

Instructor: Read me the second sentence.

→ *Student: The defenders stood and cheered in the depression above what had once been Killconey's tunnel.*

Instructor: Underline the prepositional phrase *above what had once been Killconey's tunnel*. What is the object of the preposition *above*?

→ *Student: What had once been Killconey's tunnel.*

Instructor: That noun clause is the object of the preposition. Draw a second line beneath the noun clause and write *OP* above it.

The defenders stood and cheered in the depression above what had once been Killconey's tunnel.

Instructor: Draw a box around the word that introduces the clause. Is it a relative pronoun, relative adverb, or subordinating conjunction?

→ *Student: Relative pronoun.*

Instructor: When a relative pronoun introduces a noun clause, it usually has an unstated antecedent. The sentence actually means something like, "The defenders stood and cheered in the depression directly above *the space that had once been Killconey's tunnel.*" *What* stands in for *the space.*

Read me the last sentence.

→ *Student: It is because you are kind and good.*

Instructor: Underline the subject of that sentence once, the predicate twice, and circle the noun clause.

<u>It</u> <u>is</u> because you are kind and good.

Instructor: The noun clause follows the linking verb *is* and *renames* the subject. What is *It*?

→ *Student: Because you are kind and good.*

Instructor: What part of the sentence does this noun clause function as?

→ *Student: Predicate nominative.*

Instructor: Draw a box around the word that introduces the noun clause. Is it a relative pronoun, relative adverb, or subordinating conjunction?

→ *Student: Subordinating conjunction.*

Instructor: Finish up your review by putting every word of each sentence on the correct frame in your workbook.

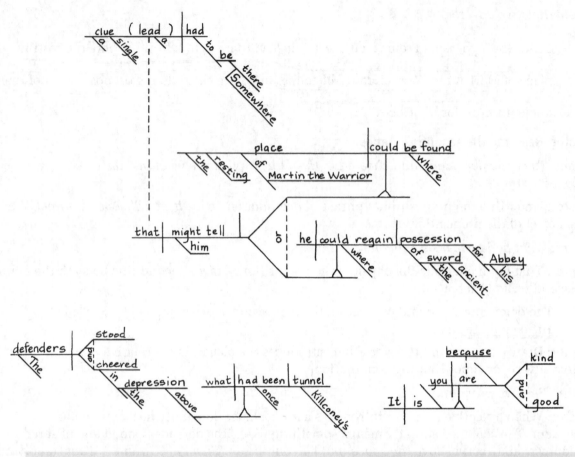

Instructor: Complete your exercises now.

—LESSON 114—

Restrictive and Non-Restrictive Modifying Clauses
Punctuating Modifying Clauses
Which and *That*

Instructor: The first two sentences in your workbook, from *How Not to Be Wrong* by Jordan Ellenberg, both contain adjective clauses beginning with *which*. What is the adjective clause in the first sentence?

→ *Student: Which seems so reasonable.*

Instructor: What does it modify?

→ *Student: Mechanism.*

Note to Instructor: If the student says *p-value*, point out that this is actually the object of the preposition *of*, and the adjective clause modifies the subject of the sentence, *mechanism*.

Instructor: What is the adjective clause in the second sentence?

→ *Student: Which happens 1/4 of the time.*

Instructor: What does it modify?

→ *Student: Event.*

Instructor: What is the difference between those two adjective clauses?

→ *Student: The first is set off by commas and the second is not.*

> **Note to Instructor:** If necessary, prompt the student by saying, "What is the difference in punctuation?"

Instructor: Read me the first definition that follows the sentences.

→ *Student: A non-restrictive modifying clause describes the word that it modifies. Removing the clause doesn't change the essential meaning of the sentence. Only non-restrictive clauses should be set off by commas.*

Instructor: Which of those two adjective clauses is non-restrictive?

→ *Student: Which seems so reasonable.*

Instructor: Read me the first sentence without the non-restrictive clause.

→ *Student: Why does the mechanism of the p-value work so very badly in this setting?*

Instructor: Leaving the clause out doesn't change the essential meaning of the sentence! But now try reading the second sentence without the adjective clause.

→ *Student: If the first throw is tails and the second is heads, an event, Paul gets two ducats.*

Instructor: When you remove the restrictive clause *which happens 1/4 of the time*, the sentence doesn't make sense any more. Read me the definition of a restrictive clause.

→ *Student: A restrictive modifying clause defines the word that it modifies. Removing the clause changes the essential meaning of the sentence.*

Instructor: You should never put a comma before a restrictive modifying clause. Adding the comma can change the meaning of a whole sentence! Look at the next two sentences from *How Not to Be Wrong*. Read the first version of the sentence, pausing at the comma.

→ *Student: I especially like the "Methods" section, which starts "One mature Atlantic Salmon (Salmo salar) participated in the fMRI study."*

Instructor: Now you know that the *Methods* section of the paper the author is discussing begins with *One mature Atlantic Salmon*. Read the second version of the sentence without pausing.

→ *Student: I especially like the "Methods" section which starts "One mature Atlantic Salmon (Salmo salar) participated in the fMRI study."*

Instructor: This sentence tells you that there are several different *Methods* sections, and that the author has an especial fondness for *one* of them—the one that starts "One mature Atlantic Salmon."

(By the way, the first sentence is the original one.)

Sometimes, writers who aren't sure about their grammar put commas in front of noun clauses. Review the definition of a noun clause one more time by reading it out loud.

→ *Student: A noun clause takes the place of a noun. Noun clauses can be introduced by relative pronouns, relative adverbs, or subordinating conjunctions.*

Instructor: In each of the next sentences from *How Not to Be Wrong*, a comma has been inserted incorrectly in front of each noun clause. Underline each noun clause and use a proofreader's deletion mark to remove the unnecessary commas.

                                                                                DO
In principle, if you carry out a powerful enough study, you can find out ℓ<u>which it is</u>.

                                                                      PN
The reason the 0.999 . . . problem is difficult is ℓ <u>that it brings our intuitions into conflict</u>.

> **Note to Instructor:** In the following dialogue, prompt the student as needed.

Instructor: In the first sentence, what part of the sentence is *which it is*?

→ *Student: The direct object.*

Instructor: Write *DO* above it. In the second sentence, what part of the sentence is *that it brings our intuitions into conflict*?

→ *Student: The predicate nominative.*

Instructor: Write *PN* above it.

Instructor: There's one exception to the rule that noun clauses shouldn't have commas around them. Read me the next rule.

→ *Student: An appositive is a noun, noun phrase, or noun clause that usually follows another noun and renames or explains it. Appositives are set off by commas.*

Instructor: When a noun clause is acting like an appositive, it has commas around it—because appositives that are longer than one word usually do have commas around them! Underline the noun clause acting as an appositive in the next sentence.

The Goldbach conjecture, <u>that every even number greater than 2 is the sum of two primes</u>, is another one that would have to be true if primes behaved like random numbers.

Instructor: Now you've reviewed almost every important rule about clauses! But before we finish, you should know about one more odd little rule.

The relative pronouns *which* and *that* can both be used of *things*. Read me the next two sentence fragments. (These are *not* from *How Not to Be Wrong*!)

→ *Student: The chocolate brownies that . . . The chocolate brownies which . . .*

Instructor: *That* and *which* both have *brownies* as an antecedent. Now read the next two sentences.

→ *Student: The chocolate brownies that were on the counter are gone now. The chocolate brownies, which were made with olive oil instead of butter, have been sitting on the counter since lunch time.*

Instructor: What is the adjective clause in the first sentence?

→ *Student: That were on the counter.*

Instructor: The brownies *on the counter* are gone—not the brownies in the drawer or in the pantry. That is a restrictive clause. The adjective clause in the second sentence is non-restrictive. Leave it out and read the sentence.

→ *Student: The chocolate brownies have been sitting on the counter since lunch time.*

Instructor: The restrictive clause doesn't have commas around it. The non-restrictive clause does. But notice one more difference: The restrictive clause begins with *that*, and the non-restrictive clause begins with *which*. For many years, grammar books have insisted on this difference: When the relative pronoun refers to a thing rather than a person, *which* introduces non-restrictive clauses, and *that* introduces restrictive clauses. The next two sentences, which are from *A Christmas Carol* by Charles Dickens, follow this old-fashioned rule. Underline the non-restrictive adjective clause, and circle the restrictive adjective clause. Draw an arrow back from each clause to the word modified.

"These are but shadows of the things (that have been,)" said the Ghost.

It was shrouded in a deep black garment, which concealed its head, its face, its form, and left nothing of it visible save one outstretched hand.

Instructor: You should know about this rule, because you will sometimes run across a teacher, or an editor, or a college professor, who thinks it's important. But the truth is that many good writers now ignore the difference. In fact, good writers have always ignored the difference—as you can see from the next two sentences from *A Christmas Carol!* Underline the restrictive clause that describes *chambers*. What pronoun introduces it?

→ *Student: Which.*

Instructor: Underline the non-restrictive clause that describes *voice*. What pronoun introduces it?

→ *Student: That.*

He lived in chambers which had once belonged to his deceased partner.

At last she said, and in a steady, cheerful voice, that only faltered once, "I have known him walk with—I have known him walk with Tiny Tim upon his shoulder, very fast indeed."

Instructor: Like many contemporary writers, Jordan Ellenberg also uses *which* and *that* interchangeably. In the next sentence, underline the restrictive clause describing *one*. What pronoun introduces it?

→ *Student: Which.*

That's certainly an impressive figure, but one which clearly indicates that the percentage doesn't mean quite what you're used to it meaning.

Instructor: Read the italicized versions of all three sentences. These versions follow the which/that rule.

→ *Student: He lived in chambers that had once belonged to his deceased partner.*

At last she said, and in a steady, cheerful voice, which only faltered once, "I have known him walk with—I have known him walk with Tiny Tim upon his shoulder, very fast indeed."

That's certainly an impressive figure, but one that clearly indicates that the percentage doesn't mean quite what you're used to it meaning.

Instructor: The difference is very small—and it's mostly one of rhythm and sound. In the last sentence, Ellenberg probably uses *which* because otherwise the sentence would have *three* "thats" in it.

So be aware of the rule, in case you're required to follow it, but generally, choose whatever sounds better in the sentence: *which* or *that*.

Finish your exercises now.

—LESSON 115—

Conditional Sentences
Conditional Sentences as Dependent Clauses
Conditional Sentences with Missing Words
Formal *If* Clauses

Instructor: If you are ready, read me the first sentence in your notebook. If you're not familiar with it, I can tell you that it's from the book *Pride & Prejudice & Zombies.*

→ *Student: I have nothing to say against him; he has felled many a zombie; and if he had the fortune he ought to have, I should think you could not do better.*

Instructor: The last sentence in this complex-compound sentence set, the next three sentences, and the two sentences I used to introduce our lesson are all conditionals. Use the rules in your workbook, listed below the sentences, to identify each remaining sentence as a first, second, or third conditional; underline the main predicate in each clause twice; and parse each underlined verb.

Here are two things to remember: First, action verbs are active or passive in voice, but the voice of state-of-being verbs is simply *state of being.*

Second, remember that the subjunctive mood expresses situations that are unreal, wished for, or uncertain. In a conditional sentence, the condition clause *always* expresses a situation that is unreal, wished for, or uncertain. So even though the indicative and subjunctive moods often look the same, you know that the verb of a condition clause is *not* in the indicative! It is in the subjunctive—or sometimes, modal—mood.

simple past, active,
subjunctive

I have nothing to say against him; he has felled many a zombie; and if he <u>had</u> the

simple present,
active modal

fortune he <u>ought to have</u>, I should think you could not do better. <u>SECOND</u>

simple present, state- simple present, active,
of-being, subjunctive modal

If my children <u>are</u> silly, I <u>must hope</u> to be always sensible of it. <u>FIRST</u>

perfect past, active,   present past, active,
subjunctive   modal

If I <u>had known</u> as much this morning I certainly <u>would</u> not <u>have called</u> him. <u>THIRD</u>

simple past, linking,   simple present, passive,
subjunctive   modal

If I <u>were</u> not afraid of judging harshly, I <u>should be</u> almost <u>tempted</u> to demand satisfaction. <u>SECOND</u>

Instructor: Let's look at a couple of ways in which conditional clauses and sentences can vary. First, in the next sentence, underline the main subject once and the main predicate twice. Then, circle the entire clause that follows the predicate.

In her postscript it <u>was added</u> that if Mr. Bingley and his sister pressed them to stay longer, she could spare them.

Instructor: In this sentence, the clause acts as an adverb, modifying the passive verb *was added.* Read me the clause.

→ *Student: That if Mr. Bingley and his sister pressed them to stay longer, she could spare them.*

Instructor: In the last lesson, you learned that clauses can contain other clauses within them. In this case, the clause is a conditional sentence made up of the dependent clause *if Mr. Bingley and his sister pressed them to stay longer* and the main clause *she could spare them*. The whole conditional sentence is turned into a dependent clause by the subordinating conjunction *that*.

Underline twice and parse the predicates in each clause of the conditional sentence.

simple past, active,
subjunctive

In her postscript it <u>was added</u> that if Mr. Bingley and his sister <u>pressed</u> them to

simple present,
active, modal

stay longer, she <u>could spare</u> them.

Instructor: According to the rules in your workbook, what kind of conditional sentence is this?

→ *Student: Second conditional.*

Instructor: In the next sentence, the dependent clause is also made up of a conditional sentence with a main clause and dependent clause of its own. Underline the main subject of the entire sentence once, and the main predicate twice. Then, circle the entire clause that follows the main predicate.

However, I <u>recollected</u> afterwards that if he had been prevented going, the wedding need not be put off.

Instructor: What part of the sentence does this sentence serve as?

→ *Student: Direct object.*

Instructor: Like the adverb clause in the previous sentence, this noun clause, acting like the direct object of the predicate *recollected,* is a conditional sentence, made dependent on the main clause by the subordinating conjunction *that*. Within that dependent clause, underline each predicate and parse the verbs. I'll help you by pointing out that *need* is acting like a helping verb here, and is equal to *must* or *should*.

perfect past, passive,
subjunctive

However, I <u>recollected</u> afterwards that if he <u>had been prevented</u> going, the

simple past [or present],
passive, modal

wedding <u>need</u> not <u>be put</u> off.

Note to Instructor: The student may label the second verb as either simple past or simple present—the verb *put* is identical in both tenses.

Instructor: According to the rules in your workbook, what kind of conditional sentence is this?

→ *Student: Third conditional.*

Instructor: Now that you've seen conditional sentences behaving like dependent clauses, let's look at another variation. Read me the next sentence in your workbook.

→ *Student: If he fears me, why come hither?*

Instructor: English sentences drop words in all sorts of situations. In this sentence, the condition clause is complete, but the consequence clause has lost some of its words. Insert a caret between *why* and *come* and write the words *should he* above it.

> should he
>   If he fears me, why∧come hither?

Instructor: Now, read me the sentence.

→ *Student: If he fears me, why should he come hither?*

Instructor: Underline twice and parse both predicates.

> simple present,   simple present, active, modal
> active, subjunctive   should he
>   If he <u>fears</u> me, why∧<u>come</u> hither?

Instructor: What kind of conditional sentence is this?

→ *Student: First conditional.*

Instructor: Examine the second sentence carefully. Try to insert the missing words. Then, double underline and parse both predicates.

>   simple present, state of
>   being indicative
>   simple present,   is he
>   active, subjunctive
>   If he no longer <u>cares</u> for me, why∧silent?

> **Note to Instructor:** If the student has trouble, say, "Like the first sentence, this one is missing a subject and a helping verb in the consequence clause."

Instructor: What kind of conditional sentence is this?

→ *Student: First conditional.*

Instructor: English speakers are lazy—we tend to drop words whenever possible to make it easier to talk and write! That's why we have so many contractions—like *that's*, which is easier to say than *that is*! But there is one form of a conditional sentence that drops an important word not out of laziness, but as a way to become more formal. Read me the next sentence in your workbook.

→ *Student: Should you wish to, meet me in the drawing room.*

Instructor: Now listen carefully to the full version of that same sentence: "If you should wish to, meet me in the drawing room." I inserted the missing *if*, but what other change did I make?

> **Note to Instructor:** Repeat the full sentence as often as necessary. This encourages the student to listen carefully rather than simply look.

→ *Student: You* and *should switched places.*

Instructor: In very formal speech and writing, conditional sentences sometimes drop *if* and change the order of the subject and helping verb. Read me the rule, and then read me the next formal conditional sentence in your workbook.

→ *Student: **Formal conditional sentences drop if from the condition clause and reverse the order of the subject and helping verb.** Were you not otherwise agreeable, I should be forced to remove your tongue with my saber.*

Instructor: Now read the sentence again, changing the condition clause into a less formal version.

→ *Student: If you were not otherwise agreeable, I should be forced to remove your tongue with my saber.*

Instructor: One last note: When you diagram a conditional sentence with missing words, place an *x* in the place of each missing element. Look carefully at the diagrams in your workbook, and then place the sentences on the frames provided.

If he fears me, why come hither?

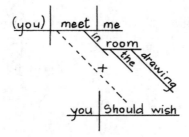

If he no longer cares for me, why silent?

Should you wish, meet me in the drawing room.

Were you not otherwise agreeable, I should be forced to remove your tongue with my saber.

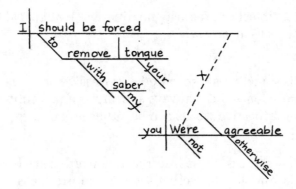

Instructor: Complete your exercises now.

—LESSON 116—

Words That Can Be Multiple Parts of Speech
Interrogatives
Demonstratives
Relative Adverbs and Subordinating Conjunctions

Instructor: We're going to finish up your clause work this week with some review.

Back in Week 27, you learned some of the most common words that can act as several different parts of speech. Review those—and learn a few new ones—by completing your first exercise now. *[Give the student time to complete Exercise 116A.]*

Instructor: All the way back in Lesson 59, you first learned about the words *who, whom, whose, what,* and *which*. Read me the two definitions in your workbook.

→ *Student: Interrogative pronouns take the place of nouns in questions. Interrogative adjectives modify nouns.*

Instructor: Some of these interrogative words are only pronouns, some are only adjectives, and some can be either. In the two columns of sentences, circle each interrogative word. Label the pronouns with the correct part of the sentence. Draw an arrow from the adjectives to the word modified.

Interrogative Pronouns   **Interrogative Adjectives**

subject
(Who) was Dragging Canoe?   (Whose) side was Dragging Canoe on?

   object of preposition
With (whom) did Dragging Canoe fight?   (What) war did he fight?

direct object
(What) did Dragging Canoe do?   (Which) tribe did Dragging Canoe belong to?

subject
(Which) of his countrymen followed him?

Instructor: Which interrogative words *only* act as pronouns?

→ *Student: Who and whom.*

Instructor: *Who* is always a subject or predicate nominative. *Whom* is always an object. Which interrogative word *only* acts as an adjective?

→ *Student: Whose.*

Instructor: This adjective is sometimes also called a possessive pronoun, because *whose* refers back to an unknown antecedent—but it always appears as an adjective, not by itself as a stand-alone pronoun. Which interrogative words can be either pronouns or adjectives?

→ *Student: What and which.*

Instructor: In the next five sentences, these interrogative words have become something else. Circle each one and underline the clause that each word introduces.

In the American Revolution, Dragging Canoe fought against the colonists (who) were rebelling against the British.

Dragging Canoe and his brother chiefs, (whom) he had known for many years, joined together and allied with the British.

Dragging Canoe told his tribesmen to consider the case of the Delaware, (whose) land had been swallowed by the American colonies.

At first, the American colonists did not know (what) Dragging Canoe was planning.

Dragging Canoe led attacks on the settlements (which) were in southeast North America.

Instructor: Four of these clauses are adjective clauses. In each, the interrogative word has become a relative pronoun, referring back to the noun described by the clause. Draw an arrow from each relative pronoun back to its antecedent. Then, tell me which clause is *not* an adjective clause.

→ *Student: What Dragging Canoe was planning.*

> **Note to Instructor:** If the student needs help, go through each sentence and rephrase each clause as a question: "Who were rebelling against the British" and "Whom had he known for many years." When you get to "What was Dragging Canoe planning," point out that the sentence doesn't *say* what he was planning, so the clause can't describe anything else in the sentence.

Instructor: This is a noun clause, serving as the direct object of the verb *did know*. The pronoun *what* introduces the clause, but it doesn't relate back to an antecedent in the sentence. Read me the next rule in your workbook.

→ *Student: The interrogative words* who, whom, whose, what, *and* which *can also serve as relative pronouns in adjective clauses or introductory words in noun clauses.*

Instructor: That last sentence follows the last part of the rule—it is an introductory word in a noun clause, but *not* a relative pronoun.

To see the different usages even more clearly, put the next four sentences on the frames in your workbook. In the blank, write the function of each interrogative word: interrogative pronoun, interrogative adjective, introductory word in noun clause, or relative pronoun.

What was the name of Dragging Canoe's father?   interrogative pronoun

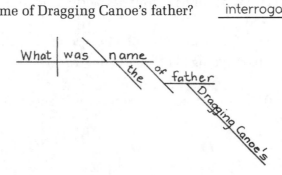

What five towns did Dragging Canoe build?   interrogative adjective

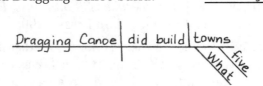

Dragging Canoe did not believe what the
governor of North Carolina told him.

<u>introductory word in noun clause</u>

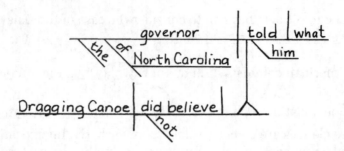

Dragging Canoe led the Cherokees who
refused to stay neutral.

<u>relative pronoun</u>

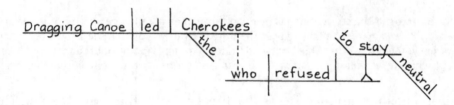

Instructor: Just like interrogatives, demonstratives can be either pronouns or adjectives. (You learned this back in Lesson 58.) Read me the demonstratives, and the two rules about them.

→ Student: *This, that, these, those. Demonstrative pronouns demonstrate or point out something. They take the place of a single word or a group of words. Demonstrative adjectives modify nouns and answer the question* which one.

Instructor: In the next set of sentences, circle each demonstrative and label it as PRO for pronoun or ADJ for adjective.

PRO
(Those) were the first Spanish ships to touch American shores.

ADJ
While a young boy, (this) future chief wanted to accompany his father, Attakullakulla, and a Cherokee war party going to battle the Shawnee.

ADJ
During one of (these) council sessions, a young chief named Dragging Canoe exploded into prominence.

ADJ
Now (that) hope is gone.

PRO
(This) was the first invasion of the Middle Towns by an enemy force on record.
—Pat Alderman, *Nancy Ward: Cherokee Chieftainess, Dragging Canoe: Cherokee-Chickamauga War Chief* (Overmountain Press, 1990).

Instructor: Although demonstratives can be either pronouns or adjectives, they are different from interrogatives in another important way. All of the interrogatives can introduce clauses—but only one of the demonstratives can. In the next three sentences, circle only the demonstrative that is introducing a clause, and underline the clause.

He had come to the council because of his admiration for that great chief.

They set off at a rapid pace, little guessing (that) a silent scout followed them.

That would be a catastrophe for the Cherokee and their allies.

Instructor: We'll finish up by looking at one last set of words. I want you to start out by reading these two sets of rules that you've already learned out loud.

→ *Student: An adverb describes a verb, an adjective, or another adverb. Adverbs tell how, when, where, how often, and to what extent. Relative adverbs introduce adverb clauses and refer back to a place, time, or reason in the independent clause. Where, when, why.*

Instructor: In the next sentence, the relative adverb links a descriptive clause back to a word in the main clause. Circle the relative adverb, underline the descriptive clause, and draw an arrow back to the word modified.

It was the orderly village to which he was heir, and (where) his mother was the pivot of the world.

Instructor: Although this descriptive clause describes a noun, it is an adverb clause because it modifies a *place*. It is diagrammed in the same way as a descriptive clause introduced by a relative pronoun—like *to which he was heir*. Place the sentence on the diagram frame provided.

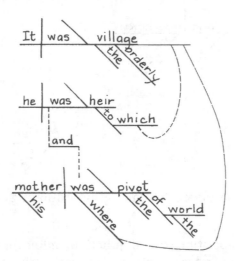

Instructor: Put your finger on each part of the diagram as I describe it. The adjective clause *to which he was heir* is connected to the main clause by a dotted line connecting *which* to its antecedent *village*. The adverb clause *where his mother was the pivot of the world* is connected to the main clause by a dotted line connecting *where* to its antecedent *village*. The only difference is that *which* is diagrammed as a pronoun within its own clause (the object of the preposition *to*), and *where* is diagrammed as an adverb within its own clause.

Where, *when*, and *why* are always adverbs—but they're not always *relative* adverbs, even when they introduce subordinate clauses. In the next sentence, circle the adverb and underline the clause that it introduces.

My heart rejoices (when) I look upon you.

Instructor: The clause *when I look upon you* doesn't refer back to a reason, time, or place in the main clause. It just answers the question *when*. It's an adverb clause, but not introduced by a relative adverb. Draw an arrow from the circled adverb back to the verb *rejoices*, and then read me the rule out loud.

→ *Student: Adverbs can act as subordinating conjunctions when they connect adverb clauses to a verb, adjective, or adverb in the main clause.*

Instructor: Place the sentence on the diagram frame in your workbook.

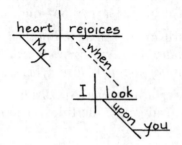

Instructor: Put your finger on the adverb acting as a subordinating conjunction. What is it?

→ *Student: When.*

Instructor: Look at the next sentence, where the adverb clause answering the question *why* is introduced by a word that is *not* an adverb.

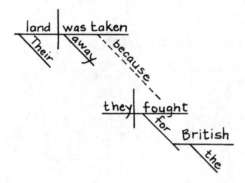

Instructor: Put your finger on the adverb acting as a subordinating conjunction. What is it?

→ *Student: Because.*

Instructor: *Because* can be a preposition or a conjunction, but never an adverb. So when subordinating conjunctions and adverbs introduce adverb clauses, they act in the same way. When a relative adverb introduces an adverb clause, it refers back to a time, place, or reason in the main clause. And when an adverb just acts like an adverb—like *away* on the diagram does— it simply modifies a verb, adjective, or adverb.

Finish your exercises now.

WEEK 31

Filling Up the Corners

After the feast (more or less) came the Speech. Most of the company were, however, now in a tolerant mood, at that delightful stage which they called "filling up the corners." They were sipping their favourite drinks, and nibbling at their favourite dainties, and their fears were forgotten. They were prepared to listen to anything, and to cheer at every full stop.

—J. R. R. Tolkien, *The Fellowship of the Ring*

— LESSON 117—

Interrogative Adverbs
Noun Clauses
Forming Questions
Affirmations and Negations
Double Negatives

Instructor: Grammar may not be as much fun as a feast, but you're now in the same stage as the hobbits at Bilbo's birthday party: You've had a full course, with plenty of grammar entrees, and now there are just a few corners left to fill up.

This week, we'll be looking at a few remaining grammar tidbits that don't really fit anywhere else. Let's start by going back to a few of those adverb rules from the end of the last lesson. Read me the first two sets of rules in your workbook.

→ Student: *An adverb describes a verb, an adjective, or another adverb. Adverbs tell how, when, where, how often, and to what extent. Relative adverbs introduce adverb clauses and refer back to a place, time, or reason in the independent clause. Where, when, why.*

Instructor: Although those adverbs can introduce adverb clauses, they can also introduce noun clauses—or stand by themselves. Underline the adverb clause in the first sentence and circle the relative adverb *where*. What does it modify?

→ Student: *Shop.*

Instructor: Place the sentence on the diagram frame.

I found a shop (where) I could buy cheese and chocolate.

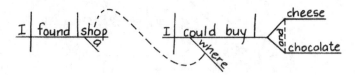

345

Instructor: In the second sentence, circle the adverb *where*. In this sentence, *where* isn't attached to a subordinate clause at all. It's just helping to ask a question. Place the sentence on the next diagram frame.

(Where) did you get the cheese and chocolate?

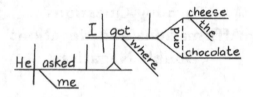

Instructor: Now underline the clause beginning with *where* in the third sentence, and circle the adverb. What did he ask?

→ *Student: Where I got the cheese and chocolate.*

Instructor: *Where* introduces the noun clause serving as a direct object. It doesn't relate back to a place, time, or reason in the main clause—it simply modifies the verb of the noun clause. Place the sentence on the third diagram frame.

He asked me (where) I got the cheese and chocolate.

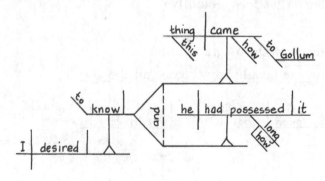

Instructor: *Where*, *when*, and *why* can be either relative adverbs or adverbs that ask a question. But there's one more interrogative adverb. Read the next two rules in your workbook now.

→ *Student: An interrogative adverb asks a question. Where, when, why, how. The interrogative adverbs can also introduce noun clauses.*

Instructor: Which interrogative adverb is *not* also a relative adverb?

→ *Student: How.*

Instructor: *How* can also be just a regular adverb, not an interrogative. Examine the next two sentences from *The Fellowship of the Ring*, and then place them on the diagram frames provided. Then, circle the one time that *how* is acting as an interrogative.

I desired to know how this thing came to Gollum, and how long he had possessed it.

How do the Wise know that this ring is his?

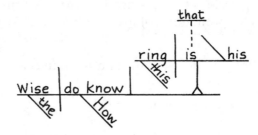

Instructor: You have now learned that there are at least three ways to form questions. Here's the simplest: Simply reverse the subject and predicate of a statement. What is the first statement in your workbook?

→ Student: *You are hungry.*

Instructor: When *you* and *are* swap places, you have a question. What is the question?

→ Student: *Are you hungry?*

Instructor: When the predicate of the sentence consists of a main verb and a helping verb, just the subject and helping verb switch places. What is the next statement?

→ Student: *You would like a big bowl of pozole.*

> **Note to Instructor:** If the student is not familiar with pozole, tell her that it is a Mexican dish made with hominy and pork. It is pronounced "po ZO lay."

Instructor: To make this into a question, the subject and the helping verb swap places—but the main verb, *like*, doesn't. What is the question?

→ Student: *Would you like a big bowl of pozole?*

Instructor: You learned the second way to make a question back in Lesson 81. Review that rule by reading it out loud.

→ Student: *Use the helping verbs* do, does, *and* did *to form negatives, ask questions, and provide emphasis.*

Instructor: What is the next statement?

→ Student: *He fixed green pozole with sliced avocados.*

Instructor: What tense is the verb *fixed*?

→ Student: *Simple past.*

Instructor: When the helping verb is added to turn this into a question, the helping verb takes on the tense of the main verb, and the main verb just takes the first person present form. What does the verb *fixed* turn into when the statement is made into a question?

→ Student: *Did fix.*

Instructor: *Did* is the simple past of the helping verb. Read the next statement and tell me what tense the main verb is in.

→ Student: *They love to nibble on chalupas. Simple present.*

Instructor: Now read me the question.

→ Student: *Do they love to nibble on chalupas?*

Instructor: *Do* is the simple present of the helping verb.

The third way to ask a question is to use an interrogative word—a pronoun, adjective, or adverb. In the next sentences, circle each interrogative word that turns the statement into a question, and label it as PRO for pronoun, ADJ for adjective, or ADV for adverb.

PRO
(Who) is bringing the bread pudding with flaming brandy?

ADJ
(What) kind of frosting are you using for the cake?

ADV
(When) will the mangos be ripe enough to make mango cake?

ADJ
(Which) limes did you use in the lime pudding?

PRO
(Whom) have you invited to the party?

ADV
(How) many loaves of challah did you bake?

ADJ
(Whose) presents are those?

Instructor: When someone asks you a question, you can answer in one of two ways. You can say "yes" or "no," or you can answer with a statement. Answer each of the following questions with a statement.

What is your favorite food?

→ *Student: My favorite food is X.*

Instructor: Do you enjoy beets?

→ *Student: I do [not] enjoy beets.*

Instructor: Can you bake bread?

→ *Student: I can/can't bake bread.*

Instructor: Would you like to go to a birthday feast and then sit around filling up the corners?

→ *Student: I would like to go to a birthday feast and then sit around filling up the corners!*

Instructor: Would you rather do grammar than go to a birthday feast?

→ *Student: I would not rather do grammar than go to a birthday feast.*

Instructor: The positive statements you made, telling me what you enjoy, what you can do, and what you would like to do, are **affirmations**. What does an affirmation do?

→ *Student: **An affirmation states what is true or what exists.***

Instructor: The negative statements, telling me what you don't enjoy, can't do, and don't want to do, are **negations**. What is a negation?

→ *Student: **A negation states what is not true or does not exist.***

Instructor: Although any positive statement is an affirmation, there are also adverbs of affirmation that make positive statements even *more* affirming! *Yes* is only one of those adverbs. Look at the partial list in your workbook, and circle each adverb of affirmation in the affirming sentences that answer each italicized question.

Adverbs of affirmation

yes, surely, definitely, certainly, absolutely, very

Did he invite her in?

And he invited her in; (yes) he did.

Were they merry?

(Surely) they were (very) merry.

Was the roast chicken ready?

The roast chicken was (definitely) ready to eat.

Were the mushrooms good?

The mushrooms were (absolutely) delicious.

Instructor: Now read the sentences without the adverbs of affirmation.

→ *Student: And he invited her in; he did. They were merry. The roast chicken was ready to eat. The mushrooms were delicious.*

Instructor: They still make sense: they're just not quite as affirming.

Adverbs of negation don't work in quite the same way. There are three adverbs of negation: *no*, *not*, and *never*. *No* can also be an adjective when it describes a noun or pronoun. In the next three sentences, circle each adverb or adjective of negation.

Adverbs of negation   **Adjective of negation**

no, not, never   no

Did anyone go hungry?

(No) man, woman or child went hungry.

When did they stop feasting?

They did (not) stop feasting until well after sundown.

How much merriment was there?

(Never) was there so much merriment.

Instructor: Try reading that first sentence without the adjective of negation *no*.

→ *Student: Man, woman, or child went hungry.*

Instructor: The sentence doesn't mean the same thing, does it? Although affirming words are usually optional, negative words are not. And there's one more thing to remember about negations. You can pile affirming adverbs on top of each other—but you can't use more than one adverb or adjective of negation! This is called a *double negative*.

You probably wouldn't use a sentence like the next one in your workbook. What does it say?

→ *Student: There is not no doubt.*

Instructor: But when you're using contractions and compound words, sometimes it's easy to use two negatives together. In the next sentence, what does *haven't* stand for?

→ *Student: Have not.*

Instructor: So the sentence actually says that you have *not* heard *no* good. That means you *have* heard *some* good. Using a double negative actually turns a negative sentence back into a positive statement! In the third sentence, what does *don't* stand for?

→ *Student: Do not.*

Instructor: The compound noun *nothing* is made up of the noun *thing* and the adjective *no*. So if you do not know *no* thing, you must know *something!* Read me the rule in your workbook.

→ *Student: **Do not use two adverbs or adjectives of negation together.***

Instructor: Finish your exercises now.

—LESSON 118—

Diagramming Affirmations and Negations
Yet More Words That Can Be Multiple Parts of Speech
Comparisons Using *Than*
Comparisons Using *As*

> **Note to Instructor:** Begin this lesson with a question that has a definite "yes" answer, and then continue with a question that has a "no" answer.

Instructor: Are you [sitting, standing, eating . . .]?

→ *Student: Yes.*

Instructor: Are you [swimming, flying, sleeping . . .]?

→ *Student: No.*

Instructor: You just used the affirmative adverb *yes* and the negative adverb *no*, but you used them as interjections. Let's read the following dialogue together. I will begin.

> Are you ready for your lesson?
> *Absolutely.*
> Do you remember the definition of a noun?
> *Definitely.*
> How sure are you?
> *Very.*
> Have you forgotten it?
> *No.*
> Will you ever forget it?
> *Never.*

Instructor: In all of your responses, the affirmative and negative adverbs can also act as interjections. If you were going to diagram one of your answers (which you probably wouldn't bother to do), you would just put it on a line all by itself, like this:

> Never

> Absolutely

Instructor: However, when these adverbs are acting within a sentence, you diagram them like adverbs. In the following sentences from the novel *I, Juan de Pareja*, by Elizabeth Borton de Treviño, place each bolded affirmative or negative adverb on the diagram.

> I can be **very** deaf when I need.

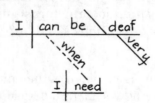

Yes, I will paint you, Juanico.

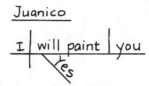

You will **never** be beaten again.

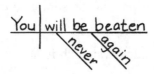

I am **no** longer a slave.

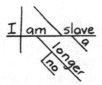

Instructor: *Yes* and *no* can be interjections or adverbs—and they can also be one other part of speech! Study the next sentence and diagram in your sentence.

> Yes, I said.
> —From *Drown* by Junot Diaz

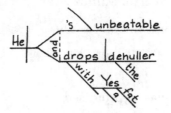

Instructor: What part of the sentence is *Yes*?

→ *Student: The direct object.*

Instructor: Sometimes, *yes* and *no* can actually be *nouns*! Put the next three sentences onto the diagram frames provided.

> He's unbeatable and drops the dehuller with a fat Yes.
> —From *Drown* by Junot Diaz

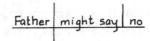

> Father might say no.
> —From *The Dreamer*, by Pam Muñoz Ryan

It has no shoestrings.

—From *The Dreamer*, by Pam Muñoz Ryan

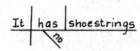

Instructor: In the first sentence, what part of the sentence is the noun *Yes*?

→ *Student: Object of the preposition.*

Instructor: In the second sentence, what part of the sentence is the noun *no*?

→ *Student: The direct object.*

Instructor: In the third sentence, what part of speech is *no*?

→ *Student: Adjective.*

Instructor: It is an adjective modifying the noun *shoestrings*. *No* is an unusual word—it can be an adjective, an adverb, *or* a noun!

Let's look at one more important word that can work in an unusual combination of ways: the word *as*. Back in Lesson 106, you learned that *as* can serve as an adverb, a subordinating conjunction, a preposition, or part of a quasi-coordinator. Look carefully at the next four sentences, and label each *as* with the correct abbreviation. If you need help, ask me.

> **Note to Instructor:** Use the following notes to prompt the student as necessary.

The stone was black and shiny, so you could see your reflection as well as the blooming trees and the clouds in the sky.
QC

—From *Return to Sender,* by Julia Alvarez

> **Note to Instructor:** The quasi-coordinator *as well as* links the double direct object *reflection* and *trees* (the third direct object, *clouds*, is linked by a regular coordinating conjunction). All three are direct objects of the verb *could see*.

Mamadre nodded and smiled as she left the room.
SC

As my partner, how do you think we should proceed?
PREP

—From *The Dreamer,* by Pam Muñoz Ryan

> **Note to Instructor:** The prepositional phrase *as my partner* acts as an adjective and modifies the pronoun *you*.

When we arrived, nothing was as promised.
ADV

—From *Esperanza Rising,* by Pam Muñoz Ryan

> **Note to Instructor:** *As* modifies the predicate adjective *promised*.

Instructor: Often, an adverb *as* and a subordinating conjunction *as* work together in a comparison. Read me the next sentence, which describes the work of the poet Pablo Neruda.

→ *Student: His affections became poems, as warm and supple as the wool of a well-loved sheep.*

Instructor: The first *as* is an adverb, describing the adjective *warm*. But to properly identify the second *as*, we'll need to look back at a rule you learned in Lesson 105. Read me that rule now.

→ *Student: When* than *is used in a comparison and introduces a clause with understood elements, it is acting as a subordinating conjunction.*

Instructor: Read me the sentence using *than* in a comparison.

→ *Student: That wool is warmer than my wool.*

Instructor: In Lesson 105, you learned that a comparison using *than* usually leaves words out of the subordinate clause that finishes the comparison. Draw a caret after *wool* and insert the words *is warm*.

That wool is warmer than my wool^{is warm}∧.

Instructor: Now look at the diagram in your workbook. Put your finger on each element of the diagram as I describe it. When you diagram a comparison, use *x* for the understood elements. Draw a dotted line from the comparative word in the main clause to the thing or person in the subordinate clause being compared. (You learned that back in Lesson 66.) The comparative word here is *warmer*. The thing being compared in the subordinate clause is *wool*. The subordinating conjunction *than* is placed on the dotted line.

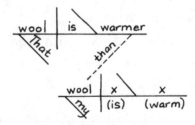

Instructor: A comparison using *as* is very similar—except that you're comparing two things that are similar, or equal. Insert a caret at the end of the sentence about Pablo Neruda, and write *is warm and supple* above it.

His affections became poems, as warm and supple as the wool of a well-loved sheep^{is warm and supple}∧.
—From The Dreamer, by Pam Muñoz Ryan

Instructor: Now, try to put that sentence on the diagram frame in your workbook.

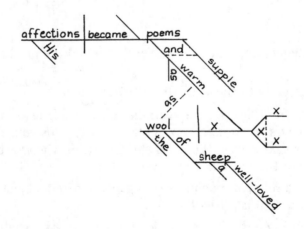

Instructor: Now, label each *as* in the sentence.

ADV   SC

His affections became poems, as warm and supple as the wool of a well-loved sheep.
—From *The Dreamer*, by Pam Munoz Ryan

Instructor: Let's look at *as* in one last role. Read me the next sentence.

→ *Student: I did as he asked.*

Instructor: Underline the subject once and the predicate twice, and circle the clause *as he asked*.

I̲ d̲i̲d̲ (as he asked)

Instructor: In this sentence, the noun clause *as he asked* is the direct object of the verb *did*. Here's a difficult question: What did he ask?

> Note to Instructor: Give the student a chance to answer, "We don't know" or "Something" or "The thing that was done."

Instructor: Although we don't know exactly what *he* asked, the word *as* stands in for *the thing he asked me to do*. In this sentence, *as* is actually acting as a *pronoun*. It is the direct object of *asked*. We don't know what the antecedent of the pronoun *as* is, because we don't know *what* he asked. In the second sentence, though, we *do* know what the antecedent is. Read that sentence out loud.

→ *Student: He had the same concerns as you have had.*

Instructor: Underline the subject once, the predicate twice, label the direct object with *DO*, and circle the subordinate clause.

DO

H̲e̲ h̲a̲d̲ the same concerns (as you have had)

Instructor: Once again, *as* serves as a pronoun. It is the direct object of *have had*, and stands in for *the thing you have had*. But in this sentence, we know what that *thing* is. It is *the same concerns*. In this clause, *as* is a relative pronoun, renaming *concerns*.

Place these two sentences on the frames provided.

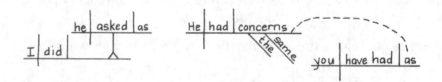

Instructor: In the next sentence, underline the subject once and the predicate twice.

struggled with

The f̲a̲r̲m̲e̲r̲ s̲t̲r̲u̲g̲g̲l̲e̲d̲ with the same difficulties (as you∧.)

Instructor: *With the same difficulties* is a prepositional phrase acting as an adverb; it modifies *struggled* and answers the question *how*. Now look carefully at *as you*. This is an incomplete subordinate clause. Draw a caret after the word *you* and insert the words *struggled with*, and then circle the entire subordinate clause.

In this sentence, *as* is a relative pronoun serving as the direct object of the understood preposition *with*. Its antecedent is *difficulties*.

Place the entire sentence on the frame provided, inserting *x* for each understood word.

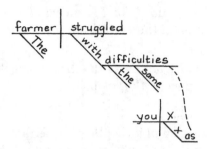

Instructor: Remember this: If you can't figure out what a phrase or clause is doing in a sentence, always ask yourself if a word has been left out. English *loves* to leave words out!

Finish your exercises now.

—LESSON 119—

Idioms

> **Note to Instructor:** Throughout this lesson, provide the meaning of any idioms that the student is not familiar with.

Instructor: You've certainly kept your nose to the grindstone, but this is no time to rest on your laurels. It's time to go back to the salt mines and ramp up your grammar efforts.

I just used four different *idioms*. Idioms are phrases that have one meaning on the surface—and a different meaning when you actually use them. You have a nose, but there's no grindstone. What does *keep your nose to the grindstone* actually mean?

→ *Student: To keep working hard.*

Instructor: *Resting on your laurels* means to relax and enjoy what you've already achieved—like an ancient Greek athlete who already won his footrace and can just wave his laurel wreath around. *Back to the salt mines* means going back to hard work. What does *ramp up* mean?

→ *Student: Increase.*

Instructor: It's not always clear how an idiom gets started—but back in the Middle Ages, *to ramp* meant "to climb," and if you *ramped* a vine, you gave it a head start on climbing and growing. Maybe that's why *ramping up* means "increasing." But when you're trying to write grammatically, it doesn't really matter what the origin (or "etymology") of an idiom is. You just need to know how to use it correctly—and that can be tricky, because many idioms don't follow regular rules of grammar.

Look at the first two sentences and accompanying diagrams in your workbook. In the first sentence, *driving at* means "implying" or "suggesting."

I'm confused because I don't know what you are **driving at**.

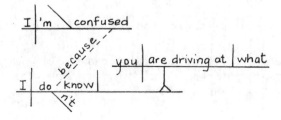

Instructor: The writer could also have said, *I don't know what you mean* or *I don't know what you are suggesting.* The combination of the verb *driving* and the preposition *at* unite to form a single meaning.

What *you are driving at* is a clause acting as the direct object of the verb *do know*. What three words are in the predicate space of that clause?

→ Student: *Are driving at.*

Instructor: In this idiom, the preposition *at* joins the progressive present verb *are driving* to create a new verb—one that doesn't mean "driving" any more. So all three words go on the same diagram space. Separating *at* would change the meaning of the verb back to driving—and the clause wouldn't make sense. When the words of an idiom form a single meaning, you shouldn't try to break them up. Just treat them like a single part of speech.

In the second sentence, what does *back to the drawing board* mean?

→ Student: *Starting over.*

Instructor: What part of the sentence is the entire phrase *back to the drawing board*?

→ Student: *Predicate nominative* OR *Predicate adjective.*

> **Note to Instructor:** Because the idiom is not clearly either a noun or adjective in function (it's an idiom, which means it doesn't follow rules), it is hard to say whether it describes or renames the subject. Either answer is acceptable.

Instructor: Within the phrase, which two words are acting as a single preposition (and are diagrammed on a single line)?

→ Student: *Back to.*

Instructor: The other parts of the idiom are the object of the preposition, *board*, and the adjectives describing *board: drawing* and *the*. Each one of those words is acting as a single part of speech and occupies its own line on the diagram.

For the rest of this lesson, we'll examine specific idioms, and decide which phrases within them are acting as single words.

> **Note to Instructor:** This lesson, including additional dialogue, is continued in the Answer Key; please refer to it now.
>
> Because English has so many different and common idioms, each year explores a different set of idioms. However, the purpose of each year's instruction is the same—to give the student practice in recognizing and using common idioms.

—LESSON 120—

Troublesome Sentences

Instructor: So what *is* grammar? (There's an answer in your workbook.)

→ *Student: Grammar is the art of speaking or writing a language correctly.*

Instructor: As we've seen this week, *correctly* can sometimes mean *breaking the rules you previously learned.* What does Mark Twain say about perfectly consistent grammar?

→ *Student: Perfect grammar—persistent, continuous, sustained—is the fourth dimension, so to speak: many have sought it, but none has found it.*

Instructor: English is what we call a *living* language. Because it is constantly used, it is always changing—and finding exceptions to its own rules. But learning the rules of grammar is the most important step towards understanding sentences that *don't* follow those rules. Read me the final quote in your workbook.

→ *Student: Grammar is to literary composition what a linch-pin is to a waggon. It is a poor pitiful thing in itself; it bears no part of the weight; communicates nothing to the force; adds not in the least to the celerity; but, still the waggon cannot very well and safely go on without it; she is constantly liable to reel and be compelled to stop, which, at the least, exposes the driver to be laughed at, and that, too, by those who are wholly unable to drive themselves.*

> **Note to Instructor:** If the student is not familiar with the adjective *celerity*, you may either ask him to look it up, or simply tell him that it means "speed, swiftness."

Instructor: As you can see from the illustration in your workbook, a linch-pin holds a wheel onto the axle of a wagon. William Cobbett is saying that grammar isn't important in itself—it's only important because it makes clear expression possible.

Today, we're going to look at some perfectly good sentences that use strange grammar. But before we do, review your diagramming rules by placing the entire William Cobbett quote onto the frames in your workbook. If you need help, ask me.

> **Note to Instructor:** Use the notes below to give all possible help. This quote is intended both to review basic diagramming structure and to illustrate some of the possible ambiguities in a well-constructed sentence. It could undoubtedly be diagrammed in other ways, but the diagrams below are legitimate interpretations.

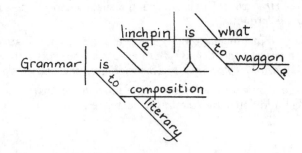

> **Note to Instructor:** It is not grammatically incorrect to diagram *what* as the subject of the direct object noun clause and *linch-pin* as the predicate nominative. Since *linch-pin* is the actual object under discussion, I have chosen to put it in the subject space.

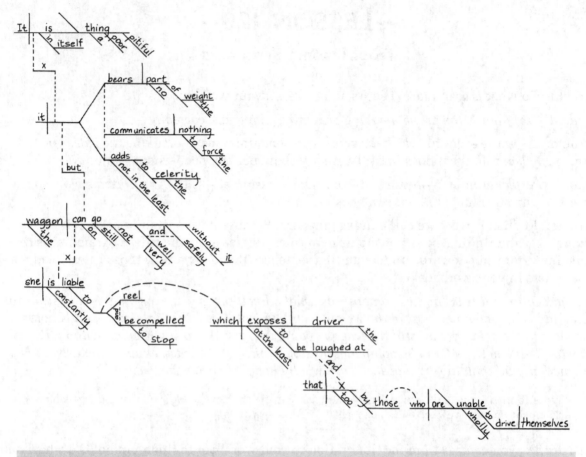

Note to Instructor: *Not in the least* is diagrammed as a single idiom because *in the least* never occurs without *not*. Instead, it becomes the idiom *at the last*, which modifies *exposes* later in the sentence.

To serves to introduce two adverbial infinitives, *reel* and *be compelled.*

Which exposes the driver . . . is an unusual construction—it is a relative clause that describes an infinitive. Technically, it functions as an adverb, but *which* remains a relative pronoun, not a relative adverb.

Laugh at is an idiom. (Notice that the preposition *at* has no object; it is part of the verb itself.)

The clause *that too by those who are wholly unable to drive themselves* is also unusual. *That* is actually the understood clause *that is.* It serves as an adverb, answering the question *how* about the infinitive *to be laughed at. And* has been transformed from a coordinating conjunction to a subordinating conjunction. *Those* is the object of the preposition by and is described by the relative clause *who are wholly unable to drive themselves.* This is another unusual construction—a relative pronoun describing a demonstrative pronoun!

Final note: Another diagrammer might possibly interpret *and* as a coordinating conjunction, since *that is* is grammatically an independent clause. But because of the explanatory function of *that too by those who are wholly unable to drive themselves*, I have interpreted the clause as an adverb clause.

Note to Instructor: The dialogue for this lesson is continued in the Answer Key. Each year of the program covers different additional *oddly constructed* sentences.

WEEK 32

—REVIEW 10—

The review exercises and answers are found in the Student Workbook and accompanying Key.

Mechanics

—LESSON 121—

Capitalization Review
Additional Capitalization Rules
Formal and Informal Letter Format
Ending Punctuation

Instructor: Read me the unpunctuated, uncapitalized sentence in your workbook, giving each word equal time and not pausing until you reach the end.

→ *Student: what an amazing place london was to me when i saw it in the distance and how i believed all the adventures of all my favourite heroes to be constantly enacting and re-enacting there and how i vaguely made it out in my own mind to be fuller of wonders and wickedness than all the cities of the earth i need not stop here to relate*

Instructor: Now, read it again, this time pausing correctly at each punctuation mark.

→ *Student: What an amazing place London was to me when I saw it in the distance, and how I believed all the adventures of all my favourite heroes to be constantly enacting and re-enacting there, and how I vaguely made it out in my own mind to be fuller of wonders and wickedness than all the cities of the earth, I need not stop here to relate.*

Instructor: No matter how good your grasp of English grammar is, you'll have trouble understanding sentences if the *mechanics*—the punctuation and capitalization—aren't right. So now that you know so much about grammar, we're going to take a week to review all of the rules you've learned, all year long, about mechanics. And we'll add a few rules as we go.

Let's start with proper nouns. What is a proper noun?

→ *Student: A proper noun is the special, particular name for a person, place, thing, or idea. Proper nouns always begin with capital letters.*

Instructor: Read each rule about proper nouns out loud, and then correct each example that follows by crossing out the incorrect small letter and writing a capital letter above it.

Note to Instructor: The rules and the correct examples follow.

1. Capitalize the proper names of persons, places, things, and animals.

boy	Manuel
store	Macy's
car	Ford
horse	Secretariat

2. Capitalize the names of holidays.
> Lent
> Ramadan
> New Year's Day

3. Capitalize the names of deities.
> Zeus
> Buddha
> Holy Spirit
> God

4. Capitalize the days of the week and the months of the year, but not the seasons.

Wednesday	February	spring
Thursday	April	fall
Saturday	September	winter

5. Capitalize the first, last, and other important words in titles of books, magazines, newspapers, movies, television shows, stories, poems, and songs.

book	*Green Eggs and Ham*
magazine	*The New Yorker*
newspaper	*The Philadelphia Inquirer*
movie	*The Hunger Games: Catching Fire*
television show	*Agents of S.H.I.E.L.D.*
story	"The Lottery"
poem	"Stopping by Woods on a Snowy Evening"
song	"Happy Birthday to You"
chapter in a book	"An Unexpected Party"

6. Capitalize and italicize the names of ships, trains, and planes.

ship	*Santa Maria*
train	*Hogwarts Express*
plane	*Air Force One*

Instructor: Let's add one more useful rule. Read the rule and the illustration out loud.

→ Student: **The titles mister, madame, and miss are capitalized and abbreviated Mr., Mrs., and Miss when placed in front of a proper name.** *Miss Snevellicci made a graceful obeisance, and hoped Mrs. Curdle was well, as also Mr. Curdle, who at the same time appeared.*

> **Note to Instructor:** We have simplified this explanation. The modern titles Mister and Miss/Mrs. are derived from the old titles Master and Mistress. In eighteenth century England, these titles were used for men and women who were wealthy enough to have servants. In pre-Civil War America, they also referred to slaveowners. Their modern forms have lost this association with servants and slaves. However, if students have the maturity to understand the historical context, you may want to investigate the evolution of these titles, and the reasons why freed African-Americans had to struggle to claim them during the Jim Crow era.

Instructor: What is a proper adjective?

→*Student: A proper adjective is formed from a proper name. Proper adjectives are capitalized. Words that are not usually capitalized remain lowercase even when they are attached to a proper adjective.*

Instructor: Correct each example that follows by crossing out the incorrect small letter and writing a capital letter above it.

	Proper Noun	**Proper Adjective**
Person	Shakespeare	the Shakespearean play
	Kafka	a Kafkaesque dilemma
Place	Italy	an Italian city
	Korea	a non-Korean tradition
Holiday	Labor Day	the Labor Day picnic
	Christmas	an anti-Christmas sentiment
Month	September	September storms
	December	the post-December blues

Instructor: Now read me the next two rules in your workbook. You've already learned the first two—but not the third.

→*Student: Capitalize the personal pronoun I. Interjections express sudden feeling or emotion. They are set off with commas or stand alone with a closing punctuation mark.*

Instructor: You've already learned these two rules. They are illustrated in the sentences from *David Copperfield*. Who prayed, in the first sentence?

→*Student: I.*

Instructor: That is a capitalized personal pronoun. What three interjections are in the sentences?

→*Student: Oh, ahem, ha.*

Instructor: Each of those interjections follows the rule. But there is one interjection that doesn't. You probably won't use it much in your own writing, but you'll often see it in older books. Read the rule about the interjection *O*.

→*Student: **Capitalize the interjection** O. **It is usually preceded by, but not followed by, a comma.***

Instructor: You can see this rule illustrated in the sentences from *The Wind in the Willows*. Read me those two sentences.

→*Student: For a few weeks it was all well enough, but afterwards, O the weary length of the nights! But, O dear, O dear, this is a hard world!*

Instructor: Your next new rule governs interjections generally—*including* O! Read it to me.

→*Student: **After an interjection followed by an exclamation point, the next word may be lowercase.***

Instructor: In the two sentences from *Nicholas Nickleby*, what two lowercase words follow the interjections and exclamation points?

→*Student: Let and how.*

Instructor: Let's cover a few more rules. What parts of a letter should always be capitalized?

→*Student: **The address, date, greeting, closing, and signature of a letter.***

Instructor: This rule is illustrated in the two sample letters in your workbook. Examine them as I explain.

When you are writing a letter with a word processing program, it is correct to double space after each element—as you can see in both letters. It is also correct, in a U.S. address, to abbreviate the state and leave out the comma between the state and ZIP code. In a formal letter, use a colon after the name of the person you're writing to; in an informal letter, use a comma.

Notice that each letter is slightly different, though. It is correct to align every element (first your address, then the date, address you're writing to, greeting, each paragraph, closing, and signature) with the left-hand margin, as in the first letter. But it is also correct to center your address and the date, take the address you're writing to back to the margin, indent each paragraph, and then indent the closing and signature to the middle of the page, as shown in the second letter. You would also sign your name by hand between the closing and the signature. Sign both of your letters now. (You can either sign your actual name or "Your Greatest Fan.")

Your Street Address
Your City, State, and ZIP Code

June 14, 2018

Well-Trained Mind Press
18021 The Glebe Lane
Charles City, Virginia 23030

Dear Editors:

Thank you for *Grammar for the Well-Trained Mind.* It is the most exciting grammar book I have ever read. I only wish I could spend more time doing grammar.

Please publish more grammar books immediately.

Sincerely,

SIGNATURE

Your Greatest Fan

Your Street Address
Your City, State, and ZIP Code

June 14, 2018

Well-Trained Mind Press
18021 The Glebe Lane
Charles City, Virginia 23030

Dear Editors:

Thank you for *Grammar for the Well-Trained Mind.* It is the most exciting grammar book I have ever read. I only wish I could spend more time doing grammar.

Please publish more grammar books immediately.

Sincerely,

SIGNATURE

Your Greatest Fan

Instructor: Read me the next capitalization rule.

→ Student: **Abbreviations are typically capitalized when each letter stands for something.**

Instructor: Do you know what the capitalized abbreviations in your next sentences stand for?

> **Note to Instructor:** You may either tell the student what the abbreviations mean, or ask the student to look the information up.

The WHO has expressed concern about the Zika virus and its rapid spread.
(World Health Organization)

Why did NASA cancel the lunar exploration program?
(The National Aeronautics and Space Administration)

OPEC was founded in 1960 in Baghdad.
(Organization of the Petroleum Exporting Countries)

Instructor: What is the next rule?

→ Student: **Capitalize the first word in every line of traditional poetry.**

Instructor: Modern poetry often breaks this rule, but most poetry written before 1920 (and a lot of poems written after) follow it. Read "The Elephant," by Hilaire Belloc, and notice that it *does* follow the rule.

→ Student: *When people call this beast to mind,*

            They marvel more and more

            At such a little tail behind,

            So large a trunk before.

Instructor: The last set of five rules governs sentences—both beginnings and ends. What does every sentence begin with?

→ Student: *A capital letter.*

Instructor: What does every sentence end with?

→ Student: *A punctuation mark.*

Instructor: Insert the correct punctuation mark at the end of each of the four sentences that come after the rules.

Look ahead, Rat! [or, Look ahead, Rat.][command]
Hooray, this is splendid! [exclamation]
I wonder which of us had better pack the luncheon-basket? [question]
Presently they all sat down to luncheon together. [statement]

Instructor: Practice all of these rules now by completing your exercises.

—LESSON 122—

Commas
Semicolons
Additional Semicolon Rules
Colons
Additional Colon Rules

Instructor: The first 19 sentences in your workbook will probably give you a hint about the answer to this question: What is the most common punctuation mark in the English language?

→ *Student: The comma.*

Instructor: Commas can do at *least* 19 different things. Let's read them together. I'll begin with the first thing in the list, you read the second, I'll read the third, and so on. We'll read number 19 together.

A comma *and* coordinating conjunction join compound sentences.

→ *Student: Commas separate three or more items in a series.*

Instructor: Commas separate two or more adjectives that come before a noun (as long as the adjectives can exchange position).

→ *Student: A comma precedes the* and *before the last item in a series of three or more (the "Oxford comma").*

Instructor: Commas set off terms of direct address.

→ *Student: Commas set off non-restrictive adjective clauses.*

Instructor: Commas set off parenthetical expressions that are closely related to the sentence.

→ *Student: Commas set off most appositives (unless the appositive is only one word and very closely related to the word it renames).*

Instructor: Commas may surround or follow interjections.

→ *Student: Commas may surround or follow introductory adverbs of affirmation and negation.*

Instructor: Commas may set off introductory adverb and adjective phrases.

→ *Student: In dates, commas separate the day of the week from the day of the month and the day of the month from the year.*

Instructor: In addresses, commas separate the city from the state.

→ *Student: Commas follow the greeting and closing of a friendly letter, and the closing of a formal letter.*

Instructor: Commas divide large numbers into sets of thousands.

→ *Student: A comma follows a dialogue tag or attribution tag that precedes a speech or quote.*

Instructor: A comma comes after a speech or quote if a dialogue tag or attribution tag follows.

→ *Student: A comma may divide a partial sentence from the block quote it introduces.*

→ *Together: Commas may be used at any time to prevent misunderstanding and simplify reading.*

Instructor: Stop and finish Exercise 122A now.

Instructor: Although semicolons and colons aren't as common as commas, they're indispensable in just a few situations. Review the rules you've already learned about these two punctuation marks by reading the next two sets of rules out loud, and then circling the punctuation marks described in each example that follows.

→ *Student: The independent clauses of a compound sentence must be joined by a comma and a coordinating conjunction, a semicolon, or a semicolon and a coordinating conjunction. They cannot be joined by a comma alone.*

> He knew—as the Athenians and Persians did not—exactly when the flooding of the Nile was about to occur, and he managed to hold the combined invasion force off until the waters began to rise rapidly around him.

> Thousands of years ago, groups of hunters and gatherers roamed across Asia and Europe, following mammoth herds that fed on the wild grasses. Slowly the ice began to retreat; the patterns of the grass growth changed; the herds wandered north and diminished.

> They eat and drink, and thank him for his generosity; but Atrahasis himself, knowing that the feast is a death meal, paces back and forth, ill with grief and guilt.

> —Susan Wise Bauer, *The History of the Ancient World*

→ *Student: Block quotes should be introduced by a colon (if preceded by a complete sentence) or a comma (if preceded by a partial sentence).*

> Piankhe did not try to wipe out his enemies. Instead, he chose to see Egypt as a set of kingdoms, with himself as High King over them:

> Amun of Napata has appointed me governor of this land,

> he wrote in another insapcription,

> > as I might say to someone: "Be king," and he is it, or: "You will not be king," and he is not.

> —Susan Wise Bauer, *The History of the Ancient World*

Instructor: You've only learned one of the next three rules, but you probably know the other two already. Insert colons into the three examples provided.

Use a colon after the salutation of a business letter.

> The White House
> 1600 Pennsylvania Ave NW
> Washington, DC 20500
>
> Dear Mr. President:

Use a colon to separate the hour from minutes in a time.
> I went to bed at 11:59 on December 31.

Use a colon to separate the chapter from verse in a Biblical reference.
> According to Ecclesiastes 12:12, "much study wearies the body."

Instructor: We'll finish up this lesson by examining four more ways colons—*and* semicolons—can be used. Read me the next two rules.

→ *Student: **If items in a series contain commas within the items, semicolons may separate two or more items in a series. If semicolons separate items in a series, a colon may set off the series.***

Instructor: If your items in a series are phrases, or even clauses, they might contain commas—so separating them *with* commas could be very confusing. Instead, you can use semicolons to separate them. And when semicolons are used to separate them, you can use a colon to introduce them. That gets rid of *all* of the commas except for the ones within the items themselves.

In the three examples that follow the rules, circle each item in the lists that follow the colons.

> Around the tomb complex, buildings recreated in stone the materials of traditional Egyptian houses: walls of stone, carved to look like reed matting; stone columns shaped into bundles of reeds; even a wooden fence with a partly open gate, chiseled from stone.
> Like the Great Pyramid, the Sphinx has attracted its share of nutty theories: it dates from 10,000 B.C. and was built by a disappeared advanced civilization; it was built by Atlanteans (or aliens); it represents a zodiacal sign, or a center of global energy.
> Between 4000 and 3000 B.C. is known as the Naqada Period, and was once divided into three phases: the Amratian, which runs from 4000 to 3500 B.C.; the Gerzean, from 3500 to 3200 B.C.; and the Final Predynastic, from 3200 to 3000 B.C.
> —Susan Wise Bauer, *The History of the Ancient World*

Instructor: How many items are in each list?

→ *Student: Three.*

Instructor: In the first sentence, how many items have a comma in them?

→ *Student: Two.*

Instructor: In the second sentence, how many items have a comma in them?

→ *Student: One.*

Instructor: In the third sentence, how many items have a comma in them?

→ *Student: All three.*

Instructor: Whenever items in a series contain any commas, using a colon to introduce them and semicolons to separate them prevents confusion. But sometimes you might want to use a colon to introduce a list with *no* commas in it. In the next three sentences, circle the items introduced by the colon.

> Stripped of personality, prehistoric peoples too often appear as blocks of shifting color on a map: moving north, moving west, generating a field of cultivated grain, or corralling a herd of newly domesticated animals.
> Many thousands of years ago, the Sumerian king Alulim ruled over Eridu: a walled city, a safe space carved out of the unpredictable and harsh river valley that the Romans would later name Mesopotamia.

(Plague,) (drought,) (and war:) these were enough to upset the balance of a civilization that had been built in rocky dry places, close to the edge of survival.

—Susan Wise Bauer, *The History of the Ancient World*

Instructor: In these sentences, the colon allows the writer to avoid adding unnecessary words before the list, such as, *They were moving north, they were moving west*, or *which was a walled city*. Read me the rule governing these sentences.

→ *Student: A colon may introduce a list.*

Instructor: And now for one last rule. What is the last thing that a colon can do?

→ *Student: For emphasis, a colon may introduce an item that follows a complete sentence, when that item is closely related to the sentence.*

Instructor: In the first sentence after the rule, what is the complete sentence that comes before the colon?

→ *Student: But the historian's task is different.*

Instructor: The infinitive phrase *to look for particular human lives that give flesh and spirit to abstract assertions about human behavior* describes *task*. The writer could have written this sentence in several ways. I'd like you to read the original sentence and then the first italicized version of it out loud, listening carefully to the sound of each sentence.

→ *Student: But the historian's task is different: to look for particular human lives that give flesh and spirit to abstract assertions about human behavior. But the historian's task, to look for particular human lives that give flesh and spirit to abstract assertions about human behavior, is different.*

Instructor: In the first sentence, the emphasis falls on *to look for particular human lives*. In the second sentence, the emphasis falls on *different*. Placing a colon before a phrase puts emphasis on that phrase.

Go ahead and complete your final exercise now.

—LESSON 123—

Colons
Dashes
Hyphens
Parentheses
Brackets

Instructor: Your lesson begins with two different versions of a sentence we read in the last lesson. Read both sentences out loud.

→ *Student: But the historian's task is different: to look for particular human lives that give flesh and spirit to abstract assertions about human behavior.*

But the historian's task is different—to look for particular human lives that give flesh and spirit to abstract assertions about human behavior.

Instructor: What is the difference between those two sentences?

→ *Student: The first one has a colon and the second has a dash.*

Instructor: You have already learned how to use both colons and dashes in this way. Read the two sets of rules in your workbook.

→ *Student: A colon may introduce an item that follows a complete sentence, when that item is closely related to the sentence. Dashes —— can enclose words that are not essential to the sentence. Dashes can also be used singly to separate parts of a sentence.*

Instructor: In this case, the dash is used in the second way. How does using a dash instead of a colon (which is the original punctuation) change the sentence?

Note to Instructor: Accept any reasonable answer from the student.

Instructor: Generally, using a colon instead of dash puts a little more emphasis on the words that follow the colon. But using a colon, a dash, or a comma would all be fine in that sentence. When you're dealing with colons, dashes, commas, *and* parentheses, which ones you use to enclose words is often a matter of style, not correct or incorrect grammar.

Let's take some time to review the rules you've already learned about these punctuation marks—and add a few more. Begin by reminding yourself of the difference between a hyphen and a dash. Which is longer?

→ *Student: The dash.*

Instructor: Hyphens are shorter and connect compound words. You've already learned that some compound nouns are joined by hyphens—although you often have to check a dictionary to find out which ones take hyphens, which ones you can put together into one word, and which are just written as two separate words. Hyphens can also connect compound adjectives—in one position. What is that?

→ *Student: The attributive position.*

Instructor: What is the attributive position?

→ *Student: Before the noun.*

Instructor: Let's add two more rules about hyphens. Read me the next rule.

→ *Student: **Hyphens connect spelled-out numbers between twenty-one and ninety-nine.***

Instructor: When these numbers are spelled out, they are always hyphenated, even if they're in the predicate position. Now look at the last rule. You probably won't use this one very much, but you'll see it in some books. If you have to divide a word at the end of a line, you can place a hyphen between the syllables. This is really only necessary if you're typing and right-justifying your margin, as in the first example from *Robinson Crusoe*. Normally, you should just use left justification, as in the second example, and let the right-hand margin be uneven.

Now let's review the rules about using parentheses by reading them alternately. I'll begin. Parentheses ( ) can enclose words that are not essential to the sentence.

→ *Student: Parenthetical expressions often interrupt or are irrelevant to the rest of the sentence.*

Instructor: Punctuation goes inside the parentheses if it applies to the parenthetical material; all other punctuation goes outside the parentheses.

→ *Student: Parenthetical material only begins with a capital letter if it is a complete sentence with ending punctuation.*

Instructor: In the first sentence from *Robinson Crusoe*, what is the parenthetical expression?

→ *Student: Whatever it was.*

Instructor: Does the sentence mean the same thing without it?

→ *Student: Yes.*

Instructor: Is it a complete sentence?

→ *Student: Yes.*

Instructor: Why doesn't it begin with a capital letter?

→ *Student: It doesn't have ending punctuation.*

Instructor: What other punctuation marks could go on either side of this clause?

→ *Student: Commas or dashes.*

Instructor: How would this change the sentence? You can read the answers from your workbook.

→ *Student: Commas make a parenthetical element a part of the sentence. Dashes emphasize a parenthetical element. Parentheses minimize a parenthetical element.*

Instructor: The next four sentences from *Robinson Crusoe* all illustrate proper use and punctuation of parentheses. Take a moment and read them carefully.

> **Note to Instructor:** You may either ask the student to read these aloud, or allow her to read silently. Students who have difficulty staying focused generally need to read aloud. Prompt the student for the following answers as necessary.

Instructor: In the first sentence, what is the parenthetical phrase?

→ *Student: Though to myself.*

Instructor: What is the entire phrase set off by the two commas?

→ *Student: Aloud (though to myself).*

Instructor: Because the second comma applies to the entire phrase, not just the parenthetical phrase, it goes outside the closing parenthesis. In the second sentence, what function does the first semicolon serve?

→ *Student: It connects two independent clauses.*

Instructor: What is the parenthetical clause?

→ *Student: So I must now call my tent and my cave.*

Instructor: Why is the semicolon outside the closing parenthesis?

→ *Student: It follows the whole independent clause, not just the clause in parentheses.*

Instructor: In the third sentence, what is the clause inside the parentheses?

→ *Student: But who grudge pains who have their deliverance in view?*

Instructor: This is an independent clause—a complete sentence. What kind of sentence is it?

→ *Student: A question.*

Instructor: Because it is a question, the question mark applies to all of the words inside the parentheses. Where does the question mark go?

→ *Student: Inside the closing parenthesis.*

Instructor: What is the function of the semicolon that comes after the parentheses?

→ *Student: It connects two independent clauses.*

Instructor: Why does it come outside the closing parenthesis?

→ *Student: It follows the whole independent clause, not just the clause in parentheses.*

Instructor: In the final sentence, one set of words is separated from the rest of the sentence by a single dash, and another by a pair of parentheses. First, underline the entire set of words set off by the single dash.

> I first laid all the planks or boards upon it that I could get, and having considered well what I most wanted, I got three of the seamen's chests, which I had broken open, and emptied, and lowered them down upon my raft; the first of these I filled with provisions—<u>bread, rice, three Dutch cheeses, five pieces of dried goat's flesh (which we lived much upon), and a little remainder of European corn, which had been laid by for some fowls which we brought to sea with us, but the fowls were killed.</u>
> —Daniel Defoe, *Robinson Crusoe*

Instructor: What does this set of words describe or rename?

→ *Student: Provisions.*

Instructor: The provisions were bread, rice, cheese, dried goat's flesh, and corn. Which of those five delicious foods does the parenthetical expression tell you more about?

→ *Student: The dried goat's flesh.*

Instructor: What about the dried goat's flesh?

→ *Student: They lived much upon it.*

Instructor: In this sentence, the five foods that make up the provision are definitely more important than the fact that they ate more goat's flesh than anything else.

Now that you've reviewed hyphens, dashes, and parentheses, finish your exercises. If you do a good job, I'll reward you with some dried goat's flesh.

—LESSON 124—

Italics
Quotation Marks
Ellipses
Single Quotation Marks
Apostrophes

Instructor: The first sentence in your workbook has two italicized names in it. What are they?

→ *Student: Around the World in Eighty Days and Mongolia.*

Instructor: *Mongolia* is the name of a ship, so you've already learned the rule governing that. What is it?

→ *Student: Capitalize and italicize the names of ships, trains, and planes.*

Instructor: You also use italics for a few other kinds of proper names. Read the next rule.

→ *Student: **Italicize the titles of lengthy or major works such as books, newspapers, magazines, works of art, and long musical compositions.***

Instructor: There's absolutely no good reason for this, but in English, we treat shorter works differently. Read the next rule.

→ *Student:* **Use quotation marks for minor or brief works of art and writing or portions of longer works such as short stories, newspaper articles, songs, chapters, and poems.**

Instructor: The examples show you how the first chapters of *The Hobbit* and *Watership Down* are punctuated differently than the books themselves. You also have examples of a newspaper, magazine, major work of art, minor work of art, and long musical composition. What is one of the shorter songs from the opera *Carmen*?

→ *Student:* "Toreador Song."

Instructor: "Scarborough Fair" is a song. "The Lottery" is a short story. What are "Stopping by Woods on a Snowy Evening" and "The Raven"?

→ *Student:* Poems.

Instructor: The *Odyssey* is also a poem—but it's as long as a book, so we italicize it. *Mona Lisa* is a major work of art, so it is usually italicized. "Saint Jerome in Penitence" is a sketch, so it isn't.

This rule, particularly for works of art, is very often applied differently by different writers and publishers, so don't worry too much about the major/minor distinction. Often, it's correct to write a work of art either way.

If you're not sure whether something should be italicized or put into quotation marks, you can look it up in an online reference tool.

Let's look at two additional rules about italics. Read me the next rule.

→ *Student:* **Italicize letters, numbers, and words if they are the subject of discussion. In plural versions, do not italicize the s.**

Instructor: If you are talking *about* a word, or a letter, or a number, rather than using it to talk about something *else,* you should italicize it. What letters are italicized in the first sentence?

→ *Student: A* and *Z.*

Instructor: That's because the sentence is about *A* and *Z.* What word is italicized in the second sentence?

→ *Student: Moist.*

Instructor: That's because the sentence is about the word *moist.* Notice, in the third sentence, that *A* and *F* are plural—but only *A* and *F* are italicized, not the *-s* that makes them plural.

Read your final rule about italics now.

→ *Student:* **Italicize foreign words not adopted into English.**

Instructor: Whenever you use words from a foreign language, you put them in italics—*unless* those words are so commonly used in English that they've become part of the English language. In the first sentence, the French phrase for REM sleep is italicized. But in the second sentence, a French phrase is *not* italicized. What is the phrase?

→ *Student: Nom de plume.*

Instructor: Nom de plume is French for "pen name." Literally, it means "name of the plume"—the plume is a feather pen. But English speakers have been using nom de plume for so long that it now qualifies as an English word, so it is not italicized.

English steals a *lot* of words from other languages. In fact, English is one of the greediest languages on earth. Terry Pratchett once said that English doesn't just borrow from other languages—it mugs them and steals their stuff!

In your exercises, you'll look at other foreign words and phrases that aren't italicized because they have been stolen by English.

Let's move on to quotation marks. You've already learned that quotation marks set off dialogue, as well as one new use for quotation marks. Read me that new rule one more time.

→ *Student: Use quotation marks for minor or brief works of art and writing or portions of longer works such as short stories, newspaper articles, songs, chapters, and poems.*

Instructor: Using quotation marks correctly is a complex skill—so we'll do a more complete review (and add a few more rules) next week. But let's look at one particular punctuation challenge. First, look at the excerpt from *Glinda of Oz*. What do the spiders actually say?

→ *Student: "The web is finished, O King, and the strangers are our prisoners."*

Instructor: What is the dialogue tag?

→ *Student: And said.*

Instructor: What punctuation mark comes between the dialogue tag and the speech?

→ *Student: A comma.*

Instructor: What kind of letter does the speech itself start with?

→ *Student: A capital letter.*

Instructor: What punctuation mark does the speech end with?

→ *Student: A period.*

Instructor: Does it come inside or outside the closing quotation marks?

→ *Student: Inside.*

Instructor: This speech follows all the rules for using quotation marks that you've already learned. But now, imagine that you want to quote from this passage in your own writing. How do you set off direct quotes?

→ *Student: With quotation marks.*

Instructor: Look at the next short paragraph in your workbook. This is from an imaginary essay about spiders, and the author quotes from *Glinda of Oz*. What is the direct quotation from Baum's book?

→ *Student: ". . . great purple spiders, which . . . said, 'The web is finished, O King, and the strangers are our prisoners.'"*

Instructor: Instead of using an attribution tag, the writer has made this direct quotation part of her own sentence. She has also cut out some words. What punctuation marks show where words have been left out?

→ *Student: Ellipses.*

Instructor: The direct quotation is surrounded by quotation marks. But there's a line of dialogue *within* the direct quotation. Look carefully at it. What punctuation marks set off the dialogue?

→ *Student: Single quotation marks.*

Instructor: When you use a quotation that contains another quotation or line of dialogue within it, use regular quotation marks for the whole quote, and single quotation marks for the dialogue or quotation within it. Punctuation marks that apply to the entire sentence go within *both* sets of quotation marks. How many total quotation marks come after the period?

→ *Student: Three.*

Instructor: One is for the line of dialogue, and the next two are for the whole quote. Read me the rule that governs quotes within quotes.

→ *Student:* **A quote within a quote is surrounded by single quotation marks.**

Instructor: When a single quotation mark occurs by itself, we call it an *apostrophe*. You've learned two uses for apostrophes. Read me the first set of rules, and then finish each example by making it possessive.

> **An apostrophe is a punctuation mark that shows possession. It turns a noun into an adjective that tells whose.**
>
> **Form the possessive of a singular noun by adding an apostrophe and the letter *s*.**
>
> spider's   wand's
> web's   sorceress's
>
> **Form the possessive of a plural noun ending in *-s* by adding an apostrophe only.**
>
> spiders'   troubles'
> fields'   lakes'
>
> **Form the possessive of a plural noun that does not end in *-s* as if it were a singular noun.**
>
> sheep's   hangmen's
> geese's   teeth's

Instructor: Finally, read me the very last rule.

→ *Student: A contraction is a combination of two words with some of the letters dropped out. An apostrophe shows where the letters have been omitted.*

Instructor: Write the contraction for each form in the blank provided.

> **A contraction is a combination of two words with some of the letters dropped out. An apostrophe shows where the letters have been omitted.**
>
> they are   they're
> was not   wasn't
> were not   weren't
> I am   I'm

Instructor: You have now reviewed all of your punctuation and capitalization rules—and added a few more! Complete your exercises now.

Advanced Quotations & Dialogue

> **Note to Instructor:** The final two weeks of instruction in this course are designed to give the student an initial chance to put all of the grammatical knowledge gained to use in actual writing. The intensive study of grammar should be followed by training in rhetoric (persuasive writing); these weeks begin that transition.
>
> Weeks Thirty-Four and Thirty-Five begin with an instructional session; the rest of the week is devoted to using the skills taught in composition. The comprehensive review in Week Thirty-Six goes back through all rules covered and then offers several different opportunities for the student to write grammatically.
>
> You should feel free to adjust and adapt the content of all writing assignments to fit the student's skill level and needs.

—LESSON 125—

Dialogue
Additional Rules for Writing Dialogue
Direct Quotations
Additional Rules for Using Direct Quotations

Instructor: In these last weeks of your grammar course, you'll spend a little more time *writing*. After all, you're not studying grammar so that you can do grammar exercises. You're studying grammar in order to become a better writer (and speaker).

This week, we'll review the rules for dialogue and quotations, add a couple of new rules, and then practice. Let's start with dialogue. The first rule in your workbook tells when you might want to use dialogue in your writing. Read it out loud to me.

→ Student: **Use dialogue in fiction and to bring other voices into memoir, profiles, and reporting.**

Instructor: When you're writing a story, you use dialogue very naturally to show your characters speaking to each other—but you can also use dialogue to make nonfiction more interesting. In the quote from the *New York Times* story, the reporter uses quotation marks twice. What does the first set of quotation marks set off?

→ Student: *The name of a minor work of art.*

Instructor: The second set of quotation marks sets off words that someone spoke—an expert whose exact words make the story more interesting. What is the dialogue tag that identifies the person making the speech?

→ *Student: Mr. Grosvenor said.*

Instructor: As I read the next two rules, point to the punctuation mark under discussion.

Note to Instructor: As you read the rule, the student should point to the punctuation marks underlined in the sentences below.

Instructor: When a dialogue tag comes after a speech, place a comma, exclamation point, or question mark inside the closing quotation marks before the tag.

> "There goes Tommaso the painter," the people would say, watching the big awkward figure passing through the streets on his way to work.

Instructor: When a dialogue tag comes before a speech, place a comma after the tag. Put the dialogue's final punctuation mark inside the closing quotation marks.

> Diamante said to Filippo, "You have learned well, and it is time now to turn your work to some account."

Instructor: Speeches do not need to be attached to a dialogue tag as long as the text clearly indicates the speaker. In the next example, who is speaking?

→ *Student: The father.*

Instructor: Usually, a new paragraph begins with each new speaker. In the next example, what two characters are speaking?

→ *Student: Michelangelo and another artist.*

Instructor: Each speech begins a new paragraph. But when short speeches by two different people are very closely related, it is also correct to keep them in the same paragraph. Read me the next example.

→ *Student: "I am growing too old to help you," Leonardo said, but Raphael shook his head. "I will go with you to the ends of the earth," he said.*

Instructor: Read me the final dialogue rule.

→ *Student: When a dialogue tag comes in the middle of a speech, follow it with a comma if the following dialogue is an incomplete sentence. Follow it with a period if the following dialogue is a complete sentence.*

Instructor: In the two examples that follow, which one follows the dialogue tag with an incomplete sentence?

→ *Student: The first one.*

Instructor: *Has found his brains at last* is just the predicate of the complete sentence, so it begins with a lowercase letter. In the second example, what complete sentence follows the dialogue tag?

→ *Student: This is indeed marvellous talent.*

Instructor: Let's review the rules for using direct quotations. As you'll see from the examples, dialogue and direct quotations definitely overlap. All of the following contain direct quotations that were documented in writing, but often those direct quotations *are* lines of dialogue! So the rules will overlap as well.

> I'll read the first rule, you read the second, and I'll read the third.

> Direct quotations are set off by quotation marks.

→ *Student: Every direct quote must have an attribution tag.*

Instructor: When an attribution tag comes after a direct quote, place a comma, exclamation point, or question mark inside the closing quotation marks. In the quote below, notice that *asked* begins with a lowercase letter even though the speech before the attribution tag ends with a question mark.

Read me the next rule.

→ *Student: When an attribution tag comes before a direct quote, place a comma after the tag. Put the quote's final punctuation mark inside the closing quotation marks.*

Instructor: As you can see in the example, the attribution tag may include other descriptive phrases and clauses. The *comma after the tag* actually goes after the tag *and* any descriptive phrases and clauses that go with it. In this sentence, *and then thundered* is the attribution tag. What does the prepositional phrase *in a voice* describe?

→ *Student: Thundered.*

Instructor: This is an adverb phrase. What adjective clause describes *voice*?

→ *Student: That thrilled his audience with prophetic intimations.*

Instructor: All together, the complete attribution tag is *and then thundered in a voice that thrilled his audience with prophetic intimations.* It is followed by a comma, and then the direct quote itself, beginning with a capital letter. What ending punctuation mark goes inside the closing quotation marks?

→ *Student: An exclamation point.*

Instructor: Read me the next rule.

→ *Student: When an attribution tag comes in the middle of a direct quotation, follow it with a comma if the remaining quote is an incomplete sentence. Follow it with a period if the remaining quote is a complete sentence.*

Instructor: Which example shows you the attribution tag followed by a comma and an incomplete sentence?

→ *Student: The second.*

Instructor: In the first example, where the tag is followed by a complete sentence, what punctuation mark comes after the tag?

→ *Student: A period.*

Instructor: A direct quote doesn't have to be a complete sentence. Read me the next rule.

→ *Student: Direct quotes can be words, phrases, clauses, or sentences, as long as they are set off by quotation marks and form part of a grammatically correct original sentence.*

Instructor: In the example given, what part of the sentence does the partial quote "*noble-hearted hospitality and manly character*" serve as?

→ *Student: Object of the preposition* for.

Instructor: You wouldn't put a comma between a preposition and its object, and you don't put a comma here because the quote forms part of a grammatically correct original sentence.

The next example in your workbook illustrates the next *two* rules. I'll read the first and you read the second. Ellipses show where something has been cut out of a sentence.

→ *Student: If a direct quotation is longer than three lines, indent the entire quote one inch from the margin in a separate block of text and omit quotation marks.*

Instructor: How many sets of words have been left out of the block quote from the book *Life and Times of Garrison*?

→ *Student: Two sets of words.*

Instructor: If you change or make additions to a direct quotation, what should you use?

→ *Student: Brackets.*

Instructor: What clarifying word has been added to the next direct quotation?

→ *Student: Douglass.*

Instructor: Finally, a quote within a quote is surrounded by single quotation marks. When you see an example of this in the remainder of the lesson, let me know.

Now let's finish up with just a few additional rules. First, when should you use a direct quotation?

→ *Student: **Use direct quotations to provide examples, cite authorities, and emphasize your own points.***

Instructor: Don't use direct quotations in place of your own writing—use them to improve your own writing!

Every quote needs an attribution quote, but **it could be indirect**. In the next sentence, who exactly is using the phrase *old master*?

→ *Student: The slaves.*

Instructor: The writer doesn't say, "The slaves said 'old master.'" But the quote makes clear that those words come from the songs of the slaves.

In previous examples, a comma has introduced a direct quote. What else can introduce a direct quote?

→ *Student: A colon.*

Instructor: When a quotation has multiple commas and other punctuation marks in it, it is sometimes clearer to introduce it with a colon. What multiple punctuation marks does this direct quotation contain?

→ *Student: Commas, dashes, single punctuation marks.*

> **Note to Instructor:** If the student does not recognize the quote within the quote, point out that Douglass's thought "I am a slave—a slave for life" comes within Douglass's other words, which are themselves quoted by Chestnutt in his biography.

Instructor: The next three rules have to do with quoting poetry—which has slightly different punctuation. Read me the first poetry rule.

→ *Student: **To quote three or fewer lines of poetry, indicate line breaks by using a slanted line and retain all original punctuation and capitalization.***

Instructor: What lines of poetry are quoted in the example?

→ *Student: We wear the mask that grins and lies,/It hides our cheeks and shades our eyes,—/This debt we pay to human guile.*

Instructor: Each line has the exact same punctuation as in the original—the slanted lines just represent the places where each line breaks. You'll see the same quote, with additional lines, in the next example. Read me the next rule.

→ *Student: **Four or more lines of poetry should be treated as a block quote.***

Instructor: If you're going to quote more than three lines, just write the poem out, indented from the margin, exactly as in the original.

Read me the last rule about quoting poetry now.

→ *Student:* ***Any poetic citation long than one line may be treated as a block quote.***

Instructor: If you're quoting two or three lines of poetry, it might read more clearly if you indented them from the margin. That is a judgment call.

Those are ALL of the rules that we need to know about direct quotations. But there's one more important rule. What is it?

→ *Student:* ***Direct quotes should be properly documented.***

Instructor: Whenever you use a direct quote, you should insert a footnote, an endnote, or an in-text citation giving the source.

> **Note to Instructor:** If the student has already learned correct documentation styles in a composition course, you may conclude this lesson now and move on to Lesson 127 tomorrow. If not, take additional time this week to complete Optional Lesson 126 before continuing on to 127.

—LESSON 126—

(Optional)
Documentation

> **Note to Instructor:** The following lesson is adapted from the *Writing With Skill* series by Susan Wise Bauer (Well-Trained Mind Press). Documentation skills overlap with composition assignments; if your writing program covers another style of citation, use that instead. This optional lesson is meant to fill in any gaps in the student's information.
>
> There's no exciting way to cover this skill, which is largely about where to put punctuation marks. The method in this lesson is intended to force the student to pay close attention to formatting details.
>
> The following information is all based on the style known as Turabian, which is the most common style used in student papers. However, the student may use any acceptable documentation style (and when taking a class, should always ask the instructor what style is preferred).
>
> Be aware that even Turabian guides differ on how to properly cite websites, ebooks, and other forms of electronic information. The method here is widely but not universally used. All documentation styles should be held lightly—the important thing for the student is to learn consistency.

Instructor: Whenever you quote from someone else's work, the quote should be followed by a *citation*.

In the first example in your workbook, the sentence containing the direct quote is followed by a *superscript*—a small number that sits up above the middle of the line. That superscript leads to a citation. Read me the first two rules in your workbook.

→ *Student:* ***A sentence containing a direct quote should be followed by a citation. A superscript number may lead to a citation at the bottom of the page (a footnote) or the end of the paper (an endnote).***

Instructor: If you use a word processing program to write, you can use the program's tools to insert either footnotes or endnotes (both are correct). If you are handwriting a paper, it is much simpler to use endnotes.

Let's go over the formatting rules for footnotes and endnotes. You read the guidelines, and I'll read the examples while you look at them carefully.

→ *Student: Footnotes and endnotes should follow this format.*

Instructor: Author name, comma, title of book italicized, open parentheses, name of publisher, comma, year of publication, close parentheses, comma, p, period, page number of quote, period.

→ *Student: If there are two authors, list them like this.*

Instructor: Author name and author name, comma, title of book italicized, open parentheses, name of publisher, comma, year of publication, close parentheses, comma, p, period, page number of quote, period.

→ *Student: If your quote comes from more than one page of the book you're quoting, use* pp. *to mean "pages" and put a hyphen between the page numbers.*

Instructor: Author name, comma, title of book italicized, open parentheses, name of publisher, comma, year of publication, close parentheses, comma, pp, period, first page number of quote, dash, second page number of quote, period.

→ *Student: If a book is a second (or third, or fourth, etc.) edition, put that information right after the title.*

Instructor: Author name, comma, title of book italicized, comma, edition number followed by ed and a period, open parentheses, name of publisher, comma, year of publication, close parentheses, comma, p, period, page number of quote, period.

→ *Student: If no author is listed, simply use the title of the book.*

Instructor: Title of book italicized, open parentheses, name of publisher, comma, year of publication, close parentheses, comma, p, period, page number of quote, period.

→ *Student: All of this information can be found on the copyright page of the book.*

Footnotes should be placed beneath a dividing line at the bottom of the page. If you are using a word processing program, the font size of the footnotes should be about two points smaller than the font size of the main text.

Endnotes should be placed at the end of the paper, under a centered heading, like this.

Instructor: Endnotes, all caps, centered, double space. Superscript number, author name, title of book italicized, open parentheses, name of publisher, comma, year of publication, close parentheses, comma, p, period, page number of quote, period.

→ *Student: For a short paper (three pages or less), the endnotes can be placed on the last page of the paper itself. A paper that is four or more pages in length should have an entirely separate page for endnotes.*

The second time you cite a book, your footnote or endnote only needs to contain the following information.

Instructor: Author last name, comma, p, period, page number, period.

→ *Student: If a paragraph contains several quotes from the same source, a single citation at the end of the entire paragraph can cover all quotations.*

Instructor: That covers the basic rules for footnotes and endnotes. But just putting footnotes or endnotes into your paper isn't quite enough. You also need a *Works Cited* page. What is on a Works Cited page?

→ Student: **Every work mentioned in a footnote or endnote must also appear on a final Works Cited page.**

Instructor: The title Works Cited should be capitalized and centered at the top. Then, after a space, list every source quoted in your paper. Let's alternate reading the next five guidelines. You begin.

→ *Student: List sources alphabetically by the author's last name.*

Instructor: The format should be: Last name of author, comma, first name, period. Title of Book italicized, period. City of publication, colon: Name of publisher, comma, year of publication, period.

→ *Student: If the work has no author, list it by the first word of the title (but ignore the articles* a, an, *and* the*).*

Instructor: If the city of publication is not a major city (New York, Los Angeles, London, Beijing, New Delhi, Tokyo), include the state (for a U.S. publisher) or country (for an international publisher).

→ *Student: For a short paper (three pages or less), the Works Cited section may be at the bottom of the last page. For a paper of four or more pages, attach a separate Works Cited page.*

Instructor: In your workbook, you will see some additional formatting rules for citing different kinds of sources. You will need to refer back to this as you complete the week's work.

Just one more thing. When you're writing scientific or technical papers, sometimes it's simpler to use an **in-text citation**. For an in-text citation, put a parenthesis after the closing quotation marks, write the last name of the author and the date of the work with no comma between them, put a comma and the page number with no *p.*, add a closing parenthesis, and finish out with the rest of the sentence and/or closing punctuation.

In-text citations stop the flow of the sentence forward, so you wouldn't want to use them in most expository writing. But with scientific writing, the flow forward is less important than documenting your claims, so the in-text citation reassures readers that they can take your conclusions seriously. The rest of the information in the Works Cited is the same as if you were using an endnote or footnote.

This lesson concludes with two more things.

First, you have a brief explanation of why these rules are called **Turabian rules**.

> **Note to Instructor:** You may give the student time to review the following explanation now or later; you may also choose whether to allow the student to read silently, or require him to read aloud.

About Turabian

The style described in this lesson is the most common one for student papers. It is known as "Turabian," after Kate Turabian, the head secretary for the graduate department at the University of Chicago from 1930 until 1958. Kate Turabian had to approve the format of every doctoral dissertation and master's thesis submitted to the University of Chicago. These papers were supposed to follow the format of the *University of Chicago Manual of Style*, but the *Manual of Style* is huge and complicated and many students couldn't figure out exactly how to use it. So Kate Turabian wrote a simplified version of the *Manual of Style,* intended just for the use of students writing papers. It was called *A Manual for Writers of Research Papers, Theses, and Dissertations*, and her book has sold over eight million copies.

Instructor: Second, your workbook contains a reference list of other styles. There are other ways to cite sources that use slightly different formats. Turabian style is almost always acceptable, but once you begin writing for other teachers and professors, you might find that one of them prefers another style.

The brief summary of how each of the major styles formats a footnote/endnote, in-text citation, and Works Cited entry is just for your reference. All of these refer to traditional print books. If you were using any of these styles, you would need to go to specialized websites for directions on how to cite articles, websites, ebooks, and other formats.

Notice differences in capitalization, punctuation, author's name, and placement of the different elements.

> **Note to Instructor:** You may choose to have the student review these rules now, or simply be aware of their existence. Citation and documentation is a complicated (and annoying) field. Even professional writers struggle to use citation rules consistently. This lesson is simply intended to teach the basics of *one* acceptable system, and to make the student aware of the existence of others as preparation for advanced work later on.

Alternative Styles for Citation

A. Turabian (most common for students)

FOOTNOTE/ENDNOTE

[1] Susan Cooper, *Silver on the Tree* (Atheneum, 1977), p. 52.

IN-TEXT CITATION

(Cooper 1977, 52)

WORKS CITED

Cooper, Susan. *Silver on the Tree.* New York: Atheneum, 1977.

B. Chicago Manual of Style

FOOTNOTE/ENDNOTE

[1] Susan Cooper, *Silver on the Tree* (New York: Atheneum 1977), p. 52.

IN-TEXT CITATION

(Cooper 1977, 52)

WORKS CITED

Cooper, Susan. 1977. *Silver on the Tree.* New York: Atheneum, 1977.

C. APA (American Psychological Association, the standard for science writing)

FOOTNOTE/ENDNOTE

APA does not recommend the use of footnotes or endnotes.

IN-TEXT CITATION

(Cooper, 1977, p. 52)

WORKS CITED

Cooper, S. (1977). *Silver on the tree.* New York: Atheneum.

D. MLA (Modern Language Association, more often used in the arts and humanities)

FOOTNOTE/ENDNOTE

MLA does not recommend the use of footnotes or endnotes for citations. They should only be used to direct the reader to additional books or resources that should be consulted.

IN-TEXT CITATION

(Cooper 52)

WORKS CITED

Cooper, Susan. *Silver on the Tree.* New York, NY, United States: Atheneum, 1977. Print.

— LESSON 127—

Practicing Direct Quotations and Correct Documentation

Instructor: For the rest of this week, you'll work on a short composition that shows proper use of direct quotations, and the correct formatting of footnotes and the Works Cited section.

Take some time to read the instructions carefully, and then read the resources provided.

If you need help, ask for it.

Note to Instructor: The rest of this lesson is found in the Answer Key.

Introduction to Sentence Style

> **Note to Instructor:** This week is a simple introduction to sentence style, intended to show the student the connection between grammatical knowledge and effective writing. As the student moves on to rhetoric, he will learn a more complex set of definitions (for example, a parallel sentence can also contain subordinate elements, and a cumulative sentence, which here is defined as *subordinating*, can be classified as *equal* because the subordinate elements carry the weight of meaning). However, the definitions in this lesson will provide a good foundation for the student to continue on into rhetoric, which follows grammar and puts grammatical expertise to use.
>
> The definitions in this week's work follow the categories laid out by Thomas Kane in *The New Oxford Guide to Writing*. As Kane notes, there are several different ways to classify sentences, and rhetoricians often differ in their definitions.

—LESSON 128—

Sentence Style: Equal and Subordinating
Sentences with Equal Elements: Segregating, Freight-Train, and Balanced

Instructor: In your workbook, you'll see four famous sentences, written in two different styles. Read me the first sentence, from "The Gettysburg Address."

→ Student: *But, in a larger sense, we cannot dedicate—we cannot consecrate—we cannot hallow this ground.*

Instructor: *We cannot dedicate, we cannot consecrate,* and *we cannot hallow* are all the same. They are all independent clauses. When a sentence is made up of a series of similar elements, we call it an **equal sentence,** because all the major parts of it are equal. Read me the next equal sentence.

→ Student: *We shall defend our island, whatever the cost may be; we shall fight on the beaches, we shall fight on the landing grounds, we shall fight in the fields and in the streets, we shall fight in the hills; we shall never surrender.*

Instructor: In this famous speech, Winston Churchill uses *six* different short independent clauses: *We shall defend our island, we shall fight on the beaches, we shall fight on the landing grounds,* and so on. Read me the definition of an equal sentence.

→ Student: **An equal sentence is made up of a series of independent grammatical elements.**

Instructor: An equal sentence can contain a few elements that are *not* similar. Notice that the first sentence begins with *But, in a larger sense.* Also, there are three independent clauses, but only one shared direct object. In the second sentence, what clause breaks the pattern of short independent clauses?

→ Student: *Whatever the cost may be.*

Instructor: Also, two of the clauses contain one adverbial prepositional phrase; one of the clauses has two adverbial prepositional phrases, *in the fields and in the streets*, instead of one; and two clauses don't have a prepositional phrase at all. In an equal sentence, there can be some small differences between the elements, but they are *essentially* similar.

Now let's look at the other type of sentence. Read me the sentence from the poet Dylan Thomas.

→ *Student: Years and years ago, when I was a boy, when there were wolves in Wales, and birds the color of red-flannel petticoats whisked past the harp-shaped hills, when we sang and wallowed all night and day in caves that smelt like Sunday afternoons in damp front farmhouse parlors, and we chased, with the jawbones of deacons, the English and the bears, before the motor car, before the wheel, before the duchess-faced horse, when we rode the daft and happy hills bareback, it snowed and it snowed.*

Instructor: The last five words of this sentence are different than everything that came before. *It snowed* and *it snowed* are two simple independent clauses linked together with a coordinating conjunction. Everything that comes before them is subordinate. What kind of grammatical construction is *when I was a boy*?

→ *Student: A subordinate clause.*

Instructor: What kind of grammatical constructions are *with the jawbones of deacons* and *before the motor car*?

→ *Student: Prepositional phrases.*

Instructor: A sentence which is a combination of independent and subordinate elements is called a **subordinating sentence**. Your final sentence is also a subordinating sentence. What is the independent clause in Martin Luther King's sentence?

→ *Student: Men do not easily assume the task of opposing their government's policy.*

Instructor: There's a dependent element on either side of that independent clause. *Even when pressed by the demands of inner truth* is a subordinate clause with an understood subject and helping verb: *Even when [they are] pressed by the demands of inner truth*. *Especially in time of war* is an adverb phrase—*especially* is an adverb describing when *men do not easily assume*, and *in time of war* is a prepositional phrase describing *especially*.

Read me the definition of a subordinating sentence.

→ *Student: **A subordinating sentence is made up of both independent and dependent elements.***

Instructor: Today, we're going to look at three different kinds of equal sentences: **segregating, freight-train,** and **balanced**. Read me the first definition.

→ *Student: **Segregating sentences express a single idea each, and occur in a series.***

Instructor: To *segregate* something means "to divide it off from the rest," and segregating sentences are all divided off from each other. Segregating sentences are usually short and simple, although they may also contain phrases and brief subordinate clauses. They come in series of three or more, and are particularly good for descriptions and for summing up actions. Read the first set of segregating sentences from *Charlotte's Web*.

→ *Student: The barn was still dark. The sheep lay motionless. Even the goose was quiet.*

Instructor: Usually, segregating sentences are written with periods, each as a completely separate sentence. But sometimes a semicolon or comma and coordinating conjunction might be added in. Read me the sentences from *I Am Legend*.

→ *Student: He hadn't found any doweling that day. He hadn't checked the generator. He hadn't cleaned up the pieces of mirror. He hadn't eaten supper; he'd lost his appetite. That wasn't hard. He lost it most of the time.*

Instructor: In this series of seven segregating sentences, the fourth and fifth are connected by a semicolon, because the two ideas in those sentences are so closely connected.

You may also sometimes see a sentence fragment in a series of segregating sentences. In the next set of sentences, John Fowles uses a fragment to continue to describe what else, besides the meadow, is empty. He also uses a comma and coordinating conjunction to link the final two sentences together. Read those to me now.

→ *Student: They disappear among the poplars. The meadow is empty. The river, the meadow, the cliff and cloud. The princess calls, but there is no one, now, to hear her.*

Instructor: What is a freight-train sentence?

→ *Student: **Freight-train sentences link independent clauses together to express a combined idea.***

Instructor: Segregating sentences break ideas and actions down into separate parts; freight-train sentences link ideas together into a chain, like train cars all hooked to an engine. Usually, freight-train sentences are linked by semicolons or by commas and coordinating conjunctions. Read me the first two examples, from *Eminent Victorians* by Lytton Strachey and *In Another Country* by Ernest Hemingway.

→ *Student: He was energetic and devout; he was polite and handsome; his fame grew in the diocese. There was much game hanging outside the shops, and the snow powdered in the fur of the foxes and the wind blew their tails.*

Instructor: In the first sentence, all three of the ideas link together to tell you all the good qualities of the subject. In the second sentence, all three ideas fill out the picture of a winter landscape filled with wild beasts.

The third example of a freight-train sentence seems to break a grammar rule you've already learned! What links the first three short sentences together?

→ *Student: Commas.*

Instructor: Normally, you shouldn't join independent sentences with just commas. But in a freight-train sentence, the independent clauses act like items in a series—so you can connect them with commas until you get to the last sentence in the series, which should be connected to the one before with a coordinating conjunction and an Oxford comma. Read the freight-train sentence from *Charlotte's Web* out loud.

→ *Student: I'm very young, I have no real friend here in the barn, it's going to rain all morning and all afternoon, and Fern won't come in such bad weather.*

Instructor: The third type of equal sentence we'll look at is a balanced sentence. What is a balanced sentence?

→ *Student: **Balanced sentences are made up of two equal parts, separated by a pause.***

Instructor: A balanced sentence is like a seesaw that always ends up balanced straight and horizontal, because both ends weigh the same. A balanced sentence can simply be made up of two simple sentences, connected. Read the sentence from *A Christmas Carol,* and listen to how the two simple sentences are exactly the same length.

→ *Student: Darkness is cheap, and Scrooge liked it.*

Instructor: A balanced sentence may be two complex sentences joined together, rather than two simple sentences—but the two complex sentences still have the same sound, length, and weight. Read the sentence from *A Tale of Two Cities* out loud, pausing at the semicolon.

→ Student: *It is a far, far better thing that I do, than I have ever done; it is a far, far better rest that I go to than I have ever known.*

Instructor: In a balanced sentence, the two halves may have very different meanings and structure—but they will still have the same sound and feel. Notice, in the final example from "I Have a Dream," that the balanced sentence is made up of two sentences connected by a colon. The first sentence has two halves. The first half is an independent clause with a subordinate adjective clause, *that I must say to my people*, and the second half, connected to the first by a comma, is an adjective clause that contains a second adjective clause, *which leads into the palace of justice*, within it. The second sentence also has two halves, connected with a comma, but they are grammatically different. What is *In the process of gaining our rightful place*?

→ Student: *A prepositional phrase [serving as an adverb].*

Instructor: What is *we must not be guilty of wrongful deeds*?

→ Student: *An independent clause.*

Instructor: Even though the two parts of this balanced sentence are structured differently, they sound the same. Read the sentence out loud, pausing at the comma and listening carefully to the entire sentence.

→ Student: *But there is something that I must say to my people, who stand on the warm threshold which leads into the palace of justice: In the process of gaining our rightful place, we must not be guilty of wrongful deeds.*

Instructor: Now that you know three different kinds of equal sentences, complete your exercise.

—LESSON 129—

Subordinating Sentences:
Loose, Periodic, Cumulative, Convoluted, and Centered

Instructor: In the last lesson, we talked mostly about independent clauses and how they relate to each other to form segregating, freight-train, and balanced sentences. These kinds of equal sentences may contain different kinds of phrases and dependent clauses—but the focus is on how the *independent* clauses relate to each other.

In this lesson, we'll look at the relationship between independent clauses and the subordinate elements—phrases and dependent clauses—and how that changes the way sentences sound.

Let's start with *loose* sentences. You've already seen these many, many times; in fact, they're the most common kind of complex sentence. What is a loose sentence?

→ Student: **In a loose sentence, subordinate constructions follow the main clause.**

Instructor: A loose sentence introduces the main idea first, and then qualifies it with various kinds of phrases and dependent clauses. The three examples in your workbook show three different kinds of loose sentences. In each one, underline the subject of the main clause once, and the predicate twice.

<u>People</u> always <u>think</u> that happiness is a far away thing, something complicated and hard to get.
—Betty Smith, *A Tree Grows in Brooklyn*

He <u>was pacing</u> the room swiftly, eagerly, with his head sunk upon his chest and his hands clasped behind him.
—A. Conan Doyle, "A Scandal in Bohemia"

The <u>spotlight</u> <u>has</u> often <u>been focused</u> on me because I was a late bloomer who turned out to be a prodigy, and perhaps, more than that, because I am a black woman excelling in a white world.
—Misty Copeland, *Life in Motion: An Unlikely Ballerina*

Instructor: In the first sentence, the main independent clause is *People always think that happiness is a far away thing*. The dependent clause *that happiness is a far away thing* is part of the main clause—it is the direct object of the verb *think*. The next phrase, *something complicated and hard to get*, is an appositive that renames *happiness*—and follows the main clause, which makes this a loose sentence.

What is the main clause of the second sentence?

→ *Student: He was pacing the room swiftly, eagerly.*

Instructor: What kind of phrase follows the main clause?

→ *Student: A prepositional [adverbial] phrase.*

Instructor: In the third example, the main clause *The spotlight has often been focused on me* is followed by two dependent clauses introduced by the same word. What is that word?

→ *Student: Because.*

Instructor: It is also followed by the conjunction *and perhaps* and the phrase *more than that*. Read me the rule about loose sentences one more time.

→ *Student: In a loose sentence, subordinate constructions follow the main clause.*

Instructor: A **periodic sentence** reverses the order of a loose sentence. What is a periodic sentence?

→ *Student: **In a periodic sentence, subordinate constructions precede the main clause.***

Instructor: As you can see in the next three examples, in a periodic sentence, phrases and dependent clauses come *before* each main clause. Underline the subject and predicate of each main clause.

To be, or not to be: <u>that</u> <u>is</u> the question.
—William Shakespeare, *Hamlet*

When Galileo and Newton looked at nature, <u>they</u> <u>saw</u> simplicity.
—Edward Dolnick, *The Clockwork Universe: Isaac Newton, the Royal Society, and the Birth of the Modern World*

Some years ago—never mind how long precisely—having little or no money in my purse, and nothing particular to interest me on shore, <u>I</u> <u>thought</u> I would sail about a little and see the watery part of the world.
—Herman Melville, *Moby Dick*

Instructor: In the first sentence, what phrases come before the main clause?

→ *Student: To be, or not to be.*

Instructor: In the second sentence, what dependent clause comes before the main clause?

→ *Student: When Galileo and Newton looked at nature.*

Instructor: In the third sentence, three phrases come before the main clause. The first is *Some years ago*. What is the second?

→ *Student: Never mind how long precisely.*

Instructor: The third is the present participle phrase *having little or no money in my purse, and nothing particular to interest me on shore*. *Little or no money in my purse* and *nothing particular to interest me on shore* are the compound objects of the present participle *having*.

   Once a periodic sentence has three or more phrases or clauses in front of the main clause, it has started to edge over into the next category: the **cumulative sentence**. What is a cumulative sentence?

→ *Student: **A cumulative sentence puts multiple subordinate constructions before or after the main clause.***

Instructor: A cumulative sentence is a loose or periodic sentence with *many* phrases or dependent clauses. Your next two examples are cumulative sentences. In each one, underline the subject and predicate of the main clause.

> Beyond the obvious facts that he has at some time done manual labour, that he takes snuff, that he is a Freemason, that he has been in China, and that he has done a considerable amount of writing lately, I can deduce nothing else.
> —A. Conan Doyle, "The Red-Headed League"

> Lastly, she pictured to herself how this same little sister of hers would, in the after-time, be herself a grown woman; and how she would keep, through all her riper years, the simple and loving heart of her childhood; and how she would gather about her other little children, and make their eyes bright and eager with many a strange tale, perhaps even with the dream of Wonderland of long ago; and how she would feel with all their simple sorrows, and find a pleasure in all their simple joys, remembering her own child-life, and the happy summer days.
> —Lewis Carroll, *Alice's Adventures in Wonderland*

Instructor: In the sentence from "The Red-Headed League," the main clause is preceded by the prepositional phrase *beyond the obvious facts* and *five* dependent clauses that are all appositives, renaming *that*. In the sentence from *Alice's Adventures in Wonderland*, what part of the sentence is the dependent clause *how this same little sister of hers would, in the after-time, be herself a grown woman*?

→ *Student: A direct object.*

Instructor: The three additional dependent clauses beginning with *how* are also direct objects—so the four clauses are four direct objects of the verb *pictured*. It doesn't matter what *kind* of phrases or dependent clauses make up a cumulative sentence—if there are many of them, and they all come either before or after the main clause, you're looking at a cumulative sentence.

   Look carefully at the sentences one more time. Which main clause sounds more important—*I can deduce nothing else* or *Lastly, she pictured to herself*?

> **Note to Instructor**: Ideally, the student will choose "*I can deduce nothing else.*" Landing on the main subject and predicate at the very end of the sentence emphasizes it. When the main clause comes at the beginning of the sentences, its importance tends to get lost as the rest of the sentence winds itself away. If necessary, read the sentences out loud to the student, emphasizing the words *I can deduce nothing else*, and de-emphasizing *Lastly, she pictured to herself*.

Instructor: Placing the main clause at the end of a cumulative sentence tends to emphasize it; placing it at the beginning tends to pull the reader's attention away from it.

There are two other variations on subordinating sentence style. What is a **convoluted sentence**?

→ *Student: **In a convoluted sentence, subordinate constructions divide the main clause.***

Instructor: Usually, in a convoluted sentence, phrases or dependent clauses come between the subject and the predicate. In the first two examples, underline the subject of the main clause once and the predicate twice.

The <u>dorm</u>, with two narrow beds to a room, <u>didn't</u> just <u>house</u> dancers studying with ABT.
—Misty Copeland, *Life in Motion: An Unlikely Ballerina*

<u>We</u>, the people of the United States, in order to form a more perfect union, establish justice, insure domestic tranquility, provide for the common defense, promote the general welfare, and secure the blessings of liberty to ourselves and our posterity, <u>do ordain</u> and <u>establish</u> this Constitution for the United States of America.
—The Constitution of the United States

Instructor: What kind of phrase is *with two narrow beds to a room*?

→ *Student: Prepositional [or, Adjectival prepositional].*

Instructor: In the first sentence of the Constitution, two different kinds of phrases come between the subject and predicate. What is *the people of the United States*?

→ *Student: An appositive.*

Instructor: What about the rest?

→ *Student: Prepositional phrase [or, Adverbial prepositional phrase]*

Note to Instructor: Prompt the student as necessary. The compound preposition *in order* introduces the phrase; the six infinitives that follow (all but the first with an understood *to*) are all objects of the preposition, and each has an object of its own.

Instructor: Less often, the main clause is divided between the predicate and direct object. In the third sentence, underline the subject once and the predicate twice, and then label the direct objects as *DO*.

DO   DO
<u>They</u> <u>knew</u>, without my needing to spell it out, every setback or curve in the road: that I had fought for ten years to be recognized, to show that I had the talent and ability to dance in classical ballets.
Misty Copeland, *Life in Motion: An Unlikely Ballerina*

Instructor: What phrase interrupts the main clause?

→ *Student: Without my needing to spell it out.*

Instructor: One last type of sentence. What is a **centered sentence**?

→ *Student: **In a centered sentence, subordinate constructions come on both sides of the main clause.***

Instructor: In the two examples, underline the entire main clause of each sentence.

With an apology for my intrusion, <u>I was about to withdraw</u> when Holmes pulled me abruptly into the room and closed the door behind me.
—A. Conan Doyle, "The Red-Headed League"

And having got rid of this young man who did not know how to behave, <u>she resumed her duties as hostess and continued to listen and watch</u>, ready to help at any point where the conversation might happen to flag.
—Leo Tolstoy, *War and Peace*

Instructor: Any sentence that has dependent phrases and clauses both before and after the main clause is a centered sentence. In the first sentence, how many phrases or clauses come before the main clause?

→ *Student: One.*

Instructor: After?

→ *Student: One.*

Instructor: The adverbial prepositional phrase comes before, and the adverbial dependent clause comes afterwards. In the second sentence, a participle phrase comes before the main clause, but that phrase contains a dependent clause. What is it?

→ *Student: Who did not know how to behave.*

Instructor: The adverb phrase that comes after the main clause also contains a dependent clause. What is it?

→ *Student: Where the conversation might happen to flag.*

Instructor: So in this sentence, a phrase *and* a clause come before *and* after the main clause.

As you study rhetoric, you'll learn much more about how to structure sentences—and why you might choose one style over another. But now you have all the grammatical tools you need to understand how these sentences work. Finish your exercise now.

> **Note to Instructor:** Classifying sentences is not an exact science.
>
> For example: Generally, a brief adverbial or adjective phrase is considered part of the main clause, not an interrupting element. So, "The man in the high castle gazed at the sky" would not be considered, by most grammarians, a convoluted sentence, but "The man, a prisoner in the high castle, gazed at the sky" probably would be.
>
> In the same way, in a long cumulative sentence, there may be a brief adverb or adjective phrase that comes after the main clause, but in most cases this does not change the presentation of the sentence from cumulative to centered.
>
> Encourage the student not to get hung up on uncertainties or to worry too much about the *correct* answer—instead, learning these sentence styles should improve the student's attention to the relationship between grammar and meaning.
>
> Explanatory notes in the Answer Key are attached to potentially ambiguous sentences.

—LESSON 130—

Practicing Sentence Style

Instructor: For the rest of this week, you'll work on a short composition that uses all eight
sentence styles covered in the last two lessons.

Take some time to read the instructions carefully, and then read the resources provided.

If you need help, ask for it.

Note to Instructor: The rest of this lesson is found in the Answer Key.

—REVIEW 11—

Final Review

Note to Instructor: At this point, the student has done enough exercises on individual grammatical rules. The four lengthy exercises in this final section should be completed over the course of the week (one exercise per day), and are designed to encourage the student to apply grammatical thinking to real written English.

This is not a *test*—it is a review and a challenge to the student to use the knowledge acquired. Give all necessary assistance.